JEWISH STUDIES

教育部人文社会科学重点研究基地
山东大学犹太教与跨宗教研究中心

第21辑

犹太研究

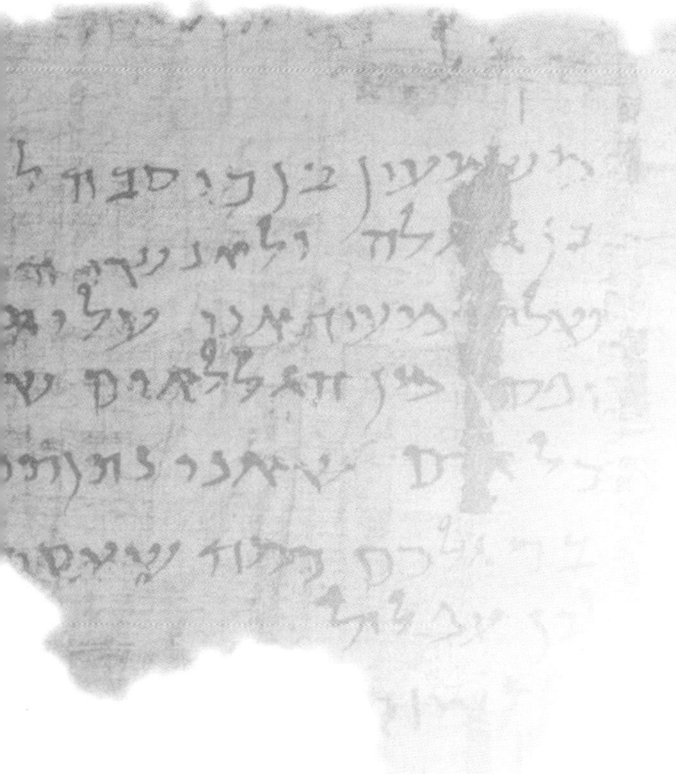

主编
傅有德
副主编
陈家富
董修元

山东大学出版社

图书在版编目(CIP)数据

犹太研究.第 21 辑/傅有德主编.—济南:山东大学出版社,2023.6

ISBN 978-7-5607-7853-2

Ⅰ.①犹… Ⅱ.①傅… Ⅲ.犹太教—宗教哲学—研究 ②犹太人—研究 Ⅳ.①B985 ②K18

中国国家版本馆 CIP 数据核字(2023)第 096769 号

责任编辑 武迎新
封面设计 牛 钧 王秋忆

犹太研究
YOUTAI YANJIU
第 21 辑

出版发行 山东大学出版社
社 址 山东省济南市山大南路 20 号
邮政编码 250100
发行热线 (0531)88363008
经 销 新华书店
印 刷 济南华林彩印有限公司
规 格 787 毫米×1092 毫米 1/16
17.25 印张 350 千字
版 次 2023 年 6 月第 1 版
印 次 2023 年 6 月第 1 次印刷
定 价 59.00 元

目录

A.以色列的极端正统派

The Ultra-Orthodox in Israel

B.观念、历史与文本

Ideas, History and Texts

目 录

A

以色列的极端正统派
The Ultra-Orthodox in Israel

Foreword

Uriya Shavit

The recent Israeli elections have handed the ultra-Orthodox minority unprecedented and outsized political power. Demographic trends suggest that by 2065, one in three Israelis will belong to this group. Given the religious dogmatism of the ultra-Orthodox, their regressive social views, and their minimal contribution to the Israeli economy and to its armed forces, some Israelis have begun to seriously doubt the viability of the Zionist enterprise, or at least to consider it gravely endangered.

This special issue comprises five research articles and one exceptional document that explore different aspects of the ultra-Orthodox in Israel. The articles, all written especially for this special issue by secular, Religious Zionist, and ultra-Orthodox scholars, engage with political, social, cultural, educational, psychological, and theological dimensions of ultra-Orthodox existence in the modern State of the Jews.

The special issue originates in the first annual conference of the Shandong-Tel Aviv Institute for Israel and Jewish Studies, which took place on May 9, 2021. The conference was attended by a particularly large audience from China, Israel, the United States, France, and other countries, indicating the growing interest in a social group whose importance and uniqueness invite more academic attention.

前言

乌利亚·沙维特

近期的以色列大选赋予极端正统派这一少数群体前所未有且与其规模不相称的政治权力。人口增长趋势显示，到 2065 年，三分之一的以色列人将属于这个群体。考虑到极端正统派的教条性、保守的社会观点以及他们对以色列经济和武装力量微乎其微的贡献，一些以色列人开始忧虑复国主义事业的前途，或至少认为后者被严重威胁。

本专栏包含五篇论文和一篇访谈录，考察以色列极端正统派的不同面向。这组特别约稿文章由世俗、宗教复国主义和极端正统派背景的学者撰写，涉及现代以色列极端正统派生活的政治、社会、文化、教育、心理、神学等诸多方面。

这组文章出自山东大学—特拉维夫大学犹太与以色列联合研究所第一届年会(2021 年 5 月 9 日)，来自中国、以色列、美国、法国等各个国家的众多学者出席此次会议，反映出对这一重要而独特的社群日益增长的学术关注。

The Ultra-Orthodox in Israel: Who They Are, Where They Are Headed

Sara Zalcberg

Abstract: This article aims to analyze current developments and trends in the ultra-Orthodox (Haredi) society in Israel. It begins with a discussion of who the ultra-Orthodox are and why it is not easy to define them, followed by an overview of the group, with particular attention to the tensions and conflicts with the majority society. Exploring the ultra-Orthodox as a society in change, which nevertheless manages to maintain its enclave mentality, the article concludes with several predictions as to how it may evolve in the coming decades.

Key Words: the Ultra-Orthodox, Israel, Identity

Introduction

Israel's ultra-Orthodox (Haredi) population is a minority group comprising 13% of the total population (including non-Jews).[1] In recent years, amidst demographic trends suggesting that within less than two generations, one in three Israelis will be a Haredi, research on this group has blossomed.[2]

---

① Lee Cahaner and Gilad Malach, *Statistical Report on Orthodox Society in Israel* 2020 (Jerusalem: The Israel Democracy Institute, 2021), 11. [Hebrew]

② Kimmy Kaplan and Yael Becher, *Studying Israeli Haredi Society: A Scholarly Inventory* (Jerusalem, September 2022), 11. [Hebrew]

This article aims to analyze current processes and trends in Haredi society and offers several predictions regarding the future of the ultra-Orthodox over the coming decades. It begins with a discussion of who the ultra-Orthodox are and why it is not easy to define them, followed by an overview of the group and its social, political, cultural, and educational characteristics, with particular attention to the main tensions and conflicts with the majority society. Exploring the ultra-Orthodox as a society in change that nevertheless manages to maintain its enclave mentality, the article concludes with several predictions as to how it may evolve in the coming decades.

Ⅰ. Who Is Ultra-Orthodox (Haredi)?

In the last two decades, ultra-Orthodox society in Israel has experienced change in various areas and expanded its boundaries. These changes have raised questions regarding what ultra-Orthodox Judaism is, who is "ultra-Orthodox," and, accordingly, what defines whether a person is ultra-Orthodox.

Friedman, who laid the foundation for research on the group in Israel, claimed that the term "ultra-Orthodox Judaism," in the modern era, refers to a defined and distinct part of Jewish society that considers itself committed to *halakha* (Jewish law) as interpreted and delineated by authorities in Jewish religious tradition ("orthodoxy").①

Unlike non-ultra-Orthodox forms of religious Judaism, such as Religious Zionism, the ultra-Orthodox are characterized, according to Friedman, by the following criteria: commitment to the strict interpretation of Jewish law; (male) total commitment to the study of Torah (specifically, the Babylonian Talmud); total obedience to religious authority; differential rejection of modernity; resistance to Zionism or at least its ideological rejection; and separation from the non-ultra-Orthodox majority.②

---

① Menachem Friedman, *Ultra-Orthodox Society: Sources, Trends and Processes* (Jerusalem: Institute for Israel Studies, 1991), 6-7. [Hebrew]

② Ibid.

Brown emphasized the concept of "faith of the sages" as a definer of Haredi society.[1] This concept underscores the obligation of ultra-Orthodox to obey religious authority not only in matters of *halakha* but also in non-*halakhic*, everyday matters. Brown further highlighted the *halakhic* limitations that ultra-Orthodox Jews adopt and pointed to the "traditional" external appearance that distinguishes them from others in society. This "traditional" appearance includes modesty rules regarding appropriate dress, mainly applied to women.[2]

The ultra-Orthodox community in Israel is diverse and comprised of different sub-groups. These sub-groups are distinguished from each other according to the extent to which they deviate from tradition and have been influenced by modernity.[3] Writing more than three decades ago, Friedman suggested four main types of ultra-Orthodox:

"Lithuanian Jews" (also known as Litvak or Yeshivish) represent the way of life that emerged in Poland-Lithuania at the end of the 19th century. This stream holds to the educational-value ethos of a "community of learners," according to which men must devote themselves to the study of Torah in yeshivas, while women raise the children and earn a living. This ethos gives the ultra-Orthodox community in Israel its unique character.

"Polish-Hasidic Jews" represent the Hasidic tradition that emerged in Poland. This stream is organized around a Hasidic "court" led by a rebbe, who shapes the nature of his congregation. One of the most influential courts in this stream is the Gur Hasidim, whose members constituted one of the pillars of the Agudath Israel movement. This international ultra-Orthodox movement worked to advance the interests of Haredim in the fields of education and welfare.

"Hungarian Jews" represent both the Hasidic tradition and Hungarian orthodoxy, which was inspired and shaped by Rabbi Moshe Sofer (Hatam

---

① Benjamin Brown, *The Haredim: A Guide to Their Beliefs and Sectors* (Jerusalem: Am-Oved/The Israel Democracy Institute, 2017), 11-12, 25. [Hebrew]

② Ibid., 12.

③ Menachem Friedman, *Ultra-Orthodox Society: Sources, Trends and Processes*, 6-7; Benjamin Brown, *The Haredim: A Guide to Their Beliefs and Sectors*, 18-31.

Sofer, 1762-1839), his sons, and his students. This group expresses positions against modernity, enlightenment ideals, and Zionism, which are stricter than those of the other Lithuanians and Hasidim.

"The Jerusalemites (*Yerushalmim*)" represent the tradition that was created in the old Ashkenazi (whose origins are in Europe) community in Jerusalem. Strict observance and anti-Zionist attitudes characterized this group and brought it closer to the "Hungarians" and, especially, to the Satmar Hasidism, which comprises several "courts" and strict anti-Zionist groups.

Another group, which Friedman located (at the time) on the fringes of ultra-Orthodox society, is the Sephardim. That is, ultra-Orthodox whose ethnicity is of Spanish, North African, and Middle Eastern descent. Friedman did not research the Sephardim and emphasized that this group requires further research.

Two decades later, Leon filled this lacuna. He included in the definition of ultra-Orthodox also religious and traditional Sephardic Jews, who in the 1980s united around the figure of Rabbi Ovadia Yosef (1920-2013) and his *halakhic* rulings, with the assistance of the Shaspolitical-social movement (*Shomrei Torah Sephardim*, or Sephardic Guardians of the Torah). This community adopted the Lithuanian ultra-Orthodox model but was characterized by a less strict approach to most areas of life compared to the Ashkenazi ultra-Orthodox groups. Therefore, Leon referred to the Sephardim as "soft ultra-Orthodox."①

Indeed, compared to Ashkenazi ultra-Orthodox groups, the Sephardic stream is more open to modernity and the non-ultra-Orthodox majority; is less strict regarding modesty rules and gender segregation; expresses less resistance to Zionism, and even identifies with it; and is not strongly opposed to military service, with some of the men serving in the Israel Defense Forces (IDF). Accordingly, Ashkenazi ultra-Orthodox do not consider Sephardic ultra-Orthodox an integral part of the ultra-Orthodox. Their exclusion is seen in the separation between the two groups in the education system and in marriage.

① Nissim Leon, "Mizrahi Ultra-Orthodoxy: Strict Ideology, Liquid Identity," *Journal for the Research of Haredi Society* 1 (June 2014): 1-20. [Hebrew]

Doron included in his definition of ultra-Orthodox Judaism also *baaleiteshuva*, "reborn" Jews who were not religious originally or did not come from an ultra-Orthodox background but have since adopted ultra-Orthodox worldviews and way of life.[①] Some *baalei teshuva* identified with Sephardic ultra-Orthodoxy; others wholly detached from their previous lives and adopted extremely pious views; and others, while adopting ultra-Orthodox views, remained, to varying degrees, part of their previous life, mainly in their professional vocation.

Some *baalei teshuva* are highly educated and employed in critical professions and are generally characterized by relative openness to modernity and the majority. Some have integrated into the less introverted Hasidic groups such as *Chabad* or the new current of *Breslav*.[②]

Malach and Cahaner expanded the definition to include "modern ultra-Orthodox" — those who originate from various ultra-Orthodox groups and have, in recent years, integrated more into the non-ultra-Orthodox majority and also adopted modern Western worldviews and values.[③] Individuals who belong to this group (which makes up about 7% of the ultra-Orthodox population) no longer see the "society of learners" as an ideal, and their sons are not committed totally to Torah study. This group also does not entirely obey religious authority. They strive for higher education, to become accomplished professionals, to integrate into the labor market, and, in general, to integrate into Israeli society. They serve in the military and turn to professional authority as an alternative to religious authority.[④]

The expanding boundaries of the definition of ultra-Orthodoxy, and the

---

① Shlomi Doron, "Changing Identities Through Rituals: Newcomers to and Defectors from Ultra-Orthodox Judaism," *Journal of Ritual Studies* 27 (2013): 13-32.

② Yoram Bilu and Tzvi Mark, "Between the Righteous and the Messiah: Outlines for a Comparative Analysis of Chabad Hasidism and Breslav Hasidism," *Iyunim Bitkumat Israel* 23 (2013): 350-377; Benjamin Brown, *A Society in Motion: Structures and Processes in Ultra-Orthodox Judaism* (Jerusalem: The Israel Democracy Institute, 2021), 248-253. [Hebrew]

③ Gilad Malach and Lee Cahaner, "Elements of Modern Life or 'Modern Ultra-Orthodoxy'? Numerical Assessment of Modernization Processes in Ultra-Orthodox Society," *Democratic Culture* 17 (2017): 19-51. [Hebrew]

④ Lee Cahaner, *Ultra-Orthodox Society on the Axis between Conservatism and Modernity* (Jerusalem: The Israel Democracy Institute, 2020), 19-70, 259-300. [Hebrew]

wide variety of groups it includes leads to the question of how to define who is ultra-Orthodox for research and discussion. The Israel Central Bureau of Statistics (CBS) proposed three criteria for the definition of a household as ultra-Orthodox.①

According to the educational institutions where the family members studied: a household is defined as ultra-Orthodox if it has at least one yeshiva graduate. This definition is problematic because it does not include families of *baalei teshuva*, who did not graduate from a yeshiva, nor does it include households with women only.

According to residence: a household is defined as ultra-Orthodox if it is in a city where the majority voted for Shas (Sephardic Guardians of the Torah), and YahadutHatorah (United Torah Judaism, UTJ), the two primary ultra-Orthodox political parties. This definition is also problematic, primarily because Shas is also supported by voters from traditional and Religious Zionist Sephardic families that are not identified with the ultra-Orthodox community.

According to self-definition: an ultra-Orthodox is someone who defines themselves as such. This, too, is problematic since, among the ultra-Orthodox population, there is often more difference than similarity. For example, a person who defines himself as an ultra-Orthodox but does not adhere to absolute gender segregation or legitimizes Zionism, may not be defined as ultra-Orthodox by other and less moderate ultra-Orthodox.

Ⅱ. Background on the Ultra-Orthodox in Israel

The roots of ultra-Orthodox Judaism lie in Europe. In the 18th and 19th centuries, religious values and traditions began to disintegrate in the face of emancipation and secularization. The division in the Jewish community between those who wanted to continue adhering to Jewish law and those who wanted to abandon or change it led to the use of the term "orthodoxy" in the Jewish context. This term expressed the perception of *halakha*, as interpreted in the Talmud and by the Sages, as relevant for all times, without change.

① Israela Friedman et al., "Measurement and Estimates of Population of Ultra-Orthodox Jews," *Technical Paper no*. 25 (Jerusalem: Israel Central Bureau of Statistics, 2011), 4-14. [Hebrew]

The term "ultra-Orthodoxy" describes the streams that went further and sought to adhere to the strictest interpretations of *halakha*, accepting additional and new limitations that had not been part of Jewish tradition as a means to fend off the dangers of modernization.[1] These streams were influenced by the ruling of Rabbi Moshe Sofer, who stated that "new things are forbidden from the Torah" in all aspects of life, including those that do not contradict Jewish law.[2]

The emergence of Zionism exacerbated the split between Orthodoxy and ultra-Orthodoxy. The division between these two streams deepened after Israel's establishment due to differences regarding their attitudes towards Zionism and in their socio-religious ethos, with one striving to separate from the majority society and the other striving to integrate and be involved in building the country (while maintaining its practiced religiosity).

The split between the two streams reached its peak in 1951 when the "United Religious Front" —the political bloc that united Religious Zionist Jews and the ultra-Orthodox since Israel's establishment — disbanded. Since then, the ultra-Orthodox have formed separate political parties representing particular ultra-Orthodox subgroups.

Ⅲ. The Ultra-Orthodox and the Zionist State

As described above, the ultra-Orthodox population in Israel comprises a range of approaches to Zionism. The vast majority (about 95%) identify with the more moderate view, which, despite its principle objection to Zionism as a secular ideology, recognizes the Zionist state and tends to obey its laws and avoid confrontations with its authorities.[3]

From their split with the Religious Zionists until the 1980s, the ultra-Orthodox were represented in the Knesset mainly by Agudath Israel, dominated by the Gur Hasidic group. In the November 1988 elections, this political party split into two parties: "Agudath Israel," representing the

---

① Benjamin Brown, *The Haredim: A Guide to Their Beliefs and Sectors*, 18-22.

② Menachem Friedman, *Ultra-Orthodox Society: Sources, Trends and Processes*, 7.

③ Benjamin Brown, *The Haredim: A Guide to Their Beliefs and Sectors*, 211-231.

Hasidic current, and "Degel Hatorah" (the flag of the Torah), representing the Lithuanians.[①] The two reunited before the 1992 elections as YahadutHatorah and remained united ever since, with seven seats in the current Knesset—the exact number of combined seats they had in 1988.

Why the representation of Yahadut Hatorah in the Knesset has not significantly grown despite the high fertility rates of its electorate has been one of the mysteries of Israeli politics. Part of the answer is that over the past 30 years, the demographic surge of the ultra-Orthodox was checked by waves of secular migration, mainly from the former USSR; another is that larger numbers of Haredim do not obey the Rabbis and vote for non-Haredi political parties, while some ceased voting at all for ideological reasons.

The strongest ultra-Orthodox political force since the mid-1980s has been Shas, representing the Sephardic ultra-Orthodox. Shas gained four seats when it first ran for parliament in 1984 and 11 in the most recent elections. Despite (but also because of) stormy criminal scandals in which members of its political leadership were embroiled, since its inception, Shas has maintained, with few interruptions, its electoral base and a kingmaker role in Israeli politics. It has steadily grown independent of the influence of non-Sephardic Rabbis and has elevated the status of Haredi Sephardic sages within the Haredi public at large.

Since 1977, the year Agudath Israel joined the first right-wing governing coalition in a country established and shaped by secular socialists, the ultra-Orthodox have enjoyed exceeding political influence. From that year on, ultra-Orthodox parties have been part of every right-wing-led coalition except for 2003-2004 and 2013-2015, when their exclusion was part of the agenda of centrist parties.

The 18 seats secured by the ultra-Orthodox in the most recent November 1, 2022, Knesset elections make up almost a third of the number required to form the majority. The centrist and left-leaning political parties made it clear that they would not join a coalition led by the largest faction in parliament, the right-wing Likud, whose head, Benyamin Netanyahu, the longest-serving

---

① Menachem Friedman, *Ultra-Orthodox Society: Sources, Trends and Processes*, 20-30.

prime minister in the history of the state, stands for trial on bribery breach of trust charges. The political survival of Netanyahu, and his hopes to remain in power and possibly out of prison, have thus become entirely dependent on the Haredi factions, whose voters vehemently and unconditionally sympathize with Netanyahu and distrust the Israeli judiciary.

As a result, the Haredim currently wield more power than ever before in Israeli political history. During coalition negotiations, the Haredi factions demanded inflated budgets, the continuation of the almost absolute deference of army service for ultra-Orthodox, and the passing of a law allowing gender segregation at public events without it being considered discrimination. Their outsized influence has raised doubts among secularist and traditional-secularist Israelis, who are still the majority in the country, whether Israel can maintain its democratic and liberal essence, and whether its economy and security can endure of Haredi population and influence.

A small minority of ultra-Orthodox in Israel (about 5%) are anti-Zionists who do not recognize the state. The circles associated with this camp have tended over the years to violate state laws in a blatant, provocative, and even violent manner.① The anti-Zionist camp comprises groups and communities who identify as "Eda Haredit." The Eda Haredit (or "Eda") is the communal, religious, and economic framework that unites the segment of ultra-Orthodox society that sought to separate itself from the organizational-community frameworks of the Zionist Yishuv during the British Mandate. To this day, it does not recognize the legitimacy of the State of Israel as a Jewish state and does not cooperate with its institutions.②

This camp adopted a fierce and uncompromising anti-Zionist position and demanded that its members separate from the Zionist enterprise and the State of Israel. Zionism, according to the Eda, is blasphemy against the hope of Messianic redemption, reflecting a rebellion against God and a betrayal of the

---

① Menachem Friedman, "Haredi Violence in Contemporary Israeli Society," *Studies in Contemporary Israeli Society* 18 (2002): 186-198; Sima Zalcberg Block, "Religious Coercion and Violence Against Women: The Case of Beit Shemesh," in *Women's Rights and Religious Law*, eds. Fareda Banda and Lisa Fishbayn Joffe (London: Routledge, 2016), 152-176.

② Menachem Friedman, *Society and Religion* (Jerusalem: Yad Yitzhak Ben-Zvi, 1977), 31. [Hebrew]

Jewish faith.[①] The Eda Haredit includes several circles such as the "Yerushalmim," Brisk, Dushinsky, and Neturei Karta, as well as Hasidic "courts" such as Munkacs, Pinsk-Karlin, Satmar, Spinka, Toldot Aharon, and Toldot Avraham Yitzhak.[②] In the past decade, an anti-Zionist trend has also been adopted by the "Jerusalem faction" — a Lithuanian faction that became radicalized—and among peripheral groups of *baalei teshuva*.[③]

Ⅳ. Characteristics and Trends

Although ultra-Orthodox society comprises a wide range of groups and streams, it is possible to observe several crucial common shared characteristics and trends relating to demography, education, higher education, employment, and military service.

A. Demography

The ultra-Orthodox population in Israel is particularly young (about 60% are under the age of twenty, compared to 35% of the total population in Israel) and is characterized by extremely high fertility rates (about 6.6 children on average per ultra-Orthodox woman compared to less than two children on average per woman in the Western world).[④] This is due to the strict observance of the command "to be fruitful and multiply" (Genesis 9:7) and the prohibition on using contraceptives.[⑤]

The high fertility rates affect the community's rapid growth rate. Forecasts indicate that within fifteen years, the ultra-Orthodox proportion of the total population (including non-Jews) will be 16%, and the proportion of ultra-Orthodox of working age will be 11%. According to long-term forecasts,

---

① Benjamin Brown, *The Haredim: A Guide to Their Beliefs and Sectors*, 153-183.

② Menachem Keren-Kratz, "Wall of Separation: Neturei Karta and Its Press During the Foundation of the State," *Kesher* 50 (Fall 2017): 71-88. [Hebrew]

③ Shlomi Doron, "Changing Identities Through Rituals: Newcomers to and Defectors from Ultra-Orthodox Judaism."

④ Cahaner and Malach, *Statistical Report* 2020.

⑤ Daphna Birenbaum-Carmeli, "Your Faith or Mine: A Pregnancy Spacing Intervention in an Ultra-Orthodox Jewish Community in Israel," *Reproductive Health Matters* 16 (November 2008): 185-191.

in 2065, ultra-Orthodox will make up about a third of the total population in Israel and 40% of the Jewish population in Israel—over five and a half million people.[1] According to Ben David, in less than forty-five years, about half of Israel's children will be from the ultra-Orthodox community![2]

Still, there has been a 0.4% decrease in fertility rates since the late 1990s, when the fertility rate for an ultra-Orthodox woman was seven children.[3] This resulted from an increase in the number of ultra-Orthodox women using contraceptives,[4] the concept of "family planning" spreading in ultra-Orthodox society, and, perhaps, the increase in the age of marriage.[5] According to Cahaner and Malach, fertility rates in the Haredi community may continue to decrease; if so, this will reduce its growth rate.[6]

B. Education

Even before Israel's establishment, the ultra-Orthodox had a separate education system under the auspices of Agudath Israel. As part of the guidelines for regulating religion and state relations during the transition from the pre-state period to independence, full educational autonomy was granted to the ultra-Orthodox within the framework of "independent education." It became the so-called "status quo."

Due to the refusal of ultra-Orthodox to accept the state's requirements for core studies (including core subjects such as math and science), independent education was and still is funded only partially by the state. This arrangement did not include the ultra-Orthodox circles that refused — and refuse to this day, at least formally — to receive state funds.[7]

---

[1] Cahaner and Malach, *Statistical Report* 2020, 15.

[2] Dan Ben-David, "The Shoresh Handbook: Education and Its Impact in Israel, 2017-2018," *The Shoresh Institution for Socioeconomic Research* (2018).

[3] Cahaner and Malach, *Statistical Report* 2020, 13.

[4] Lee Cahaner, *Ultra-Orthodox Society on the Axis between Conservatism and Modernity* (Jerusalem: The Israel Democracy Institute, 2020), 200; Kimmy Kaplan, *Internal Popular Discourse in Israeli Haredi Society* (Jerusalem: Zalman Shazar Center for Jewish History, 2007), 231-233. [Hebrew]

[5] Cahaner and Malach, *Statistical Report* 2020, 13.

[6] Ibid., 14.

[7] Benjamin Brown, *A Society in Motion: Structures and Processes in Ultra-Orthodox Judaism*, 74-76.

The ultra-Orthodox education system maintains complete gender segregation. Boys study in "Talmud Torah" from three to thirteen. In this framework, religious studies are emphasized, but there are a few extracurricular studies at the most basic level. At thirteen, young ultra-Orthodox men move to yeshivas, where their studies from morning until evening are devoted to religious studies, especially Talmud. At seventeen, the young men move to "big yeshivas," where they devote themselves to studying Talmud for at least a year. Some retire or partially retire from the yeshiva track to work at one point or another. However, in the Lithuanian stream, most men continue the yeshiva track until their thirties and forties. Thus, most ultra-Orthodox males do not study core subjects, and only a small minority (15%) take matriculation exams.①

Most ultra-Orthodox girls are educated in the "Beit Ya'akov" network, which includes an elementary school and a seminar equivalent to high school. Over the years, girls' studies integrated more basic studies covering broader subjects than their male counterparts. This is so girls can fulfill their destiny within the "Society of Learners"— to provide for the family so the husband can devote himself to studying Torah.

The main potential vocation of Haredi women has been teaching in the Beit Ya'akov network. This occupation was perceived as ideal for ultra-Orthodox women, as it allowed them to earn a living while remaining within the community's boundaries. The level of education at ultra-Orthodox girls' schools is much lower than that of state institutions. Indeed, only in the past ten years did educational institutions for girls begin preparing them for the state matriculation exams.②

The teaching field within the community became saturated, making teaching a less viable profession for women to pursue due to a lack of available positions. Moreover, teachers' salaries did not cover the expenses of families with many children, even more so when the woman was the sole breadwinner. Recognizing the need for additional sources of income, the Beit Ya'akov

① Benjamin Brown, *A Society in Motion: Structures and Processes in Ultra-Orthodox Judaism*, 76-95.

② Ibid.

institutions have created more training courses, some of which prepare the girls for matriculation exams so that they can pursue degrees, primarily at institutes of higher education that have been established in the last two decades that are geared toward the community. The increased preparation for the matriculation exams in the Beit Ya'akov network led to a tremendous jump in the rate of ultra-Orthodox girls who passed the exam: 58% in 2018/2019, while fifteen years earlier, only 31% passed.[1]

Given the data above, as well as the lack of core studies in educational institutions for boys and the community's rapid growth rate, some fear Israel becoming a country of "third-world education."[2] However, an encouraging trend is the moderate decrease in the number of ultra-Orthodox boys studying in ultra-Orthodox institutions between 2013-2021.

From 2003 to 2013, the growth in ultra-Orthodox education was rapid and constant at 4.2% per year. From 2013 to 2021, this trend reversed with a 2.3% decrease in total.[3] This trend stems from a decrease in ultra-Orthodox birth rates and in the attractiveness of ultra-Orthodox institutions among the more moderate trends within ultra-Orthodoxy.

At the same time, the influence and importance of ultra-Orthodox state institutions have moderately increased. Ultra-Orthodox state institutions offer a hybrid educational model to pupils from ultra-Orthodox backgrounds whose parents wish to preserve Torah-based ultra-Orthodox educational foundations and have their children obtain a broader education on core subjects and acquire more diverse study skills. This synthesis applies to approximately 4% of all ultra-Orthodox education for boys.[4] Although this rate is low, it is significant from the point of view of the ultra-Orthodox, for whom core studies for boys not only abrogate the Torah but also subvert the ultra-Orthodox ethos.

C. Higher Education

In line with the low rate of eligibility for enrollment to institutes of higher education, the rate of ultra-Orthodox studying in such institutes is also

---

① Cahaner and Malach, *Statistical Report* 2020, 98-103.

② Dan Ben-David, "The Shoresh Handbook: Education and Its Impact in Israel, 2017-2018."

③ Cahaner and Malach, *Statistical Report* 2020, 26-43.

④ Ibid., 27.

particularly low. While the ultra-Orthodox comprise 13% of the general population, only 4.5% of all university and college students in Israel are ultra-Orthodox. Most students study for a bachelor's degree (82%), while only a few pursue graduate degrees (18%). Most students are female (67%).

While the rate of ultra-Orthodox enrollment is relatively low, it has more than doubled in the last decade, while the rate in the general population has not changed significantly.[①] It is, therefore, possible to speak of a process of academization emerging in ultra-Orthodox society, especially for women, but it is still in its infancy.

Most ultra-Orthodox students — both men and women — apply to special academic frameworks that are culturally and religiously adjusted to the values and practices of the ultra-Orthodox student. These frameworks include courses and programs that do not differ in their level and requirements from non-Orthodox academic institutions. In recent years, the number of these institutions has risen, and studying in them has become normative and part of the ultra-Orthodox mainstream.[②]

The existence of an "ultra-Orthodox" academic framework expresses a significant change that ultra-Orthodox society is going through and the long way it has come. Once, the concept of "Orthodox academic education" was considered an oxymoron, and higher education was seen as a real threat. Still, the demand for special frameworks also signifies the insistence of the Haredi population to limit the influence of the non-ultra-Orthodox majority and to maintain its autonomy.

D. Employment

In line with the high rate of ultra-Orthodox men who devote themselves to Torah study (or at least claim to) and the low rate of ultra-Orthodox men who pursue higher education, only 52.5% of ultra-Orthodox men of working age (25-64) join the labor market, compared to 86% of men of working age in the

① Cahaner and Malach, *Statistical Report* 2020, 32-33.
② Novis Deutsch and Rubin, "Ultra-Orthodox Women."

general populace.[1] In the last decade, the rate of ultra-Orthodox men of working age who devote themselves to studying Torah (or at least claim to) and avoid integration into the labor market increased by one-third: in 2012, the number of ultra-Orthodox men of working age who studied in "Kollel" was 70,000, and in 2020 it was 94,000.[2]

Furthermore, the lack of professional experience and education among ultra-Orthodox men limits their possible employment in certain occupations. Thus, over the last decade, ultra-Orthodox men have found work in education more than in any other field: about one in three, compared to one in twenty in the general population. It is a low-income profession. Thus, the grim reality is that much of the Haredi contribution to the labor force is the creation of a new generation of Haredi men who will not be able to compete in the job market.

In contrast, the rate of ultra-Orthodox men working in management and high-tech, high-income professions, is particularly low (4.5% and 3%, respectively, compared to 13% and 14%, respectively, in the general population). Furthermore, while the rate of non-ultra-Orthodox men working in the high-tech industry has increased by almost 2% in the last decade, the rate of ultra-Orthodox men in the industry has not changed.[3]

These data explain the disparity in average income between ultra-Orthodox men and non-ultra-Orthodox men, which is increasing: the average gross monthly income among ultra-Orthodox men aged 25-64 is twice as low as the average income of men aged 25-64 from the general population.[4] The data illustrates the link between low education and low income in the ultra-Orthodox community, which led Ben David to argue that "third world education" will lead to a "third world economy."[5]

Employment data regarding ultra-Orthodox women indicates an increase in their participation in the labor market over the past two decades. This

① Ariel Karlinsky, "Education, Employment and Earnings of Ultra-Orthodox Men, a Long-Term View: Are the Gaps Narrowing?," *Policy Paper no.* 70 (Jerusalem: Kohelet Policy Forum, 2021), 5-7. [Hebrew]

② Ibid., 39-40.

③ Cahaner and Malach, *Statistical Report* 2020, 61.

④ Ibid., 58-59.

⑤ Dan Ben-David, "The Shoresh Handbook: Education and Its Impact in Israel, 2017-2018."

increase coincided with their increasing pursuit of academic studies. In 2003, only about half of ultra-Orthodox women worked, while in 2020, almost 80% of them were working. The data also show the gap between the percentage of working ultra-Orthodox women and the percentage of working non-ultra-Orthodox women (82.5%) has narrowed and that the rates of occupational integration among the two groups are almost equal.①

Moreover, unlike ultra-Orthodox men, whose main occupation is still education, the occupations of ultra-Orthodox women are similar to those of non-ultra-Orthodox women. For example, between 2014-2020, the rates of ultra-Orthodox women employed in education decreased by 5% in favor of other occupations (39%), while the rates of non-ultra-Orthodox women employed in education did not change significantly (17%). In these years, there was also an increase in the rate of ultra-Orthodox women engaged in high-tech (from 3% to 5%), while among non-ultra-Orthodox women, there was an increase in this industry, but at a lower rate (from 6% to 7%).②

Despite ultra-Orthodox women increasingly joining the workforce, the reality that in at least half of ultra-Orthodox families, most of which have multiple children, they are the primary or sole breadwinners, means that the ultra-Orthodox population is characterized by extremely high poverty rates (over half of the ultra-Orthodox population lives below the poverty line compared to 21% of the total population), and high levels of housing and population density.③ Given this, Ben David warns that Israeli society is facing an existential threat.④

E. Military Service

According to the Israeli Defense Service Law (1986), men and women 18 years of age are conscripted into the IDF; men are required to serve three years and women two years. Citizens can be exempted from military service because of different conditions, including religious practices. Ultra-Orthodox youth are

---

① Cahaner and Malach, *Statistical Report* 2020, 64.

② Ibid., 63-64.

③ Assaf Tsachor-Shai and Nitsa Kasir, "Covid-19, Population Density, and Haredi Cities," The Haredi Institute for Public Affairs (April 2020), 3-4.

④ Dan Ben-David, "The Shoresh Handbook: Education and Its Impact in Israel, 2017-2018."

encouraged torequest service exemptions or deferrals based on their being yeshiva students whose "profession" is studying the Torah. Ultimately, they postpone their enlistment until their duty to serve expires, thereby avoiding military service entirely.①

Ultra-Orthodox opposition to military service stems from several factors: (a) the perception that military service harms Torah study and, given the Torah is of supreme importance, religious study surpasses military service in importance; (b) the perception that the military's secular framework threatens to undermine or erode the faith of ultra-Orthodox youth even though the IDF goes to great lengths to accommodate their religious and cultural needs; (c) lack of identification with the values of the IDF and the state; and (d) theperception of military service involving risk that contravenes Jewish law.②

The roots of the generous exemption policy are in a decision taken by Israel's first prime minister and minister of defense, David Ben-Gurion. In the early years of independence, Ben-Gurion exempted 400 yeshiva students from service in order to enable them to study Torah and revive the yeshiva world that was destroyed in the Holocaust. According to Ben-Gurion, "Based on Section 12 of the Security Service Law, I released yeshiva students from mandatory service. This release applies only to yeshiva students who are engaged in Torah study in yeshivas, as long as they are engaged in Torah study in yeshivas."③

The exemption from military service does not allow those who wish to leave the yeshiva and integrate into the labor market to do so without being obliged to enlist. Over the years, the number of yeshiva members has grown; today, over 135,000 yeshiva students are exempt from military service.④

Until 2007, the rate of ultra-Orthodox who joined the army reached a few hundred at most; it then began to rise until 2015, when enlistment reached more than 2,000 recruits, although it is questionable whether all of these were

---

① Benjamin Brown, *The Haredim: A Guide to Their Beliefs and Sectors*, 14.

② Yohai Hakak, *Haredi Masculinities Between the Yeshiva, the Army, Work and Politics—The Sage, the Warrior, and the Entrepreneur* (Leiden: Brill, 2016), 39-56.

③ Zvi Tal, "The Committee to Formulate the Appropriate Arrangement Regarding the Recruitment of Yeshiva Students—A Report [Hebrew]," Knesset of Israel, 2002.

④ Cahaner and Malach, *Statistical Report* 2020, 72.

actually Haredi at all. However, since 2015, the enlistment rate has decreased significantly; in 2019, only 1,222 ultra-Orthodox enlisted.①

The ultra-Orthodox attitude toward military service has not changed, except among certain circles that see military service as a default for boys the ultra-Orthodox framework cannot deal with. Indeed, most ultra-Orthodox recruits do not represent the mainstream of the ultra-Orthodox public. Rather, they are young people who did not last in the yeshiva framework, and the military framework provides them with an alternative supportive framework. Others turned to military service so they could join the labor market when discharged from service.②

Ⅴ. Conflicts and Tensions

The characteristics and trends detailed above result from the ultra-Orthodox's religious stringencies, its separation from the majority, and the obligation of the men to devote their time to Torah study.③ These characteristics create points of tension and conflict between the ultra-Orthodox and the non-ultra-Orthodox majority around three main issues: (a) lack of participation in the workforce; (b) opposition to military service; and (c) opposition to the legal system.

About half (47%) of ultra-Orthodox men still prefer the world of the yeshiva or at least the resources their membership provides them, over entering the general labor market, and they rely on allowances they receive from the yeshiva.④ These allowances are paid for by donations, as well as by the state, which has provided (and provides) funds as part of coalition agreements with ultra-Orthodox parties.

As a result, under the auspices of the state, it has been possible to perpetuate the ignorance of ultra-Orthodox men in worldly matters and their

① Cahaner and Malach, *Statistical Report* 2020, 72.

② Yohai Hakak, *Haredi Masculinities Between the Yeshiva, the Army, Work and Politics—The Sage, the Warrior, and the Entrepreneur*, 39-56.

③ Benjamin Brown, *The Haredim: A Guide to Their Beliefs and Sectors*, 11-12.

④ Cahaner and Malach, *Statistical Report* 2020, 31.

inability to integrate into the workforce. This reality has provoked anger and frustration among the majority, who feel those among the ultra-Orthodox, who do not work or pay taxes, are living at their expense, and do not share the economic burden. "Exploiters, parasites, and freeloaders" are only some of the pejorative terms used by Israelis in the majority to describe the ultra-Orthodox.[1]

Another source of tension is the ultra-Orthodox's failure to share the country's security burden with the majority. Over the years, efforts have been made to change the Israeli Defense Service Law. These efforts involved bills requiring yeshiva students to enlist in the IDF and civil service.

However, whenever such a bill is raised, ultra-Orthodox hold mass demonstrations and prayer rallies led by the community's leading rabbis to protest the potential law and to prevent its adoption and implementation. Attempts to change the Israeli Defense Service Law have failed so far. Still, efforts to advance legislation have had an unintended consequence: they have contributed to increasing already existing ultra-Orthodox suspicions of the judiciary and their lack of faith in it.

According to Zicherman,[2] ultra-Orthodox distrust of the judiciary stems from three conflicts:

The obligation to obey the law when it contradicts religious law.[3] This was most recently seen, for example, during the Covid-19 lockdowns, when ultra-Orthodox violated state-mandated restrictions on public gatherings by obeying their rabbis' orders to continue attending congregational prayers and study in yeshivas.[4]

The common perception among ultra-Orthodox is that the Israeli judiciary is "the courts of Gentiles," mainly due to its adoption of the British legal system and general reliance on so-called human-made laws. "Gentile courts" are prohibited in Jewish law, while rabbinical courts are considered the

---

① Cahaner, *Ultra-Orthodox Society*, 230.

② Haim Zicherman, "One Trial You Will Have: The Triple Confrontation of Haredi Society," *Law, Society and Culture—Tel Aviv University* (2018): 37-68. [Hebrew]

③ Ibid.

④ Zalcberg and Zalcberg Block, "Covid-19 Amongst the Ultra-Orthodox."

appropriate venue for legal proceedings.

Confrontation with the Supreme Court over rulings on issues of religion and state, which the ultra-Orthodox view as restrictive and encroaching on their way of life.[①]

These three conflicts led to a crisis of trust. The only three demonstrations organized by ultra-Orthodox leaders in recent decades that attracted hundreds of thousands of protestors were directed against the Supreme Court and its rulings. Surveys indicate a very high degree of distrust in the judiciary among the ultra-Orthodox (83%).[②]

Ⅵ. Where Is Ultra-Orthodox Society Headed?

What is the future of ultra-Orthodox society? Has it and will it become an existential threat to the Zionist enterprise as a rational and modern expression of Jewish identity, or will a moderate trend emerge that bridges the widening gaps between the community and the majority?

Studies suggested that the development of religious movements is a process that includes several key stages. (a) The foundation stage of the movement; (b) the expansion stage — in which the movement expands and recruits new members to its ranks; and (c) the institutionalization stage — in which members are born into the movement, into an existing reality, with almost no scope for choosing an alternative reality.

Intergenerational changes and changes in the socio-economic status of religious movements and groups over time make them more "compromising" in their relations with the "outside world," and they take on a more institutional and "calm" character. The religious zeal of the founders' generation is moderated among the members of subsequent generations, and some may even rebel against it.

The data presented so far indicate a trend of perpetuating ignorance among the ultra-Orthodox population, especially among ultra-Orthodox men, and a trend of low integration of ultra-Orthodox men into the labor market.

---

① Zicherman, "One Trial You Will Have."

② Ibid.

However, looking at the processes that ultra-Orthodox society has undergone in recent decades paints a broader, more profound, and more complex picture.

This picture does not ignore the impact ultra-Orthodox society has on Israeli society. At the same time, it identifies changes and trends that may minimize the threat to Israeli society that some policymakers and researchers see emanating from the ultra-Orthodox community.

Recent years have seen increasing participation, presence, inner resilience, and self-confidence of different factions in ultra-Orthodox society.[1] Some ultra-Orthodox are strong enough to integrate into the majority without feeling threatened by it. At the same time, ultra-Orthodox society has become more receptive to its members who integrate into the majority and to members that deviate from the ultra-Orthodox ethos.[2] Extensive discourse has developed among the ultra-Orthodox on issues that until recently were considered taboo, such as domestic violence and sexual abuse, even in the most conservative circles.[3]

Part of the change originates from grassroots ultra-Orthodox female activism— ultra-Orthodox women who dared to challenge social conventions and challenge the community's leading rabbis.[4] Ultra-Orthodox women's activism, which some also define as "ultra-Orthodox feminism," involves female activists who raise the issues of women's education, women's employment in the public discourse, and their political representation.[5] Their activity is seen by others in the ultra-Orthodox public as a challenge to

---

① Kimmy Kaplan and Nurit Stadler, *From Survival to Consolidation: Changes in Israeli Haredi Society and Its Scholarly Study* (Tel Aviv-Jerusalem: HakibbutzHameuchad and Van Leer Jerusalem Institute, 2012), 11-28.

② Neri Horowtiz, "Haredi Disaffiliation: Risk, Potential and Social Policy," Out for Change Association (Jerusalem, 2018), 22-24.

③ Sara Zalcberg, "Changes in Coping Patterns of Ultra-Orthodox Society in Israel Regarding Sexual Abuse," in *Sexual Offenses in Israel: Trends in Legislation, Assessment, and Treatment*, eds. Mili Shhory-Biton, Yehudit Aboulafia and Lisa Tzvi (Jerusalem: Carmel Publishing House, 2021), 455-480. [Hebrew]

④ Michal Kravel-Tovi, "They Must Join Us, There is No Other Way: Haredi Activism, the Battle Against Sexual Violence, and the Reworking of Rabbinic Accountability," *Nashim* 37 (2020): 66-86.

⑤ Cahaner, *Ultra-Orthodox Society*, 203-205.

fundamental values such as modesty, the family, and obedience to the rabbis.①

In general, ultra-Orthodox women today are more educated, established, assertive, and opinionated. As such, they have become significant agents of change for the ultra-Orthodox population, initiating innovative and revolutionary developments. Meanwhile, their conduct consciously and unconsciously has contributed to challenging the prevailing ideal type of ultra-Orthodox family—the husband who devotes himself to Torah study while his wife, in addition to raising the kids, works as the primary breadwinner, often as a teacher.②

Several other agents of change have contributed to transformations in ultra-Orthodox society in recent years. One is those who leave the ultra-Orthodox world. Throughout the years, such people were denounced and ostracized by their families and the community.③ However, in recent years, the attitude of ultra-Orthodox society regarding "dropouts," as they are called in Haredi discourse, has changed and shifted from an exclusive to an inclusive approach. Following this, a significant portion of dropouts tend to maintain ties with their family members, unlike before, and they influence them in one way or another.④

Another major agent of change is the internet. Despite some rabbis' objection to any such usage, whereas only 28% of the Haredim used the internet in 2008, no less than 64% did so in 2020.⑤ The internet revolution penetrated ultra-Orthodox society, exposing it to previously inaccessible content, which is now only a click away. This revolution broke the boundaries of the "Orthodox ghetto."

The changes in employment and the increasing integration, even if still

① Helene Sinnreich, "(In)visible Women: Ultra-Orthodox Jewish Women's Faces and the Internet," *Shofar: An Interdisciplinary Journal of Jewish Studies* 38 (Summer 2020): 61-91.

② Orly Tsarfaty, "From Transparent Women to Present Women: The Struggle of Ultra-Orthodox Women for Representation in the 20th Knesset," *Gender* 4 (December 2015): 1-29.

③ Shlomi Doron, "Changing Identities Through Rituals: Newcomers to and Defectors from Ultra-Orthodox Judaism," 13-32.

④ Neri Horowtiz, "Haredi Disaffiliation: Risk, Potential and Social Policy," 9-39.

⑤ Cahaner and Malach, *Statistical Report* 2020, 74.

very moderate, into the labor market have created, in recent years, an ultra-Orthodox middle class, a class that did not exist previously. This is a more academic, open, and consumerist ultra-Orthodox, which has adapted to modern Western consumer culture and even to a luxurious lifestyle that it did not know before. This group has adopted a standard of living that will be very difficult to give up.

To maintain this standard of living, the new middle class will have no choice but to continue to pursue education, lucrative professions, and further integration into the labor market.[1] This group is not only a product of changes within ultra-Orthodox society, but is itself an agent of change that may impact the future of ultra-Orthodox society. It is not impossible that this class will continue to expand and will contribute to increasing integration, perhaps even through military service. A counter-reaction of resistance to such a trend is expected but, according to Brown, will appear at much lower rates.[2]

The great triumph of the ultra-Orthodox in the recent elections may prove counter-productive, as the non-ultra-Orthodox majority appears to be losing patience. Future governments may back away from coalition agreements with ultra-Orthodox parties that force them to finance yeshiva members, as was the case in 2003 when child allowances were significantly cut and ultra-Orthodox had no choice but to enter the labor market.[3]

It is also possible that future governments will sever the link between exemption from military service and the inability to enter the workforce and allow and encourage yeshiva members who refuse to serve in the army to go to work. Such a decision will indeed further damage the perception of conscription as egalitarian. Yet it will decrease the huge gap in economic contribution.

Even if the rate of ultra-Orthodox who adopt modern Western worldviews and the rate of ultra-Orthodox men who study in institutions of higher education and integrate into the workforce remain very low today, they

---

① Haim Zicherman and Lee Cahaner, *Modern Ultra-Orthodoxy: The Emergence of Haredi Middle Class* (Jerusalem: The Israel Democracy Institute, 2012), 145-161. [Hebrew]

② Benjamin Brown, *A Society in Motion: Structures and Processes in Ultra-Orthodox Judaism*, 401-403.

③ Eitan Regev, "Patterns of Haredi Integration into the Labor Market: An Inter- and Multi-Sector Analysis and Comparison," in *The State of the Nation Report* 2017 (Jerusalem: Taub Center, 2017), 6.

represent an increase compared to the rates in the past and a significant change whose weight is far beyond its quantitative significance. These are indeed very small steps for the majority but important steps for ultra-Orthodox society. Just as the ultra-Orthodox community of two decades ago did not look the same as it does today, in two decades, it may look different than today.

以色列的极端正统派:身份与趋向

萨拉·扎尔克伯

【摘要】本文旨在分析以色列极端正统派(Haredi)社群的当下发展趋势。首先讨论极端正统的身份界定难题,然后概要刻画这一群体,聚焦于其与主流社会间的张力和冲突。通过探讨极端正统派作为一个社群如何在变化中维持其飞地特质,本文对其未来数十年的演化趋势作出若干预测。

【关键词】极端正统派;以色列;身份认同

JEWISH STUDIES
犹太研究
第21辑

Better Left Unsaid: Sexual Offenses and the Haredim

Carl Yonker

Abstract: The article examines when and how ultra-Orthodox news media reports on sexual scandals involving public figures within and outside the community, focusing on three recent cases involving Donald Trump, Yehuda Meshi-Zahav, and Chaim Walder. Through a comparative analysis of the reporting (or non-reporting) of these scandals in leading ultra-Orthodox dailies (*Hamodia*, *YatedNe'eman*, *Hapeles*, and *Hamevaser*), the weekly *Mishpacha*, and online news websites (*B'HadreiHaredim*, *KikarHaShabbat*, and *Haredim* 10) it explores the strategies employed by Haredi media when reporting on sexual offenses. It demonstrates that ultra-Orthodox media do not primarily serve as platforms for reporting news of public interest, but rather as agents delineating the borders of legitimate public speech.

Key Words: Sexual Offenses, the Haredim, Silence

Introduction

Unlike the secular press in Israel and elsewhere, the purpose of ultra-Orthodox news media is to provide Haredim with "information they should be thinking about and [protect the community] from information that may be contrary to the desired moral values."① Its (self-conceived) role is thus not to provide a critical perspective of its community or "objective" reporting, but to

① Matt Evans, "Exacerbating Social Cleavages: The Media's Role in Israel's Religious-Secular Conflict," *Middle East Journal* 65 (Spring 2011): 246.

reinforce Haredi values and "build what they see as the model society" by "[reflecting] less of what reality is and more of what reality should be."[1]

Producing "clean" news that adheres to the community's religious values and norms in an effort to maintain "a holy community" is paramount, resulting in a high level of self-imposed censorship to avoid publishing "inappropriate" and "forbidden" content that violates their religious standards, including matters related to gossip, sex, and modesty such as prohibiting publishing photos of women or using their first names.[2] The purpose is not to ignore issues or silence discussion, but to mark the boundaries of legitimate discussion.

To do so, *mashgichim* (content supervisors, i.e., censors) "read every word before it goes to print,"[3] carefully ensuring readers, including children, are not exposed to "forbidden" content. In the case of the daily newspapers, these censors are the official representatives of the rabbis who oversee and supervise their community's newspaper.

Reporting on sexual offenses or even on controversial sexual behavior has long been considered a taboo and is extremely rare, particularly in the traditional printed press, whose censors are far more rigid in defining the boundary between what is fit and unfit to print. This resistance to report on sexual offenses increases when they involve members of the community. When compelled to cover cases of sexual abuse because they involve prominent public figures or officials, Haredi media outlets are careful to frame the story and use language that upholds avoiding gossip (*lashon hara*), avoiding public shaming (*halvanatpanim*), and maintaining modesty (*tziniut*).

For example, euphemistic and coded language is used to describe sexual offenses instead of words like "sexual harassment," "abuse," and "rape." The use of coded language does not assume a reader's ignorance of the subject being addressed. On the contrary, the language is well-understood by readers, and

---

① Yoel Cohen, "Religion News in Israel," *Journal of Media and Religion* 4 (2005): 181.

② Matt Evans, "Exacerbating Social Cleavages: The Media's Role in Israel's Religious-Secular Conflict," 246.

③ Simeon D. Baumel, "Communication and Change: Newspapers, Periodicals, and Acculturation Among Israeli Haredim," *Jewish History* 16 (2002): 164-166.

censors are aware the public likely knows and gossips about the taboo subject.

Scholarly literature on ultra-Orthodox news media is rich and has explored different aspects.[①] When scholarship addressed the topic of sexual offenses and Haredi news media, it did so within the broader context of discussions on modesty and on generally avoided topics. Two examples are usually provided but not broadly elaborated on and comprehensively analyzed—the August 1990 scandal that erupted when *YatedNe'eman* published an article on an attack on a female soldier that accidentally included the word "rape," and when former Israeli president Moshe Katzav was indicted on rape charges in 2007 and forced to resign.[②]

Other, more recent examples, particularly several that occurred within the community, are yet to be examined and compared. Further, in the above examples, analysis was limited to the established Haredi printed press and did not account (and in the case of the 1990 scandal, could not) for the evolution of the Haredi media landscape, including the rise of online news websites that have largely freed themselves from stringent rabbinical editorial oversight and new newspapers.

Given the diversity of ultra-Orthodox media, a thorough comparative analysis of when Haredi media outlets choose to report on sexual offenses and how they do so (how stories are framed and described, and what linguistic tools are used, such as omission and euphemistic language), is important for a broader understanding of the community and the nuances of Haredi media.

This article examines when and how ultra-Orthodox news media reports on sexual scandals involving public figures within and outside the community,

① See, for example: Menachem Michelson, "The Ultra-Orthodox Press in Israel," *Kesher* No. 8 (November 1990): 12e-21e; Kimmy Kaplan, "The Media in Haredi Society in Israel [Hebrew]," *Kesher* No. 30 (November 2001): 18-30; Simeon D. Baumel, "Communication and Change: Newspapers, Periodicals, and Acculturation Among Israeli Haredim," 161-186; Yoel Cohen, "The Media Challenge to Haredi Rabbinic Authority in Israel," *ESSACHESS. Journal for Communication Studies* 10 (2017): 113-128; Oren Golan and Nahki Mishol-Shauli, "Fundamentalist Web Journalism: Walking a Fine Line Between Religious Ultra-Orthodoxy and the New Media Ethos," *European Journal of Communication* 33 (2018), 304-320.

② See, for example: Simeon D. Baumel, "Communication and Change: Newspapers, Periodicals, and Acculturation Among Israeli Haredim,"164; Yoel Cohen, "The Media Challenge to Haredi Rabbinic Authority in Israel," 117.

focusing on three recent cases involving Donald Trump, Yehuda Meshi-Zahav, and Chaim Walder. To do so, the study comparatively analyzes the reporting (or non-reporting) of these scandals in the main ultra-Orthodox dailies (*Hamodia*, *YatedNe'eman*, *Hapeles*, and *Hamevaser*), the weekly *Mishpacha*, and online news websites (*B'HadreiHaredim*, *KikarHaShabbat*, and *Haredim* 10).

Through the case studies, the study addresses and engages with several interrelated questions. What factors influence the decision to cover or not cover a sexual offense scandal? When covered, how is the scandal framed? What words and expressions are used or omitted? Though all are committed to avoiding engaging in gossip and public shaming, and preserving modesty, what are the similarities and differences in how independent Haredi media outlets and printed dailies interpret and define these borders?

Ⅰ. Ultra-Orthodox Media—Reinforcing the Believers

The Haredi movement emerged in Europe in the early 19th century in response to the *Haskalah* (Jewish Enlightenment) movement, Reformism, and Secularism, insisting on strict observance of *halakha* (Jewish law) and resisting and opposing modernism and changes to Jewish social and religious practices.[1] This observant community "lives in exile among Jews," separate from its less or non-observant co-religionists in an "enclave" or "bounded" community — a group that endeavors to maintain a cohesive group identity by creating its own culture and distancing itself from outsiders by establishing physical and symbolic boundaries.[2]

For the ultra-Orthodox, these boundaries function as "walls of virtue" designed to protect the community from malign and insidious outside influences of modern secular society.[3] The "wall of virtue" creates a distinction and separation between the holy, morally superior community of insiders

---

① Kimmy Kaplan, "The Media in Haredi Society in Israel," 18.

② Oren Golan and Heidi A. Campbell, "Strategic Management of Religious Websites: The Case of Israel's Orthodox Communities," *Journal of Computer-Mediated Communication* 20 (2015): 467.

③ Gabriel A. Almond et al., *Strong Religion: The Rise of Fundamentalism around the World* (Chicago: The University of Chicago Press, 2003), 23-24, 31-34.

following God's commands and the "evil," immoral outsiders who ignore God's commands and pose an existential threat to corrupt and destroy the community's observant way of life through the temptations of secular modernity.①

However, the boundary separating inside from outside is not uniform, nor is it static; the ultra-Orthodox community is comprised of different groups divided over divergent religious interpretations and outlooks, each of which negotiates and defines its interaction with modern secular society in Israel.② Nevertheless, the boundary exists even if it is in flux.

The ultra-Orthodox press was intended to be an alternative to the secular press, protecting the community from its influences while satisfying the demand for news within their own communities. These alternative media outlets adhered to Torah values and *halakhic* principles as understood by rabbinical authorities, and were intended to help develop the community's culture, forge common identities, and shape the perception of the world, both inside and outside the community.③

The earliest Haredi newspapers were established by and affiliated with ultra-Orthodox political parties, and the four main daily newspapers today remain so. *Hamodia* was inaugurated in 1950 following the establishment of the Jewish state by Agudath Israel, connected to the Gur Hasidic dynasty. Until the 1980s, it was the ultra-Orthodox community's most important newspaper when a split within Agudath Israel between Hasidic and non-Hasidic currents resulted in the 1985 establishment of a new daily, *YatedNe'eman*. Founded by Rabbi Menachem Man Shach, *YatedNe'eman* became the paper of the Ashkenazi political party DegelHatorah and of the non-

① Gabriel A. Almond et al., *Strong Religion: The Rise of Fundamentalism around the World*, 34.

② Ibid., 85; Kimmy Kaplan, "The Media in Haredi Society in Israel," 18; Matt Evans, "Exacerbating Social Cleavages: The Media's Role in Israel's Religious-Secular Conflict," 240-241.

③ Kimmy Kaplan, "The Media in Haredi Society in Israel," 20-21; Yoel Cohen, "Israeli Haredi Media and the 'Female Factor,'" 367-368; Yoel Cohen, "The Media Challenge to Haredi Rabbinic Authority in Israel," 116.

Hasidic Lithuanian current.①

More recently, two new newspapers emerged from splits with *Hamodia* and *YatedNe'eman-Hamevaser* and *Hapeles*. First published in 2009, *Hamevesar* is the newspaper of the Shlomi Emunei faction of Agudath Israel that former Knesset member Meir Porush established due to a split with the Gur Hasidim, who dominate *Hamodia*. *Hapeles* was founded in 2012 due to a leadership dispute in the Lithuanian Haredi community, becoming the mouthpiece of the more radically anti-Zionist "Jerusalem Faction" (*HapelegHayerushalmi*) aligned with Rabbi Shmuel Auerbach, which broke away from the BneiBrak-based Lithuanian leadership. Headed by former longtime editors of *YatedNe'eman*, the two dailies are fierce and bitter rivals, articulating different outlooks within the Lithuanian Haredi community.②

The readership of ultra-Orthodox dailies has declined over the last decade due to the general fall in demand for the printed press, increasing internet access, and the appeal of "independent" outlets in print and online. According to the last available surveys on Haredi media in Israel, *Hamodia* had the largest exposure rate within Haredi society (16.6%) compared to *YatedNe'eman* (16.2%), *Hamevaser* (13.5%), and *Hapeles* (11.2%), but only *Hamevaser*'s exposure increased compared to previous years (up from 11.0%), while the other papers' exposures declined (*Hamodia* from 18.1%, *YatedNe'eman* from 17.1%, and *Hapeles* from 13.7%).③

Among the "independent" outlets, i.e., those not directly tied to a party or faction and whose target audience is the Haredi public as a whole (Hasidic and non-Hasidic), are the commercial weekly magazines *Mishpacha* (est. 1984) and *B'Kehila* (est. 1997) and the websites *B'HadreiHaredim* (est. 2008), *Kikar HaShabbat* (est. 2009), and

① Matt Evans, "Exacerbating Social Cleavages: The Media's Role in Israel's Religious-Secular Conflict," 244; Simeon D. Baumel, "Communication and Change: Newspapers, Periodicals, and Acculturation Among Israeli Haredim," 164-167.

② Yoel Cohen, "The Media Challenge to Haredi Rabbinic Authority in Israel," 116. On the newspapers' rivalry see, for example: Yehuda Halevi and Avi Greenzieg, "Torah Scholars: Hapeles Desecrates Heaven and Spreads Hatred [Hebrew]," *B'HadreiHaredim*, February 17, 2014, https://www.bhol.co.il/news/750837.

③ "TGI Survey of the Haredi Press — All the Stats [Hebrew]," *Kikar HaShabbat*, March 22, 2018, https://www.kikar.co.il/journalism/271693.

Haredim 10 (est. 2014). *Mishpacha* has significantly greater exposure within the community than *B'Kehila* (21% to 11%),[①] while *B'HadreiHaredim* and *Kikar HaShabbat* are the most frequently visited Haredi websites.

"Independent" outlets are considered to be more "open" (i.e., publishing news on all Haredi parties) and tend to operate independently from rabbinic authority and their appointed censors—*Mishpacha* being an exception—while remaining careful to avoid upsetting the community's sensitivities regarding immoral content.[②] Their emergence has been an intensely contested issue, with Haredi leaders and the dailies frequently attacking the weeklies and websites as not being "kosher" enough and a threat to Torah values.[③]

In 2009, for example, *YatedNe'eman*, *Hamodia*, and *Hamevaser* published warnings on the dangers of the internet that singled out for reproach "websites that call themselves Haredi," accusing them of printing gossip and lies, spreading discord, and attempting to "Hellenize" (i.e., secularize) the community.[④] Similar accusations were leveled at the weekly magazines by rabbis, but, as noted above, independent publications, in general, are careful to adhere to and respect the community's religious boundaries when considering what is fit to print, though they negotiate the boundaries differently.

At the core of rabbinic criticism lies the fear that the more independent weeklies and news websites erode their traditional authority rather than affirm it.[⑤] If Haredi weeklies and websites, like secular media, exist beyond rabbinical authority and the reach of their appointed censors, then the rabbis have no control over the information, the narrative, and defining the

---

① "TGI Survey of the Haredi Press—All the Stats [Hebrew]," *Kikar HaShabbat*, March 22, 2018, https://www.kikar.co.il/journalism/271693.

② Yoel Cohen, "The Media Challenge to Haredi Rabbinic Authority in Israel," 122.

③ Menachem Michelson, "The Ultra-Orthodox Press in Israel," 14e.

④ ShacharIlan, "The Commercial Department of the Hellenists [Hebrew]," *The Seventh Eye*, December 14, 2009, https://www.the7eye.org.il/19860.

⑤ Heidi Campbell, "Whose Got the Power? Religious Authority and the Internet," *Journal of Computer-Mediated Communication* 12 (April 2007): 1043-1062; Karine Barzilai-Nahon and Gad Barzilai, "Cultured Technology: The Internet and Religious Fundamentalism," *The Information Society* 21 (2005): 25-40; Oren Golan and Heidi A. Campbell, "Strategic Management of Religious Websites: The Case of Israel's Orthodox Communities," 1044; Yoel Cohen, "The Media Challenge to Haredi Rabbinic Authority in Israel," 120.

boundaries between what is permitted and what is forbidden. In a survey conducted by Yoel Cohen, "82% of Haredi rabbis favored 'to a large extent' the supervision of newspapers, and a further 13% favored this 'to some degree.'"[1] Cohen's survey also revealed that 77% of Haredi rabbis favor separate, Haredi newspapers under their supervision "to a large extent," while another 9% favor it "to some extent."[2]

Rabbinical control over the media is intended to maintain the community's boundaries by preserving and protecting it from outside influences deemed harmful to its way of life and religious worldview. Thus, the purpose and role of rabbinically-appointed censors are to ensure unacceptable content and ideas are not published while publishing content that reinforces its religious values and sense of holiness.[3]

Natan Grossman, the former editor of *YatedNe'eman*, put it thus: "All in all, our role is to reinforce the believers. We provide them with information that will assist them in confronting the secular public and in persuading unbelievers. The paper is a propaganda tool."[4] Content, therefore, "reflects less what reality is and more what it should be."[5]

Haredi editors ensure their paper's content is "clean" and "family-friendly" and does not "defile" the homes of its readers, avoiding controversial topics involving gossip, crime, and sexual offenses, lest they lose subscribers as *YatedNe'eman* almost did when it published a story about an attempted sexual assault on a female soldier that used the word "rape," which had been accidentally overlooked by an exhausted censor.[6] This approach does not assume the ignorance of readers who are likely aware of the controversial topics. Rather, it allows readers to remain ignorant while also protecting them from exposure to controversial matters they do not wish to be exposed to.

---

① Yoel Cohen, "The Media Challenge to Haredi Rabbinic Authority in Israel," 117-118.

② Ibid., 118.

③ Matt Evans, "Exacerbating Social Cleavages: The Media's Role in Israel's Religious-Secular Conflict," 246.

④ Quoted in Menachem Michelson, "The Ultra-Orthodox Press in Israel," 20e.

⑤ Matt Evans, "Exacerbating Social Cleavages: The Media's Role in Israel's Religious-Secular Conflict," 246; Yoel Cohen, "The Media Challenge to Haredi Rabbinic Authority in Israel," 116.

⑥ Menachem Michelson, "The Ultra-Orthodox Press in Israel," 12e.

These limitations pose a serious challenge that often prevents Haredi media from dealing with problematic topics, but not always. When articles on problematic topics like sexual offenses are published in newspapers, magazines, and websites, journalists employ a variety of techniques to carefully frame and report the controversial subject matter to avoid crossing boundaries of modesty and *lashon hara*.

Framing defines how reality is interpreted and understood by determining what issues are addressed and what is ignored, what details are included and what is excluded, where information is placed, and what is emphasized. All can impact the reader's perception of events and public opinion, as well as express the position of the media outlet itself on particular events.①

In addition to framing, a variety of linguistic techniques are at journalists' and editors' disposal when reporting on problematic topics "through nuances of style and language,"② including using neutral terms, euphemistic language, or omitting problematic words and phrases. These linguistic nuances reveal the diversity of ultra-Orthodox society and its media, distinguishing each outlet from another "by fine lines...that often mark the divide between the permitted and the forbidden."③

Ⅱ. Donald Trump—The Preferred (Immoral) Candidate

Few consider Donald Trump, the 45th president of the United States, to be a man of character and high moral standards. He is crude and rude, erratic and impulsive, arrogant and disruptive, a cheater and philanderer.

Yet, despite his character flaws, moral shortcomings, and immoral behavior, Trump still managed to secure a great deal of support from ultra-Orthodox Jews in the US and Israel. According to Deutsch, Haredi voters "appear to be a distinct exception" when it comes to Jewish voting patterns in the United States, as "a large majority [of Haredi Jews] supported Trump in

---

① Thomas Nelson, Zoe Oxley, and Rosalee Clawson, "Toward a Psychology of Framing Effects," *Political Behavior* 19 (1997): 221-246.

② Simeon D. Baumel, "Communication and Change: Newspapers, Periodicals, and Acculturation Among Israeli Haredim," 168.

③ Ibid., 162.

the [2016] general election, though there were also pockets of dissent for a variety of reasons."[1]

How could ultra-Orthodox support a candidate who essentially embodied everything the community opposes? Part of the answer lies in the ultra-Orthodox's traditional support for the Republican party; another was due to who his opponent was in 2016—Hillary Clinton.

Deutsch suggested that "not only did Clinton inherit the bad feelings toward President Obama that had long existed among many in the Haredi community, but her gender also likely hurt her with at least some Haredi voters."[2] Rabbi Gershon Edelstein urged his American yeshiva students in BneiBrak not to vote for Clinton and follow the advice of Rabbi Shmuel Kaminetzky, the head of the Philadelphia Yeshiva, to support Trump, declaring, in reference to Clinton, that "people who do not behave honestly and tell the truth, success is not their lot."[3]

Other rabbis in BneiBrak had urged American followers to "vote for the man and not the woman" because "death and poverty" follow the rule of a woman, while others could not conceive of a woman ruling the greatest power in the world, declaring there "would have been a flaw in creation" were Clinton elected.[4] This broad support for Trump was reflected in Haredi media, influencing how they framed and wrote about news damaging to his candidacy or involving his immoral behavior.

On the eve of the second presidential debate in October 2016, Haredi support for Trump faced a new and disturbing challenge. A recording of Trump making vulgar and lewd comments about women, saying he could do anything he wanted, just "grab 'em by the pussy," was released, igniting a

---

① Nathaniel Deutsch, "'Borough Park Was a Red State': Trump and the Haredi Vote," *Jewish Social Studies* 22 (2017): 160. The Satmar community was a notable exception, supporting Hillary Clinton, and "roughly 70 percent of the Jewish electorate" supported her, in line with previous elections. Ibid.

② Ibid., 167.

③ Eli Yakobi, "Rabbi Kaminetzky Explains: Trump Has Always Acted Truthfully and Honestly [Hebrew]," *B'HadreiHaredim*, November 10, 2016, https://www.bhol.co.il/news/772605.

④ See, for example: Moshe Weisberg, "Kabballist Rabbi Kook: We Were Saved from the Amalekite Clinton [Hebrew]," *B'HadreiHaredim*, November 9, 2016, https://www.bhol.co.il/news/772544; Moshe Weisberg, "Rabbi Gross: If Clinton was Elected — It Would Be a Flaw in Creation [Hebrew]," *B'HadreiHaredim*, November 9, 2016, https://www.bhol.co.il/news/772561.

political storm in the United States.① In the days that followed, more women came forward and publicly accused Trump of sexually harassing and sexually assaulting them, adding fuel to the political drama.② While numerous allegations of sexual misconduct have been made against Trump, he has never been criminally investigated or charged, though there have been several cases of civil litigation against him.

Given the centrality of the story to the presidential campaign and the importance of the American election to the ultra-Orthodox community in the US and Israel, Haredi media outlets were confronted with a development they could not ignore and that damaged their preferred candidate's electoral chances. How, then, did they choose to report on the scandal, and what similarities and differences emerged in the reports that appeared in independent outlets and party newspapers?

While not excusing Trump's unacceptable behavior and speech, stories that appeared online and in print nevertheless adopted his talking points and absolved him of wrongdoing. The reports described Trump as the victim of a political smear campaign and did not seriously engage with his sexual misconduct and infidelity. Moreover, as will be seen below, Haredi media outlets employed various euphemisms to convey that Trump had made unacceptable remarks about women without mentioning the sexually explicit nature of his remarks.

Articles on *KikarHaShabbat*, *B'HadreiHaredim*, *Haredim* 10 referred to "embarrassing recordings" that contain "problematic statements" and "harsh and ugly remarks toward women" and where he can be heard "speaking

① David Fahrenthold, "Trump Recorded Having Extremely Lewd Conversation About Women in 2005," *The Washington Post*, October 7, 2016, https://www.washingtonpost.com/politics/trump-recorded-having-extremely-lewd-conversation-about-women-in-2005/2016/10/07/3b9ce776-8cb4-11e6-bf8a-3d26847eeed4_story.html.

② See, for example: Megan Twohey and Michael Barbaro, "Two Women Say Donald Trump Touched Them Inappropriately," *The New York Times*, October 13, 2016, https://www.nytimes.com/2016/10/13/us/politics/donald-trump-women.html.

rudely about women" using "derogatory language."[1] Online Haredi outlets noted the scandal had hurt Trump politically within his own party and threatened to unravel his candidacy, but none elaborated on the sexually explicit nature of what Trump specifically said about women. To do so would have crossed the boundaries of legitimate discourse and modesty. Given the general fervor with which Haredi readers follow political intrigue and the particular attention paid to the American elections, such elaboration was unnecessary; informed readers knew exactly what Trump had said.

Reports on the election scandal in Haredi dailies varied significantly in length, detail, and tone, and tended to be more reticent than the online outlets in reporting about the tape and its contents. In a short article, *Hamodia* related some of the accusations exchanged by the candidates, including the Clinton email scandal, Trump's refusal to release his tax records, and Trump's proposed "Muslim ban," but avoided touching on the recording or the drama surrounding it.[2]

Several days later, in an article reporting Clinton had widened her lead on Trump in the polls, *Hamodia* referred to Trump's loss of support within the Republican party but did not explain why or that it had to do, in part, with the tape in which he made lewd comments about women.[3] *Hapeles* was only slightly more forthcoming than *Hamodia* , noting the second debate was held at the height of a public and media storm around Trump due to "problematic statements that he had made" that had caused the Republican candidate to lose significant support within his own party. While characterizing the debate as filled with "heavy barrages of insults," the article did not elaborate on the

---

① Yoni Gabai, "A Battle of Tapes and Leaks on the Way to the White House [Hebrew]," *Kikar HaShabbat*, October 8, 2016, https://www.kikar.co.il/world-news/211892; David Leibovitz, "After a Collapse in the Polls: The Trump Brand Also Suffers a Painful Drop [Hebrew]," *Haredim* 10, October 25, 2016, https://ch10.co.il/news/318886/; Daniel Hertz, "Trump Versus Clinton: A Particularly Stormy Confrontation [Hebrew]," *Kikar HaShabbat*, October 10, 2016, https://www.kikar.co.il/world-news/212015; Yoel and Bitelman, "Hilary Clinton Versus Donald Trump: Round Two [Hebrew]," *B'HadreiHaredim*, October 10, 2016: https://www.bhol.co.il/news/770690.

② "Survey: The Democratic Candidate Won the Second Debate as Well [Hebrew]," *Hamodia*, October 11, 2016.

③ "A Sense of Panic in the Republican Party After New Poll [Hebrew]," *Hamodia*, October 13, 2016.

nature of "the problematic statements."①

In contrast to *Hamodia* and *Hapeles*, *YatedNe'eman* adopted a different but common approach when covering controversial subject matter—employing condemnatory language to distinguish between the "holy" community and the secular outside, right from wrong. While this approach typically appears in editorials, *YatedNe'eman*'s A. Ben Aharon employed it in his news article, expressing his — and the paper's — utter disgust with the state of American politics — and the state of American culture in general. Characterizing the second debate as a "mudslinging contest in front of the cameras," *YatedNe'eman* lamented the level to which the American Republic — and its presidential candidates—had sunk, comparing the debate to something seen in "a banana republic" that revealed America's "new and repulsive face."②

Unfortunately, the paper told its readers, the ugliness of the debate and the revolting manner in which the candidates spoke and conducted themselves by dragging skeletons out of each other's respective closets had become the central story of the elections. Thus, it had to be covered.

The article related that Trump had been asked multiple questions about "the tape," including whether "he had changed since the days he spoke so harshly." The lewdness of Trump's remarks and the fact that they were directed at women was omitted. The article even reported Trump's response to a question regarding his outrageous comments, in which he rhetorically asked whether Bill Clinton was not even worse than him, leaving only the knowledgeable reader to make the connection on their own between the former president's sexual assault scandals and Trump's lewd remarks.③

Though *Hapeles* and *YatedNe'eman* had reported on the recordings, neither they nor the other Haredi dailies followed up with articles on additional sexual assault allegations against Trump. Only the online outlets covered the mounting complaints of sexual misconduct against Trump after the second

① Eliyahu Adler, "The US Presidential Race: The Candidates Debated a Second Time; Trump Loses Support of Republican Party [Hebrew]," *Hapeles*, October 13, 2016.

② A. Ben Aharon, "The Second Debate: A Mudslinging Contest Before the Cameras—Skeletons in the Closet Against Skeletons in the Closet [Hebrew]," *YatedNe'eman*, October 13, 2016.

③ Ibid.

debate until election day. For the dailies, the story about the recording was too big not to cover when it broke, but after that, there was no need to follow and expose their readers to the ins and outs of Trump's sexual escapades and dalliances.

In January 2018, as Trump was completing his first year in office, the above reports regarding his sexual misconduct were in the news again and at the center of American political discourse. According to a report by *The Wall Street Journal*, Trump's then-personal attorney Michael Cohen negotiated a US $130,000 non-disclosure agreement with Stormy Daniels, the porn star who claimed she had had an affair with Trump in 2006 prior to the election.① The hush money payment to Daniels was connected to a broader Federal Bureau of Investigation (FBI) probe into Russian interference in the election and resulted in the FBI raiding Cohen's home and seizing documents.

However, unlike in 2016, revelations about Trump paying hush money to a porn star or his personal attorney being at the center of an FBI investigation were not addressed in online and print Haredi media save for a single article on *B'HadreiHaredim*, which focused on Russia and made passing mention of hush money paid to a "source" (*gorem*) before the election.② It was not newsworthy, and editors and censors deemed ignoring a controversial story involving bribes and porn stars a more prudent course of action that upheld the values of modesty and avoiding gossip.

This changed dramatically in August 2018 when Cohen, appearing in a US District Court in Manhattan, implicated Trump in a federal crime. Having reached a plea deal with the government by pleading guilty to breaking campaign finance laws and tax fraud, among other charges, Cohen admitted to making two illegal payments to two women "in coordination with and at the direction of a candidate for federal office" during the 2016 election campaign to

① Joe Palazzolo and Michael Rothfeld, "Trump Lawyer Used Private Company, Pseudonyms to Pay Porn Star 'Stormy Daniels,'" *The Wall Street Journal*, January 18, 2018, https://www.wsj.com/articles/trump-lawyer-used-private-company-pseudonyms-to-pay-porn-star-stormy-daniels-1516315731.

② Yanky Farber, "The FBI Raided the Offices of Trump's Personal Attorney. He Fumes: This is a Disgrace [Hebrew]," *B'HadreiHaredim*, April 10, 2018, https://www.bhol.co.il/news/899486.

silence them and influence the election.[①]

Cohen's stunning admission in court and agreement to turn state's witness against Trump, his former client and the president, was a political bombshell that Haredi media could not ignore. Yet, while both online and print Haredi outlets, except for *Haredim* 10, were careful to avoid any direct mention or suggestion that the story involved women, let alone women who were porn stars, each outlet adopted a slightly different approach to (not) reporting on the hush money payments.

In a snippet on its fourth page, *Hamodia* reported that Cohen had reached a plea agreement with authorities regarding Russian involvement in the elections, but did not offer further details and did not report on developments in the story that emerged in the days that followed.[②] Like *Hamodia*, *YatedNe'eman* published only one report on Cohen, but provided readers with far greater detail. The article related the charges against Cohen, noting the lawyer's role in trying to influence the election by "paying hush money to figures outside the campaign who had embarrassing information about the president," and having done so on Trump's orders.[③] No details were given as to why the information would have embarrassed the president.

Similar to *YatedNe'eman*, *Hapeles* reported on the "dramatic development" that Cohen had hidden information from the public at Trump's direction prior to the election, arranging two payments to "sources" that could have revealed "negative information about Trump" to the public without providing further details. Moreover, the article obscured the fact that the unnamed "sources" were women.[④]

Striking a far different tone from the other three was *Hamevaser*. In a

① William K. Rashbaum, Maggie Haberman, Ben Protess, and Jim Rutenberg, "Michael Cohen Says He Arranged Payments to Women at Trump's Direction," *The New York Times*, August 21, 2018, https://www.nytimes.com/2018/08/21/nyregion/michael-cohen-plea-deal-trump.html.

② "The Trump Investigations: Campaign Manager Convicted; Former Attorney Entered into a Plea Agreement [Hebrew]," *Hamodia*, August 22, 2018.

③ R. Hofner, "The President's Former Attorney, Michael Cohen, Signed a Plea Deal [Hebrew]," *YatedNe'eman*, August 23, 2018.

④ P. Koren, "Trump's Lawyer Testifies: I Hid Information from the Public at His Direction before the Election [Hebrew]," *Hapeles*, August 23, 2018.

cover story for the paper, journalist Yaakov Lustigman claimed American law enforcement was conducting a "witch hunt" against Trump and had succeeded in turning Cohen into a state witness.[1] Essentially repeating Trump's talking points, Lustigman portrayed Cohen as a turncoat who had succumbed to the pressure and turned his back on Trump. Not a single mention of the hush money payments, the only charges on which Trump was directly implicated, appeared.

In contrast to the articles that appeared in the printed dailies, Nathan Pearl, writing for *Haredim* 10, was the most forthcoming on the nature of the hush money. Pearl wrote that Cohen had "admitted to paying hush money to two women so they would not speak about the relationships they allegedly had with Trump," and "claimed Trump himself had ordered him to make the payments."[2] In comparison, Eli Rothman, writing for *Kikar HaShabbat*, wrote that Cohen had signed a plea deal in which he admitted that Trump ordered him to pay "to avoid serious embarrassment for himself [Trump] in the last presidential election."[3] Rothman left it up to the reader to guess to whom or to what entity Cohen had paid the money and why the latest development in the "forbidden funds affair" was so dramatic.[4]

Ⅲ. Yehuda Meshi-Zahav — The "Good" Haredi

In March 2021, the Israeli daily *Haaretz* published a disturbing investigative piece revealing multiple allegations of sexual assault and sexual harassment of minors and women against Yehuda Meshi-Zahav (1959-2022), the media-savvy ultra-Orthodox founder and chairman of the ZAKA voluntary

[1] Yaakov A. Lustigman, "Drama in the United States: Trump's Attorney Turned Himself In and Signed an Agreement as a State Witness with the FBI [Hebrew]," *Hamevaser*, August 22, 2018.

[2] Nathan Pearl, "Trump: Looking for a Good Lawyer? I Recommend Against Hiring Michael Cohen [Hebrew]," *Haredim* 10, August 22, 2018, https://ch10.co.il/news/454396/.

[3] Eli Rothman, "Trump: If They Impeach Me, You Will All Be Poor [Hebrew]," *Kikar HaShabbat*, August 23, 2018, https://www.kikar.co.il/world-news/288597.

[4] Ibid.

community emergency response organization.① His picture plastered across the front page of *Haaretz*'s weekend edition, the article related how Meshi-Zahav had taken advantage of his position and fame to sexually abuse six victims over the course of several decades, the earliest dating to 1983 and the latest to 2011.

The investigative report came just days after Meshi-Zahav was declared the winner of the Israel Prize, the highest state-awarded prize, for his contributions to Israeli society. In the following days, more complaints of sexual abuse arose, and the first sexual assault complaint against Meshi-Zahav was filed with the police, which opened a broader investigation. In light of the accusations against him and amid the frenzy in mainstream Israeli media over the story, Meshi-Zahav announced he had resigned from his role in ZAKA and was giving up the Israel Prize.②

Raised in Jerusalem's ultra-Orthodox neighborhood of Mea Shearim as part of the Eda Haredit community, in his youth, Meshi-Zahav was known for his public anti-Zionist activism within the ultra-Orthodox community, leading protests against the state of Israel and its institutions. He also served as the editor of the community's newspaper, *HaEda*.

Over time, however, he changed his views, infuriating some within the anti-Zionist Haredi community.③ In the early 1990s, he founded the volunteer organization ZAKA to help identify and recover the remains of disaster victims, particularly those killed in suicide attacks. Through ZAKA, he worked closely with the Israel Police and other government institutions. Through his efforts, he was honored in 2003 as a torchbearer for Israel's Independence Day with torch-lighting ceremony. He also promoted reconciliation between the religious and secular communities in Israel and advocated for ultra-Orthodox recruitment into the Israel Defense Forces (IDF) and integration into

① Shira Elek and Aaron Rabinowitz, "Testimonies: Yehuda Meshi-Zahav Sexually Assaulted and Exploited Children, Minors, and Women [Hebrew]," *Haaretz*, March 12, 2021.

② Aaron Rabinowitz, Shira Elek, Josh Brenner, Bar Peleg, and Jonathan Lis, "Police Will Check the Complaints Against Meshi-Zahav, Who Gave Up Israel Prize [Hebrew]," *Haaretz*, March 14, 2021.

③ Shai Eisenberg, "Yehuda Meshi-Zahav Returns to 'Eda' [Hebrew]," *B'HadreiHaredim*, January 6, 2009, https://www.bhol.co.il/news/70376.

Israel's workforce.[1]

Due to his activism, his work with the state, and his background as an ultra-Orthodox Jew, Meshi-Zahav became accepted among Israel's secular social and political elite, who viewed him as a bridge-building figure and symbol of unity within Israeli society. However, the things that made him, as an ultra-Orthodox person, acceptable among the Israeli establishment did little to endear him to the Haredi public, which considered him a marginal figure at best and someone who had "left" the community at worst.[2]

While the Meshi-Zahav affair grabbed headlines in the mainstream Israeli press, as can only be expected of such a sensational criminal story, it went almost entirely unreported in ultra-Orthodox media. The dailies *YatedNe'eman*, *Hamodia*, *Hamevaser*, and *Hapeles*, as well as the weekly *Mishpacha*, did not mention the investigation at all and avoided reporting on subsequent developments in the affair, including Meshi-Zahav's suicide attempt in April 2021 and his death in June 2022 after more than a year of being in a coma. Like the printed dailies and weeklies, the oldest ultra-Orthodox website *B'HadreiHaredim* also did not cover the story. It would only mention it in June 2022, when it published an obituary about him.[3]

The case of Meshi-Zahav presented a triple-fold discursive challenge because of (a) his eager cooperation with the Zionist state and his eagerness to accept the honors it bestowed on him; (b) the nature of the alleged offenses he committed, which allegedly involved homosexual acts with minors; and (c) the long, long period of the silencing of these acts in communities that take pride in their morality.

The decision of Haredi dailies not to cover the affair at all reflected a strict adherence to maintaining the "modesty" and "purity" of the "family-friendly" publications; they completely ignored a story that was no doubt the talk of the town regardless of having the techniques and tools at their disposal to cover it

---

① Eli Rotman, "Committee Member: The Time Has Come to Burst the Bubble of Ultra-Orthodox Recruitment [Hebrew]," *Kikar HaShabbat*, February 20, 2020, https://www.kikar.co.il/haredim-news/348438.

② Zalczberg, "A Shaken Ship."

③ Avrumi Pearlstein, "The Activist Yehuda Meshi-Zahav (z"l) Passed Away [Hebrew]," *B'HadreiHaredim*, June 29, 2022, https://www.bhol.co.il/news/1405732.

without offending the community's religious and moral sensibilities. In this instance, they chose not to use any of those techniques.

Only *B'HadreiHaredim*'s online competitors, *Kikar HaShabbat* and *Haredim* 10, chose to cover the affair, publishing their first articles after Meshi-Zahav resigned from ZAKA.① Explaining the decision to cover the story despite its taboo subject matter, Chaim Iloz, the editor of *Kikar HaShabbat*, in an interview with the Religious Zionist newspaper *Makor Rishon*, explained the website could not ignore a case of this magnitude.②

Iloz, however, emphasized that there were boundaries the website would not cross when writing on the issue of sexual abuse. He stressed that the website "did not need to go into details" but only needed to make readers aware of and "understand the seriousness of the actions and suspicions."③ Further, he added that the website is careful about publishing names and issuing judgment out of concern that the accusations may turn out to be unfounded and indictments against alleged criminals, dropped.④

To stay within those boundaries, *Kikar HaShabbat* used indirect language to describe the sexual abuse allegations, stating that police were investigating "serious allegations" against Meshi-Zahav based on the testimonies of six victims he allegedly "attacked," as reported by *Haaretz*, without elaborating further. The article quoted Meshi-Zahav at length, enabling him to portray himself — and for the article to reinforce the perception — that he was the victim of a smear campaign.

According to Meshi-Zahav, the accusations were "part of the price [he paid] for the path [he] had chosen," while the article was no more than "an attempt to settle old scores and eliminate him."⑤ While informed readers could

① "Meshi-Zahav Takes a Break from ZAKA and Gives Up the Israel Prize [Hebrew]," *Kikar HaShabbat*, March 12, 2021, https://www.kikar.co.il/haredim-news/387419; Avi Katz, "Yehuda Meshi-Zahav Gives Up the Israel Prize and Takes a Break from ZAKA [Hebrew]," *Haredim* 10, March 12, 2021, https://ch10.co.il/news/660106/.

② Bethel Coleman, "Silk Gloves: How Did the Ultra-Orthodox Media Deal with the Meshi-Zahav Affair? [Hebrew]," *Makor Rishon*, March 18, 2021, https://www.makorrishon.co.il/news/327093/.

③ Ibid.

④ Ibid.

⑤ "Meshi-Zahav Takes a Break from ZAKA and Gives Up the Israel Prize," *Kikar HaShabbat*.

fill in the details regarding the allegation, as the affair was a topic of discussion among the Haredi public, allowing the accused to portray himself as the victim, unchallenged, suggests greater sympathy with the accused than with the alleged victims of his abuse.

Similarly, *Haredim* 10 reported police were investigating allegations that Meshi-Zahav had "committed serious acts against women and minors" before printing, in full, Meshi-Zahav's letter to ZAKA volunteers and workers in which he referred to the allegations as "unfounded plots," "gossip," and efforts to "close accounts [with him]."[①] In the weeks that followed, *Haredim* 10 covered the Meshi-Zahav affair extensively, publishing a dozen articles on developments in the criminal investigation in which it continued to use indirect language so as to avoid explicitly stating the allegations had to do with sexual offenses, maintaining its use of "serious crimes" and "attacks against women and minors."[②]

A little over a month after accusations against him became public, Meshi-Zahav attempted suicide hours before a new expose on the allegations against him was to air on *Uvda* , an investigative program on Israel's Channel 12. The macabre development presented Haredi editors with yet another choice and challenge—whether to address the taboo subject of suicide in addition to the taboo of sexual abuse and, if so, how. The dailies, as well as *Mishpacha* and *B'HadreiHaredim*, which had chosen not to address the sexual abuse allegations, remained consistent and ignored his attempted suicide as well, despite it being common knowledge within the community and within Israeli society at large.

Reporting on the suicide attempt, *Kikar HaShabbat* and *Haredim* 10 wrote that the former ZAKA chairman had been taken to the hospital in critical

---

① Avi Katz, "Yehuda Meshi-Zahav Gives Up the Israel Prize and Takes a Break from ZAKA."

② See, for example: "New Information Reaches the Police: Woman Claims Meshi-Zahav Attacked [Her] Four Years Ago [Hebrew]," *Haredim* 10, March 17, 2021, https://ch10.co.il/news/660995; "Meshi-Zahav Affair: Some of the Victims were Summoned to Testify or File a Complaint [Hebrew]," *Haredim* 10, March 19, 2021, https://ch10.co.il/news/661181/.

condition after being found in his home by one of his sons.[①] Without directly mentioning or suggesting Meshi-Zahav had tried to kill himself, both articles portrayed him as someone who had suffered a medical emergency whose causes were unknown.

The articles, however, indirectly suggested the possible reason for the deterioration of Meshi-Zahav's health was the combination of the recent *Haaretz* investigation into "serious acts" and "a series of abuses" attributed to him, the police investigation, and the about-to-air investigative piece on *Uvda*. No mention was made that the investigations were into alleged incidents of sexual abuse of young men and women and other minors.[②]

Following Meshi-Zahav's death in June 2022 after more than a year of being in a coma, the three ultra-Orthodox websites published obituaries. *B'HadreiHaredim*, writing about the affair for the first time, referred to the sexual abuse allegations that prompted Meshi-Zahav's resignation from ZAKA as "a media storm" before stating he passed away after being in a coma without mentioning what caused his coma.[③]

Its obituary, more than those that appeared in *Kikar HaShabbat* and *Haredim* 10, embodied the community's complicated and ambivalent views of the man, paying homage to Meshi-Zahav's early activism on behalf of the community, his work in ZAKA, and for raising a Torah-observant family while also characterizing him as an outsider who had "left" the Haredi community and adopted "Israeliness."[④]

In contrast to *B'HadreiHaredim*'s obituary, those of *Kikar HaShabbat* and *Haredim* 10 distinguished themselves from their online and print competitors in their respective attempts to acknowledge that Meshi-Zahav had attempted suicide. Both websites stated that Meshi-Zahav had entered a coma

---

① "Yehuda Meshi-Zahav Taken to the Hospital in Critical Condition [Hebrew]," *Kikar HaShabbat*, April 22, 2021, https://www.kikar.co.il/haredim-news/390210; Chaim Twil, "Yehuda Meshi-Zahav Evacuated in Critical Condition: Sedated and Ventilated with Signs of Life [Hebrew]," *Haredim* 10, April 22, 2021, https://ch10.co.il/news/666644/.

② Ibid.

③ Avrumi Pearlstein, "The Activist Yehuda Meshi-Zahav (z"l) Passed Away."

④ Ibid.; "A Year After: The Former Head of ZAKA Yehuda Meshi Zahav Passed Away at the Age of 62 [Hebrew]," *Haredim* 10, June 29, 2022, https://ch10.co.il/news/752564/.

after he had "harmed himself" and "tried to end his life" following the publication of a harsh investigation into "serious suspicions against him" that he had "committed serious acts against men and women, boys and girls."[1] Yet, even while acknowledging that Meshi-Zahav had committed a serious and reprehensible act forbidden by Jewish law by attempting to commit suicide, the websites maintained their stance that going into detail about the sexual nature of the allegations would cross a line—readers did not need to hear it from them, they already knew.

Ⅳ. Gossip Kills—The Chaim Walder Affair

Eight months after journalists Aaron Rabinowitz and Shira Elk published their expose on the Meshi-Zahav affair, the two published a second shocking report on sexual abuse allegations against Chaim Walder, a highly regarded and revered Haredi author and educator.[2] Published in *Haaretz*'s weekend edition, the investigation was based on the testimonies of several women who accused Walder of sexually abusing them while they were minors.[3]

Until the allegations were published, Walder had been considered a beloved and celebrated figure, particularly among the Lithuanian Haredi community. For over thirty years, he authored a weekly column in the community's newspaper, *YatedNe'eman*, and hosted a radio program on *Kol Chai*. He wrote dozens of books, including the widely-read children's series "Children Speak," that filled the shelves of ultra-Orthodox homes. He was a prominent children's advocate and educator who established a child and family therapy center in BneiBrak, among other things.[4]

Given his advocacy on behalf of children and families, the accusations of

① "After a Year in a Coma, Yehuda Meshi-Zahav Passed Away [Hebrew]," *Kikar HaShabbat*, June 29, 2022, https://www.kikar.co.il/death-notices/421938; "A Year After: The Former Head of ZAKA Yehuda Meshi Zahav Passed Away at the Age of 62."

② Aaron Rabinowitz and Shira Elk, "Women Testify: The Author Chaim Walder Took Advantage of Us Sexually When We Were Minors [Hebrew]," *Haaretz*, November 12, 2021.

③ Ibid.

④ Eli Bitan, "Ultra-Orthodox Society Falls Into Line and Renounces Walder [Hebrew]," *Makor Rishon*, January 7, 2022, https://www.makorrishon.co.il/news/443905/.

sexual abuse caught the community off-guard and left it in a state of shock, confusion, and anger. Searching for answers and clarity, the sexual abuse allegations against Walder were widely discussed and debated among the ultra-Orthodox public (to say nothing of Israeli society at large), even among rabbis, particularly on social media sites.①

Answers and clarity, however, would not come from the Haredi media, which initially reacted to the *Haaretz* investigation, as with the Meshi-Zahav affair, with silence. Not a single story about the sexual abuse allegations appeared online or in print.

Why did these outlets — their censors and editors — choose to strictly adhere to the default approach of not reporting on such topics, particularly when they occur within the community and, in this case, involve a celebrated figure? How could *YatedNe'eman*, in light of the allegations and, to a certain degree, indirectly acknowledging their veracity, suspend Walder from the newspaper and cease printing his weekly column less than a week after the *Haaretz* investigation, but not publish a report on the matter?

Censors and the rabbis they represented considered addressing the accusations to be crossing a red line. They feared that giving publicity to a scandal (about which most likely every Haredi household had already learned from other sources) would indicate that public and transparent discussion of the matter was considered legitimate — something the leaders of the community were eager to avoid.

However, Haredi media subject to less rabbinical control were not entirely silent. *Kikar HaShabbat* initially published an article on the affair before falling silent again, noting Walder had been suspended from the Haredi radio station *Kol Chai* due to "a series of allegations" regarding his conduct, including "serious allegations... he had behaved inappropriately towards his patients."②

The weekly magazine *Mishpacha*, in an editorial published two weeks

① Dana Bezalel, "This is How the Conspiracy of Silence Around the Write Chaim Walder Crumbled [Hebrew]," *Makor Rishon*, November 20, 2021, https://www.makorrishon.co.il/news/423359/.

② "The Author and Educator Chaim Walder Suspended from Kol Chai Radio [Hebrew]," *Kikar HaShabbat*, November 17, 2021, https://www.kikar.co.il/haredim-news/405626.

after the allegations came to light, departed from the consensus approach of not covering stories on the subject of sexual abuse.[1] It did so in an unprecedented manner, its editors having concluded that the affair, the topic dominating public discussion, could not and should not be ignored and that their magazine must play a role and express its views.[2] However, the editors argued that they were adhering to the community's boundaries regarding modesty and public shaming, which remained of utmost importance.

In an editorial entitled "No Time to Whisper," the magazine acknowledged the pain and shock within the community while reminding readers that it was not the role of the magazine or of individuals in the community to pass judgment on serious and immoral behaviors.[3] Further, it emphasized that the discourse on the allegations, particularly ones so serious, should accord with *halakhic* guidelines, but the public domain was not the place for these discussions as they "could lead to public shaming, [figuratively] opening one's wounds and shedding their blood."[4] Indeed, "one injustice will not be corrected by another injustice, and not all means are kosher to achieve an objective."[5] Without specifically mentioning Walder or the affair, *Mishpacha* suggested Haredi media adopt a different approach that engaged with the challenge confronting the press—confronting the sin of sexual abuse within the community without committing sin by publicly shaming victims and the accused.

It was only after Walder committed suicide more than a month later, in late December 2021, at his son's graveside that Haredi media would engage in the affair to a greater extent, albeit to differing degrees.[6] As they had from the beginning, *Hamodia* and *Hamevaser* ignored Walder's suicide and the affair entirely, neither publishing an obituary for him nor publishing an article

---

① "Editorial — No Time to Whisper [Hebrew]," *Mishpacha*, November 25, 2021.

② Amy Spiro, "Six Months After the Walder Abuse Scandal Broke, Has the Haredi World Seen Change?," *Times of Israel*, May 16, 2022, https://www.timesofisrael.com/6-months-after-the-walder-abuse-scandal-broke-has-the-haredi-world-seen-change/.

③ "Editorial — No Time to Whisper."

④ Ibid.

⑤ Ibid.

⑥ On Walder's suicide, see: Yehoshua Brenner, "The Author Chaim Walder Committed Suicide After Testimonies Published Against Him [Hebrew]," *Haaretz*, December 28, 2021.

discussing the affair and acknowledging his death.

YatedNe'eman published an obituary for Walder, which was expected given Walder's status within the Lithuanian Haredi community and that he had authored a weekly column for the paper for decades. It also published a religious opinion of Rabbi Gershon Edelstein, the paper's overseer, which argued why the media was not the place for addressing issues like those involved in the Walder affair in an effort to justify and explain the silence of the Haredi press.

The obituary made no mention of the circumstances regarding his death, writing that the "renowned author" was "suddenly taken at an early age... to his heavenly home" while visiting his son's grave.① Regarding the affair, the paper wrote that Walder "recently had been asked to temporarily stop writing his regular column and take a break from writing [in general]."② Censors ensured that the sexual abuse allegations were not mentioned, nor was there even a hint that Walder was suspected—even convicted by a rabbinical court—of being a sexual predator. Instead, the paper maintained its "purity" by ignoring the issue so as not to present an immodest topic to its readers or publicly shame Walder.

Hapeles, despite its long disdain and criticism of Walder, and its rivalry with *YatedNe'eman*, the paper from which it split in 2012, considered *YatedNe'eman*'s flattering eulogy for Walder a provocation. It published a scathing full-page rebuke reminding readers of the strict prohibition against praising the wicked who have sinned and erred.③ The harsh rebuke appeared in the form of an exegesis without mentioning its journalistic rival, Walder, or the affair.

Employing this "condemnatory" editorial approach enabled *Hapeles* to maintain its "purity" while also reinforcing its own sense of "holiness" by teaching its rivals a moral lesson. Taking its title from Psalms 50:21, in which

① M. Berger, "Rabbi Chaim Eliezer Walder, May His Memory Be a Blessing [Hebrew]," *YatedNe'eman*, December 28, 2021.

② Ibid.

③ Rabbi AryehChaimson, "On the Agenda: 'I Will Rebuke You and Present the Case Before Your Eyes [Hebrew],'" *Hapeles*, December 31, 2021.

God tells the wicked that He will rebuke them for their transgressions and lay the case against them before their eyes, the article proceeded to lay out "the case" against "the wicked" — Walder and *YatedNe'eman*. Urging readers not to follow *YatedNe'eman*'s path by justifying the wicked, calling evil good, and darkness light, it warned against strengthening transgressors with words and to not associate with those who agree with injustice; one does not praise an individual who transgresses the Torah and violates its commandments. Recalling Proverbs 17: 15 ("One who justifies the wicked and one who condemns the righteous, Both of them alike are an abomination to the Lord"), the article condemned those who knew an injustice had been committed yet continued to justify the transgressor.

On the same day that *Hapeles*'s rebuttal appeared, *YatedNe'eman* published the views of Rabbi Gershon Edelstein. In his "Torah Views" (*da'at Torah*) column, entitled "And You Showed Them the Way," Edelstein, pushing back against critics, defended the decision by his paper and other Haredi outlets to not address any aspect of the Walder affair on their pages or websites.

Edelstein went so far as to suggest that Walder's death was not a suicide, but murder, claiming public gossip and criticism drove him to take his own life. Referencing a passage from the Gemara that states, "one who publicly shames his friend [*hamalbinpaneihavero*] has no share in the World to Come,"[1] Edelstein accused those openly discussing the affair of publicly shaming Walder, thereby endangering their share in the World to Come.[2] His arguments addressed a core question raised in public discourse and *Mishpacha*'s November editorial — whether Haredi media has a role in addressing taboo subject matter. Edelstein's answer was clear — no, it did not, and to do so would amount to engaging in sin and emulating the behavior of secular Jews.

---

① *b.BavaMetzia* 59a. The passage in the Gemara addresses King David's affair with Bathsheba and what God's judgment is on one who engages in intercourse with a married woman. According to the text, such a man's punishment is execution, but he has a share in the World to Come. However, the one who publicly humiliates another in public does not have a share in the World to Come, rendering the transgression of public shaming worse than adultery.

② Rabbi Gershon Edelstein, "And You Showed Them the Way [Hebrew]," *YatedNe'eman*, December 31, 2021.

Without mentioning Walder by name, Edelstein's opinion made a series of interrelated points on the issues of gossip and public shaming surrounding the affair — both the sexual abuse allegations and his suicide. Edelstein argued victims must consult with the appropriate authorities so the matter can be dealt with confidentially and with discretion, emphasizing that giving testimony (about sexual abuse) does not constitute "gossip" (*lashon hara*) and that "with discretion, there is wisdom." Those spreading information, especially explicit and obscene descriptions of sexual abuse, in the media who are not personally affected by the matter are not helping the victims, but causing greater harm rather than good. Edelstein expressed his shock at how "the children of Abraham, Isaac, and Jacob" — the Haredim — could follow the path of "the evildoers" (*harasha'im*, e.g., secular Jews) by engaging in public gossip and seeking "revenge" through public shaming, stating the one who does so transgresses the Torah and is considered a murderer.①

Turning his attention to the media, Edelstein bluntly stated that the media was not the place for addressing issues like those involved in the Walder affair. Newspapers and journalists covering the story were committing the prohibited act of public shaming and were responsible for ruining lives, "shedding blood," and murdering those about whom they were publishing. In ruining people's lives, newspapers and journals were not acting in accordance with Jewish law, which dictates matters must be dealt with in a professional and discreet manner. His unambiguous and broad criticism of the "terrible faults" of modern mass media that covered the affair, however, was not enough.

Going further, Edelstein asserted the moral superiority of Haredi newspapers and of rabbinical editorial oversight and censorship, stating that ultra-Orthodox newspapers stood a world apart from their contemporaries by continuing to act responsibly by deferring to the rabbis in determining what issues should not be reported and what should be ignored. In other words, rabbinical authority would be upheld, and no one should expect the traditional ultra-Orthodox printed press to change its approach to these matters.

---

① Rabbi Gershon Edelstein, "And You Showed Them the Way [Hebrew]," *YatedNe'eman*, December 31, 2021.

Edelstein suggested that other Haredi media outlets should consider themselves warned that deviating from the accepted approach would amount to transgressing Jewish law. Yet, was his warning warranted?

Given the perception of Haredi news sites as "free and independent" news sources that abjure the rabbinical editorial oversight of the daily press, it was assumed their coverage of the affair would match or even exceed *Mishpacha*'s. Yet, until Walder's death, only *Kikar HaShabbat* had published anything about the affair, *B'HadreiHaredim* and *Haredim* 10 choosing to ignore it like the traditional press. All three, however, published obituaries for Walder that differed only slightly in their content, euphemistically noted his committing suicide, and carefully avoided casting judgment on or shaming Walder.

B'HadreiHaredim and *Kikar HaShabbat* ran similar headlines on their websites stating that "at the age of 53, the author Chaim Walder, of blessed memory, passed away,"[①] while *Haredim* 10's headline stated, "the author and educator Chaim Walder was found lifeless next to his son's grave."[②] Their obituaries euphemistically spoke of the circumstances of Walder's death as being "unfortunate" and "tragic."[③] *B'HadreiHaredim* did not mention the affair, while *Kikar HaShabbat* and *Haredim* 10 wrote of "serious accusations that he had behaved in an inappropriate manner" and "serious suspicions [Walder] had committed serious acts."[④] The most fundamental difference between the obituaries published online and that published in *YatedNe'eman* was *Kikar HaShabbat* and *Haredim* 10's decision to mention the accusations against Walder.

Haredim 10, however, set itself apart further from the other two online outlets and the printed press. Its obituary was the only one to mention that Walder's death came shortly after Rabbi Shmuel Eliyahu, the head of the Safed

① "At Only Age 53, the Author Chaim Walder, May His Memory Be a Blessing, Passed Away [Hebrew]," *Kikar HaShabbat*, December 27, 2021, https://www. kikar. co. il/death-notices/408708; "Blessed be the True Judge: The Author Chaim Walder Passed Away at 53 [Hebrew]," *B'HadreiHaredim*, December 27, 2021, https://www.bhol.co.il/news/1318641.

② Chaim Twil, "The Author and Educator Chaim Walder was Found Lifeless Next to His Son's Grave [Hebrew]," *Haredim* 10, December 27, 2021, https://ch10.co.il/news/711348/.

③ Ibid.; "At Only Age 53," *Kikar HaShabbat*; "Blessed be the True Judge," *B'HadreiHaredim*.

④ Chaim Twil, "The Author and Educator Chaim Walder was Found Lifeless Next to His Son's Grave."

rabbinical court, had announced his ruling against him based on the testimonies of 22 women.① Further, the website published multiple articles on the affair, including on the rabbinical court's proceedings, exploring the affair's impact on Walder's victims and Haredi society at large, and how to discuss the affair with children.②

Haredim 10 reported on an interview Eliyahu gave to the Israeli radio station *Reshet Bet* in which he declared that he was not surprised that Walder committed suicide, calling it "an attempt to silence the victims." Going further, Eliyahu stated, "such people do not go to Heaven," comparing the severity of Walder's acts to murder and even expressing a degree of relief that Walder was dead, stating "the world had become a bit purer" as "dozens of other girls had been saved from harm."③

Only the weekly *Mishpacha* raised, in the context of the affair, the question of what the role of the Haredi press is when such scandals arise. Though not a direct response to Edelstein's *da'at Torah*, *Mishpacha* published a column entitled "We Cannot Ignore," in which the magazine's editors doubled down on their position. As they had in November, the magazine argued that the ultra-Orthodox community, including its major media outlets, must not evade addressing the serious allegations against Walder (though it did not mention his name). To remain silent and try to run away from it would be irresponsible; the easy, evasive path was to be avoided. The moment demanded a response, despite the complicated nature of the

---

① Chaim Twil, "The Author and Educator Chaim Walder was Found Lifeless Next to His Son's Grave." On the Safed Rabbinical Court and its judgment against. Walder, see, for example: Dana Betzalel, "Rabbi Eliyahu: We Received Serious Testimonies from Individuals Harmed by Chaim Walder [Hebrew]," *Makor Rishon*, November 21, 2021, https://www.makorrishon.co.il/news/423931/.

② See, for example: "How Will the Chaim Walder Tragedy Affect the Ultra-Orthodox Public's Attitude Toward Assaults? [Hebrew]," *Haredim* 10, December 28, 2021, https://ch10.co.il/news/711639/; "The Chaim Walder Affair: What Do You Say to Children Now? A Parental Educator Explains [Hebrew]," *Haredim* 10, December 28, 2021, https://ch10. co. il/news/711704/; "Chaim Walder Affair — Court Secretary Reveals: They Presented Evidence, They Burst into Tears [Hebrew]," *Haredim* 10, December 29, 2021, https://ch10.co.il/news/711886/.

③ "Rabbi Shmuel Eliyahu on the Late Writer Chaim Walder: He Will Not Reach Heaven [Hebrew]," *Haredim* 10, December 28, 2021, https://ch10.co.il/news/711635.

affair, declaring, "woe to us if we speak and woe to us if we don't."[1]

The editorial acknowledged that "these issues have never been discussed in the ultra-Orthodox community nor in an ultra-Orthodox newspaper. On the other hand, the ultra-Orthodox community has never faced such a complex, difficult, talked about, and irrepressible hour."[2] Further, it lamented that the affair managed to break down the defensive walls the community has built to protect its children and those used by the ultra-Orthodox press to avoid dealing with difficult issues, as avoiding the issue offers "protection" in difficult times and "protects children from information that may harm their souls."[3] Yet, the unprecedented manner in which the affair was being discussed among the Haredi public rendered the above meaningless in the eyes of the magazine's editors. They asked, what good is a policy of silence when children are already aware?

Challenging the common view that media was not the place for such talk, the editors stated that the role of the media was to be a responsible, involved actor that leads the desired social process under the guidance of spiritual authorities. However, as they had before, the editors emphasized that the magazine would do so "only according to the Torah and rabbinic authority, and will guard against crossing halakhic and moral boundaries that are forbidden to cross."[4]

Conclusion

The way in which the scandals above were (and more often were not) reported reveals Haredi media outlets, regardless of rabbinical editorial oversight, adhere to and respect the community's religious boundaries on gossip, public shaming, and modesty when considering what is fit to print. Ultra-Orthodox media does not serve as a platform for reporting news of public interest, but rather as an agent delineating the borders of legitimate public speech.

---

① "Editorial — We Cannot Ignore [Hebrew]," *Mishpacha*, December 30, 2021.

② Ibid.

③ Ibid.

④ Ibid.

Yet the boundaries are negotiated differently. This results in a degree of diversity among Haredi media outlets, whose differences are nuanced by the taboo subjects they choose to (not) cover, how they are framed, and what language is (not) used.

The dailies, directly and tightly controlled by censors on behalf of rabbinical leaders, are the most averse to publishing stories on sexual offenses, particularly those that emerge from within the community, but the above examples illustrate that the weeklies and websites also share the aversion. Still, websites are more likely to publish articles on sexual offenses, employing a variety of linguistic techniques, including using neutral terms, euphemistic language, or omitting problematic words and phrases.

Yet, the commitment to publishing "clean" news that avoids "inappropriate" or "forbidden" content remains paramount, as not doing so may result in the loss of subscribers and readers. The result of this commitment means Haredi media outlets remain spaces where meaningful discourse on sexual offenses within and outside the community is absent.

Some thought the Walder scandal would constitute a turning point in the relationship between the Haredi community and the media it consumes when it comes to the subject of sexual offenses. Given that the dailies maintained their traditional approach to not address these issues at all and that websites largely failed to be free and independent voices, it is doubtful whether any significant change has indeed occurred in recent years. Only with the revelation of a new scandal will one be able to tell if the walls of silence have been broken and the Haredi media is more ready to serve as a space for such discourse.

避而不谈:性侵害与极端正统派

卡尔·扬克尔

【摘要】本文审视极端正统派新闻媒体何时以及如何报道涉及社群内外公共人物的性丑闻,聚焦于涉及唐纳德·特朗普、犹大·默什-扎哈夫和哈依姆·瓦尔德的近期事件。通过比较分析极端正统派主流日报、周报、线上新闻网络对这些丑闻的报道(或不报道),探讨极端正统派媒体在报道性侵害时所采取的策略,揭示极端正统派媒体的首要功能不在报道涉及公共利益的新闻,而在划定合法公共话语的界线。

【关键词】性侵害;极端正统派;沉默

JEWISH STUDIES
犹太研究
第21辑

Why Are the Self-Isolated Ultra-Orthodox Happier?

Shlomo Black

Abstract: Despite their modest financial standing, a significant majority of the ultra-Orthodox in Israel report high levels of life satisfaction — higher than any other group. Yet, the research at the center of this article reveals that the more individuals with a strong ultra-Orthodox identity integrate into general Israeli society, the lower their rate of satisfaction with life. This article presents the research findings and analyzes the reasons for this correlation between isolation and life satisfaction.

Key Words: Self-Isolated, Ultra-Orthodox, Happiness

Introduction

According to the latest estimate by Israel's Central Bureau of Statistics (CBS), people who identify as ultra-Orthodox (Haredim) in Israel's general population number 1.2 million, or 16.5% of the Jewish population. The average secular Jewish-Israeli woman will give birth, on average, to 1.9 children, while an ultra-Orthodox woman will give birth to 6.6 children, the highest rate in the OECD.[①]

The growth rate for the ultra-Orthodox population is four percent a year. Fifty-eight percent of the ultra-Orthodox population consists of youth under the age of 19. According to CBS estimates, about one in three of Israel's

① "Family Database," OECD, May 21, 2017, http://www.oecd.org/els/family/database.htm.

population will be ultra-Orthodox by 2065.[1] Since employment and military enlistment rates are significantly lower amongst ultra-Orthodox than that in the general Jewish population, coupled with especially high poverty rates, these demographic trends may have grave implications for Israeli society.

In the past decade, Israel's governments, through governmental and non-governmental offices, have tried to increase the integration of the ultra-Orthodox into the Israeli economy and society. Initiatives have included workforce participation incentives, including in the high-tech sector, as well as incentives for studying in higher education institutes and developing programs to encourage military enlistment. However, it is broadly agreed that these initiatives are far from achieving their goals, and the degree of ultra-Orthodox integration remains limited.[2]

This article examines the relationship between the isolation of the ultra-Orthodox and their life satisfaction rates. The article is based on research the author conducted with a sample size of 315 ultra-Orthodox individuals. The study found that ultra-Orthodox individuals who strongly identify as ultra-Orthodox, and acquire an additional Israeli identity (integrate), are less satisfied with their lives compared to ultra-Orthodox individuals who strongly identify as ultra-Orthodox and who maintain their isolation by not acquiring an Israeli identity.

Erich Fromm argues that in order to understand the individual, we must understand the environment in which he or she lives.[3] This article is divided into three parts. The first discusses the unique characteristics of the ultra-Orthodox community. Research data are presented in the second part, and the framework for understanding the data is presented in the third part.

---

① Israel Shlezinger, "One in Three will be a Haredi by 2065," *Israel Hayom*, June 27, 2018, https://www.israelhayom.co.il/article/567065.

② Shlomo Black, Tomer Fadlon, and Meir Elran, "Integrating the Ultra-Orthodox into the Labor Market," *The Institute for National Security Studies*, August 15, 2021, https://www.inss.org.il/publication/orthodox-jews-labor-force/.

③ Erich Fromm, *Escape from Freedom* (New York: Henry Holt and Company, 1941), 6.

Ⅰ. The Ultra-Orthodox: Between Self-Isolation and Integration

On the one hand, the ultra-Orthodox population feels a sense of discrimination;① on the other hand, its life satisfaction rates are high, higher than any other group in Israel.② The ultra-Orthodox city of BneiBrak, a symbol of the self-isolated ultra-Orthodox city, is consistently among the cities with the highest life expectancy and life satisfaction rates in Israel.③

The history and sociology of the ultra-Orthodox community explain this apparent contradiction.

In the second half of the 18th century, when traditional trends began spreading among Jewish communities, some community leaders feared the extinction of traditional Judaism, which they perceived as "true Judaism."④ This birthed the Jewish ultra-Orthodox movement as an ideological faction that opposes any compromises concerning the observance of Jewish religious commandments (*mitzvot*) and integrating non-Torah values into everyday life.⑤

This opposition took the form of a self-isolating way of life and adopting an even stricter approach to observing religious commandments. The ultra-Orthodox identity that was formed was characterized by a commitment to *halakha* (Jewish law) and tradition, and the elevation of the importance of Torah study and of the family unit. It was also characterized by the outspoken rejection of modern norms and innovations and complete adherence to rabbinic authority (*da'at Torah*) in every aspect of life.

The rabbinical leaders of Israel's ultra-Orthodox during the country's early years of independence, headed by Rabbi Avraham Yeshaya Karelitz, also

---

① "The Social Survey [Social Survey Generator]," Israel Central Bureau of Statistics (2022), https://www.cbs.gov.il/he/subjects/Pages/הסקר-החברתי.aspx.

② Ibid.

③ "Annual Health Statistics for Israel 2021," *Israel Central Bureau of Statistics* (2021), 72, https://www.cbs.gov.il/he/publications/pages/2021/72-בריאות-שנתון-סטטיסטי-לישראל-2021-מספר.aspx.

④ Menachem Friedman, *Ultra-Orthodox Society*: *Sources*, *Trends and Processes* (Jerusalem: Institute for Israel Studies, 1991), 40-80. [Hebrew]

⑤ Jeffrey Blutinger, "'So-Called Orthodoxy': The History of an Unwanted Label," *Modern Judaism* 27 (2007): 310-328.

known as the Chazon Ish (1878-1953), felt the need to increase the number of Torah students. This was in order to recover from the disaster of the Holocaust, which decimated the community. They decreed that the majority of ultra-Orthodox men must study the Torah for many years and postpone joining the workforce and engaging in practical life as much as possible.[1]

Thus, the ultra-Orthodox Society of Learners (*HevratHalomdim*) was founded. The Society of Learners established a life routine that revolves entirely around the study of the Torah. Ultra-Orthodox society evolved into an "enclave society" that emphasized its moral superiority over the modern outside world.[2]

Its leaders nurtured the principles (or advantages) of isolation to counter the temptations of modern society. Students in the Society of Learners were required to study the Torah while minimizing their exposure to the world outside the *beit midrash* (house of study).[3] Within ultra-Orthodox society, even those who do not attend the yeshivas (schools for studying the Torah), and do not spend their days studying the Torah, see the yeshiva instructors and students as examples and role models whose path should be followed.[4]

A routine dedicated to studying the Torah requires living a materially modest lifestyle. Israeli ultra-Orthodox yeshiva students receive a scholarship equal to one-fifth of the minimum wage, while the burden of managing the household as well as providing a steady income falls on the woman's shoulders.

While various studies show that affinity between high religiosity and life

---

① Jeffrey Blutinger, "'So-Called Orthodoxy': The History of an Unwanted Label," 40-80.

② Emmanuel Sivan, *The Enclave Culture*, trans. Ada Paldor (Jerusalem: Alpayim, 1991), 75-76. [Hebrew]

③ Nissim Leon, "Responsibility for the Other: On the Question of the Student Society in the Tradition of Rabbi Ovadia Yosef," in *From Survival to Consolidation: Changes in Israeli Haredi Society and Its Scholarly Study*, eds. Kimmy Kaplan and Nurit Stadler (Jerusalem: The Van Leer Jerusalem Institute and Hakibbutz Hameuchad, 2012), 233-251. [Hebrew]

④ Gideon Aran, "Haredi Body: Chapters from an Ethnography in Progress," in *Israeli Haredim: Integration Without Assimilation?*, eds. Emmanuel Sivan and Kimmy Kaplan (Jerusalem: The Van Leer Jerusalem Institute and Hakibbutz Hameuchad, 2003),99-133 [Hebrew]; Haim Soloveitchik, "Rupture and Reconstruction," *Tradition* 28 (1994): 61-130.

satisfaction is significantly connected to economic stability,① Israeli ultra-Orthodox society is an exception to the rule. Despite generally difficult living conditions, 73% of ultra-Orthodox individuals in Israel reported high levels of life satisfaction.② This rate is higher than any other life satisfaction rate in any other Israeli population.③

However, life satisfaction rates among ultra-Orthodox Jews are not uniform. The study conducted by the author shows that within the ultra-Orthodox community, life satisfaction depends on the strength of an additional Israeli identity. The more an ultra-Orthodox individual who strongly identifies as ultra-Orthodox integrates, or adopts an Israeli identity, the lower their level of life satisfaction, and the less they integrate, the higher their level of life satisfaction.

Ⅱ. The Research

This study included 315 respondents from the ultra-Orthodox community, aged between 18 and 69 ($M = 32.60$, $SD = 9.43$). Two hundred two (202) respondents were male (64.3%) and 112 female (35.7%); two participants did not report their gender identity.

Studies have found that there is no difference between the results of questionnaires filled out online and those filled out using "pencil and paper."④ However, a lone study that examined this point among the ultra-Orthodox community found that there is a difference, in some items, between electronic questionnaires and "pencil and paper" questionnaires. Hence, this difference does not lie in items that refer

---

① Kayonda H. Ngamaba and Debbie Soni, "Are Happiness and Life Satisfaction Different Across Religious Groups? Exploring Determinants of Happiness and Life Satisfaction," *Journal of Religion and Health* 5 (December 2018): 2118-2139.

② "The Social Survey [Social Survey Generator]," *Israel Central Bureau of Statistics* (2021), https://www.cbs.gov.il/he/Pages/הסקר-החברתי.aspx.

③ This compared to 50% of religious Jews, 41% of traditional religious Jews, 38% of slightly religious traditional Jews, and 41% of non-religious secular Jews.

④ Leigh W. Jerome et al., "The Coming of Age of Telecommunications in Psychological Research and Practice," *American Psychologist* 55 (2000): 407- 421.

to ultra-Orthodox integration with the Israeli population.[1]

I tried recruiting participants to complete pencil and paper questionnaires among yeshiva Students of Kollels in BneiBrak and Jerusalem, but the response rate was low. Out of 65 questionnaires delivered, only 18 were completed. Therefore, I decided not to include the paper questionnaires in the reported findings.

Hence, the participants were recruited online using a "snowball sampling" method through the help of social media. Prior to filling out the questionnaire, participants signed a consent form and were guaranteed complete anonymity. This guarantee was ensured by not asking participants for personal details.

The research included the following questionnaires:

1. A single item examining identification with ultra-Orthodox culture.
2. A single item examining identification with Israeli culture.
3. A questionnaire examining life satisfaction levels — Life Satisfaction Index (LSI).

Two single items were used to examine participant identity and their identification levels with ultra-Orthodox and with Israeli cultures.[2] Participants were asked to rate how strongly they identify with each specific culture on a scale of 1 (do not identify at all) to 7 (strongly identify). One question referred to identification with ultra-Orthodox culture, and another referred to identification with Israeli culture. Though it is assumed that when a variable is heterogenous, it is better to use a questionnaire consisting of numerous items,[3] some researchers claim that, in some cases, questionnaires with multiple items might obscure and even skew conclusions.[4] In recent years, we

---

① Yitzhak Trachtingot, "Ultra-Orthodox Yeshiva Students and Entry into the Workforce: Reasons, Concerns, and Perceptions Regarding Employment," *The Jerusalem Institute for Policy Studies* 1 (2014): 42-65. [Hebrew]

② Tom Postmes, S. Alexander Haslam, and Lise Jans, "A Single-Item Measure of Social Identification: Reliability, Validity, and Utility," *British Journal of Social Psychology* 52 (December 2013): 597-617.

③ Robert Loo and Peter Kelts, "A Caveat on Using Single-Item Measures," *Employee Assistance Quarterly* 14 (1998): 75-80.

④ Richard Y. Bourhis, Léna C. Moïse, Stéphane Perreault, and Sacha Senécal, "Toward an Interactive Acculturation Model: A Social Psychological Approach," *International Journal of Psychology* 32 (1997): 369-386.

have witnessed an increase in single-item questionnaires in psychology studies.①

I side with Postmes and his colleagues,② who conducted a series of studies to measure the validity of single items to examine individual identification with the group. They found that single items are efficient and, in some cases, even preferred to standard identification questionnaires. Another consideration for using single items to examine the degree of identification was the wish to avoid creating a cognitive burden for participants while filling out the questionnaires without compromising the quality of the results.

In order to measure the participants' level of life satisfaction,③ a Life Satisfaction Index (LSI) questionnaire was used. In it, participants were asked to rate their stances on a Lickert Scale from 1 (Strongly Disagree) to 7 (Strongly Agree). The questionnaire included five items that measured the participant's life satisfaction (e.g., "my living conditions are excellent"; "I am content with my life"). High scores indicate a high life satisfaction rate. The questionnaire was found valid in other studies,④ and Cronbach's alpha reliability for this current study stood at 0.86.

Ⅲ. Results

In the following, means, standard deviations, and simple correlations are presented (see Table 1).

---

① Richard W. Robins, Holly M. Hendin, and Kali H. Trzesniewski, "Measuring Global Self-Esteem: Construct Validation of a Single-Item Measure and the Rosenberg Self-Esteem Scale," *Personality and Social Psychology Bulletin* 2 (2001), 151.

② Tom Postmes, S. Alexander Haslam, and Lise Jans, "A Single-Item Measure of Social Identification: Reliability, Validity, and Utility."

③ Ed Diener, Robert Emmons, Randy Larsen and Sharon Griffin, "The Satisfaction With Life Scale," *Journal of Personality Assessment* 49 (1985): 71-75.

④ Dana Anaby, Tal Jarus, and Bruno D. Zumbo, "Psychometric Evaluation of the Hebrew Language Version of the Satisfaction with Life Scale," *Social Indicators Research* 96 (2010): 267-274.

Table 1 Means, Standard Deviations, and Correlations for Tested Variables

	Mean	Standard Deviation	1	2
Identifying as Ultra-Orthodox	5.23	1.70	-	
Identifying as Israeli	3.88	1.70	-0.21**	-
Life Satisfaction	5.22	1.36	0.27**	-0.12*

Notes: * $=P<0.01$, ** $=P<0.05$

There was a significant negative correlation between identification with ultra-Orthodox culture and identification with Israeli culture [t (1, 312) = 9. 084, $p=0.001$]. The CBS findings were validated,① as a positive correlation between life satisfaction and identification with ultra-Orthodox culture was found ($r=0.27$, $p<0.001$). In contrast, a negative correlation was found between the level of identification as an Israeli and life satisfaction levels ($r=-0.12$, $p=0.032$). These findings show that the more an ultra-Orthodox holds to an ultra-Orthodox identity, their life satisfaction rates increases. On the contrary, the more an ultra-Orthodox holds to an Israeli identity, their life satisfaction decreases.

Is maintaining an ultra-Orthodox identity, isolated from the Israeli one, what allows for high life satisfaction rates? In order to test this assumption, a Hayes plugin was used in the Process Command in Model 1 (see Figure 1).②

This model tested the negative correlation between identifying as an Israeli and life satisfaction. Accordingly, the degree of identifying as an Israeli was set as the predictor variable and life satisfaction was set as the predicted variable. The degree of identification as ultra-Orthodox was set as the moderating variable (the summary of the model is presented in Table 2). The calculated model was found significant [F (3,309) = 10.95, $p<0.001$, $R^2=0.096$]. As the table shows, a primary effect was found for the degree of identification as ultra-Orthodox. In other words, ultra-Orthodox and Israeli identities, each in their own way, affect levels of life satisfaction. Additionally, a significant

① "The Social Survey [Social Survey Generator]," *Israel Central Bureau of Statistics* (2021) https://www.cbs.gov.il/he/Pages/מחולל-סקר-חברתי-חדש.aspx.

② Andrew Hayes, *An Introduction to Mediation, Moderation, and Conditional Process Analysis: A Regression-Based Approach* (New York: Guilford Press, 2018).

interaction effect was found (see Figure 1). The effect indicates that when both identities are taken into account, there is still an effect on life satisfaction levels.

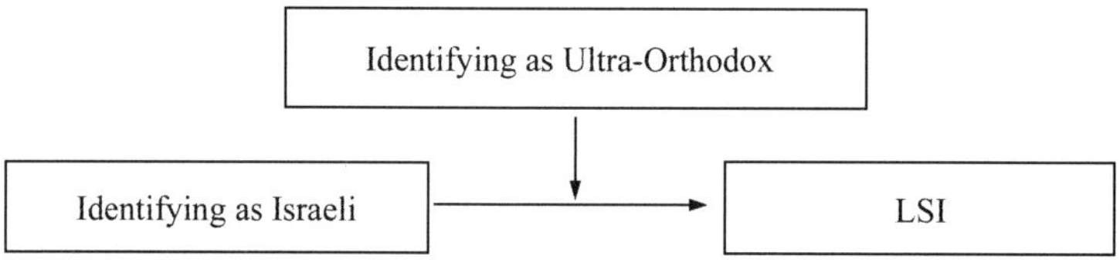

Figure 1 Test Model — The Effect of Identifying as Ultra-Orthodox on the Relationship between Identifying as an Israeli and Life Satisfaction Levels

Table 2 Summary of the Model to Test the Moderation of the Relationship between Israeli Identification (X) and Life Satisfaction (Y) by Ultra-Orthodox Identification (M)

	ΔR^2	*B*	*SE*	*T*	*P*
Israeli Identification		0.28	0.15	1.89	0.060
Ultra-Orthodox Identification		0.47	0.12	3.94	<0.001
Interaction	0.016	-0.06	0.03	-2.34	0.020
Total R^2	0.096				
N	313				

However, the situation is even more complex. By analyzing simple effects, I divided Israeli and ultra-Orthodox identities into three levels (low, average, and high). I then tested how mixing these identities at various levels affects life satisfaction.

This analysis shows that Israeli identification has a significant negative effect when a high level of ultra-Orthodox identification is present (b=-0.12, P=0.021). This means that life satisfaction for an individual with a high level of ultra-Orthodox identification will decrease the more they identify as Israeli. Conversely, for ultra-Orthodox individuals who have low (b=0.08, P=0.185) or medium (b=-0.06, P=0.134) levels of ultra-Orthodox identification, identification as Israeli has not shown a significant effect on life satisfaction (see Figure 2). Therefore, for ultra-Orthodox individuals who do not strongly identify with their ultra-Orthodox identity, Israeli identification does not decrease their life satisfaction in a statistically significant way.

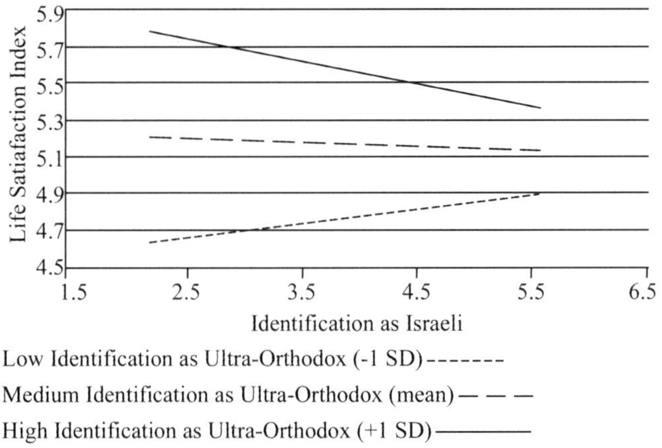

Figure 2 Interaction of Identification as Ultra-Orthodox and Identification as Israeli in Predicting Life Satisfaction

Ⅳ. The Challenge of the Acculturative Integration Assumption

Berry's Acculturation Model is one of social psychology's most cited and famous models.① According to this model, a person who lives in a multicultural environment adopts some norms and values from both cultures. However, the level of integration between identities varies from one person to the next.

Berry suggested four different patterns of behavior that might result from an individual's migration into a multicultural environment: (a) abandon their original identity and adopt the identity of the majority (assimilation); (b) identify with the majority and with their original identity at the same time (integration); (c) ignore the majority identity and solely retain their original identity (isolation); or (d) lose the original identity while rejecting the majority identity (marginalization).

Berry and Hou② use single items and calculate the four strategies by

① John W. Berry, "Immigration, Acculturation, and Adaptation," *Applied Psychology* 46 (1997): 5-68.

② John Berry and Feng Hu, "Immigrant Acculturation and Wellbeing in Canada," *Canadian Psychology/Psychologie Canadienne* 57 (2016): 254-264.

clustering them into four dimensions. In the current study, I used only one dimension (i.e., integration). This method is used frequently.①

Berry and his colleagues relied on the Acculturation Model when they presented the integration hypothesis. This hypothesis argues that a person who chooses to integrate will be more satisfied with their life than someone who adopts the other alternatives.② Berry relied on studies that showed a positive correlation between the integration strategy and multiple positive characteristics and properties, including: psychological,③ social, and health adjustability,④ creativity, mental well-being,⑤ pro-social behavior,⑥ educational and professional success,⑦ satisfaction and commitment to work, little feeling of weariness, increased salary, and more.⑧ These results were validated across groups and cultural contexts.⑨

The results of the research conducted for this article, which indicates the integration of the ultra-Orthodox into the broader Israeli identity as a predictor of lower life satisfaction, contradicts Berry's and his colleagues' integration

① See also: Fons Van de Vijver, John Berry, and Ozgur Celenk, "Assessment of Acculturation," in *Cambridge Handbook of Acculturation Psychology*, eds. David Sam and John Berry (Cambridge, United Kingdom: Cambridge University Press, 2016), 93-114.

② John Berry, Zarina Lepshokova, MIRIPS Collaboration, and Dmitry Grigoryev, "How Shall We All Live Together? A Meta-Analytical Review of the Mutual Intercultural Relations in Plural Societies Project," *Applied Psychology* 71 (2022): 1014-1041.

③ Maria Stogianni et al., "Sample Characteristics and Country Level Indicators Influencing the Relationship Between Biculturalism and Adjustment: An Updated Meta Analysis," Unpublished manuscript (2021).

④ Eunju Yoon et al., "A Meta-Analysis of Acculturation/Enculturation and Mental Health," *Journal of Counseling Psychology* 60 (2013): 15-30.

⑤ Paul Schmitz and Florian Schmitz, "Correlates of Acculturation Strategies: Personality, Coping, and Outcome," *Journal of Cross-Cultural Psychology* 53 (August 2022): 875-916.

⑥ Angela-MinhTu Nguyen and Verónica Benet-Martínez, "Biculturalism and Adjustment: A Metanalysis," *Journal of Cross-Cultural Psychology* 44 (2013): 122-159.

⑦ M. Dalal Safa and Adriana Umaña-Taylor, "Biculturalism and Adjustment Among U.S. Latinos: A Review of Four Decades of Empirical Findings," *Advances in Child Development and Behavior* 61 (2021): 73-127.

⑧ Marcus Valenzuela, Angela-MinhTu Nguyen, and Vasyl Taras, "A Review of Organizational Research on Acculturation from a Nonwork — Work Spillover Perspective: Content Analysis and Future Research Guidelines," *International Journal of Management Reviews* 23 (2021): 516-540.

⑨ Thuy Pham and Richard Harris, "Acculturation Strategies Among Vietnamese Americans," *International Journal of Intercultural Relations* 25 (2001): 279-300.

hypothesis.

The possible explanation for this contradiction lies in the characteristics of ultra-Orthodox isolation and in the possible results of its undoing.

Ⅴ. Hypotheses and Discussion

The findings show that ultra-Orthodox who more strongly identify as Israelis are less happy. Two hypotheses as to why this is the case can be suggested.

First, integrating into Israeli identity is considered an offense, and even betrayal, of the cultural ethos in which they were raised and educated — which requires total emotional and identity isolation from the non-Orthodox majority. Second, they develop a "neither here nor there" consciousness of one who no longer belongs fully to ultra-Orthodox society, but who also is not accepted by, nor feels a sense of belonging to general society.

The ultra-Orthodox group ethos asserts that ultra-Orthodoxy is the continuation of authentic Judaism that has existed since the biblical Exodus. According to this ethos, all other Jewish factions have deviated from the original way of life. For example, this ethos sees secular Judaism as a faction a few decades old, perhaps a little older, originating in the Jewish Enlightenment or *Haskalah*.[1] This, while ultra-Orthodox society carries the burden of every wrong suffered by the Jewish people during their years of exile. According to the ultra-Orthodox ethos, other nations' persecution of the Jews throughout two thousand years of exile has fundamentally targeted Jews who looked and acted like the ultra-Orthodox of today.[2]

Studies show that feelings of victimhood increase the likelihood that a group will cultivate sentiments and practices of convergence,[3] which may

---

① Aviezer Ravitzky, *Freedom Inscribed: Diverse Voices of Jewish Religious Thought* (Tel Aviv: Am Oved, 1999). [Hebrew]

② Benjamin Brown, *The Haredim: A Guide to Their Beliefs and Sectors* (Jerusalem: Am Oved/ The Israel Democracy Institute, 2017). [Hebrew]

③ Michael Wohl and Nyla Branscombe, "Group Threat, Collective Angst, and Ingroup Forgiveness for the War in Iraq," *Political Psychology* 30 (2009): 193-217.

include hostility towards and self-isolation and distancing from the majority group.①

The feeling of victimhood serves the satisfaction levels of the ultra-Orthodox. A study the author conducted along with Itzhak Trachtingot and Gabriel Horenczyk showed that the ultra-Orthodox believe that they become stronger the more they are discriminated against.② Discrimination sharpens and emphasizes the difference between the ultra-Orthodox and the other groups: "The more they afflicted them, the more they multiplied and grew."

Another study by Bergman, Horenczyk, and Abramovsky-Zitter shows that the more discriminated against the ultra-Orthodox feel, the more satisfied they are with their lives.③ In a follow-up study, we found that the ultra-Orthodox individual prefers his ultra-Orthodox peers to integrate at a lower level than the individual would allow himself or herself.④

Ultra-Orthodox identity is an ethnic-communal identity, while Israeli identity is a national-civil identity. It is not necessary for these identities to coincide.⑤ Those who identify as ultra-Orthodox find it easy to ignore other identity frameworks, deny them, and maintain their opinion that they are the sole authentic representatives of Judaism. The ChazonIsh based ultra-Orthodox

---

① Gilad Hirschberger, TsachiEin-Dor, Bernhard Leidner, and Tamar Saguy, "How is Existential Threat Related to Intergroup Conflict? Introducing the Multidimensional Existential Threat (MET) Model," *Frontiers in Psychology* 7 (2016): 1877-1889.

② Shlomo Black, ItzhakTrachtingot, and Gabriel Horenczyk, "Community Post Traumatic Growth: Israeli Haredim Coping with Corona Virus," *Contemporary Jewry* 42 (2022): 85-112.

③ Yoav Bergman, Gabriel Horenczyk, and Rachel Abramovsky-Zitter, "Perceived Discrimination and Well-Being Among the Ultra-Orthodox in Israel: The Mediating Role of Group Identity," *Journal of Cross-Cultural Psychology* 48 (2017): 1320-1327.

④ Shlomo Black, "Acculturation Integration Discrepancies Between the Individuals and Groups: The Case of the Ultra-Orthodox Community in Israel," PhD Dissertation, The Hebrew University of Jerusalem, 2020. [Hebrew].

⑤ Uzi Ben-Shalom and Gabriel Horenczyk, "Cultural Identity and Adaptation in an Assimilative Setting: Immigrant Soldiers from the Former Soviet Union in Israel," *International Journal of Intercultural Relations* 28 (November 2004): 461-479.

ideology on the idea of delegitimizing Israeli culture.[1] Thus, ideology generated a self-isolating society, not the other way around.

This explains the connection between isolation and life satisfaction. An ultra-Orthodox who was raised believing in the benefits of self-isolation, and chooses to turn from these and join the general public, feels a sense of guilt for breaking the Haredi ethos via integration into Israeli society. Thus, integrated individuals who retain a strong ultra-Orthodox identity feel a sense of guilt.

Moreover, the integrated ultra-Orthodox who is still embedded in ultra-Orthodox society sometimes feels rejected by members of his or her community. Their standing in the synagogue is undermined, their children find it harder to join the local community's educational institutions, and their peers' esteem of them decreases.[2] Therefore, such a situation, even if integration was the individual's choice, can be expected to include numerous and difficult choices.

The correlation between life satisfaction and the sense of security that the ultra-Orthodox community instills may explain why there are ultra-Orthodox individuals who, though they stopped following the Torah and stringently observing the commandments, insist on maintaining an ultra-Orthodox appearance and on belonging to their community, at least superficially.

In a focus group organized to analyze these findings, one of the participants argued that an ultra-Orthodox who integrates wants with all their heart to belong to their original group, and that's why they spend their free time studying the Torah or "hanging out with ultra-Orthodox friends" in order to have some sense of belonging. Still, even if they try to maintain two identities, the community does not always allow for that. Therefore, an individual who holds two identities might find himself or herself alone and without any sense of belonging. This creates a feeling of "neither here nor there" and traps the

---

① Yoav Bergman, Gabriel Horenczyk, and Rachel Abramovsky-Zitter, "Perceived Discrimination and Well-Being Among the Ultra-Orthodox in Israel: The Mediating Role of Group Identity"; Yedidia Stern, "The Identity Crisis of the State of Israel," *Democratic Culture* 14 (2012): 257-275 [Hebrew]; Yitzhak Trachtingot, "Ultra-Orthodox Yeshiva Students and Entry into the Workforce: Reasons, Concerns, and Perceptions Regarding Employment."

② Yitzhak Trachtingot, "Ultra-Orthodox Yeshiva Students and Entry into the Workforce: Reasons, Concerns, and Perceptions Regarding Employment."

individual in a state of acculturative "marginalization."[①]

Exposure to the secular world might also undermine well-informed beliefs and offer ideological alternatives, provoking questions and doubts. This, too, might hurt the levels of life satisfaction.

The rabbinic authority that controls every aspect of life allegedly harms the freedom of the faithful.[②] Still, life satisfaction is not necessarily dependent upon an individual's freedom of choice. The decisive question is to what extent a person wants to be free to choose and whether the person is happy with the degree of freedom he or she has. A person who cedes freedom due to ideological motives and accepts rabbinical authority willingly does not feel unsatisfied with the consequences of that choice.

Conclusion

It should be noted that the current study was not conducted under experimental/operative conditions, so the findings can imply patterns, or at the most, they can describe the participants' concept and understanding of their own experiences. To explore which of the variables studied suppresses/increases the other, follow-up studies are necessary, which will allow for testing the order of the variables' appearance.

One may claim that because the ultra-Orthodox identity item was rated at high levels, the interpretation of the interaction was affected. To that end, it is important to note that such a claim does not significantly weaken the research findings regarding the correlations between the two identities, and between each identity and life satisfaction. Furthermore, the distribution of participants that rated the Likert scale between five to seven is roughly equal.

A majority of participants in this study were male (65%), and a minority were female. It is possible that female respondents would react differently than the average found.

Another limitation has to do with the volatile nature of the relationship

① Shlomo Black, "Acculturation Integration Discrepancies Between the Individuals and Groups: The Case of the Ultra-Orthodox Community in Israel."

② Menachem Friedman, *Ultra-Orthodox Society: Sources, Trends and Processes*, 40-80.

between ultra-Orthodox society and Israeli society as a whole. There are periods in which the conflict increases and the legitimacy of integration decreases. Conversely, there are periods of collaboration that the ultra-Orthodox consider fertile (mostly when their representatives are part of the government). Additional research is necessary, therefore, to better clarify the relationship between ultra-Orthodox integration and their life satisfaction.

Still, the research does allow a measure of familiarity with the subjective experiences and beliefs of the ultra-Orthodox.

Since 2010, Israel's governments have invested large sums to integrate the ultra-Orthodox in various fields.[①] Some of these integration efforts were successful, but some failed remarkably.[②] Attempts at integration were based on socio-economic data but neglected the psychological understanding of the ultra-Orthodox individual.[③]

It is appropriate for decision-makers to respond to the results of this research. The majority group must take the psychological profile of the minority group, which it aims to integrate, into consideration. Understanding the results of this research might furnish policymakers with important tools to better integrate the ultra-Orthodox into society. The key to successfully managing this integration, as the research results show, is to do so in a way that would help avoid feelings of spiritual decline and that would not damage the feelings of belonging to ultra-Orthodox society.

On the other hand, as long as young ultra-Orthodox individuals are taught to self-isolate from the general population and to see the non-ultra-Orthodox majority as a negative influence that might lead them to deviate from the original ultra-Orthodox way of life, relations with non-ultra-Orthodox society will often be accompanied by suspicion and antagonism.[④]

The ultra-Orthodox and the majority are thus both required to create a meaningful dialogue that would remove walls of suspicion and allow for painless integration.

---

① For additional information see: Government Resolutions 1994/10, 869/15.

② For more information see: Report of The State Comptroller of Israel 2019.

③ Shlomo Black, Tomer Fadlon, and Meir Elran, "Integrating the Ultra-Orthodox into the Labor Market."

④ Thomas Pettigrew and Linda Tropp, "How Does Intergroup Contact Reduce Prejudice? Meta-Analytic Tests of Three Mediators," *European Journal of Social Psychology* 38 (2008): 922-934.

自我隔离的极端正统派为何更具幸福感

所罗门·布莱克

【摘要】尽管经济拮据,但以色列的大部分极端正统派都声称具有很高的生活满足感,高于任何其他群体。本研究显示,具有强烈极端正统派身份认同感的个体融入以色列主流社会的程度越高,其生活满足感程度越低。本文陈述这些研究发现,并分析隔离与生活满足感之间的相关性的原因。

【关键词】自我隔离;极端正统派;幸福感

Ultra-Orthodox and Prolonged Singlehood: Finding a Partner, Negotiating with God

Sara Zalcberg　Sima Zalcberg Block

Abstract: The ultra-Orthodox community in Israel is witnessing a phenomenon of prolonged singlehood. Based on semi-structured interviews with 20 ultra-Orthodox prolonged male and female singles of diverse affiliations, the study suggests that prolonged singlehood has impacted participants' faith and practiced religiosity. Interviewees described their disappointment in God and their sense that He is testing their faith. They also testified to a decrease in their observance, especially concerning praying, abiding by kosher rules, and maintaining modesty. The decline in religious practice and belief was attributed to a crisis of faith, the loosening of imposing social ties, and the need to satisfy physical and emotional needs.

Key Words: Ultra-Orthodox, Singlehood, Crisis of Faith

Introduction

The ultra-Orthodox Jewish community is a minority group in Israel, albeit a growing one. Israel is home to about 1.25 million ultra-Orthodox Jews, comprising 13% of the Jewish population.[①] The community is diverse, with streams and subgroups differing in dress, community lifestyles, leadership, educational systems, and attitudes toward secular society and the modern

① Lee Cahaner and Gilad Malach, *Statistical Report on Orthodox Society in Israel* 2020 (Jerusalem: The Israeli Democracy Institute, 2021), 11. [Hebrew]

world.

Still, all ultra-Orthodox Jews share several core attributes. These include observing a strict version of Jewish law, obedience to the decrees of rabbinical leaders on everyday life issues, including politics, and the commitment of men to the study of religious texts.① They differ from Religious Zionists, another large religious minority, in their notional rejection of Zionist ideology.

Ultra-Orthodox society dictates an almost absolute separation between the sexes and emphasizes women's modesty, with strict rules governing female attire. It also dictates that marriage should occur at an early age (18-23, varying according to the stream and subgroup) to maintain the community's pureness and encourage the constitution of large families (birth rates in Haredi families are over six children per family).②

"Traditional" or "arranged" marriages are the norm in Haredi society, similar to arranged marriages that historically existed in traditional Jewish society.③ Couples meet and agree to marry in line with the expectations and preferences of the prospective couple's parents and without a pre-marriage period of shared life, in contrast to the "modern marriage" in the West, which is based on the personal relationship of the couple and often takes place only after a significant period of non-marital sexual relations.④

Since the mid-1990s, the ultra-Orthodox community in Israel has undergone significant changes due to its increasing, even if still limited, interactions with the majority of society. These interactions have led to greater openness toward non-Haredi practices in different aspects of life, including education, occupation, communication, health, leisure culture, and

① Benjamin Brown, *The Haredim: A Guide to Their Beliefs and Sectors* (Jerusalem: Am Oved/The Israeli Democracy Institute, 2017), 13-14, 24-33 [Hebrew]; Menachem Friedman, *Ultra-Orthodox Society: Sources, Trends and Processes* (Jerusalem: Institute for Israel Studies, 1991), 7-9. [Hebrew]

② Sima Zalcberg Block, "Gender Differences in the Involvement of Young People in the Matchmaking Process in an Extreme Ultra-Orthodox Community," *Journal of Jewish Identities* 5 (2012): 27-50.

③ David Lehmann and Batya Siebzehner, "Power, Boundaries and Institutions: Marriage in Ultra-Orthodox Judaism," *European Journal of Sociology* 50 (2009): 273-308; Avraham Grossman, *Pious and Rebellious: Jewish Women in Medieval Europe* (Waltham: Brandeis University Press, 2004), 98.

④ Karen Dion and Kenneth Dion, "Individualistic and Collectivistic Perspectives on Gender and the Cultural Context of Love and Intimacy," *Journal of Social Issues* 49 (1993): 53-69.

consumption, as well as openness toward various ideas, concepts, and practices such as feminist discourse.[1] They had some effect also on ultra-Orthodox marriage patterns.

Prolonged singlehood, including in Israel, has received substantial scholarly attention.[2] However, this phenomenon has not yet been studied in the context of Israeli ultra-Orthodox. This study seeks to fill this gap in the literature by focusing on the experiences of ultra-Orthodox who remained single into their mid-20s and beyond, particularly how their situation affected their religiosity.

In his rich review, Engelberg noted the prolific discourse on singlehood versus family.[3] Several studies suggested that a "strong family" is necessary for strong religiosity.[4] The reason is that most religious ceremonies are celebrated in the family environment, and most religious practices are based on the traditional family structure.[5] Studies further demonstrated that since the second half of the twentieth century, Orthodox Judaism, like other conservative religions, emphasized the importance of family life as one of its central motifs in its war against secularism.[6]

Studies among various conservative religious communities in the West showed that social pressure is often applied on singles to get married and that

---

① Orna Braun-Lewensohn and Tehila Kalagy, "Between the Inside and the Outside World: Coping of Ultra-Orthodox Individuals with Their Work Environment After Academic Studies," *Community Mental Health Journal* 55 (2019): 894-905; Gilad Malach and Lee Cahaner, "Elements of Modern Life or 'Modern Ultra-Orthodoxy'? Numerical Assessment of Modernization Processes in Ultra-Orthodox Society," *Democratic Culture* 17 (2017): 19-51. [Hebrew]

② For example, Ari Engelberg, *Prolonged Singlehood among Religious Zionists: Religiosity and Individualization in Late Modernity* (Ramat Gan: Bar-Ilan University Press, 2020) [Hebrew]; Kinneret Lahad, *A Table for One: A Critical Reading of Singlehood, Gender and Time* (Manchester: Manchester University Press, 2017).

③ Ari Engelberg, *Prolonged Singlehood among Religious Zionists: Religiosity and Individualization in Late Modernity*, 149-197.

④ Kristen Heimdal and Sharon Houseknecht, "Cohabiting and Married Couples' Income Organization: Approaches in Sweden and the United States," *Journal of Marriage and Family* 65 (2003): 525-538.

⑤ Mark Chaves, "Family Structure and Protestant Church Attendance: The Sociological Basis of Cohort and Age Effects," *Journal for the Scientific Study of Religion* 30 (1991): 501-514.

⑥ Air Engelberg, *Prolonged Singlehood among Religious Zionists: Religiosity and Individualization in Late Modernity*, 149-152.

prolonged singlehood leads to being pushed to the margins of the devout group. These studies describe religious singles as being "in the middle," torn between the values of their community and mainstream cultural values, i.e., Western secular values.

For example, American Muslim singles struggle with the American mainstream's norms regarding sex;① and modern Orthodox Jewish singles in the United States and Israel were found to experience mental stress due to the requirement to avoid sexual relations before marriage altogether.②

Engelberg identified three patterns in his study of prolonged singlehood among the Religious Zionists in Israel. The most common sees the period of singlehood as a religious moratorium in which singles allow themselves to be less strict with various religious practices. The second sees singles who do not reduce their religious observance, and, in fact, their level of religiosity remains as it was before they entered the phase of prolonged singlehood. The third pattern sees singles who increasingly reduce their religious observance and move towards secularism.③

In light of the review presented above, the hypotheses of this study were:

Some ultra-Orthodox singles describe themselves as being in a state of "between" the values of their religious minority community and the mainstream cultural values, i.e., Western secular values. This tension is reflected especially regarding relations with the opposite gender.

Some describe a period of religious moratorium, during which they are less strict about the observance of religious practices, intending to resume their religious observance once they marry. On the other hand, some remain observant, perhaps even more observant, believing that righteousness will advance a divine intervention that will change their personal status. Still, some

---

① Zarinah El-Amin Naeem, *Jihad of the Soul: Singlehood and the Search for Love in Muslim America* (Detroit: Niyah Press, 2009).

② Air Engelberg, *Prolonged Singlehood among Religious Zionists: Religiosity and Individualization in Late Modernity*, 165-167; Yaakov Frances, "A Qualitative Study of Sexual-Religious Conflict in Single Orthodox Jewish Men," PhD Dissertation, City University of New York, 2008.

③ Air Engelberg, *Prolonged Singlehood among Religious Zionists: Religiosity and Individualization in Late Modernity*, 169-199.

become less observant to the point of leaving the ultra-Orthodox world and identity altogether and adopting a Religious Zionist identity or a secular identity that allows for a more inclusive attitude towards prolonged singlehood.

The article opens with a brief review of the institution of marriage and the traditional partner selection process in ultra-Orthodox communities. A discussion of the methodology is followed by a presentation of findings. The article concludes with a comparative discussion of the findings.

Ⅰ. The Institution of Marriage and Matching in the Ultra-Orthodox Community

Present-day ultra-Orthodox are classified today into four major streams: (a) Hasidim, whose society is organized around a Hasidic "court" led by a rebbe, who is a fatherly figure to the congregation at large through a direct connection to the divine. (b) Lithuanian Jews (Litvak or Yeshivish), who regard the study of religious texts (Torah) as the central and constitutive value of life for males. The Lithuanian stream is more modern than the Hasidic stream, both in lifestyle and appearance. (c) The Sephardic, a stream comprised of Jews from North Africa and the Middle East.[1] The Sephardic joined the ultra-Orthodox in the last quarter century, adopting the Lithuanian style, including in their partner selection process. (d) Modern ultra-Orthodox, who originate from all three streams and, in recent years, demonstrate increasing integration into Israeli society, adopting "modern" concepts, values, and norms from the majority society surrounding them.[2]

All ultra-Orthodox streams and groups attribute great importance to the institution of marriage and see it as central to the community. For this reason, over the years, ultra-Orthodox parents could not allow the process of choosing a partner to be decided by the sentiments of their children and took charge of matching their grown children, with the soon-to-marry preferences playing a

---

① Benjamin Brown, *The Haredim: A Guide to Their Beliefs and Sectors*, 17-24; Menachem Friedman, *Ultra-Orthodox Society: Sources, Trends and Processes*, 6-7.

② Gilad Malach and Lee Cahaner, "Elements of Modern Life or 'Modern Ultra-Orthodoxy'? Numerical Assessment of Modernization Processes in Ultra-Orthodox Society."

minor role in the process.①

The traditional process of searching for a partner in the ultra-Orthodox community is considered, first and foremost, a business arrangement between the two sides, mainly the parents, overseen by a matchmaker who proposes partners for the children.② Parents from both sides of prospective matches examine and weigh the projected value offered by the counterparty.

The barter value, or "matchmaking capital," is the properties and characteristics of prospective marriage candidates that parents consider when selecting a match for their son or daughter.③ The parents receive the matchmaker's offers and research those that seem suitable, paying close attention to family background.

The degree of involvement young ultra-Orthodox have in the decision about whom to marry varies from group to group within the community and sometimes even from family to family. Couples who match may be given many or few opportunities to meet before their engagement is announced, as well as more or less freedom to refuse a proposed match recommended by their parents.

Among Hasidic communities, the most conservative of the ultra-Orthodox on marriage, parents have almost exclusive control over the choice of the spouse. They arrange for the prospective couple to meet once or twice, usually at the girl's home, for no longer than an hour. The girl and the boy sit in a room with the door open to prevent *yichud* — being alone together in private. At the end of these meetings, the pair must decide whether they agree to the match offered.④

Among the Lithuanians, as well as the Sephardic, both more modern than

---

① Sima Zalcberg Block, "Gender Differences in the Involvement of Young People in the Matchmaking Process in an Extreme Ultra-Orthodox Community."

② David Lehmann and Batya Siebzehner, "Power, Boundaries and Institutions: Marriage in Ultra-Orthodox Judaism"; Sima Zalcberg Block, "'The Art of the Deal': Preferences in Spouse Selection among Parents in a Hasidic Community," *Israel Studies Review* 28 (2013): 61-82.

③ Sima Zalcberg Block, "'The Art of the Deal': Preferences in Spouse Selection among Parents in a Hasidic Community."

④ Sima Zalcberg Block, "Gender Differences in the Involvement of Young People in the Matchmaking Process in an Extreme Ultra-Orthodox Community."

the Hasidic stream, the financial arrangements between the parents are also crucial, but there is greater individual freedom in choosing a spouse.[1] A prospective couple meets about five to eight times, without parental supervision, usually in a busy public place such as the lobby of a respectable hotel or on walks in public locations to avoid *yichud*. After these meetings, they must decide whether they want to formalize the relationship through marriage.

Among all ultra-Orthodox, premarital sex is forbidden, as is physical contact before marriage.[2] This prohibition is called *shmirat negiah* (observance of touching).

These patterns have been the norm in traditional Jewish society for years. However, prolonged singlehood has been shown to increase the degree of freedom that singles have in choosing their partner, including the number and length of the meetings between prospective couples and the location of these meetings, which for some, have moved to more intimate settings.[3]

Ⅱ. The Research Paradigm and Methodology

The current study utilized a qualitative paradigm that focuses on reality, as perceived by those living it, while emphasizing a context-informed approach.[4] This approach allows for insights into participants' experiences through their unique socio-cultural context and the significance that they attach to those experiences.

According to the verse "at eighteen the bridal canopy" (Pirkei Avot 5:

① Benjamin Brown, *The Haredim: A Guide to Their Beliefs and Sectors*, 18-31; Menachem Friedman, *Ultra-Orthodox Society: Sources, Trends and Processes*, 6-7.

② Avidan Milevsky, Deborah Shifrah Niman, Atara Raab, and Ruchie Gross, "A Phenomenological Examination of Dating Attitudes in Ultra-Orthodox Jewish Emerging Adult Women," *Mental Health, Religion & Culture* 14 (2011): 311-322.

③ Sima Zalcberg Block, "'I Wanted to Choose for Myself': Changing Marriage Patterns in the Ultra-Orthodox Society in Israel," in *Arranged Marriage: The Politics of Tradition, Resistance, and Change*, ed. Peter Berta (New Brunswick: Rutgers University Press, 2023), 190-205.

④ Norman Denzin and Yvonna Lincoln, *The SAGE Handbook of Qualitative Research*, 5th *ed.* (Thousand Oaks, CA: Sage, 2017); Dorit Roer-Strier and Roberta Sands, "Moving Beyond the 'Official Story': When 'Others' Meet in a Qualitative Interview," *Qualitative Research* 15 (2015): 251-268.

21), some ultra-Orthodox families prefer to marry off their sons as young as possible. The Hasidic marry at a younger age than Lithuanians do. Hasidic girls usually get married at the ages of 18-19, and boys typically get married at the ages of 19-20. Among Lithuanians, the girls usually get married at the ages of 19-22, and the boys get married at the ages of 21-23.

No *halakhic* rulings determine at what age a person is considered a prolonged single. Therefore, we conducted a pre-test among 30 ultra-Orthodox from the various streams and groups, asking them for a definition.

The pre-test found that in ultra-Orthodox society, prolonged singlehood is considered to start at the age of 24 in all groups and streams. Accordingly, the study population included single men and women 24 years or older from various groups of the ultra-Orthodox community in Israel.

Participants were recruited through advertisements in ultra-Orthodox WhatsApp groups, some specifically for ultra-Orthodox singles, that called to participate in the research. At a later stage, some of the participants referred the authors to additional participants ("snowball sampling"). At the end of this process, the final sample included 20 participants (ten men and ten women) who were willing to share their experiences and perceptions about their personal status.

The age of participants ranged from twenty-six to forty-two. All live in urban areas. Six participants are students in college or university; five work in education; four work in the business sector or in clerical jobs; three work in health and welfare services; and two (males) dedicate their time to Torah study in a yeshiva.

Data collection consisted of semi-structured interviews conducted in Hebrew. In the interviews, participants discussed their religious faith and practice and how these were affected by prolonged singlehood.

Interviews were conducted during 2022 by phone, Zoom, and in person, according to the participant's preference. Each interview lasted between one hour to an hour and a half. All interviews were documented, recorded, and transcribed with the participants' consent.

Data analysis was based on the thematic analysis method.① Analysis based on this approach consists of two levels: the first is general-thematic, aiming to identify significant themes in the interviews and correspondence, and the second consists of uncovering the meanings underlying the surface-level data, as well as the meanings of the first-level categories.

The thematic analysis included the following steps: (a) we familiarized ourselves with the data by reading the interviews several times; (b) we developed preliminary ideas by reading the first five interviews several times and identified segments representing discrete units of meaning; (c) we manually identified codes and grouped them into initial themes, revising them where necessary; and (d) finally, we refined, named, and described the interrelationships between the themes that emerged.

Data saturation was reached when analysis of the interviews suggested that additional coding was no longer feasible.②

The study's quality assurance was based on Lincoln and Guba's criteria of qualitative research.③ The credibility of the findings as indicative of Haredim at large was established by including participants from various Haredi groups in order to obtain a broad range of opinions. In addition, in-depth interviews encouraged free and open dialogue. A repetitive review of data collection and analysis processes, and a peer review of the findings, also enhanced the credibility of our work.

To reduce authors' bias, we did our best to be conscious of our own perceptions about the topic and avoided guiding participants to focus on particular issues during the interviews.

The study was conducted per the code of ethics determined by the American Psychological Association.④ As such, the study's purpose was

---

① Michael Patton, *Qualitative Evaluation and Research Methods* (Beverly Hills, CA: Sage, 2002), 429-540.

② Patricia Fusch and Lawrence Ness, "Are We There Yet? Data Saturation in Qualitative Research," *The Quantitative Report* 20 (2015): 1408.

③ Yvonna Lincoln and Egon Guba, *Naturalistic Inquiry* (Newbury Park, CA: Sage, 1985), 239-331.

④ Linda Campbell et al., *APA Ethics Code Commentary and Case Illustrations* (American Psychological Association, 2010).

explained to participants before their participation. Participation was voluntary, and participants were notified that they could withdraw from the study at any time. Participants' confidentiality and anonymity were ensured throughout all stages of the study, including the omission of potential identifying details from the current paper.

Ⅲ. Findings

All participants reported that prolonged singlehood affects their spiritual and practiced religiosity. Some participants reported a decrease in both dimensions; some reported an increase in their faith along with a decrease in their religious practice; others reported a decrease in religious practice with no effect on their faith.

Almost without exception, those who reported a decrease in their religiosity (either in practice or faith or both) said that they do not foresee changing their religious behavior after they have married and started a family, if they do.

Ⅳ. Religious Faith

Analysis of participants' observations about the effect of prolonged singlehood on their religious faith presents three central themes. One is disappointment in God and doubts about Him. Another is constant self-reflection, reckoning, introspection (*cheshbonnefesh*), and feeling that God is testing them or putting them on trial by not matching them with an appropriate spouse. Yet another is acceptance of God's behavior and even the strengthening of faith.

Some participants reported feeling disappointed in God. They said they used to trust God, who stood by them until the time was ripe to find a spouse, and then was no longer present in their lives. One of them, a 30-year-old Sephardic female from southern Israel, explained: "We get slaps and disappointments. We say [Psalms 121:2], 'my help comes from the LORD, who made heaven and earth,' right? I expect God to stand by my side and bring me redemption, but each time I get burned again."

Another, a 33-year-old Litvak female from Jerusalem, also expressed disappointment in God: "As much as I've strived, and I continue to strive, it's frustrating. I sometimes ask myself: maybe God doesn't see me."

The concept of "striving" (*hishtadlut*) is central in Judaism. According to Meor, this is "a general term for all the acts and efforts people perform to improve their lives, their economic and social situations, and their status in any other field."[1] "Striving" is a way for people to try and entice divine assistance to improve their physical existence in this world.

A 27-year-old Hasidic female from BneiBrak, who engaged in several practices considered as striving in the hopes of finding a partner, explained: "I went to the Western Wall for 40 days; it didn't help. I went to Rashbi's [Rabbi Shimon Bar Yochai] grave; it didn't help either. I keep giving to charity; it doesn't help. I admit that I broke down a bit; I fell apart. It was a big disappointment."

Some participants stated that their prolonged singlehood raised internal doubts of faith. A 36-year-old Sephardic female from southern Israel said: "Singlehood raises many questions about faith, such as 'God, where are you,' 'why is this happening?' I dialogue with God and tell Him, 'Give me a sign of what I have not done until today that I must do in order to find my mate.'"

Another participant, a 30-year-old Litvak female from one of the new ultra-Orthodox towns in the center of Israel, described an internal struggle that haunts her every time she prays. According to her: "I struggle to pray. I tell God I have been in this cycle of matchmaking for 11 to 12 years [since the age of 18]. I pray every day, and what has changed since yesterday? What will today's prayer do that yesterday's prayer did not? It's hard for me to pray because I see things are not happening. But despite these feelings, I decided I would not let up on the prayer."

Some participants stated that their singlehood leads them to engage inself-reflection, reckoning, and introspection. They examine what they have done wrong and where they should improve religiously.

A 25-year-old Hasidic female from one of the new ultra-Orthodox towns

[1] Menachem Meor, *The Believer Versus the Striver* (Jerusalem: Hamikhlala, 1994), 15. [Hebrew]

in the center of Israel said that every Friday when she lights Shabbat candles, she reflects on her behavior over the previous week: "I ask myself, maybe the guy I met this week didn't suit me because I didn't pray with enough devotion? Maybe I wasn't modest enough? Maybe I disrespected my parents?"

Similarly, another participant, the 27-year-old Hasidic female from BneiBrak, said: "At night, before falling asleep, I always ask myself, what have I done wrong? Almost all my girlfriends [already have] a child or two or even three, and I'm the only one alone. I probably need to fix something. A few years ago, I dated a certain guy, and my parents put a lot of pressure on me to marry him. He was a very good guy. But I don't know why he didn't suit me. My parents and the matchmaker told me it was a pity I rejected him and would regret it, but I insisted. Sometimes I wonder, maybe what I'm going through now is because I rejected the guy and also caused my parents agony."

"Testing" in the Jewish religious context means that God puts a person to a test of faith by exposing that person to certain adversity, giving the person an opportunity to express faith through adherence to Him, despite the adversity experienced. Some participants expressed this sentiment.

A 29-year-old Litvak female from Jerusalem said: "Singlehood is one big test. God puts me through tests. Thank God I have been able to meet those tests so far. Lately, I am starting to feel that maybe He is putting me through tests more than others."

Similarly, a 35-year-old Sephardic female from Jerusalem said: "They say that God tests only those who can stand it...even though I would have given up this experience. Each one and his own test. [For] one [it] is making a livelihood, [for] another coping with a health issue; I have prolonged singlehood. What shall I do? I pray I'll succeed with God's help."

In contrast, some participants stated that despite the pain and agony caused by their prolonged singlehood, they accept reality as it is and explain it to themselves as an integral part of God's way of leading the world that cannot be disputed. The 35-year-old Sephardic female explained: "I tell myself that God is not working for me. I mean, He doesn't owe me anything, and He is the one who controls our lives and guides us, so there is no room for bookkeeping and complaints. He guides things as they should be. With God's help, I will find the right one at the right time."

A 26-year-old Hasidic male from one of the new ultra-Orthodox towns in the center of Israel said: "Everything in its time. There must be a reason why my pairing is delayed. Not everything is visible and known to us. The ways of God are hidden."

There were participants who not only accepted the delay in finding their match but also stated that prolonged singlehood made them spiritually stronger and increased their faith in God. One of them, the abovementioned 30-year-old Litvak female, said: "There is a great spiritual strengthening. I pray hard, talk to God and get a lot of strength from it. In terms of faith, I'm only getting stronger."

The 35-year-old Sephardic female explained that her faith has increased because she has been left with no other choice: "I am strengthened by faith. Clinging to faith is the anchor of my sanity. Without faith in God, I would not have survived. I believe in God by the power of inertia. I have no choice but to believe; otherwise, there is no hope and no meaning."

Some participants attributed the strengthening of their faith mainly to a parallel process that occurred during the years of singlehood: their departure from the religious-educational framework in which they were brought up — the yeshiva or the seminar. In these institutions, strict adherence to religious practices was the default and an inseparable part of their daily routine. Being on their own and single, faith became a different kind of challenge with particular rewards.

A 42-year-old Sephardic male from Jerusalem said: "My faith grew stronger because I am not really supervised by any authority since I left the yeshiva. I am not in a setting where observance is automatic [the default] nor with family and wife, a space that also demands a commitment to a certain religious behavior. Now I have no supervision of that kind that requires me to inquire and think about what I am doing and why. This has led me to believe more strongly. Not simply to observe but [to believe] due to reason, understanding, and strong faith."

For this participant and others, mainly men, the years of prolonged singlehood led to self-inquiry about religiosity and contemplation about which rigidities are indeed important and required according to Jewish law (*halakha*) and what the observance of religious practices actually means for them. Their self-reflection strengthened their faith, although in some cases, at the same time, it led to a decrease in observance of religious practices.

Ⅴ. The Practical Dimension

All participants reported a decrease in their practice of religion, especially prayer, keeping kosher laws, and maintaining modesty. The analysis of participants' answers points to five primary reasons for this process: (a) a loosening of social control on their religious observance; (b) a detachment from social frameworks with strict norms of religious practice; (c) a change in outlook and perspectives regarding religious practices and values; (d) a crisis of faith; and (e) emotional and physical needs.

While for some participants, leaving the educational institutions in which they were raised — the *yeshiva* or the seminar — led to a strengthening of their faith, some became less observant as a result (including several who claimed their faith had been strengthened).

They said that being outside the authority of a controlled system and without intense supervision, they allowed themselves to "let loose," as they described it. A 36-year-old Litvak male from the center of Israel explained: "Changing the framework, no longer being in the yeshiva, requires setting your limits. The boundaries blur, and setting the boundaries for yourself becomes more difficult and complex. That is, at this stage in my life, what I used to see as a red line, I [now] dare to cross it."

A 30-year-old Hasidic male from Jerusalem said: "[my] religious practice has weakened. I am less strict about prayers and minyans [the minimum quorum for prayer]. [It's] more liberating. [My] level of religious practice has decreased due to a change in the course of [my] life — leaving the yeshiva."

The 25-year-old Hasidic female from central Israel said: "Over the years, you can definitely see a decrease in the [level of] observance. It is noticeable in my prayer. I used to pray every morning, but that has changed since I left the seminar. Now, I am less strict about prayers. The framework has changed, and the agenda has changed."

Another area in which a decrease in religious observance was revealed, mainly due to not being part of a religious institution, is the observance of kosher laws. The ultra-Orthodox world is strict about eating only food subject to particularly rigid kosher inspections. In Israel, there are over 40 panels that grant kosher certifications, with community affiliation being a significant parameter in kosher acceptance. The choice of supervising authority is an important aspect of affiliation with one community or another.

Kosher certifications divide into two main types — one, known as "ordinary kosher," which is supervised and approved by the Chief Rabbinate of Israel (therefore also known as "rabbinic" kosher), and the "strictly kosher" (*mehadrin*), to which the ultra-Orthodox public adheres. The difference between them is the level of *halakhic* standards.

Almost without exception, participants stated that during their prolonged singlehood, they began to be less meticulous about eating food with the "strictly kosher" label and were satisfied with the "ordinary kosher" of the Rabbinate.

The 35-year-old Sephardic female said: "All these years, I was meticulous about eating *mehadrin*. Since I left the seminar, I still keep kosher, but not *mehadrin*. I live alone; I don't eat with my parents; I am less strict."

A 28-year-old Litvak male from BneiBrak explained: "If, as a young yeshiva guy, I didn't dare to put food in my mouth that wasn't *mehadrin*, after leaving the framework [the yeshiva], I allowed myself to eat Rabbinate as well. You don't have the supervision of your parents, on the one hand, nor the supervision of the yeshiva, where you eat most of the time anyway. The food is strictly kosher, and I hang out in many places that are not *mehadrin* kosher."

Ultra-Orthodox modesty requirements dictate that men and women who are not married should avoid closeness, bodily exposure, and intimacy. Women should dress in a way that exposes their bodies as little as possible to men so they will not arouse men's sexual desire.[1] Modesty norms are intended, first and foremost, to prevent sexual intercourse outside marriage, which is prohibited according to Jewish law.

As with kosher laws, with modesty, there are differences in the degree of

---

① Sima Zalcberg Block, "Shouldering the Burden of Redemption: How the 'Fashion' of Wearing Capes Developed in Ultra-Orthodox Society," *Nashim* 22 (2011): 32-55.

strictness between the various ultra-Orthodox groups. However, all streams dictate that women walk with stockings, with sleeves down to the elbow, and with a skirt that falls below the knee.

Several female participants stated that they stopped adhering to some of these norms, as the 29-year-old Litvak said:"I am no longer in the seminar, so I stopped wearing stockings. And the shirts and the skirt are not so long anymore [...]. Sometimes, I travel alone to Tel Aviv and sit by the beach, not swimming, with clothes on, but still at the mixed beach."

Several participants stated that the years of prolonged singlehood and being outside religious educational institutions made them ponder what religious practices mean to them. This investigation led to a change in outlook and perceptions regarding some religious practices and values, resulting in a decrease in observance in certain areas. A 39-year-old Litvak male from Jerusalem said: "I can say that the examination and study in depth led me to be less strict about some commandments."

In this context, the 26-year-old Hasidic male referred to observing kosher laws and defined his process as "development." He said that in the past, he believed that products not bearing the "*mehadrin*" stamp were not kosher, but over the years and with exposure to more information about the subject, he learned that the kosher issue in Israel is political and that in practice there is no real difference between most koshers types. He said: "Over time, I matured. I learned that *mehadrin* is no more kosher than the Rabbinate and that there is mainly a lot of politics here, so I allow myself to eat Rabbinate kosher."

Another participant who testified to a change in her perspective said:"I am less strict today about wearing socks. Over the years, I have developed and realized that this is not what is important, and it will not make me more religious. I want a home of Torah and values, and I am looking for an ultra-Orthodox partner for whom these things are important. I hope that the fact that I am not careful about socks will not label me as unsuitable for marriage in the eyes of ultra-Orthodox men."

A 40-year-old Sephardic male from southern Israel referred to a perceptual change regarding modesty norms:"The first time I approached a girl in an online ultra-Orthodox matchmaking forum was, for me, crossing a red line of modesty. Even though the content of the message I sent her was a request to communicate with her via a matchmaker, who would be a third party, I felt uneasy with my actions. I felt I had done something very wrong regarding modesty. This experience changed my essence, and I didn't feel the same after it happened. Something in me changed. I was a guy who never dared to approach a girl. The first conversation with a girl would only be on the first date arranged by a matchmaker. This step was a defining moment because I, as a bachelor, took the most guarded, sacred, and pure thing in ultra-Orthodox society, which up to that day I had adhered to strictly, and threw it away while daring to build a different world of my own, with other concepts. It was a dramatic, life-changing moment."

Some participants reported decreased observance of religious practices due to a crisis of faith they experienced due to their prolonged singlehood. One of them, the 30-year-old Sephardic female, related an internal struggle about faith she was experiencing that led her to decrease her religious observance, especially regarding modesty. She said: "Singlehood definitely caused me to slack in my observance. I constantly struggle internally [over whether my] skirt will remain long enough or whether I will shorten my sleeves. I am always at war: should I shorten by one centimeter or lengthen by one centimeter? It's a feeling of defiance, a kind of rebellion. I know it doesn't make sense that I'm sort of punishing God, but...in the past, for example, I didn't dare to go without stockings, and I expected things to happen as they were supposed to, that I would find a match. And it didn't happen. I did what I had to do; I observed the way I should, and that's the breaking point. It didn't help me with God."

These words indicate a decrease in strict observance as an expression of rebellion against God, or even punishing Him, for not rescuing them from singlehood. Still, the participant knew God's punishment was irrelevant and inapplicable.

The 29-year-old Litvak female spoke about a decrease in the frequency of her prayers in light of doubts and disappointment with God: "I try to pray at least once a day, at least the *dawn blessings*. But I skip prayers; I'm not as strict as I was in the past. It's not intentional; it's just hard for me to pray. I'm really fighting with myself about this, but I don't feel God's presence in my life, so it's very hard to pray to Him."

A number of participants reported a decrease in adherence to avoiding *yichud* and adherence to *shmirat negiah*.

A 27-year-old Litvak male from one of the new ultra-Orthodox towns in the center of Israel explained: "In recent years, I do meet with girls alone and violate the prohibition of *yichud*. Every now and then, I also violate the prohibition of *shmirat negiah*. The body and mind demand theirs."

Several female interviewees made similar observations. For example, a 29-year-old Litvak attested that a decrease in adherence to strict modesty norms is an attempt to create a feminine presence, not to mention a sexual presence, to be attractive and attract potential partners: "At school, we talked a lot about modesty and the prohibitions of *yichud* and *shmirat negiah*. Yet, it is hard to maintain it as physical contact and hugs are so necessary in this difficult time. This causes us to break the boundaries of modesty we have been raised with all these years. We were taught that a man must not enjoy his little pinky. And the clothing, it's a kind of statement, when you're looking for a relationship, and you expose yourself, your body, a little, you basically say [to the guys], 'Hey, look, I'm here. Come.'"

Another reason for the decrease in strictly observing modesty norms that several participants mentioned was the need to give themselves a "discount," to make it easy for themselves during the difficult time they go through as a sort of compensation for their bitter fate.

The 27-year-old Hasidic female explained: "In recent years, with my prolonged singlehood, I allow myself to be less strict. I still keep my sleeves down to the elbow, but not necessarily beyond that. I want to give myself a better feeling about myself."

Ⅵ. Future Plans

Participants stated that they do not expect their religious behavior to change in the future, even if they marry, because of what they described as "reaching a different place in life," a place in which their opinion is correct and appropriate. They described a return to stricter religiosity as "going back."

For example, the 36-year-old Litvak male explained: "I don't believe things will change after I start a family. I am now in a different place, which, in my opinion, is correct, better, and more real. So why go back?"

The 30-year-old Litvak female said: "I became more modern, I developed, I went through a process. I am in a place from which there is no return. Nor would I want to [return] because I believe that everything I went through led me to a lifestyle with no fewer values."

Another participant, the 40-year-old Sephardic male, clarified: "I underwent a fundamental change. I built a different world for myself. You can't go back to what was."

Only a handful of interviewees reported a desire to return to their former level of observance once they marry and start a family. Their main motivation is to be a model for their future children.

The 27-year-old Hasidic female explained: "In the future, when I get married and have children, I will return to being stricter with modesty. It is important for me to be an example for my future children." Similarly, the 30-year-old Hasidic male said, "I guess I will go back to observing the three daily prayers and strict kosher standards. This is how I grew up, and this is how I would like to raise my children."

Ⅶ. Comparative Dimensions and Conclusion

A number of studies demonstrated that women tend to believe more than men in a personal God and almost see Him as a partner in a relationship.[1] Engelberg found that this pattern applies to Religious Zionist singles.[2] The reason is that, unlike Religious Zionist women, Religious Zionist men are educated in the *yeshiva*, which exposes them to a system of thought deeply rooted in the Torah, and becomes their main religious point of reference. The main attitude of the yeshivas is rationalist and sees God as sublime and supreme. Accordingly, the students strive to approach Him through spiritual

---

① Robert Wuthnow, *Sharing the Journey: Support Groups and America's New Quest for Community* (New York: The Free Press, 1994), 239; Susan Starr Sered, "Mother Love, Child Death and Religious Innovation: A Feminist Perspective," *Journal of Feminist Studies in Religion* 12 (1996): 5-23.

② Air Engelberg, *Prolonged Singlehood among Religious Zionists: Religiosity and Individualization in Late Modernity*, 188-195.

ascension, not through negotiating with Him.

The study indicated this is also the case for the ultra-Orthodox, with female participants discussing negotiations with God as an aspect of their prolonged singlehood. At the same time, men did not testify to having such a relationship as part of their attempts to make sense of their unfavorable condition.

The study found that participants who submissively accepted their situation as an expression of God's will were not necessarily more desperate; instead, some believed God would summon the right pairing for them at the right time. These findings are in line with findings among Religious Zionist singles,① among prolonged single Malay Muslim women who mentioned the notion of "jodoh" — a soul-mate as fated by God at the perfect time,② and among prolonged single Mormons that emphasized the idea of having faith in God and marrying the right person, at the right time, in the right place.③

All participants reported a certain decrease in adherence to religious practices, especially in prayer, keeping kosher, and modesty, with some noting unsatisfied sexual urges as a reason. This reason is in line with Engelberg's study, which found that life outside a family led young Religious Zionist Israelis to deviate from religious laws.

Although the decrease in religious practice is reminiscent of the experiences documented among Religious Zionists singles, none of the ultra-Orthodox participants defined themselves as Religious Zionist. Instead, almost without exception, they situated themselves in the category of modern ultra-Orthodox. This subgroup of ultra-Orthodox developed only at the turn of the century. It is characterized by openness toward various issues and modern life practices and adopting concepts and values from modern Western society.④ Manifestations of this can be seen in exposure to the unfiltered internet,

---

① Air Engelberg, *Prolonged Singlehood among Religious Zionists: Religiosity and Individualization in Late Modernity*, 189-210.

② Rozita Ibrahim and Zaharah Hassan, "Understanding Singlehood from the Experiences of Never-Married Malay Muslim Women in Malaysia: Some Preliminary Findings," *European Journal of Social Sciences* 8 (2009): 395-405; Rozita Ibrahim, "'What Is Wrong with Me?' — Single Women's Reflections on Missing the Marriage Transition," *Asian Social Science* 12 (2016): 213-219.

③ Jana Darrington, Kathleen Piercy, and Sylvia Niehuis, "The Social and Cultural Construction of Singlehood among Young, Single Mormons," *The Qualitative Report* 10 (2005): 639-661.

④ Benjamin Brown, *The Haredim: A Guide to Their Beliefs and Sectors*.

perceptions of women's status and rabbinical authority, secular patterns of leisure activity, and the importance attributed to academic studies.[1]

In contrast to the second hypothesis, and unlike Religious Zionist singles, a majority of participants did not describe the years of prolonged singlehood as a temporary period of religious moratorium, in which they are less strict about observance yet intend to return to stricter religiosity after they finally marry. Rather, some see their newly adopted and more relaxed conduct as permanent. However, not everyone adopted this approach, and it does not apply to all aspects of life.

In one way, some participants have found new religious meaning in their lives due to their prolonged singlehood. Being alone, they find that external pressures and expectations do not dictate their faith but rather are born of inner convictions. While they are possibly less religious in the demonstrative sense, they feel more so because their beliefs were tested and have deepened.

As is the case with members of other religious groups, including the Religious Zionist, prolonged ultra-Orthodox singles do not challenge their perception of marriage as an ultimate desired existential goal.[2] This is not the case for secular singles in the Western world, where, while marriage is still the norm and the desire of most people, singlehood has become, in recent decades, a more common way of life.

With marriage still being a social default in the ultra-Orthodox world, young Haredi men and women who desire to remain part of the traditions and the society into which they were born are confronted with enormous challenges when trying to negotiate their situation. Their search for a partner thus also becomes a negotiation of faith and practice, creating new meanings and establishing new boundaries.

---

① Gilad Malach and Lee Cahaner, "Elements of Modern Life or 'Modern Ultra-Orthodoxy'? Numerical Assessment of Modernization Processes in Ultra-Orthodox Society."

② Ari Engelberg, *Prolonged Singlehood among Religious Zionists: Religiosity and Individualization in Late Modernity*, 195-199; Rozita Ibrahim and Zaharah Hassan, "Understanding Singlehood from the Experiences of Never-Married Malay Muslim Women in Malaysia: Some Preliminary Findings"; Rozita Ibrahim, "'What Is Wrong with Me?' — Single Women's Reflections on Missing the Marriage Transition"; Zarinah El-Amin Naeem, *Jihad of the Soul: Singlehood and the Search for Love in Muslim America*; Jana Darrington, Kathleen Piercy, and Sylvia Niehuis, "The Social and Cultural Construction of Singlehood among Young, Single Mormons."

极端正统派和延长的单身期:寻觅伴侣,与神协商

萨拉·扎尔克伯格　西玛·扎尔克伯格·布洛克

【摘要】以色列的极端正统派社群正出现单身期延长的现象。基于对20位出身不同宗派的极端正统派延期单身男女的半结构式访谈,本研究显示延长的单身期会影响信徒的信仰和宗教践履程度。受访者描述他们对神失望,感到神在试探他们的信仰。他们对教规的遵守程度下降,尤其是在祈祷、遵守饮食律法和保持谦卑方面。宗教实践与信念的衰退源于信仰危机、社会纽带的松弛和满足生理及心理欲求的需要。

【关键词】极端正统派;单身;信仰危机

"The Wall" and "Ascending as a Wall": Neturei Karta, Zionism, and the Holocaust

Tal Cohen

Abstract: This article examines how the Holocaust and related issues were discussed by Neturei Karta, the ultra-Orthodox faction most harshly opposed to Zionism. Based on an extensive analysis of hundreds of articles and opinion pieces published in the faction's journal, it argues that writing about the Holocaust was central to Neturei Karta's efforts to delegitimize Zionism on the eve of the State of Israel's founding and in its first decades of existence. Zionists were blamed for directly and indirectly bringing about the physical destruction of European Jewry, as well as for exacting "a spiritual holocaust" against Jewish believers. These perspectives echo to this day.

Key Words: Neturei Karta, Zionism, the Holocaust

Introduction

Neturei Karta is a faction within the Eda Haredit (The Haredi Council of Jerusalem).[①] The Eda Haredit consists of tens of thousands of people who, unlike mainstream ultra-Orthodox Jewish factions, isolate themselves from national institutions almost entirely, including abstaining from voting in

① The Neturei Karta belonged to the Eda Haredit until 1966, when it withdrew from it. At the end of the 1970s, however, some Neturei Karta members rejoined the Eda Haredit and until today, there are some in Neturei Karta who identify with the Eda Haredit and others who do not.

elections. Neturei Karta comprises several hundred individuals, most of whom live in Jerusalem's Mea Shearim neighborhood. Members of this faction are characterized by their especially harsh opposition to the Zionist state and its institutions. Some go beyond passive opposition and openly cooperate with Israel's enemies, describing Israel as occupied Palestinian territory.

One expression of Neturei Karta's radical worldview is their perspective on the Holocaust. The faction's current leader, Rabbi Meir Hirsch, publicly blames Zionism for the destruction of European Jewry and for "a spiritual holocaust" that supposedly happened to the Jewish people. ①

Radical as it may sound, Rabbi Hirsch's stance, which might have landed him in court and resulted in a lengthy prison sentence in some European countries, is not new. It reflects a perspective towards the Holocaust shaped by Neturei Karta's rhetoric since the end of the Second World War. It also echoes the way in which the faction's leadership treated different affairs related to the Holocaust, including the Kasztner Affair and — notably different — the Eichmann trial.

This article—originally a master's thesis written at Tel Aviv University under the guidance of Prof. Dina Porat—is based on a contextual analysis of hundreds of opinion pieces and articles published between 1944 and 1961 in *HaChomah* (*The Wall*), Neturei Karta's journal. The article argues that writing about the Holocaust was central to Neturei Karta's consistent effort to delegitimize Zionism.

At the height of the Holocaust, and later throughout the 1948 Palestine War and the efforts to establish a Jewish state, Neturei Karta blamed the Zionists for directly and indirectly bringing about the physical destruction of European Jewry, as well as for exacting a spiritual holocaust against Jewish believers. This article illustrates that, instead of seeking to understand the Holocaust, Neturei Karta abused history to generate lies portraying Zionism as a diabolic movement.

---

① See: "Enemy of the State: An Interview with Rabbi Israel Meir Hirsch," in the last article of this special issue.

Ⅰ. Neturei Karta: Historical Background

Neturei Karta began when some representatives of the anti-Zionist Haredi circles in Jerusalem's Old Yishuv withdrew, near the end of the First World War, from "The City Committee for Jerusalem's Jews"—an autonomous group responsible for representing the interests of the entire Jewish population in Jerusalem. They inaugurated an alternative group to represent the anti-Zionist ultra-Orthodox Jews of Jerusalem, called "The City Committee for Ashkenazi Communities" (which, since 1937, has been known as the Eda Haredit). It was led by Rabbi Yosef Chaim Sonnenfeld (1849-1932) and Rabbi Yitzhak Yerucham Diskin (1839-1925), who were, at the time, among the prevalent spiritual leaders of the Old Yishuv.

Another step in the group's self-isolation was the debate surrounding the "The Communities Ordinance of 1921" (*HukatHakehilot*). The ordinance intended to organize Jewish representation vis-à-vis British Mandate authorities in Palestine. According to the ordinance, all Jews in the Land of Israel would be represented before Mandate authorities through an umbrella organization: the Knesset of Israel. The *Kanaim* (Zealots) of Jerusalem refused to be represented by Zionists, and also opposed the establishment of a chief rabbinate.[1] As part of their struggle, they joined World Agudath Israel, the movement representing the majority of ultra-Orthodox Judaism.[2]

Following Hitler's rise to power in Germany (1933), World Agudath Israel was forced to collaborate with the Jewish Agency for Israel to acquire immigration (*aliyah*) certificates for its members. This collaboration exacerbated tensions within World Agudath Israel between those who argued a policy of total separation from the Zionist movement was obsolete and the *Kanaim*, who opposed collaboration under any circumstances. In 1935, following these tensions,

---

① Motti Inbari, "Rabbi Amram Blau Founder of the Neturei Karta Movement: An Abridged Biography," in *Jewish Radical Ultra-Orthodoxy Confronts Modernity, Zionism and Women's Equality*, ed. Motti Inbari (New York: Cambridge University Press, 2016), 195-196.

② Kimmy Kaplan, *Amram Blau: The World of Neturei Karta's Leader* (Jerusalem: Yad Yitzhak Ben-Zvi and Ben-Gurion Institute, 2017), 48-49. [Hebrew]

a faction led by Rabbi Amram Blau, the brother of Moshe Blau, the leader of Jerusalem's Agudath Israel, and Rabbi Aharon Katzenelbogen, withdrew in order to establish a new institution called HevratHahaim.①

In 1938, following their refusal to pay the tax fundraising the "Community Ransom" (*KoferHayishuv*), HevratHahaim's leadership published an announcement explaining their position. It was signed Neturei Karta. They have been using the name ever since.

Neturei Karta is an Aramaic term meaning "guardians of the city." It is first mentioned in a midrash describing three wise men whom Rabbi Judah ha-Nasi sent to wander the Land of Israel and inspect its cities and towns to correct the wrongs they might see in them. When they arrived in one of the Jewish cities, they asked to meet the city's guards and were met by armed persons. They responded that these were not the guardians of the city, but its destroyers. According to them, the true guardians of the city are those studying the Torah. From the point of view of Neturei Karta, the scouts and guards in the Jewish Yishuv during the British Mandate were the city's destroyers, while the Yishuv's true guardians remained those who dedicated their lives to the Torah and its commandments (*mitzvot*).②

Aviezer Ravitzky, a scholar of Jewish religious and political thought, explained the purpose of the name Neturei Karta was to defy the shift in values that Zionism had attempted to implement. For generations, the Jewish people were instructed to adhere to the world of the Torah and to focus on spiritual-religious matters. They had to live by an oath not to "ascend as a wall" — meaning not to migrate to Israel in an organized, political manner. Zionism's mere existence led the Jewish people to act like other nations and peoples. It

① Motti Inbari, "Rabbi Amram Blau Founder of the Neturei Karta Movement: An Abridged Biography," 196-197. Until 1945, both moderate and radical (*kanaim*) Haredim were members of the Eda Haredit. However, following the former's loss in organizational elections, Agudath Israel withdrew from the Eda Haredit. See: Menachem Friedman, "'Neturei Karta' and the Shabbat Demonstrations in Jerusalem between 1948-1950, Processes and Background," in *Divided Jerusalem—1948-1967: Sources, Summaries, Selected Affairs, and Helpful Tools*, ed. Avi Bareli (Jerusalem: Yad Yitzhak Ben-Zvi, 1994), 228-229. [Hebrew]

② Menachem Friedman, "Haredim and Palestinians in Jerusalem," in *Jerusalem: A City and Its Future*, eds. Marshall J. Breger and Ora Ahimeir (Syracuse: Syracuse University Press, 2002), 235-236.

asked the Jewish people to neglect the Torah and God and achieve its national aspirations using physical force. According to Neturei Karta, Zionism's actions defy divine ordinance.①

Ⅱ. *HaChomah* Journal

With the establishment of Neturei Karta as a body independent of The Jewish National Council and World Agudath Israel, its members, led by Blau (the editor of World Agudath Israel's journal between 1927-1933),② surmised that in order to influence Haredi public opinion, as well as general public opinion, they had to make themselves heard. They decided to create their own journal.

Despite the opposition of the Old Yishuv, Neturei Karta among them, to the use of Hebrew as an everyday language, they chose it as the language of their publications. The Hebrew language was the language of the majority in the Jewish Yishuv in Palestine, and the faction understood that for their opinions to be heard, they had to express them in Hebrew.③

The first issue of *HaChomah* was published in the Hebrew month of Sivan in 1944 (May-June). A manifesto of sorts was printed on the cover detailing the journal's roles, declaring: "The Target: To instill and establish a fortified wall for a Judaism religiously loyal to our holy Torah without compromise or concession."④ Over the years, the journal was published under different names, including *Chomatenu* (Our Wall) and *MishmeretChomatenu* (Our Wall's Guard).

Neturei Karta used their journal to polemicize on two fronts: First, against the Zionist Yishuv in Palestine during the British Mandate and against the Israeli state and its institutions after its formation. Second, against

① Aviezer Ravitzky, *Messianism, Zionism and Jewish Religious Radicalism* (Chicago: The University of Chicago Press, 1996), 61-62.

② A position he had lost due to his expressed disdain of the Chief Rabbinate and its leader, Rabbi Abraham Isaac Kook. See: Menachem Keren-Kratz, "Kol Yisrael and Crystallization of Haredi Identity in Mandate Palestine," *Kesher* 51 (2018), 149-150.[Hebrew]

③ Kimmy Kaplan, *Amram Blau: The World of Neturei Karta's Leader*, 27.

④ *HaChomah: An Issue for Religious Reinforcement*, Sivan 1944.

Agudath Israel and its affiliated movements, Poalei Agudath Israel and Poalei Agudath Israel Jerusalem, who collaborated with the Zionists and were the main target of assault.[①] The journal addressed various sensitive issues, including the decision to establish the state, the public desecration of Shabbat, the enlistment of Haredim to the Israel Defense Forces (IDF), and elections to the Israeli parliament. The Holocaust of European Jewry and its causes, along with other related affairs, were also discussed in the journal.

Ⅲ. Blaming Zionism for a Spiritual Holocaust

Separation from the Zionist enterprise and its characteristics was a central tenet of Neturei Karta's worldview. Their struggle against the Zionist movement was meant to emphasize Zionism's anti-religious character and the faction's disagreements with it. *HaChomah* was used as a platform for public protest against various issues connected with Neturei Karta's opposition to the Zionist enterprise and the State of Israel. Over the years, it published numerous articles attacking and denigrating Zionism and its leaders, along with the State of Israel and its institutions, while pointing out their "crimes" against religious Judaism.

The discussion surrounding the Holocaust of European Jewry — as it happened and after the fact—was central to Neturei Karta's radical anti-Zionist rhetoric and to its efforts to present Zionism as an illegitimate movement. This discussion included an analogy between Nazi crimes and Zionist "crimes," as well as claims concerning the alleged collaboration between Zionists and Nazis.

This article focuses on such debates published in *HaChomah* between 1944 and 1961.

HaChomah claimed that the way in which children who emigrated to Israel were raised constituted a spiritual holocaust. These claims were

① Poalei Agudath Israel saw the settlement of Israel and the State of Israel as valuable, while the Poalei Agudath Israel Jerusalem, while professing anti-Zionist views similar to those of Neturei Karta and the *Kanaim* in general, did not act to distance themselves completely from Zionist enterprise and even ran for seats in Israel's parliament. Kimmy Kaplan, *Amram Blau: The World of Neturei Karta's Leader*, 60.

motivated by the debate surrounding the Tehran Children at the beginning of the 1940s. At the time, an argument was taking place between the Religious Zionist and Haredi camps and the secular camp regarding the intake of hundreds of children, most of them orphans, who had been able to escape from Poland to Iran and were, in turn, brought to Israel by the Jewish Agency. Agudath Israel, representing Haredi Jews, argued that most children came from Haredi homes and, therefore, must be raised in the same way. Nevertheless, the great majority of children were sent to non-religious settlements and were raised in secular institutions.[①]

Already in June 1944, *HaChomah* concerned itself with child Holocaust survivors who were brought to Israel by the Jewish Agency, claiming that the children were forcefully secularized.

Therefore it [the Zionist movement] is now exploiting the terrible Holocaust which came as if in ambush, to steal the soft, inferno-struck children now reaching Israel, to take their religion away, incite them and remove them from holy Jewish law... In this manner, the ceaseless Zionist extermination machine operates. What Hitler, may his name and memory be blotted out, cannot finish abroad, the Zionist leadership completes here in Israel.[②]

Under the pen name "Man of Jerusalem," the writer used the Holocaust both directly and metaphorically to describe the Zionist movement, its targets, and its activities. He explained how it maliciously exploited the innocence and orphanhood of child Holocaust survivors to exterminate them spiritually.

This was done, according to him, by controlling their intake and education in Israel while pursuing its true objective — the extinction of the Jewish religion. He went on to emphasize the devilish act (and thus also the comparison with the Nazis) by claiming that Zionism "exploited" the Holocaust to increase Jewish emigration to Israel under the pretense of rescue, as part of a plan to establish a national home for the Jewish people.

---

① Dvora Hacohen, "History, Memory, Historiography: The 'Tehran Children' Controversy," in *Culture, Memory, and History: Essays in Honor of Anita Shapira*, eds. Meir Hazan and Uri Cohen (Jerusalem: ZalmanShazar Center and Tel Aviv University, 2012), 275-311. [Hebrew]

② "The Child Slayers [Hebrew]," *HaChomah*, August 13, 1944.

In an issue published several months later, the same line of attack persists, aiming to present the Zionist movement as a regime with Nazi objectives. The Zionists, like the Nazis, aspire to destroy Judaism:

> And while our brothers abroad are led to the gallows, and their bodies meet the stake in the evil Goy detention camps, we see in front of our very eyes the burning of thousands of clear and pure souls of the children in Israel, in the extermination camps of our own evildoers, who torture them and force upon them a mental inquisition, tearing from their soft cores the belief in one God which their holy fathers MGAT [May God Avenge Them] wished for them as their souls rose to the heavens by pure and holy avenues. Aha! Crematoriums for our brother's bodies in Nazi camps — there, and Crematoriums for our children's souls in Zionist camps — here.①

The education of immigrant Jewish children was subject to many debates in the first years of the State of Israel as well. The leaders of Neturei Karta saw public and Zionist education as an attempt to extract children from the path of true Judaism.②

The analogy between the physical Holocaust and the spiritual "holocaust" persisted in the pages of *HaChomah* during the early 1950s as well. An article from June 1950, revolving around the opposition to the education given to children in immigration camps, states that "as we know, the Zionists established extermination camps in Israel, where tens of thousands of souls burn each day, souls of Jewish children who were brought here from every corner of the earth. The Zionist Gestapo quarantined the camps and erected blockades by the camps' entrances to delay those who want to enter and alert parents to the destructive terror hovering over their heads."③

Similarly, in the preface to an article concerning the treatment of immigrants in the immigration camps (which *HaChomah* called "extermination camps"), it was said that: "While this is written, thick smoke

① "Cremating the Souls [Hebrew]," *HaChomah*, February 7, 1945.

② Kimmy Kaplan, *Amram Blau: The World of Neturei Karta's Leader*, 479-480.

③ Zvi Jacobson, "On the Souls of Our Children [Hebrew]," *Om Ani Chomah*, June 1, 1950.

is seen gathering and rising from every refugee camp across the country... The Zionists who now wield power are this very day on their spiritual extermination quest... as was their target."[1] After which, the writer pondered as to which extermination was worse since "their activity [the educational activity of Zionists] has in it an element that competes with the Nazi's actions in the Majdanek and Auschwitz gas chambers.[2]

In an issue from April 1950, an article was published under the headline: "In Auschwitz and in Israel."[3] From the headline, it is evident that the article's content aimed to create a parallel between the lives of Jews in Nazi concentration camps and the lives of religious Jews in Zionist Israel. In other words — it asserted that Nazi objectives during the Holocaust, i. e., the destruction of the Jewish people, and the desires of the Zionist regime to destroy the Jewish religion in the State of Israel, are identical.

The events that took place in Auschwitz are described by a Holocaust survivor who criticized the way Jewish prisoners who were assigned to supervise forced labor and other tasks in the camp conducted themselves. He presents them as Nazi collaborators, even though he knew full well that they had been forced, rather than chosen, to act the way they had.

In the interview, the Holocaust survivor compares the Zionist regime with the Nazi regime. He explains that by virtue of its secularism, the Zionist regime is an apostate one, sinful and blasphemous in its essence, which, through force, seeks to detach immigrants from Torah values and from *halakha* (Jewish law). The writer called the immigration camps "concentration" and "extermination" camps, the purpose of which was to force Jewish people to leave the path of the Torah and religious belief in God.[4]

Ⅳ. Zionism as Responsible for the Holocaust and the Physical Destruction of European Jewry

Gershon Greenberg, a scholar of Jewish theology, found that during the

---

① "In the Fire's Tongues [Hebrew]," *Om Ani Chomah*, July 27, 1950.

② Ibid.

③ S. Halevi, "In Auschwitz and in Israel," *Om Ani Chomah*, July 27, 1950.

④ Ibid.

first years of the Second World War, Orthodox Jewish thinkers emphasized the role of Amalek—a generic term for the traditional enemy of the Jewish people who embodies evil throughout the world as part of the divine plan to bring the Jewish people back to the righteous path of the Torah. However, as the war went on and the extent of evil increased, it became more difficult to justify the horrors with the claim of divine providence. Some turned to an explanation focused on the inner Amalek, part and parcel of the Jewish people, who encouraged the outer Amalek, meaning the Nazi gentiles (*goyim*, i.e., non-Jews).①

Years before the Holocaust, Rabbi Elchanan Wasserman (1874-1941)—a prominent rabbi and leader of Agudath Israel who was killed in the Holocaust—wrote that the inner Amalek precedes the outer Amalek and feeds it by asking Jews to assimilate into other cultures and people, leading to increased hatred towards the Jews. Wasserman believed that belief in God, as well as the Torah, is part of human existence and that without it, the "evil inclination" (*yetzer hara*) grows and manifests itself in blasphemy and idol worship (*avodazara*). Accordingly, the blasphemy brought about by national and secular Judaism — the destruction of the Torah and persecution of its followers—was, in fact, a declaration of war against God that led to the inner destruction of the Jewish people. For these reasons, Rabbi Wasserman saw those variations of Judaism as an inner Amalek, one that fueled the external hate inherent to other nations and ultimately led to the Holocaust.②

HaChomah's first issue quoted Wasserman's ideas, copied from his book *A Collection of Notes*. His ideology was adapted to fit the times:

> And it is written, God fights with Amalek from one generation to the next, and the Torah testifies that the war persists in every generation until the coming of the Messiah. But in previous generations, when the Torah ruled in Israel, the war was waged by the seed of Amalek from the gentile nations of the world. But since we unburdened ourselves from the

---

① Gershon Greenberg, "Amalek in Holocaust-Era Orthodox Jewish Thought," in *Bioethical and Ethical Issues Surrounding the Trials and Code of Nuremberg: Nuremberg Revisited*, ed. Jacques J. Rozenberg (Lewiston: Edwin Mellen Press, 2003), 203.

② Ibid., 205-206.

Torah, the seed of Amalek now sprawls in our midst and multiplies among our converted to enrage... [1]

The identification of Zionism as a blasphemous secular movement is the ideological basis for Neturei Karta's isolationism. According to them, in wishing to resemble other nations and peoples, Zionism aspired to build a national home without tradition, without the Torah and its commandments, and, in doing so, it brought about the destruction of the Jewish religion; therefore, it was seen as the root of all the evils experienced by the Jewish people.

V. Blaming Zionists for Sabotaging the Rescue of Jews in the Holocaust

According to Neturei Karta, the Zionist leadership's hatred towards diaspora Jews, especially religious Jews, was not manifested only in their forced secularization of Jewish children but also in their efforts to sabotage the rescue of ultra-Orthodox Jews in Europe. Thus, Zionists were blamed by Neturei Karta for participating, alongside the Germans, in the murder of Jews during the Holocaust.

At the end of August 1944, Neturei Karta's journal included the supposed testimonies of religious Jews who immigrated through the efforts of the Jewish Agency's "Rescue Committee" (*VaadHahatzalah*). The committee was formed in January 1943 after reports that confirmed, at the end of 1942, the systematic extermination of European Jews. The committee's goal was to act as an umbrella organization for the entire Yishuv in Mandatory Palestine, which would include the various factions and coordinate rescue efforts.

The article referred to activities aimed at rescuing Hungary's Jews that year. Its title, "Rescue Committee or Extermination Committee," implies its content:

> Some Torah-observant Jews say: Those [Zionist Jews] who were appointed agents of the rescue committee do not allow a Torah-observant

[1] "Our Condition [Hebrew]," *HaChomah*, Sivan 1944. See also: "Our Condition [Hebrew]," *HaChomah*, December 14, 1944.

> Jew to be rescued. They do not give him room to board a ship, or any means of rescue, under any circumstances... They also say: agents of the rescue committee came, carrying fortunes, to a famous place of slaughter to save a list of twenty-eight blasphemous Zionists, their friends. And when these were not found there, other Jews begged them to be saved now that they had no other choice, and those [the agents] refused to hear and went back whence they had come.①

The Zionist leadership, and the Rescue Committee as its representative, were thus presented as a cruel devil, the enemy of the Jewish people, who wished to destroy Haredi Judaism and "finish" the German mission.

Behind these claims lies a complex reality. The Nazis invaded Hungary in March 1944. Prior to the invasion, David Ben-Gurion, then the head of the Jewish Agency, had proposed to try and put pressure on Britain to increase its quota of immigration permits, while at the same time increasing the sums allocated for rescue.② A debate raged between various parties and movements regarding immigrants' demographics and the allocation of seating on the ships. Agudath Israel claimed it was marginalized, and that despite agreements promising it six percent of immigration capacity, the ships that had arrived in April and May did not include even one of its members or affiliated persons.③

It cannot be ignored that throughout the debates that took place in the Jewish Agency, complaints were raised among some of the Zionist party leaders concerning the number of anti-Zionist immigrants. On the other hand, other officials agreed with Agudath Israel that the number of immigrant members from their ranks on the ships was indeed small. The debate was mainly moot, however, since, in practice, the operator of the Romanian shipyard was a Greek man called YankiPandelis, and the people of the Mossad

---

① "Aha! Rescue or Extermination Committee God Have Mercy?! [Hebrew]," *HaChomah*, August 30, 1944.

② Tuvia Friling, *Arrows in the Dark: David Ben-Gurion, the Yishuv Leadership, and Rescue Attempts During the Holocaust*, Vol. 2 (Madison: The University of Wisconsin Press, 2005), 4-5.

③ Chaim Shalem, *A Time to Take Action to Rescue Jews: Agudat Yisrael in Eretz Israel Confronting the Holocaust* 1942-1945 (Sde Boker: The Ben-Gurion Research Institute/Ben-Gurion University of the Negev, 2007), 184-185. [Hebrew]

Aliyah Bet knew that his motivations were entirely financial.[1]

Yitzhak Gruenbaum, a Polish Jewish leader during the 1920s, was the head of the Rescue Committee. Gruenbaum, as the committee's representative, was himself put under fire in the pages of *HaChomah*, both for being a secular Zionist and for leading the rescue efforts, which were largely unsuccessful.[2] He was attacked and described as one who maliciously and intentionally acted to exterminate Haredi Judaism based on personal grudges. His son, Eliezer, who was imprisoned in Auschwitz during the war, was criticized severely:

> There is a certain Jew in Poland named Gruenbaum who, during the last five years of the war, placed himself at the service of the Nazis and became a Gestapo agent, the executor of the extermination of Polish Jews. Gruenbaum did his job with zeal, delivered his own people to the slaughter, crushed the skulls of babies and infants using his very hands, threw thousands of brothers and sisters, old folk and elderly, rabbis and *tzadikim* [righteous people] into the gas chambers and furnaces, [and] brought thousands of the Sons of Israel out of hiding and put them on the gallows... They, the Zionist leaders, know better than anyone that Gruenbaum, the son, inherited the morals and ideology of the father. He had learned from him the lesson that the goat's life is superior to that of a human being, and that standing on the blood of Jews for whichever interest is permitted, he understood that a death blow must be given to Haredi Jews...[3]

The article also claims that Gruenbaum used money allocated for the rescue of European Jews in order to save his son, who was under arrest in Paris at the time. According to the article, the leaders of the Yishuv were aware the money was being used for these purposes but kept quiet because they feared that public knowledge might turn to public outrage or, worse, that the

---

[1] Dina Porat, *The Blue and the Yellow Stars of David: The Zionist Leadership in Palestine and the Holocaust* 1939-1945 (Cambridge: Harvard University Press, 1990), 247-249.

[2] Ibid., 64-71.

[3] "The Sins of the Father [Hebrew]," *HaChomah*, January 21, 1946.

money they had been receiving might stop.①

These are baseless claims. Eliezer (Itche) Gruenbaum, son of Yitzhak Gruenbaum, was, in fact, imprisoned in Auschwitz at the end of June 1942, where he was appointed to various positions, one of which was block attendant. When the war ended, he returned to Paris.

In August 1945, he was arrested for assisting the Nazis and became subject to investigations after having been identified in the streets by some survivors. During these investigations, he met his father numerous times. He was eventually released, largely thanks to his father, who sought out witnesses to testify on his behalf, but also because he was arrested in France for an offense that neither took place within its territory nor against its citizens. Therefore, he could not be tried in the country.②

As for the allegation itself, once the scope of calamities became apparent, and even more so after 1942, the elder Gruenbaum acted prodigiously, within his position, to rescue Jews despite holding an advisory office with no executive powers.③ In deliberations within the Jewish Agency in the summer of 1944 following the occupation of Hungary, Gruenbaum asserted, contrary to Ben-Gurion's opinion, that a Zionist prerequisite should not be set for immigration. This was due both to common perception in Jewish public opinion and because in Romania, to which Jewish refugees escaped, everyone was in an appalling state that made preferences of this kind ill-advised.④

Ⅵ. The Zionist Leadership's Indifference towards the Holocaust

Along with Gruenbaum, *HaChomah* mentioned Dr. Chaim Weizmann,

① "The Sins of the Father [Hebrew]," *HaChomah*, January 21, 1946.

② Tuvia Friling, *A Jewish Kapo in Auschwitz: History, Memory, and the Politics of Survival* (Waltham, Mass.: Brandeis University Press, 2014), 31-50, 137-155.

③ Dina Porat, "'Do Your Utmost to Verify Your Cable': Yitzhak Gruenbaum, His Activities and Statements During the Holocaust," in *When Disaster Comes from Afar: Leading Personalities in the Land of Israel Confront Nazism and the Holocaust*, 1933-1948, ed. Dina Porat (Jerusalem: Yad Yitzhak Ben-Zvi, 2009), 449, 465-471 [Hebrew]; Tuvia Friling, *Arrows in the Dark: David Ben-Gurion, the Yishuv Leadership, and Rescue Attempts During the Holocaust*, 5-7.

④ Dina Porat, *The Blue and the Yellow Stars of David: The Zionist Leadership in Palestine and the Holocaust* 1939-1945, 248-250.

who served as president of the World Zionist Organization during the Holocaust. In an article published in the September 1948 issue and which was mainly a severe indictment against the Jewish Agency as representative of the Zionist movement, the two were asked to respond to allegations that numerous opportunities to rescue European Jews arose during the war and that these were intentionally blocked, despite knowing full well that this was a death sentence for Jews who were not rescued. The article argued that the supposedly reductive statements by Weizmann and Gruenbaum regarding European Jews during the Holocaust were allegedly proof of their decision to abandon European Jewry to the Nazis.①

According to the article, at the bottom of the hierarchy of European Jews, in the eyes of Zionism and its leaders, stood, allegedly, religious Jews, who did not have any right to exist as far as Zionists were concerned. That is why they did not merit being rescued, and there is no problem with them "going into the furnaces."②

The article stated that the same leaders who abandoned Jewish people to die were those whose policy of ingratiation at the feet of foreign nations—in order to normalize the idea of Jewish nationalism—had led to growing antisemitism in Europe. In this way, Zionism, according to the authors of the article, aided, directly and indirectly, the Holocaust and the deaths of millions of Jews.③

At the peak of the 1948 War, around the time Israel declared its independence, *HaChomah* published an opinion piece entitled "Is This the Love of Israel?" The writer argued that the deaths of hundreds of Jews in the war did not indicate dedication and sacrifice for ideals, as the Zionists sought to portray it, but a grave crime, an intentional mass murder. What guided Zionism and its leaders was not the love of Israel, but the hatred of it.

---

① "The Jewish Agency Is Required to Respond with a Clear Yes or No [Hebrew]," *HaChomah*, September 30, 1948. Porat indicates that even during the 1980s, Haredi allegations against the Zionist movement and its role in the Holocaust prominently included these two figures. Dina Porat, "'Amalek's Accomplices' Blaming Zionism for the Holocaust: Anti-Zionist Ultra-Orthodoxy in Israel During the 1980s," *Journal of Contemporary History* 27 (1992), 700-701.

② "The Jewish Agency Is Required to Respond with a Clear Yes or No [Hebrew]," *HaChomah*, September 30, 1948.

③ Ibid.

The proof was that the Zionists were the ones who had delivered Torah-observant Jews into the hands of the Nazis so that the former would not become an obstacle to their future plans: "And who might these be, the ones who delivered into Nazi hands in Europe those among the Jews who wouldn't take a Zionist Shekel; who might they be, who persecuted Torah-observant Jews to death during the war and afterward, who might they be, if not these so-called 'Lovers of Israel...'"

Through his words, the writer directly connected the Holocaust, the establishment of the State of Israel, and the 1948 War, and explained that on its way to fulfilling its primary objective of establishing a state, Zionism was willing to act at the expense of the suffering and deaths of many people, and drag Israel into a bloody war not only with the Arabs living in Palestine at the time but with every Arab nation surrounding it. The Zionists acted the same way, the article argued, during the Holocaust, when they intentionally sabotaged the rescue of religious Jews as part of its plan to establish a secular-Zionist state.①

In the same spirit, in 1948, two months after Israel's declaration of independence and at the end of the first temporary truce in the war, *HaChomah* published an article with a similar orientation — not only are the Zionists not really the traditional sons of Israel, but they aim to uproot the Torah of Israel. Accordingly, the secular Zionist nation is just like the other nations of the world. As such, it participated, along with other nations of the world, in the destruction of six million Jews during the Holocaust by standing aloof and out of a clear interest in achieving its ultimate goal — establishing a nation-state.

The writer argued that the Zionists persisted in this way by dragging the people into a war that resulted in the unnecessary loss of many Jewish lives for a theologically illegitimate cause, a Jewish state:

> They are a nation as low as the rest of the *goyim* [other nations]. Just like the rest of the world's nations stood aloof and killed our six million brothers in Europe with their own hands, just like them, the modern nation of the Zionists, they too have a hand in the cruel mass

① Y. P., "Is This the Love of Israel? [Hebrew]," *HaChomah*, March 4, 1948.

> murder of millions of our martyrs. It is, therefore, no wonder that when they declared a state, they favorably remembered that enemy of the Jews, Hitler, may his name and memory be blotted out, who had helped them in their efforts to establish their nation by exterminating millions. They follow him in his ways as a modern nation by destroying thousands and tens of thousands of peaceful inhabitants to achieve their false objective.[1]

Thus, according to Neturei Karta, the birth of the State of Israel constitutes heresy against God's will and, therefore, must be condemned and confronted fiercely. Moreover, Zionism, on its way to self-fulfillment, had done intentional evil—whether in the 1948 War that took the lives of many, or earlier, in not rescuing European Jews from extermination, standing by and even actively aiding their destruction.

Ⅶ. The Kasztner Trial

Attempts to link Zionism with Nazi actions did not revolve exclusively around those acting from within the Yishuv. According to Neturei Karta, the moral decline which characterized the Zionist leadership after the establishment of the State of Israel was tethered to the way its representatives acted in Europe, and generally to all those who identified as Zionists, who were seen as suspected collaborators,[2] or worse—as central causes for the extermination of European Jewry.

Dr. Israel (Rezső) Kasztner was, during the Second World War, one of the Zionists movement's most prominent leaders and a member of the Aid and Rescue Committee in Budapest. As part of his role, he negotiated with the Germans, a fact known to the Zionist leadership in Mandatory Palestine, to save Hungarian Jews. After the war, Kasztner's rescue efforts and the results thereof provoked a controversy that reached its peak in the Greenwald-Kasztner trial. The trial, which commenced on January 1, 1954, quickly turned political. At its center stood the political and ethical problems the

① "Investigation and Clarification [Hebrew]," *HaChomah*, July 21, 1948.

② See: "From One Week to The Next [Hebrew]," *Om Ani Chomah*, January 11, 1951.

Zionist leadership faced concerning rescue efforts during the Holocaust.①

The trial began with a criminal complaint for libel filed against Malchiel Greenwald, a gonzo pamphleteer who had accused Kasztner of collaborating with the Nazis and abandoning Jews. In June 1954, Kasztner turned from accuser to accused, and the trial transformed into the Kasztner affair and a fierce public debate over the policies of the Zionist leadership in Mandatory Palestine during the Holocaust. It was only at this point that Neturei Karta's journal found it apt to publish an article about the trial. Kasztner's name was not mentioned in the article. Instead, Zionism, as a movement, was blamed for participating in the destruction of Hungarian Jewry:

> And now comes the trial between two Hungarian immigrants, which places in front of the Zionist judge the shameful conduct of the Zionists in its entirety when it came to saving the Jews of Hungary. The hairs of one's head should stand on end upon hearing the atrocious details of how these ignoble murderers lent their hands in delaying and sabotaging rescue, all to help each other to establish the apostate state. The details of how, with their very hands, they misled one of the rescue agents and put a stop to the entire plan are terrible. And terrible, too, are the declarations and responses of the Zionist leaders, who openly said that they would not let the details come to light or anything concerning their Zionist inclinations, even if the cost would exceed hundreds of thousands of Jews, who were, for these reasons, led to their extermination in the fiery furnaces...②

It was for a reason that the writer chose to argue that the Kasztner Trial supplied decisive evidence that Zionism was actively and maliciously sabotaging the rescue efforts of Jews during the Holocaust. Greenwald himself had made this kind of allegation in his pamphlets when he explained that Kasztner chose, allegedly, to save his relatives and affiliates for bribe money, while everyone

---

① Yehiam Weitz, *The Man Who Was Murdered Twice: The Life, Trial, and Death of Dr. Israel Kasztner* (Jerusalem: Keter Publishing House, 1995). [Hebrew]

② A. Yehuda Cohen, "Upon Thy Walls Jerusalem: Those Destroyers [Hebrew]," *MishmeretChomatenu*, June 17, 1954.

else, Haredi Jews among them, were sent to the extermination camps.[1]

The historical truth is different. The decisions on the make-up of the passengers were made by a small committee headed by Auto Komoly, the director of the Rescue Committee. Alongside Kasztner, this committee consisted of additional representatives, including some from the Orthodox community in Cluj. Kasztner was a key figure in this affair, but he was not the only one who decided who would board which train.[2]

The proceedings, which placed the leadership of the Yishuv alongside Kasztner at the forefront of the accusations, affected public opinion and did not go unnoticed by Neturei Karta, which found it fertile grounds for their anti-Zionist ideology. In order to prove that the Zionist idea and its proponents brought about a disaster, the February 1955 issue of the movement mentioned another affair concerning the Holocaust alongside their coverage at the peak of the Kasztner trial. The affair, namely the reparations agreement between Israel and West Germany, had already led to wide public debate at the time.[3]

The writers emphasized that the trial confirmed the claim concerning Zionism's responsibility during the Holocaust; it was not merely a passive participant but actively collaborated with the Nazis, and the proof of this lay in Kasztner's deeds. As if this was not enough, according to the article, Zionism went further by taking reparation money and German commodities as part of the reparation agreement, in the manner of "Hast thou killed and also taken possession."[4]

On June 22, 1955, the verdict was passed in Kasztner's trial. In it, Judge Benjamin Halevi, the president of the district court, determined that Kasztner had "sold his soul to the devil," for in his actions as a Nazi collaborator, he had effectively supported the Nazi extermination operation.

Nine days later, an article was published in Neturei Karta's journal under

---

① Yehiam Weitz, *The Man Who Was Murdered Twice: The Life, Trial, and Death of Dr. Israel Kasztner*, 95.

② Yehuda Bauer, *Jews for Sale? Nazi-Jewish Negotiations*, 1933-1945 (New Haven: Yale University Press, 1994), 198.

③ Isaac Ashkenazi, "Herzl's Doctrine of Slaughter [Hebrew]," *MishmeretChomatenu*, February 17, 1955.

④ The term originates in the biblical tale of Naboth's vineyard, 1 Kings 21:19 (KJV).

the large, bolded headline: "The Kasztner Trial." This was the first time since this journal began reporting on the trial that the name of Israel Kasztner was mentioned as the primary defendant.

Nevertheless, the content accorded with the manner of reporting that Neturei Karta's journal had taken until then, emphasizing that "during the Kasztner trial, Zionist leaders in Israel were also accused of aiding the extermination." Furthermore, "To us, this is not new. Haredi Jews knew and still know that the Zionists are the haters of Judaism, in mind and in spirit alike."①

In mid-July 1955, the journal returned to the Kasztner trial. Again, Kasztner was not mentioned by name as a defendant, and the article began by stating: "A Zionist directly participated in the extermination of about a million Hungarian Jews."② The timing of these publications is noteworthy — shortly afterward, on July 26, Israel's third parliamentary elections were set to be held. It was a tumultuous election with the trial, especially the verdict, in the background. All sides tried to exploit the verdict during their campaigns for political gain.③

Neturei Karta did not participate in the election. Nevertheless, its leaders wanted to remind the public, especially close to the elections, that "The Zionists have ceased to be 'suspects' and are now direct defendants on trial for the mass extermination of large Jewish groups."④ Kasztner himself, it was claimed, was only one example of Zionism's crimes, and therefore mentioning him by name was of no importance; it was enough to say that he was a "*Nazo-Judes*," and that he felt that "there were a million superfluous Jews in Hungary; this 'excess' he tried, dedicated wholeheartedly to the Hitlerite Asmodeus, to remove."⑤

Why did Kasztner collaborate with the Nazis, according to the authors?

① M. H., "The Kasztner Trial [Hebrew]," *MishmeretChomatenu*, June 30, 1955.

② Porat, *The Yellow Badge*; "The Zionist Hackenritzles [Hebrew]," *MishmeretChomatenu*, July 15, 1955.

③ Yehiam Weitz, *The Man Who Was Murdered Twice: The Life, Trial, and Death of Dr. Israel Kasztner*, 287-299.

④ "The Zionist Hackenritzles [Hebrew]," *MishmeretChomatenu*, July 15, 1955.

⑤ Ibid.

They suggested that not unlike the Zionist leaders, he acted out of heartfelt hatred for Haredi Jews and to prevent their migration to the Land of Israel. He went as far as negotiating with the Nazis, which eventually led to them sending hundreds of thousands of Hungarian Haredi Jews to their deaths.[1]

In January 1957, proceedings commenced in the appeal the state had submitted against Benjamin Halevi's verdict in the hope of clearing Kasztner's name. However, on the night of March 3, 1957, Kasztner was murdered near his home. The murder struck a nerve in Israeli society despite its political and ideological polarization, which was expressed in the various newspapers that reported with shock on the assassination.[2]

Neturei Karta, for its part, chose to ignore the murder. Only at the end of that month did it mention it in a small article, which deepened the demonic image of the Zionist regime. The article argued that Kasztner's assassins had learned from their Zionist predecessors how traitors and opponents should be treated, as had been the case with Dr. Jacob Israël de Haan (1881-1924)[3]—the spokesperson for the anti-Zionist Haredi Jews in Jerusalem — who was murdered in June 1924 at the entrance to the Shaare Zedek Hospital (an operation possibly carried out by the Haganah due to De Haan's communications with British and Arab leaders).

Ⅷ. The Eichmann Trial

On May 23, 1960, David Ben-Gurion announced the capture of Adolf Eichmann and of his being brought to Israel to stand trial. Eichmann was one of the prominent architects of the Holocaust of European Jewry.[4] The announcement electrified the nation and became the main topic of discussion in

---

① "The Zionist Hackenritzles [Hebrew]," *MishmeretChomatenu*, July 15, 1955.

② Yehiam Weitz, *The Man Who Was Murdered Twice: The Life, Trial, and Death of Dr. Israel Kasztner*, 325-328.

③ "Whoso Keepeth the Fig Tree Shall Eat the Fruit Thereof [Hebrew]," *MishmeretChomatenu*, March 28, 1957.

④ "The Prime Minister's Announcement Regarding the Arrest of Adolf Eichmann [Hebrew]," *DivreiHaKnesset* 22 (May 23, 1950):1291.

the Israeli-Jewish public.[①]

In contrast, Neturei Karta referred to Eichmann's arrest only at the beginning of June and declared in their journal: "The land trembles, and a great uproar sounds from the edge of the Zionist state... after many years they were now able to catch the vile enemy of Israel, Adolf Eichmann, may his name and memory be blotted out, and bring him clandestinely to their country."[②]

While Israel's streets were brimming with national pride and hunger for vengeance, Neturei Karta chose to present the future trial as an attempt by the Zionists to "fabricate history" and clear their name after the Kasztner Trial, which had revealed to the public that they had collaborated with the Nazis.[③]

Indeed, in the years leading up to the capture of Eichmann, both right and left-wing politicians claimed Ben-Gurion was not doing enough to capture the Nazi criminal because of some fear that, if he were to stand trial, Eichmann would expose his ties to Kasztner, and the affair would return to the headlines and haunt Ben-Gurion and his party, as it indeed did during the trial itself.[④]

Neturei Karta's journal presented the trial's objectives, supposedly citing Ben-Gurion himself,[⑤] and, at the same time, claimed that the Zionists' ultimate purpose was to clear their name from their guilt which had become public knowledge. What was this guilt? The article's title, "The Inveigler and the Killer... One Judges the Other..." speaks to it. It originates in a passage from Midrash Numbers Rabbah in the name of Rabbi Shimon: "How do we know that a man's inveigler does more than his killer? For the killer kills in this world and leaves a part for the next one, while the inveigler kills him in this world and in the next one."[⑥]

---

① Hanna Yablonka, *The State of Israel vs. Adolf Eichmann* (New York: Schocken Books, 2004), 33-36.

② "The Inveigler and The Killer...One Judges the Other...[Hebrew]," *MishmeretChomatenu*, June 9, 1960.

③ Ibid.

④ Ora Herman, *The Furnace and the Reactor: Behind the Scenes at the Eichmann Trial* (Tel Aviv: Hakibbutz Hameuchad, 2017), 17. [Hebrew]

⑤ "The Inveigler and The Killer...One Judges the Other...[Hebrew]," *MishmeretChomatenu*, June 9, 1960.

⑥ Numbers Rabbah 21:4 [Hebrew].

Therefore, Zionism is the worst sin. According to Neturei Karta's journal, the Nazis might be guilty of exterminating the Jewish people by killing their bodies, but the Zionists' sin is greater because their notions of Jewish nationalism, blasphemous in themselves, led to antisemitism in Europe and to a hatred of Jews that brought about their destruction. According to the article, the Kasztner and Eichmann trials proved that the Zionists participated in the Holocaust by collaborating with the Nazis and negotiating with them.

In the following issue, Neturei Karta's journal described how the Zionists meant to clear their names of the bloodshed of millions of European Jews. They intended to do this, the article claimed, by drafting special laws that would allow for Eichmann to stand trial in Israel.[①] The issue of Israel's right to try Eichmann was at the center of the debate as soon as Eichmann was brought to the country. At that time, Ben-Gurion declared that Israel was a sovereign state and that it had the right to try Eichmann in an Israeli court, by Israeli judges, and according to Israeli laws.[②]

After discussing Eichmann's capture and its implications, Neturei Karta did not tend to the matter further. Only six months later or so, following Eichmann's formal arrest in Israel and while preparations for the trial, which was due to begin on April 11, 1961, were underway, did Neturei Karta's journal publish two articles criticizing Zionism and its role in the Holocaust.

Instead of dealing with Eichmann himself and his crimes as an enemy of the Jewish people, the journal chose to focus again on blaming the victim, as someone whose part in the destruction of European Jewry was even greater than that of the perpetrator of the crime — citing the murderer himself and treating his words as historical truth and fact.

Shortly after the trial began, the cover page of the mouthpiece published an article, spread across two pages, and titled: "The Zionists Try Eichmann,

---

① S. D. Katz, "Thee Which Frameth Mischief by a Law [Hebrew]," *MishmeretChomatenu*, June 23, 1960.

② Ora Herman, *The Furnace and the Reactor: Behind the Scenes at the Eichmann Trial*, 61-65; Yehiam Weitz, "The Holocaust on Trial: The Impact of the Kasztner and Eichmann Trials on Israeli Society," *Israel Studies* 1 (1996), 17.

May His Name and Memory be Blotted Out."① The article brimmed with criticism and accusations, according to which the primary cause for the destruction of European Jewry was Zionism, the national ambitions of which meant breaking an oath not to "immigrate as a wall" and ended ultimately in bringing about the Holocaust.

The article stated, "If one took everything into account, one would find that these blasphemous Zionists are far worse for the House of Israel than all of its enemies and opponents hitherto. All evil nations threatening Israel have not done to the people of Israel what the Zionists came to do [with their many iniquities]."②

Apart from another article that continued to blame Zionism and its leaders for the Holocaust through the Eichmann trial,③ the journal did not discuss the Eichmann trial further-not the survivors' testimonies, the verdict, or the death sentence, which was eventually given, nor the execution. This, while the trial and the testimonies heard in it were at the center of the public agenda in Israel.④

The great importance of the Eichmann trial, as explained by the historian Hanna Yablonka, was that it generated a double shift in consciousness: On the one hand, it crystallized information about the Holocaust into knowledge and consciousness, and on the other hand, it bound the Holocaust to the Israeli national ethos.⑤

According to Michal Shaul, a scholar of Haredi Holocaust memory, the Eichmann trial changed attitudes toward the Holocaust also in the mainstream ultra-Orthodox public. In the eyes of Haredi Jews, *Kiddush Hashem* (sanctification of God's name) was absent from the trial, which instead emphasized Zionist values of armed heroism and presented Israel as the only

① "The Zionists Try Eichmann, May His Name and Memory Be Blotted Out [Hebrew]," *MishmeretChomatenu*, April 27, 1961.

② Ibid.

③ "Eichmann: I Was Enthused by the Zionist Idea and its Initiator, Herzl (the Name of the Wicked Shall Rot) 'Some Country, Some Firm Ground under their Feet [Hebrew],'" *MishmeretBeitenu*, June 29,1961.

④ Yehiam Weitz, "The Holocaust on Trial: The Impact of the Kasztner and Eichmann Trials on Israeli Society," 19.

⑤ Hanna Yablonka, *The State of Israel vs. Adolf Eichmann*, 222.

refuge for the Jewish people.① The ultra-Orthodox factions felt, accordingly, that they were not permitted to take part in shaping Israeli remembrance of the Holocaust. As a result, in the early sixties, the ultra-Orthodox remembrance of the Holocaust was no longer integrated with the general historical memory, but became a counter-memory in which the two types of heroism were seen as polar opposites.②

In any case, changes in Holocaust remembrance in Israeli society at large, including among ultra-Orthodox factions, did not leave a mark on Neturei Karta. The main function of Eichmann's trial for the movement was to serve as another piece of supposedly supporting evidence to blame Zionism and its leaders for the Holocaust of European Jewry.

Conclusion

Neturei Karta's journal, like other Haredi newspapers, functioned as a tool in an ideological struggle more than as a platform for credible news articles.③ Accordingly, *HaChomah*, in its various incarnations, is a mirror that reflects the spirit and values that characterized this group.

Neturei Karta's persistent and relentless struggle against Zionism shaped the way in which their journal treated the Holocaust and related events. Neturei Karta claimed that the Zionists contributed directly and indirectly to the extermination of Jews, mainly religious Jews, and were responsible for the spiritual Holocaust that befell Jewish people.

Though Neturei Karta is numerically a small group in Haredi society, the

---

① Michal Shaul, "Holocaust Memory in Ultra-Orthodox Society in Israel: Is it a 'Counter-Memory?'" *The Journalof Israeli History* 32 (2013), 221. Roni Stauber adds that in articles written during the fifties in ultra-Orthodox parties' newspapers, the heroism of the fighters in the Warsaw Ghetto Uprising, while strongly rejecting the claim that the physical resistance was tied to Zionism ideology and explaining that the uprising was a Jewish resistance. See: Roni Stauber, *Lessons for this Generation: Holocaust and Heroism in Israeli Public Discourse in the* 1950*s* (Jerusalem: Yad Yitzhak Ben-Zvi/The Ben-Gurion Research Center/Ben-Gurion University of the Negev Press, 2000), 113. [Hebrew]

② Michal Shaul, "Holocaust Memory in Ultra-Orthodox Society in Israel: Is it a 'Counter-Memory?'" 228-229.

③ Kimmy Kaplan, "Profiles in the Haredi Press in Israel: History, Development, and Characteristics [Hebrew]," *Sectoral Media in Israel* 3 (2006): 1-47. [Hebrew]

multiple struggles they fought in the fifties were concomitant with those of the main factions in ultra-Orthodox Judaism. As Menachem Friedman explained, their ideological influence is greater than their demography, because mainstream ultra-Orthodox society regarded them, especially in the early 1950s, as martyrs who were willing to pay heavy prices for their uncompromising beliefs.①

Additional research is needed in order to learn to what extent the distorted historical representation of the Holocaust in Neturei Karta's journal affected how the Holocaust and Zionism are interpreted in ultra-Orthodox society at large.

① Menachem Friedman, *The Haredi (Ultra-Orthodox) Society—Sources, Trends and Processes* (Jerusalem: The Jerusalem Institute for Israel Studies, 1991), 94-95. [Hebrew]

“墙”与“回归如墙”：圣城守护者、复国主义与大屠杀

塔尔·科恩

【摘要】本文审视强烈反对复国主义的极端正统宗派“圣城守护者”如何谈论大屠杀及相关问题。基于对该宗派期刊发表的数以百计文章的广泛分析，本文提出，大屠杀书写对于“圣城守护者”质疑复国主义在以色列建国前后的合法性的努力至关重要。复国主义者被谴责应为欧洲犹太社群的毁灭负直接或间接责任，并对犹太教信徒实施“精神屠杀”。这些观点至今仍有回响。

【关键词】圣城守护者；复国主义；大屠杀

Enemy of the State: An Interview with Rabbi Israel Meir Hirsch

Uriya Shavit

Abstract: Rabbi Israeli Meir Hirsch is the current leader of Neturei Karta, the most radical anti-Zionist ultra-Orthodox group in Israel. They not only regard Israel as illegal state in a religious sense, but also cooperate with the "enemy" of Israel (Palestine Liberation Organization and Iran). In April, 2021, Prof. Shavit had an interview with Rabbi Israeli Meir Hirsch who directly explained the ideologies, social structure of that religious groups and the future of Israel.

Key Words: Neturei Karta, Ultra-Orthodox, Anti-Zionism

Rabbi Israeli Meir Hirsch is the current leader of Neturei Karta, the most radical anti-Zionist ultra-Orthodox group in Israel. Neturei Karta not only holds Israel to be a religiously illegitimate and criminal state and refrains from any engagement with state institutions, but also cooperates with Israel's enemies (On the historical and ideological roots of the movement, see Tal Cohen's article in this issue).

Rabbi Hirsch became Neturei Karta's leader in 2010 following the death of his father, Rabbi Moshe Hirsch. The elder Hirsch was born in New York and was married to the daughter of Rabbi AharonKatzenelbogen, one of Neturei Karta's founders. He was close to Yasser Arafat, the leader of the Palestine Liberation Organization (PLO), acted as his advisor on Jewish affairs, and considered Israel as occupied Palestinian territory. In 2006, Neturei Karta sent a delegation to Tehran to a Holocaust-denying and distorting conference hosted by the Iranian regime, a move considered extreme even for some in the movement's ranks.

The younger Hirsch follows in his father's ideological footsteps, albeit in a somewhat less public manner.

While Neturei Karta is not averse to open contacts with Israeli Zionists, including academic scholars of ultra-Orthodox society, their leadership has given very few in-depth interviews throughout its century of existence. In April 2021, ahead of the first annual conference of the Shandong-Tel Aviv Institute for Israel and Jewish Studies, which explored Haredi society, Rabbi Hirsch granted a lengthy recorded interview to Prof. Uriya Shavit. In the interview, at times in shockingly candid terms, he addressed his community's ideology, social structure, and vision for the future of Israel. Excerpts from the interview, edited for clarity, are published here.

The door of Rabbi Hirsch's modest home in the Mea Shearim neighborhood in Jerusalem bears a sign in Hebrew, Arabic, and English: "A Jew, Not a Zionist." Israel Meir Hirsch is a gracious, soft-spoken host who serves his guests Coca-Cola and cakes. He is also a religious leader who does not believe in the language of moderation or ambivalence.

Prof. Shavit: I would like to start, with your permission, with the entrance to your home, with the door. It bears a sign that says: "A Jew, Not a Zionist."

Rabbi Hirsch: That's right.

Prof. Shavit: Can the Rabbi explain what this means?

Rabbi Hirsch: We have been living here under Zionist occupation for more than 70 years, and the Zionists took over this land by force and with weapons. We try in every moment and take every opportunity to clarify to whomever we can that Zionism and Judaism are two completely opposite terms.

Zionism actually aimed to eradicate the Jewish roots of the Jewish people, to establish a new people with no ties to its heritage. This declaration [the sign at the door] started, in fact, with the late Rabbi [Amram] Blau, the leader of Neturei Karta, who died in the year 5734; you can calculate when that was [1974]. He decided at one point... He attached that sign to his clothes and wore it... in his final years. It is a declaration that we are simply Jews and unrelated to Zionism. That is basically the point of hanging the sign on the door.

Prof. Shavit: Well, before I ask about your historical and theological perception, about what were the origins of the objection to Zionism, I would first like to ask something about the present and the future. What do you wish would happen? What are you praying for? There is a given situation—the State of Israel exists. What do you wish for?

Rabbi Hirsch: We wish the people would return to its roots, of course, and know where they came from because Zionism managed to separate all the people who live here in this state from their Jewish roots.

This means that [currently] the House of Israel is like all the other non-Jewish nations, and we are not connected to any heritage or something that obligates us. What we wish is for the day described in the book of *Prophet Malachi*, at the end of the prophecy: "He will turn the hearts of the fathers to the children, and the hearts of the children to their fathers," which means that we hope that the entire nation will return to its roots. This is what we hope and pray for.

Prof. Shavit: But in practical political terms, until the arrival of the Messiah...Well, the Ottoman Empire ceased to exist, and so has the British Mandate. In pragmatic political terms, if the State of Israel ceased to exist as a Zionist state, then the only possible way to reach your desired outcome is for the Palestinian Authority or Hamas to take over. Is that something you hope for?

Rabbi Hirsch: So long as the redemption does not come from God, we would prefer any Arab-Muslim regime in order to live our religious life in peace and with no wars, and each can live his life in any way he chooses.

Prof. Shavit: But ultimately, when we look, for instance, at the situation of Christians in the Palestinian Authority, if the Zionist enterprise would collapse, the chance that Jews would live here in peace is not a real one, is not a realistic one.

Rabbi Hirsch: The real solution—without deluding ourselves that things will go one way or another—is to return the entire land to its rightful owners, which is, at present, the Palestinian people, and through them, we can live under a regime that does not intend to destroy the faith.

Even [Yasser] Arafat himself, in his first speech at the United Nations (UN) in 1973, said unequivocally that our [the Palestinian people's] battle is also for the Jewish people. This implied [that from Arafat's point of view, the Palestinians also fight for] the Jewish people that are under Zionist occupation, and [the Palestinians] will make sure that everyone can live under our rule with no discrimination, meaning that [the Palestinians] respect the Jewish religion. Anyone can watch that speech and see what he said.

Prof. Shavit: If I understand correctly, from a theological standpoint, the source of your objection to Zionism is not only or not even primarily the reality of a state that is not based on Rabbinical Law. Your fundamental problem with Zionism is the notion of the "Three Oaths" [a *midrash* in which God instructed the Jewish people not to reclaim the Land of Israel forcefully and not to rebel against the other nations] that by realizing Jewish sovereignty, Zionism is "ascending as a wall" [i.e., leading a return to the land of Israel in an organized political fashion prior to the arrival of the Messiah and thus rebelling against God]. This means that from your point of view, there is nothing that the Zionist state can do that can correct the distortion it represents.

Rabbi Hirsch: Of course not. Because we completely deny any possibility of a Jewish regime, whether by Haredim or by Jews who have already become separated from their roots. We are forbidden to establish any regime before the arrival of the Messiah, no matter the form.

And, of course, we also object to...let's say there was a state [that was] managed according to the laws of the Torah, to Jewish law. We also strongly object to this idea. Fundamentally, we support the concept of separation between church and state because this mixture of church and state is the source of all these outbursts.

Prof. Shavit: Tell me, where lies the difference between you and Agudath Israel? Because they, too, are not Zionist. They are not among Herzl's fans; they don't support the Zionist idea.

Rabbi Hirsch: As far as I see it, Agudath Israel are Reform Jews for all purposes; they are a reform movement for all purposes.

Prof. Shavit: Why is that?

Rabbi Hirsch: Because they became separated from their roots. I mean, initially, Agudath Israel fought against the Zionist idea. [Yet later] they simply distorted the path, became part of the [Zionist] establishment, and involved the Haredi public in the Zionist turmoil. This means they are a bridge for recruiting people from the Haredi community to the Zionist community.

Prof. Shavit: Where lies the difference between you and groups that are widely referred to as the Eda Haredit, such as the Toldot Aharon Hasidic sect?

Rabbi Hirsch: In fact, all of these Hasidic groups — the Eda Haredit, Toldot Aharon, Toldot Avraham Yitzhak—basically have the same view as us. They are not as extreme as going to the Arabs, but in principle, they do not accept government funds, do not study in Hebrew, and are not connected at all to any Zionist establishment in any way. This [Eda Haredit] is a very large group of 50,000 families that are practically separated from the state.

Prof. Shavit: But, after all, you do not have common leadership institutions, so what are the ideological and practical differences between you and Toldot Aharon, for example?

Rabbi Hirsch: Ideologically, it's the same. We differ in our attitude of appealing to the Arabs [which we do, and they do not] because people don't like the matter of appealing to the Arabs. In the general public, people see it as if we are collaborating with murderers, etc.; still, we [and the other Eda Haredit groups] share the same principles.

Prof. Shavit: When interacting with members of the PLO, with members of Hamas, did you honestly feel that you would be comfortable and safe living under their rule?

Rabbi Hirsch: I feel very comfortable when I go to Ramallah and to all kinds of places in the territories [the West Bank and Gaza] or in the world, whether in Egypt, Qatar, or any other state. We don't sense any inkling indicating that living together will not be possible.

Prof. Shavit: You have no connections with the state. Not only do you not vote in national or local elections, but if I remember correctly, you don't pay social security or health insurance. So, on the practical level, how do you manage? I mean...

Rabbi Hirsch: We manage. It's very hard, and, of course, we have to constantly send people to fundraise abroad to raise money for our institutions. We can't really live without those donations, but this is the path we chose, and we persevere on it.

Prof. Shavit: From a certain respect, I estimate that many from the secular and also the traditional sectors would say: there is something we appreciate here. Here are people who object to Zionism but are fully committed to this objection; they don't live at my expense.

Rabbi Hirsch: Indeed.

Prof. Shavit: But if a member of Neturei Karta is, God forbid, sick and needs to go to the hospital, how is this covered?

Rabbi Hirsch: It's very hard. For example, my late father was hospitalized for a lengthy time, and we had to pay for it ourselves. We asked for donations to do so. But it is definitely very hard.

Prof. Shavit: And what are the sources of income? What jobs do people have?

Rabbi Hirsch: Usually, the men study in the Kollel; we call it a Kollel [a college for studying Torah]. Some women work from home in various jobs that generate some income. But it's very hard, of course; daily life is not simple at all.

Prof. Shavit: Do people have jobs in the general employment market? I mean, do they go out and work in factories, for example?

Rabbi Hirsch: They don't have formal jobs, but there are all kinds of religiously-related jobs that do provide a substantial income for those who work in that area, and through this, each person earns a living one way or another.

Prof. Shavit: And there are donors.

Rabbi Hirsch: Of course. All the time.

Prof. Shavit: Who are the donors? Where do they live?

Rabbi Hirsch: Mostly the Satmar congregations in the United States and Europe. The SatmarRebbe reinforced the idea of financially supporting people living in the Holy Land who do not take anything and who decisively avoid any support, and that's the foundation of our existence here in the Holy Land.

Prof. Shavit: If I remember correctly, your criticism of the Zionist movement is much broader than the theological issue of "ascending as a wall," of compromising an important principle. In your view, the Zionist movement is responsible for a large-scale historical crime—[You hold that the Zionists] collaborated with the Nazis.

Rabbi Hirsch: Without a doubt. But we see the spiritual holocaust that

Zionism brought upon the Jewish people as much worse than the Holocaust that occurred 80 years ago. From our perspective, from the Torah's perspective, from the Torah's outlook, the sages say in the Talmud: "Whoever causes a person to sin is worse than one who kills him," which means that from our perspective, causing a Jew to sin is worse than killing him. Zionism is, in fact, guilty of this spiritual holocaust of the Jewish people.

Prof. Shavit: But if I understand correctly, in your view, it bears some responsibility for the Holocaust itself.

Rabbi Hirsch: Without a doubt. Those who are familiar with history can see the undeniable connection between the Zionist leaders and the Nazis. It is well documented, so it is not something that I am inventing. And whoever reads some history knows that they played a very big role in the crime of the Holocaust, which took place 80 years ago.

Prof. Shavit: If there had been no Zionist movement and if there hadn't already been hundreds of thousands of Jews here [in Israel] in the 1930s, they would have been murdered.

Rabbi Hirsch: By whom?

Prof. Shavit: By the Nazis.

Rabbi Hirsch: By the Nazis?

Prof. Shavit: And their collaborators, yes.

Rabbi Hirsch: Look, the Zionists declared a financial boycott of Germany, which inflamed Hitler, and only then did he decide and say that he would take a terrible revenge against the Jews.

If the Zionists hadn't provoked the German people, it would never have come to those things. This is a fact; I'm not making this up, that the Zionists upset Hitler greatly, and only then did he decide as he did. But initially, his purpose and his plan were only to deport the Jews, not to kill them, not to murder them. This happened as a result of the Zionist provocation.

Prof. Shavit: Well, one can say these things in Israel, but you know it's considered a criminal offense in Germany or Austria. It's an interesting point to think about.

Rabbi Hirsch: Holocaust deniers.

Prof. Shavit: But, and I say this not as a provocation but rather as a historical fact that should be considered, Zionism won, and your group lost.

Today there are nine million people in the State of Israel and you, Neturei Karta, are no more than 400-500 families. Maybe this is something else that should be considered?

Rabbi Hirsch: I always say that Herzl succeeded with his vision... Herzl writes in his diary that once when he was walking on the street in Paris, a Gentile yelled at him, "Jewish pig," which annoyed him very much. So he wrote in his diary that he had a brilliant idea right after [he was yelled at]. What was the idea? To take some Jews and convert them to Christianity, they would go on a Sunday openly to a monastery, and then people would stop hating us.

But actually, in practice, Herzl had good connections with August Rohling, if you've heard of him, who was the father of modern antisemitism before and during Hitler's time, and Hitler based his hatred on his findings. Herzl writes in his diary that antisemitism is his best friend because, through antisemitism, he would be able to achieve his goals. But what did Zionism actually want from the Jewish people? Just like Herzl writes, it wants to generate a new nation unconnected to Jewish heritage.

Prof. Shavit: But the question is: If you represent God's will, why did Herzl succeed?

Rabbi Hirsch: It is written: "The way of the wicked prospers."

Prof. Shavit: Well, that way, you can explain anything, but...

Rabbi Hirsch: It is a fact. It is also written: "Though the wicked spring up like grass and all evildoers flourish," but what does it say after that? "...they will be destroyed forever." This means there is an upward movement, but the decline will be very dramatic. As with Haman the Wicked, where the sages say that the king elevated him and raised him above the ministers. Why? So that his downfall would be much more forceful.

Prof. Shavit: There is another point in the Zionist victory that I think is even more interesting. We are speaking in Hebrew.

Rabbi Hirsch: Correct.

Prof. Shavit: And you speak outstanding Hebrew, contemporary Hebrew. When Eliezer Ben-Yehuda [the reviver of the Hebrew language] was persecuted in Jerusalem at the end of the 19th century, very few spoke Hebrew; almost no one spoke Hebrew. So even your beautiful Hebrew is proof of the Zionist victory. Where did you gain this proficiency in Hebrew?

Rabbi Hirsch: With no formal studies, with no academic degree, and all those things. I simply grew up here and picked up the language.

Prof. Shavit: You know, already at this point in the conversation, some people might ask the following question: Who is forcing you to stay here? If the Zionist state is so bad for you, you are invited to pack your suitcases and move to Nablus or to New York.

Rabbi Hirsch: There is no doubt on that issue. It would, of course, have been preferable. But we think we were here before the state's establishment and have entered a state of occupation. We are actually captives here in the country.

It's not as if we live a full civil life and enjoy every moment. As a result of the circumstances, we were living here, and we continue to live here despite the occupation. It doesn't mean that one can't live under occupation. You live, but it's hard; it is not a regular life. We hope that eventually this state will disappear, and then we will be able to live just like before the state's establishment in peace, tranquility, and fraternity.

Prof. Shavit: By the way, no one is truly preventing you from living your life. The state allows the Mea Shearim neighborhood to retain its autonomy.

Rabbi Hirsch: That's not really true. If you follow the news, you'll know that groups of policemen come here every day. For instance, last night, they came to the neighborhood at 3 AM, woke up the entire neighborhood, and arrested some people. Incidents like this happen daily in our life. People don't notice this, but we live under occupation and oppression. And this happens on the ground every day; I'm not making it up.

Prof. Shavit: The state doesn't force you to send your children to its schools, and it allows you to collect donations freely. This is not to be taken for granted, considering your ideology.

Rabbi Hirsch: Of course, the Zionist country declares itself the only democracy in the Middle East, although this is not true. But they need to show the world that they let people live the life they want to, even if they object to it.

Prof. Shavit: I would like to learn a little about the daily life of Neturei

Karta, about the spiritual and cultural life of Neturei Karta, and to ask about your views also on some issues that are not political. Do the children study at your own community schools?

Rabbi Hirsch: Yes, of course. We have our own schools, for boys and for girls, yeshivas, kollels, etc., which are our spiritual base.

Prof. Shavit: Television?

Rabbi Hirsch: There is no such concept.

Prof. Shavit: No such concept? Why? Television has educational and worthy content too. You can choose what to watch and what to consume.

Rabbi Hirsch: We say that we are separated from electronic media and written media. I say that when I look at a newspaper, for instance, when I read a headline or an article in a newspaper, I immediately stop being a thinking person and start believing the tall tales of the person who wrote the editorial or the article.

It means that I need to switch my mind to the thoughts of the journalist, and then my head stops thinking completely. Once I was at a snack shop on Friday, and I saw a man buying all the newspapers, everything they had on sale. I told the salesman, his name is Dudu, I told him: "Do me a favor, put all this on the scale. I want to see how much nonsense this man is going to eat on Shabbat." It simply drives you mad.

Prof. Shavit: And mobile telephones are also banned from the home? Smartphones, on which you could watch videos?

Rabbi Hirsch: Absolutely. We are absolutely separated from all that.

Prof. Shavit: In the last two decades, what is known as "Haredi cinema" has been flourishing, kosher cinema with moral narratives. Do you find it legitimate?

Rabbi Hirsch: Absolutely not. It brings in the secular cinema through the back door. It means they are bringing the Haredi community's point of view closer to the style of secular cinema. We are against...Not only us, but also the entire traditional Haredi public is against this, against bringing these ideas into the Haredi market.

Prof. Shavit: What about sports? A healthy mind in a healthy body...

Rabbi Hirsch: This is no different. You can exercise at home; you don't have to exercise elsewhere. Every person can exercise at home.

Prof. Shavit: So gyms and things like that, swimming in pools, are not permitted.

Rabbi Hirsch: They are not permitted.

Prof. Shavit: So I'll ask a question a little bluntly and naively: How do you have fun? What do you do when you want to have some fun? To rest?

Rabbi Hirsch: So sometimes, during the intermediate days of Passover and Sukkot, people take trips to the beach or somewhere to take the children, to amuse them, etc. But during the year, we don't have those things, meaning that there are no breaks—no summer break and no other break.

Prof. Shavit: It's not an easy life. Very demanding.

Rabbi Hirsch: Not easy at all.

Prof. Shavit: What is the proportion of those who defect? Those who leave the community?

Rabbi Hirsch: That is more common among the general [Haredi] public.

Prof. Shavit: But if a child from Neturei Karta would... okay, not even leave the faith but "desert" to a Litvak Yeshiva or a Hasidic group. Would you exclude him, or would you continue to respect him?

Rabbi Hirsch: No, absolutely not. So long as he doesn't leave the faith, he is still within our framework.

Prof. Shavit: What about if someone from Neturei Karta married someone from a different group? For instance, a Hasidic or Litvak group, which, so to speak, collaborates with the Zionists. Is that acceptable?

Rabbi Hirsch: Absolutely not.

Prof. Shavit: Not acceptable? How come? Love is the most important.

Rabbi Hirsch: It depends on who is involved. Since it would mean changing the entire path, the entire heritage, it is fiercely resisted. We try in any way possible to prevent those things.

Prof. Shavit: And you succeed?

Rabbi Hirsch: Yes, in general.

Prof. Shavit: I'm curious to know how is it possible, and to what degree is it possible in a 21st-century society, to keep the walls high and protective [the boundaries separating the community from secular society]. I am asking you about two to three well-known figures familiar to the Israeli public. I'm just curious if you might have heard about them and what is your attitude toward them. For example, Amos Oz [a well-known Israeli author]. Does that name mean anything to you?

Rabbi Hirsch: Yes, I've heard a lot about him. Of course.

Prof. Shavit: But you were never curious enough to read one of his books.

Rabbi Hirsch: I've heard some things he said, but reading a book is not in our scope because we have our own history books, and we are not looking for new stars to receive ideas from them.

Prof. Shavit: And let's say—ShlomoArzti [a well-known Israeli singer]. Are you familiar with that name?

Rabbi Hirsch: He's also familiar, yes.

Prof. Shavit: And what do you think about him? Maybe you've heard something...?

Rabbi Hirsch: It does not interest us at all. The secular public defines its own stars, and this [music] receives significant attention from the Israeli public. But we don't have these things in our community. We don't have the concept of highly appreciating...

Prof. Shavit: Do you have music?

Rabbi Hirsch: There is music, of course, but during the year, we hardly listen to music. Only during the intermediate days of Sukkot do we have music in the synagogues and people play music at home, but generally speaking, music doesn't have a significant role in our community.

Prof. Shavit: Do you listen to the radio?

Rabbi Hirsch: Definitely not.

Prof. Shavit: Not that either. So how do you know what's happening in the world?

Rabbi Hirsch: I hear from friends who are more connected, who listen to the news. I'm informed about what is happening.

Prof. Shavit: If, let's say, tomorrow there is a successful military operation, Israel somehow manages to neutralize the Iranian nuclear project, would it not give you any satisfaction?

Rabbi Hirsch: It [Israel] is constantly succeeding. It has had very substantial successes. But as we see it, it doesn't make us feel that we're living in a state that could protect us. In other words, the state is an existential hazard to the Jewish nation due to its provocations aimed at other nations. What we are saying is that if this obstacle weren't here, we wouldn't need protection. They create the problem, and they save us from the problem.

Prof. Shavit: Millions of people in our world were saved thanks to scientists who dedicated their lives to research and who developed a vaccine for Covid-19. And what do all of these scientists have in common? None of them is Haredi. None of them could have been Haredi since you cannot become an esteemed researcher, certainly not in the life sciences and in the exact sciences, without studying certain core subjects.

Rabbi Hirsch: Indeed.

Prof. Shavit: But the Haredim benefit from these medicines. They benefit from a world with a life expectancy — in the Western world — that has risen from around 70 and is already reaching around 85.

Rabbi Hirsch: Look, the Sages taught us that "wisdom in the Gentiles — Believe it." If you recognize wisdom in the Gentiles — believe it. What does it mean to "believe"? It means that you should believe that they made an important achievement for humanity. But it doesn't mean that we need to be part of science. God has enough representatives in the entire world who take care of the universe's existence.

Prof. Shavit: But there is a logical contradiction in this position. Because the aspiration of your group is that everyone should accept its position, that everyone should see the light that it sees. But if everyone saw the light your group sees, there will be no scientists to develop medicines.

Rabbi Hirsch: There is no contradiction. The Gentiles can continue with their science, keep contributing to humanity at large, and we will continue in our ways [and] we don't have to take part in this issue. We can continue. It's no obstacle, and it's not a factor that can put people at any risk. We agree that "wisdom in the Gentiles — believe it."

Prof. Shavit: How does one become a leader of Neturei Karta? Is there an election process, a council, or some other process?

Rabbi Hirsch: No, not at all. It simply continues over the generations. My late grandfather founded the movement, my father continued it, and I continued after my late father.

Prof. Shavit: But it is not based on a Hasidic principle.

Rabbi Hirsch: Not at all. Basically, we are Litvaks.

Prof. Shavit: So, it derives from the fact that the community accepts your authority.

Rabbi Hirsch: It's just a succession of the leadership. It's not some title to which you are elected. It's simply a continuation.

Prof. Shavit: Is it taken for granted that one of your sons will be your successor many years from now?

Rabbi Hirsch: I haven't even thought about it.

Prof. Shavit: No, but in terms of how the group works, is it taken for granted that one of your sons will be your successor?

Rabbi Hirsch: It usually works that way, but it doesn't have to. Not at all.

Prof. Shavit: And...who is the appointing body? How does it happen in practice? When your father died, at what moment did you become his successor?

Rabbi Hirsch: There was no one else to continue the contacts, etc., so I continued since I was already familiar with all these procedures from the experience I had gained in the years when my father was still alive. And at that time, there was no one else who could continue these contacts, so I succeeded him. It's not as if there was any election or anything like that.

Prof. Shavit: And what is the practical meaning of this leadership role? What does your daily life look like?

Rabbi Hirsch: In everyday life, we go out for prayers in the morning, then continue studying. Personally, I'm more occupied with deciphering manuscripts and prayer interpretations, some of which I have already published. And every person has their own daily occupations, for most studying in yeshivas and kollels.

Prof. Shavit: But are you, for example, more in charge of collecting donations, of their distribution?

Rabbi Hirsch: Yes, I'm in charge of many things.

Prof. Shavit: Does your group have its own court of law?

Rabbi Hirsch: A court of law? No.

Prof. Shavit: So, if a dispute arises inside the community, how do you settle it?

Rabbi Hirsch: Usually, it's referred for arbitration. We call it "Zabla," an acronym for "this selects one and the other selects one" [each of the sides selects one arbiter, and they both select a third arbiter, constituting a three-member arbitration panel]. In this way, each person ultimately receives the ruling he hopes for, yet basically we don't have a permanent court of law. There is the court of the Eda Haredit, and anyone who wants to can appeal to it, but we ourselves prefer arbitration.

Prof. Shavit: How much of your everyday life is occupied with contact with foreign governments, with political activists in all kinds of places?

Rabbi Hirsch: It's throughout the year; it's continuous; something different every time. But of course, first and foremost, it's spreading the message that Zionism and Judaism are two completely opposite expressions. We convey this [message] one way or another to world leaders and, of course, here in our contacts with the Palestinian Authority.

Prof. Shavit: What is your attitude toward homosexuals? If a young boy were to go to his father or mother, or if a girl would, and say they are gay, how would you react?

Rabbi Hirsch: There is no such thing as someone who would say something like that. The term doesn't even exist.

Prof. Shavit: But the lack of a term doesn't imply that what the term describes doesn't exist.

Rabbi Hirsch: Yes, but there are no such terms. There is no possibility that a boy would say something like that. There is no such term; it doesn't exist.

Prof. Shavit: But you know that just because the term doesn't exist, it doesn't mean that the boy doesn't exist.

Rabbi Hirsch: Yes, but there is no such term in our lexicon. There isn't; there simply isn't.

Prof. Shavit: You say that something like that never happened.

Rabbi Hirsch: Absolutely not.

Prof. Shavit: But there is no readiness to accept...

Rabbi Hirsch: Not at all. There would be no readiness. It is a red line.

Prof. Shavit: How are matches made [marriages arranged]? I mean, after all, yours is a fairly small community, and there are limited options.

Rabbi Hirsch: It's the same for most of Haredi society. The parents on both sides ask around about each other, and there's a matchmaker who takes care of all the details. Then they [the potential couple] have a meeting and decide upon the engagement and wedding, of course. But there is no concept of saying, "I want this person; he wants her." It does not work like that.

Prof. Shavit: Do you have a hunch... I'm not asking about a belief. I'm asking about a hunch: Where will we be in ten years? Where will your community be in ten years?

Rabbi Hirsch: Of course, "Prophecy was given to the fools," but we estimate Zionism is nearing its end. It will not be long, as we see it.

国家之敌:拉比以色列·梅尔·希尔施访谈录

乌利亚·沙维特

【摘要】拉比以色列·梅尔·希尔施是最激烈反对复国主义的极端正统派群体“圣城守护者”的现任领袖。“圣城守护者”不仅认为以色列是一个宗教上不合法的国家,还与以色列的“敌人”(如巴勒斯坦解放组织和伊朗)合作。在2021年4月,山东大学—特拉维夫大学犹太与以色列联合研究所第一次年会(主题是极端正统派)前,乌利亚·沙维特教授对拉比希尔施进行了录音采访。在访谈中,拉比希尔施坦率阐述了该宗派的意识形态、社会结构和对以色列未来的展望。

【关键词】圣城守护者;极端正统派;反复国主义

B

观念、历史与文本

Ideas, History and Texts

大希律的希腊化与罗马化策略研究*

张　帅**

【摘要】大希律是公元前1世纪罗马的犹太藩属王。在面对当时复杂的政治环境时，他采取了一系列措施来维系国家的政治地位。在文化方面，他大举推行希腊化政策，推动犹太王国融入“世界性”主流文化体系中，从而扩大了他个人和犹太国家的影响力。在政治方面，他推行罗马化的政治策略。这一策略的核心是与罗马统治者建立良好的私人关系。大希律在效忠庇护人的同时，也获得了相应的政治回报。正因如此，犹太王国才得以保持高度自治。

【关键词】大希律；希腊化；罗马化；庇护人

引言

从公元前3世纪中叶到公元前2世纪后期，随着罗马征服领土的扩大，行省的数量也在不断增加。除行省制度以外，利用当地的国王作为罗马统治的工具也是罗马人自古相承的办法。此类国王在现代术语中叫作“藩属王”(client king)，罗马人称之为“盟邦和友邦的国王”(rex socius et amicus)。①

大希律正是这样一位藩属王。在他的统治下，犹太藩属国与罗马帝国统治者保持了良好的互动。在此基础上，犹太藩属国保留了相对独立的政治权力，领土面积得以不断扩大。同时，凭借大希律的政治影响力，散居地犹太人的权益得

* 本文获得首都师范大学研究生高水平学术创新项目资助和首都师范大学历史学院2022年研究生科研立项(2022LS09)资助。

** 张帅，首都师范大学历史学院博士研究生。

① 参见宋立宏 Song Lihong，〈犹太战争与巴勒斯坦罗马化之两难〉[The Dilemma between the Jewish War and the Romanization of Palestine]，《世界历史》[World History]，2002年第1期[2002, Issue 1]，72。

到了保障。可以说,此时犹太国家的辉煌程度仅次于希伯来统一王国时期。

大希律是如何达成如此成就的?关于这一问题,学界进行了相关研究。埃米尔·舒勒(Emil Schürer)在《耶稣基督时代犹太人的历史》[*The History of the Jewish People in the Age of Jesus Christ* (175 *B.C.-A.D.* 135)]一书中认为:"大希律利用他对罗马的影响,保护流亡海外的犹太人免受非犹太人世界的压迫和对他们权利的损害。因此,犹太国王的权力地位被证明是有益的,即使对不直接在他统治下的犹太人也是如此。公元前20年到前14年是他最辉煌的统治时期,尽管对罗马有依赖性,但就外部威严而言,它可以与国内所知的最好的时期相比。"①E.玛丽·斯莫尔伍德(E. Mary Smallwood)在《罗马统治下的犹太人:从庞贝到戴克里先(古代晚期犹太教研究)》[*The Jews under Roman Rule: From Pompey to Diocletian* (*Studies in Judaism in Late Antiquity*)]一书中指出,大希律是以土买的"藩属王",并进一步论述道:"大希律的权力基础纯粹是世俗的,他缺乏哈斯蒙尼前辈作为高级祭司所拥有的威望和精神权威,因此比许尔卡努斯对罗马的依赖要大得多,这是他职业生涯的关键。"②彼得·理查森(Peter Richardson)的《大希律:犹太人的国王和罗马人的朋友(新约人物研究)》[*Herod: King of the Jews and Friend of the Romans* (*Studies on Personalities of the New Testament*)]以大希律为中心,讨论犹太王国与罗马帝国的政治关系。作者认为整个大希律家族似乎都知道如何在关键时刻转变,平衡罗马的需求和犹太的需求。③ 由于大希律的国王身份是由罗马统治者所册封,因此与罗马当权者保持良好的私人关系是维系他统治的重要因素。格萨·韦尔姆斯(Geza Vermes)在《真正的大希律》[*The True Herod*]中提出:"大希律是一个多面人格。他的优点是巨大的,缺点也是巨大的。他知道自己非常幸运成为国王,但他的成功也要归功于他良好的判断力。作为一个政治家,他被赋予了非凡的天赋。他最令人钦佩的成就是完美地处理了公元前30年在罗德岛与屋大维极其危险的会面。他一向是罗马忠实的仆人,但他也知道如何奖励那些使他高兴或为他服务的人。"④对于大希律的统治而言,最重要的是如何处理好与罗马统治者的关系。面对错综复杂的政治局势,大希律审时度势,追随罗马帝

① Emil Schürer, *The History of the Jewish People in the Age of Jesus Christ* (175 *B.C.-A.D.* 135), vol.I, Rev. and eds. G. Vermes and F. Millar (Edinburgh: T. & T. Clark Ltd., 1973), 319.

② E. Mary Smallwood, *The Jews under Roman Rule: From Pompey to Diocletian* (*Studies in Judaism in Late Antiquity*) (Leiden: E. J. Brill,1976), 60.

③ 参见 Peter Richardson, *Herod: King of the Jews and Friend of the Romans* (*Studies on Personalities of the New Testament*)(Columbia: University of South Carolina Press, 1996), xiii。

④ Geza Vermes, *The True Herod* (Edinburge: T. & T. Clark, 2014), 94.

国的统治者。格萨·韦尔姆斯进一步提出:"因为罗马帝国对他来说代表了一个神圣的新世界,奥古斯都是文明人类的救世主,大希律决心要尽其所能使他的犹太王国成为这个新秩序中不可或缺的重要组成部分。"[①]除了上述学者外,泰萨·拉贾克(Tessa Rajak)的《犹太人与希腊和罗马的对话》(*The Jewish Dialogue with Greece and Rome*)也具有一定的参考价值。[②] 综上所述,虽然学界对相关问题进行了一定的讨论,但是,大希律所采取措施的本质是什么,这些措施又对犹太王国的发展有着怎样的意义等问题尚存讨论空间。

一、大希律希腊化政策与意义

(一)大希律的希腊化政策

约瑟夫斯(Josephus)对大希律推行的希腊化措施有着充分的记载。在公共建筑建设方面,约瑟夫斯主要从三个层面进行了记载。首先,在耶路撒冷地区,"他每隔五年就要举行一次体育比赛,以纪念凯撒,并在耶路撒冷修建了剧院。然后在耶路撒冷的附近还修建了一个大型的圆形剧场,这两个建筑都非常豪华……希律王朝以最出色的方式庆祝了五年一度的节日,他向邻国人民发出了通知,并邀请了全国各地的参与者。来自世界各地的运动员和其他参赛者都受到了邀请,他们被奖项以及胜利所带来的荣耀所吸引……因为大希律为比赛的获胜者提供了非常丰厚的奖品……他还向战车的驾驶者以及骑在赛马上的骑手提供了可观的礼物"[③]。

通过分析约瑟夫斯的文本,可以得出三点结论:第一,在耶路撒冷及周围地区建有希腊式的建筑,其中包括剧院和圆形剧场。第二,大希律定期举办希腊式的体育赛会,该赛会以奥林匹亚赛会为原型。尤其是其中的马术比赛,是按照希腊风格举办的。第三,该赛会在古代近东地区有着很大的影响力,奖励丰厚,并且有效地扩大了大希律和他的王国在周边地区的影响力。然而,约瑟夫斯却对大希律的做法持批判态度。他认为,大希律违背了犹太民族传统,实践外邦人的习俗,并逐渐破坏了迄今为止不可侵犯的古老的生活方式。作为结果,犹太人在后来遭受了相当大的伤害,因为这些以前在民众中引起了虔诚信念的东西被忽

① Geza Vermes, *The True Herod*, 102.

② Tessa Rajak, *The Jewish Dialogue with Greece and Rome* (Leiden · Boston · Köln: Brill, 2001).

③ Josephus, *Jewish Antiquities*, 15. 267-272.

略掉了。[①] 显然,约瑟夫斯将犹太人日后遭遇的灾难与大希律推行的希腊化措施联系起来,这与他撰写《犹太战记》时所秉承的态度一致。事实上,早在公元前2世纪中叶,在耶路撒冷就已经存在希腊式体育馆,不少犹太贵族少年还在这里接受体育训练。对于耶路撒冷的犹太人来说,希腊式体育馆并非新鲜事物。因此,这些建筑本身没有引发犹太人大规模的反对。他们唯一在意的是建筑的装饰是否涉嫌偶像崇拜。[②] 可以说,大希律在耶路撒冷没有大量引进新的文化元素。从本质上讲,他只是继承并推动了希腊文化在犹地亚地区的进一步传播。

其次,在耶路撒冷以外的领土,大希律建造了凯撒利亚(Caesarea)并重建了塞巴斯特(Sebaste)。在大希律时期,凯撒利亚是犹太的港口城市,它取代斯特拉托塔成为近东地区的希腊化中心。在该城市的南部地区建有一座希腊式的竞技场,并建有与托勒密宫殿有着诸多共同特点的大希律宫殿。[③] 在靠近海岸的地区,港口的码头一直延伸到奥古斯都神庙附近。巨大的奥古斯都塑像俯瞰着海面,向所有过往的船只宣示着大希律的忠诚和他的希腊主义倾向。[④] 根据约瑟夫斯的说法,凯撒利亚的奥古斯都塑像是仿照奥林匹亚的宙斯像建造的。由此可见其中的希腊化元素。[⑤] 同时,罗科(Samuel Rocca)认为,整座凯撒利亚城都是仿照亚历山大城建造的。因此,它与亚历山大城有着许多共同特征。[⑥] 除凯撒利亚外,大希律还重建了希腊化城市撒玛利亚(Samaria),并将城市名称改为具有希腊化特征的塞巴斯特。该城市居住着六千移民,他们实行特殊的法律。城内建有巨大的奥古斯都神庙[⑦],而且很可能还存在着一座剧院。

最后,在犹太王国以外,大希律广泛资助希腊世界的建设。他在特里波利(Tripolis)、大马士革(Damascus)和托勒密(Ptolemais)修建了体育馆,在拜布卢斯(Byblus)修建了城墙,在贝里图斯(Berytus)和提尔(Tyre)修建了门廊、神庙和市场,在西顿(Sidon)和大马士革修建了剧院,在老底嘉(Laodicea)修建了沟渠,在阿斯卡隆(Ascalon)修建了浴场、喷泉和柱廊,为通往安条克的两英里长的

① Josephus, *Jewish Antiquities*, 15. 267-268.

② 同上, 15. 277-279。

③ 参见 Samuel Rocca, *Herod's Judaea: A Mediterranean State in the Classical World* (Tübingen: Mohr Siebeck, 2008),329。

④ 参见 E. Mary Smallwood, *The Jews under Roman Rule: From Pompey to Diocletian* (*Studies in Judaism in Late Antiquity*), 79。

⑤ 参见 Josephus, *The Jewish War*, 1. 414。

⑥ 参见 Samuel Rocca, *Herod's Judaea: A Mediterranean State in the Classical World*, 330-331。

⑦ 参见 Josephus, *The Jewish War*, 1. 403。

主要道路的铺设提供了资金,并沿道路架设了柱廊,为科斯(Cos)和其他城市提供了捐赠,雅典(Athens)、斯巴达(Sparta)、尼科波利斯(Nicopolis)等地区也得到了大希律慷慨的捐赠,[1]他还制定了五年一次的比赛,并以凯撒的名字命名。同时,他为第192届奥林匹亚运动会提供了丰厚的奖励。这些奖励不仅颁发给第一名,也颁发给第二名和第三名。[2] 大希律"不仅给希腊送了礼物,而且给全世界送了礼物"。面对奥林匹亚赛会因缺乏资金而陷入衰落的局面,大希律担任了奥林匹亚运动会的主席,并且捐助了充足的资金。[3]

在文化上,大希律重用希腊知识分子。其中包括学者安德洛马库斯(Andromachus)和吉梅勒斯(Gemellus)、演说家伊雷内厄斯(Irenaeus),最著名的是大马士革的尼古拉斯(Nicolaus),他是大希律的御用作家[4],他撰写的史书成为约瑟夫斯撰史时所使用的重要史料。尼古拉斯生于公元前64年,在大马士革接受了希腊式的教育。他曾担任安东尼和克里奥帕特拉的孩子的老师,也是大希律统治的最后十余年中最有影响力的顾问。[5] 在大希律陪同阿格里帕出访期间,尼古拉斯发表了一段精彩的演讲,从而成功地为爱奥尼亚的犹太人争取到了合法权益。在大希律与奥古斯都的关系因锡勒乌斯事件陷入危机时,尼古拉斯作为使者出使罗马,凭借自己的智慧成功地使得奥古斯都与大希律重归于好。由此可见,尼古拉斯深受大希律的信任,并深度参与王国的政治活动。

在经济上,大希律发行了仅有希腊文的钱币。这一行为打破了哈斯蒙尼王国时期的双语传统。他所造钱币上的铭文基本都是"属于大希律王"

---

① 参见 Josephus, *The Jewish War*, 1. 422-425; E. Mary Smallwood, *The Jews under Roman Rule: From Pompey to Diocletian* (*Studies in Judaism in Late Antiquity*), 81。

② 参见 Josephus, *The Jewish War*, 1. 415。

③ 参见 Josephus, *Jewish Antiquities*, 16. 148-149。

④ 参见 Norman Gelb, *Herod the Great: Statesman, Visionary, Tyrant* (Lanham: Rowman & Littlefield Publishers, 2013), 89; Emil Schürer, *The History of the Jewish People in the Age of Jesus Christ* (175 *B.C.-A.D.* 135), vol.I, 310-311。

⑤ 参见 Mark Toher, *Nicolaus of Damascus: The Life of Augustus and the Autobiography* (Cambridge: Cambridge University Press, 2017), 1-4。

(ΒΑΣΙΛΕΩΣ ΗΡΩΔΟΥ)。[①] 在图像方面,铸造于大希律时期的犹太钱币基本延续了哈斯蒙尼王朝的惯例,但是更具希腊化特征。第一枚钱币[②]正面是象征着太阳神阿波罗崇拜的三足祭坛和希腊语铭文,背面则是一个香炉,极有可能是象征着耶路撒冷的庙宇。也有一种说法认为,背面的图案是头盔。从这枚钱币可以看出,大希律时期的钱币上缺少希伯来文。在另外一些钱币上,还刻有其他希腊元素,如双丰饶角、船锚、棕树枝等,以及诸神信使赫尔墨斯使用的双蛇杖、带雕饰的翘起的船尾、带羽饰的头盔等。[③] 值得注意的是,在大希律时期铸造的钱币上,不仅有希腊化元素,还存在犹太元素和一些模糊不清的元素。比如第二枚钱币[④]上雕刻的符号,似乎既不明显是犹太人的,也不明显是异教徒的。在钱币正面,一个花环被绑在底部,主体部分是一个类似于"Ω"的符号,在它的中间出现两条交叉线。钱币背面是三条腿的桌子。雅典人可能在这里面认出了阿波罗的三脚架,犹太人可能认为这是供桌。[⑤] 第三枚钱币[⑥]出土于塞巴斯特。它的正面为马其顿头盔,通常被视为权力的象征,围绕头盔的是希腊文字"ΒΑΣΙΛΕΩΣ ΗΡΩΔΟΥ"。钱币的背面则是一个模糊的符号。罗科认为该符号是马其顿的盾牌。[⑦] 第四枚钱币[⑧]在设计上总体继承了哈斯蒙尼王国的特色。钱币正面为船锚,并且配有希腊文。钱币背面的图案略显模糊,希腊人可能会将它们视为两个丰饶角,犹太人可能会将它们视为一对羊角号。目前,学界对在二者中间的图案尚存争议:一说是石榴,这样便与哈斯蒙尼时期的钱币没有区别;一说是双蛇杖,也就是采用了异教符号;还有一说则主张是摩西的权杖,这又成了犹太符号。[⑨]

---

① 参见宋立宏 Song Lihong,〈希腊化与罗马时期犹太人的政治宗教特征——以古代犹太钱币为中心的考察〉[Jewish Political and Religious Characteristics during the Hellenistic and Roman Periods: With a Focus on Ancient Jewish Coins],《历史研究》[Historical Research],2013年第3期[2013, Issue 3],112; Donald T. Ariel and Jean-Philippe Fontanille, *The Coins of Herod: A Modern Analysis and Die Classification* (Leiden: Koninklijke Brill NV, 2012), 121; Baruch Kanael, "Ancient Jewish Coins and Their Historical Importance," *The Biblical Archaeologist* 26 (1963): 48; Peter Richardson and Amy Marie Fisher, *Herod: King of the Jews and Friend of the Romans* (Columbia: University of South Carolina Press, 1996), 308-309。

② 图片见徐龙 Xu Long,《犹太和以色列国钱币》[Money of Ancient Judaea and Israel](北京[Beijing]:世界图书出版公司[World Publishing Corporation],2010),42,"希律三足祭坛和头盔钱币"。

③ 宋立宏,〈希腊化与罗马时期犹太人的政治宗教特征——以古代犹太钱币为中心的考察〉,113-114。

④ 图片见徐龙,《犹太和以色列国钱币》,44-45,"希律王冠和三角祭桌钱币"。

⑤ Baruch Kanael, "Ancient Jewish Coins and Their Historical Importance," 49.

⑥ 图片见徐龙,《犹太和以色列国钱币》,42,"希律盾牌和头盔钱币"。

⑦ Samuel Rocca, *Herod's Judaea: A Mediterranean State in the Classical World*, 1.

⑧ 图片见徐龙,《犹太和以色列国钱币》,45,"希律船锚和双丰饶角钱币"。

⑨ 宋立宏,〈希腊化与罗马时期犹太人的政治宗教特征——以古代犹太钱币为中心的考察〉,113。

虽然学界对图像本身的文化属性存在争议,但笔者认为,大希律基本遵循了哈斯蒙尼王朝时期的钱币形式:一面采用具有鲜明特征的希腊图像,并配以希腊文;另一面则采用犹太化的图像,但是取消了钱币上的希伯来文。因此,就钱币而言,与哈斯蒙尼王朝相比,大希律希腊化政策更为彻底。显然,大希律是想在他的钱币上同时刻上异教徒的标志(虽然没有明显冒犯他的犹太臣民的标志)和犹太的标志(虽然没有像安提古努斯时期那样明显)来强调国家的"犹太—希腊"性质。①

值得思考的是,大希律是否真正热爱希腊文化?解决问题的关键在于,他为何在耶路撒冷修建希腊式的建筑并举办希腊式赛会?公元前2世纪,犹太贵族发起了自我希腊化运动。他们在耶路撒冷修建了希腊式体育馆,鼓励青年参与体育训练。这种行为造成了严重的派别对立,最终以大祭司被驱逐而告终。面对如此惨烈的历史教训和可预知的风险,大希律仍然坚持在耶路撒冷修建希腊式建筑,这是否代表着他崇尚希腊文化?答案是否定的。大希律一生出访过很多地方,但是他却从未真正到过近在咫尺的希腊本土。总体来看,他对希腊文化的推崇仅限于建筑、体育赛会等层面,没有深入更深层的文化内核。显然,大希律对希腊文化的热爱程度有待商榷。

(二)大希律推行希腊化政策的目的

事实上,修建希腊式的城市、建筑和神庙,是罗马藩属国王常见的效忠方式。② 斯皮尔曼(Spielman)认为,大希律的这些行为都是在向他的臣民做宣传,强调自己与西方伟大的巨人(奥古斯都)之间的联系。在王国各地兴建的建筑展示了国王的财富和资源,以及他与站在他身后的地中海统治者之间的联系。③同时,在耶路撒冷举办赛会并非仅仅出于私利,而是精心设计的政治策略,旨在宣传耶路撒冷作为大希律王国的首都和犹太世界的中心。④ 斯皮尔曼准确地诠释了大希律的深层用意。

第一,大希律推行希腊化政策,以此宣传自己与罗马的联系,从而巩固自身的政治地位。事实上,犹太人很早就建立了王权政制。根据《希伯来圣经》所述,犹太人的第一位国王扫罗是被先知撒母耳膏选,他是被上帝选中为以色列人的

---

① 参见 Baruch Kanael, "Ancient Jewish Coins and Their Historical Importance," 48。

② 参见 Suetonius, *Augustus*, 60。

③ 参见 Erich S. Gruen, *Constructs of Identity in Hellenistic Judaism* (Berlin/Boston: Walter de Gruyter GmbH, 2016), 387。

④ Loren R. Spielman, "Playing Roman in Jerusalem: Jewish Attitudes toward Sport and Spectacle during the Second Temple Period," *Jews in the Gym: Judaism, Sports, and Athletics*, ed. Leonard J. Greenspoon (West Lafayette: Purdue University Press, 2012), 3.

君王。犹太人的第二位国王大卫和第三位国王所罗门，都是被上帝选中而成了国王。因此，犹太人早期的国王是由神意所选，具有神学意义上的合法性。所罗门死后，犹太王国陷入了南北分裂的境地。南方的犹大王国相对稳定，北方的以色列王国则相对混乱，时常会有篡位的情况发生。公元前 2 世纪中后期建立的哈斯蒙尼王国，则是凭借自身的军事实力建立的政权。同时，马卡比家族是祭司家族，本身具备一定的合法性。相比较而言，大希律政权的建立就显得与众不同。他是被罗马元老院任命为犹太王的。从法律层面来说，他的合法性依据不再是犹太人祖先留下的法律，而是罗马法。换言之，罗马法代替《托拉》成了立国的基础。[①] 因此，他的政权在犹太人内部缺乏牢靠的政治基础。可以说，在他近 40 年的统治中，王国内部的动乱可谓接连不断。他在早年间陷入与安提古努斯的政治斗争。此后，大希律王国又经历了两次起义，即公元前 22 年的加拉达人起义和公元前 11 年的特拉可尼(Trachonitis)起义。公元前 6 年，大希律与法利赛人彻底决裂，并处决了其中的部分重要人物。公元前 4 年，也就是他统治的最后一年，耶路撒冷爆发了大规模的骚乱。[②] 正是内部动荡、宗派不满和对政权的广泛敌意促使国王展示了这些联系。[③] 他希望通过展示与罗马统治者的友好关系，威慑国内反对势力，从而巩固自身的统治。

第二，大希律的希腊化政策，极大地推动了希腊文化在王国内外的进一步传播，使大希律王国融入了希腊文化共同体中。[④] 斯莫尔伍德认为，大希律作为一个犹太人，无论是在种族还是宗教信仰方面，都在尽可能地希腊化他的王国，希腊化也可以被视为他的职责。藩属王的职能是通过介绍希腊文化的特点，为他的臣民融入罗马帝国做好准备。[⑤] 如果进一步推论斯莫尔伍德的观点，可以得出如下结论，即大希律的行为并非出于他对希腊文化的认同，而是犹太人希腊化的必然结果。也就是说，大希律只是顺应了历史发展的趋势。在公元前 2 世纪的地中海世界，希腊文化是主流文化。作为罗马帝国的藩属国，除了融入这一文化共同体，大希律别无选择。事实证明，大希律的希腊化措施，在一定程度上使他的王国成功地融入了地中海"世界性"的文化体系中。同时，他还赢得了广泛的个人声誉，并借他的声誉和犹太国王的身份，提升了整个帝国犹太社区的形

① 宋立宏，〈希腊化与罗马时期犹太人的政治宗教特征——以古代犹太钱币为中心的考察〉，112。

② 参见 Josephus, *Jewish Antiquities*, 17. 149-163。

③ 参见 Erich S. Gruen, *Constructs of Identity in Hellenistic Judaism*, 387。

④ 参见 Samuel Rocca, *Herod's Judaea: A Mediterranean State in the Classical World*, 324-325。

⑤ 参见 E. Mary Smallwood, *The Jews under Roman Rule: From Pompey to Diocletian* (*Studies in Judaism in Late Antiquity*), 82。

象。这样既有效地保护了犹太人的权利，又增强了犹太人对他的尊重。[①]

第三，推行希腊化政策是大希律统治多民族国家的必要手段。与以往犹太王国不同，大希律统治的国家民族成分复杂，其中既包括犹太人，又包括希腊人、罗马人、阿拉伯人等。换言之，大希律统治的不再是一个纯粹的犹太国家，而是一个以犹太人为主体的多民族国家。事实上，奥古斯都让大希律统治一个异质的王国就是希望借助这位东方君主的强力意志，来避免王国内部的异质因素可能对统治秩序造成的震荡，以捏合出一个有凝聚力的藩属国。[②] 因此，大希律需要兼顾各个族群的需求。在建筑方面，以神庙为例，大希律在耶路撒冷重修了第二圣殿；在罗德岛帮助当地人重修了希腊神庙；在凯撒利亚修建了凯撒神庙。但是，在耶路撒冷等犹太人聚居地，大希律仅修建了犹太圣殿和会堂，没有修建异教神庙。[③] 种种迹象表明，大希律尊重各地区和各民族不同的文化习俗，并且能够因地制宜地实施他的统治政策。总体来看，推行希腊化政策是大希律统治多民族国家的必要手段。

二、大希律的罗马化策略

罗科指出，大希律的成功之处在于他有能力在个人层面和罗马的各类人建立同盟关系。[④] 这是对大希律政治能力的高度概括。事实上，与其说大希律对罗马国家忠诚，不如说是对罗马权贵忠诚。大希律在他统治的大部分时间里，主要是在马克·安东尼和后来的奥古斯都身上，都或多或少地取得了平等的地位，这在罗马统治东方的史册上是独一无二的。[⑤] 从塞克斯图斯(Sextus Caesar)和卡修斯(Cassius)到安东尼和奥古斯都，大希律已经适应了他们每一个人的需要，并能够在恰当的时机更进一步。[⑥] 他与安东尼建立了良好的关系，并在安东尼的支持下出乎意料地成了犹太王。在此后的很长时间里，大希律积极支持安东尼的各项决定，同时也获得了相应的回报。然而，这种对个人的忠诚并非绝对的。在亚克兴海战中，由于克里奥帕特拉的缘故，大希律陷于对阿拉伯人的战争

---

① 参见 Norman Gelb, *Herod the Great: Statesman, Visionary, Tyrant*, 93。

② 参见宋立宏，《犹太战争与巴勒斯坦罗马化之两难》，73。

③ 参见 Samuel Rocca, *Herod's Judaea: A Mediterranean State in the Classical World*, 331。

④ 同上，55。

⑤ 同上，53。

⑥ 参见 Josephus, *Jewish Antiquities*, 14. 383; Norman Gelb, *Herod the Great: Statesman, Visionary, Tyrant*, 73。

中,没有直接加入安东尼与屋大维作战。这恰恰为大希律与屋大维建立友好关系创造了条件。在安东尼战败后,大希律赴罗德岛拜见奥古斯都,并成功地赢得了后者的信任。在此后的数十年间,他充分展现出自己对奥古斯都的政治忠诚和高超的政治能力,并深得奥古斯都的信任。因此,他统治下的犹太王国得以长期保持高度自治。

(一)大希律与安东尼的私人关系

大希律与安东尼友好关系的建立最初是由于安提帕特。在亚历山大二世叛乱期间,伽比尼乌斯派遣安东尼去镇压叛乱,安提帕特协同作战。① 在这次军事行动中,安东尼与安提帕特建立了深厚的友谊。② 除此之外,利益交换也是大希律与安东尼建立友好关系的重要原因。在安提帕特去世后,面对犹太上层团体的指控,安东尼保护了大希律。根据约瑟夫斯的记载,这一切都是用金钱买来的。③ 此后,收受贿赂的安东尼多次驱逐前来控告大希律的犹太使团。④

公元前 40 年,帕提亚人入侵巴勒斯坦,并围困了耶路撒冷,许尔卡努斯二世被掳。⑤ 帕提亚人任命安提古努斯为犹太王和大祭司。大希律仓皇逃到罗马,并向安东尼求助。出于对与安提帕特友谊的认可、大希律给予的利益承诺以及对安提古努斯的厌恶⑥,安东尼同意给予帮助。屋大维则是考虑到安提帕特曾经对自己的友善,也愿意帮助大希律。⑦ 在二人的授意下,大希律来到元老院,在这里他得到了元老们的支持。最终元老院决定向帕提亚宣战,并任命大希律为犹太王。⑧ 事实上,帕提亚人在黎凡特地区的行为,已经严重威胁到了罗马的利益。对于罗马来说,他们想把帕提亚人支持的安提古努斯从犹太人的王位上赶走,并在他的位置上安排一名自己指定的人。⑨ 同时,还需要一个有实力的人来保护叙利亚到埃及的路线,并为罗马的军队提供物资。⑩ 大希律正是罗马所需要的角色。对于大希律来说,安东尼送的这份大礼是他始料未及的。因为按

---

① 参见 Josephus, *Jewish Antiquities*, 14. 84-85。

② 同上,14. 326。

③ 同上,14. 302-304。

④ 同上,14. 327。

⑤ 同上,14. 348。

⑥ 同上,14. 382, 14. 382. e。

⑦ 参见 Josephus, *Jewish Antiquities*, 14. 383; Norman Gelb, *Herod the Great: Statesman, Visionary, Tyrant*, 34。

⑧ 参见 Josephus, *Jewish Antiquities*, 14. 384-385。

⑨ 同上,14. 383。Norman Gelb, *Herod the Great: Statesman, Visionary, Tyrant*, 34.

⑩ 参见 Emil Schürer, *The History of the Jewish People in the Age of Jesus Christ* (175 *B.C.-A.D.* 135), vol. Ⅰ, 389。

照犹太传统，王位应授予哈斯蒙尼王族。[①] 所以大希律从未奢求过获得王位，他来罗马的诉求也只是渴望获得四分领主的头衔。在大希律统治的第一天，安东尼设宴招待他，足见其对大希律的善意态度。此时的大希律虽有王衔，但没有任何的实际权力。犹地亚地区的实际控制权仍掌握在帕提亚人和安提古努斯手中。两年以后，大希律在安东尼的帮助下开始夺回对国家的控制权。

在这一过程中，大希律展现出他非凡的军事才能，并获得了安东尼的欣赏。[②] 公元前 37 年，安提古努斯被带到安东尼面前。根据《犹太古史》第 14 卷的记载，由于大希律担心安提古努斯的王室血统会对自己不利，因此，在他的贿赂下，安东尼处决了安提古努斯，哈斯蒙尼王国正式灭亡。[③]事实上，大希律担心罗马人对他的支持会发生改变。这一担忧不无道理，因为通常来说，罗马人往往会任命传统的王族成员为国王，这样更有利于地区稳定。[④] 对于犹太人来说，大希律的个人财产并不能弥补他王室血统的缺乏。许多犹太人将大希律视为非法篡夺者。[⑤] 大希律之所以成为藩属王，一方面是由于安东尼的支持，另一方面则是因为帕提亚人的介入。对于多数元老来说，与其说是支持大希律成为犹太王，不如说是为了反对帕提亚人及其任命的犹太王。对大希律来说，将安提努斯处决对他最为有利。对安东尼来说，他听闻犹地亚仍有不少人忠诚于安提古努斯，于是他将后者斩首，以此来稳定犹太局势。[⑥] 关于采取“斩首”的方式来处决安提古努斯的原因，约瑟夫斯引用了斯特拉波的观点，认为安东尼用这种不光彩的处决方式，是为了削弱犹太人对安提古努斯的记忆，从而更好地接受大希律。[⑦] 从传世文献来看，罗马人很少会以斩首的方式处决国王。安东尼对安提古努斯的处决方式很可能与大希律有关，是大希律对安提古努斯杀害自己兄弟约瑟夫(被安提古努斯斩首)的报复。[⑧] 安东尼遵从了大希律的请求，以斩首的方式提前处决了本应该送到元老院的安提古努斯。事实上，对罗马在东方的统治来说，安提古努斯是一个巨大的威胁。即便没有大希律的劝说，安东尼也很可能会处

① 参见 Josephus, *Jewish Antiquities*, 14. 386-387。事实上，将王位传给哈斯蒙尼家族继承人也不符合犹太传统。根据《希伯来圣经》的规定，王位应传给大卫的后裔。

② 参见 Josephus, *Jewish Antiquities*, 14. 445-446。

③ 同上，14. 488-490。

④ 参见 Aryeh Kasher, *King Herod: A Persecuted Persecuted* (Berlin & New York: Walter de Gruyter, 2006), 91。

⑤ 参见 David M. Jacobson, "Three Roman Client Kings: Herod of Judaea, Archelaus of Cappadocia and Juba of Mauretania," *Palestine Exploration Quarterly* 133 (2001): 24。

⑥ 参见 Josephus, *Jewish Antiquities*, 15. 8-9。

⑦ 同上，15. 9-10。

⑧ 参见 Aryeh Kasher, *King Herod: A Persecuted Persecuted*, 87。

决他。总之,处决安提古努斯符合大希律和安东尼的共同利益。在大希律攻占耶路撒冷后,他收集了大量的金银,将它们制作成礼物送给安东尼及其朋友们。[①] 这实际上是大希律对自己的庇护人的一种回报。

事实上,大希律对安东尼并不足够信任。在大希律密谋溺死大祭司阿里斯多布鲁斯后,安东尼要求他到老底嘉对阿里斯多布鲁斯的死亡原因作出解释。[②] 大希律对此次出行非常悲观。阿里斯多布鲁斯的母亲亚历珊德拉与克里奥帕特拉的友好关系,克里奥帕特拉对自己的仇视,以及她与安东尼之间的特殊关系,使得大希律未来的政治生涯充满不确定性。[③] 于是在临行前,他对自己死后王国的事务进行了安排。他嘱咐自己的叔叔约瑟夫,如果自己遭遇不幸,就处死米利暗,一方面是出于自己对她的爱,另一方面他担心安东尼会对米利暗图谋不轨。[④] 然而,安东尼不仅没有惩罚大希律,反而还设宴款待他。[⑤] 随后,大希律护送安东尼前往叙利亚,然后返回耶路撒冷。关于大希律与安东尼在老底嘉谈话的细节,约瑟夫斯没有详细地记载。但是,安东尼很可能知道事情的真相。显然,如何把握与大希律合作的政治利益是他首要考虑的问题。[⑥] 对于安东尼来说,阿里斯多布鲁斯是个无足轻重的人物。为此惩罚大希律,反倒是有损罗马和他本人的政治利益。在此次谈话后,大希律对安东尼更加信任。为表达自己的忠诚(抑或是对安东尼知遇之恩的感谢),大希律在圣殿附近修建了一座堡垒,将具有重大意义的祭司袍放在该堡垒中,并命名为"安东尼亚"(Antonia)。这显然是在纪念他的罗马庇护人。[⑦]

根据约瑟夫斯的记载,在公元前 31 年爆发的亚克兴海战中,在克里奥帕特拉的蛊惑下,安东尼命令大希律进攻阿拉伯人。[⑧] 因此,大希律缺席了安东尼与屋大维之间的战争。根据约瑟夫斯的说法,大希律的缺席是由于克里奥帕特拉的缘故。但是,卡舍尔却认为,大希律有意将自己陷入对阿拉伯人的征战中,这表明他并非毫无保留地支持安东尼。[⑨] 尽管在这次内战中他处于被动状态,不得不站在安东尼一边,但是,事实上,避免在内战中站队是大希律的惯用手法。

---

① 参见 Josephus, *Jewish Antiquities*, 15. 5。

② 同上,15. 63-65。

③ 参见 Aryeh Kasher, *King Herod: A Persecuted Persecuted*, 132-133。

④ 参见 Josephus, *Jewish Antiquities*, 15. 65-67; Josephus, *The Jewish War*, 1. 441。

⑤ 原因分析参见 Aryeh Kasher, *King Herod: A Persecuted Persecuted*, 129。

⑥ 同上,115。

⑦ 参见 Josephus, *The Jewish War*, 1. 401-402。

⑧ 参见 Josephus, *Jewish Antiquities*, 15. 109-111; Josephus, *The Jewish War*, 1. 364-365。

⑨ 参见 Aryeh Kasher, *King Herod: A Persecuted Persecuted*, 137-143。

罗科对此有准确的概括:大希律支持统治土地的一方。[1] 虽然大希律的动机我们已经很难考证,但是,不论原因如何,与阿拉伯的征战使他避免陷入和屋大维直接为敌的境地。[2] 在与阿拉伯人的战争中,大希律和他率领的犹太人展现出英勇的精神。[3] 但是,由于克里奥帕特拉的偷袭,犹太人损失惨重并陷入被动地位。面对士气低落的犹太士兵,大希律发表了一段言语激昂的演讲。在演讲中,他强调了自己与安东尼的友谊。[4] 同时,他也提到自己送给安东尼总价两百塔兰特的礼物,以此获得了安东尼提供的安全保障。[5] 但是,在《犹太战记》中,约瑟夫斯呈现了一段与《犹太古史》存有差异的演讲,其中没有涉及与安东尼有关的内容。因此,两段演讲内容的真实性尚存疑。不论如何,《犹太古史》中大希律的演讲却直接透露出他与安东尼关系的本质,即通过利益交换获得安全保障。之后的情节更能表现二者关系的本质特征。当大希律得知安东尼在亚克兴海战中失败时,他唯一担心的是自己能否逃脱屋大维的惩罚。[6] 事实上,大希律早已产生了转变阵营的想法。在亚克兴海战爆发后,一群角斗士欲前往埃及支援安东尼。大希律协助叙利亚总督狄迪乌斯(Didius)阻止了角斗士继续前进[7],这无疑表现出他立场的转变。并且在安东尼自杀前,大希律就已经通过在罗德岛的出色表现成功地加入了屋大维的阵营。

总体来看,大希律与安东尼保持着良好的关系,维系这一关系的重要因素是利益,既包括政治利益,又包括经济利益。在约瑟夫斯的记载中,大希律多次贿赂安东尼,后者则以相应的政治利益回报大希律。除此之外,安东尼对安提帕特的良好印象,以及对大希律个人能力的欣赏,都是大希律与安东尼建立友好关系的重要因素。大希律与安东尼构成了罗马政治环境中的利益共同体。即便如此,大希律也有过改变阵营的想法。由此可见,这种共同体并非绝对牢靠。

(二)大希律与奥古斯都的私人关系

公元前 31 年,安东尼在亚克兴海战中战败。得到消息的大希律惊恐万分,自知难逃屋大维的惩罚。[8] 为减少许尔卡努斯二世对自己的威胁,大希律将他

---

① 参见 Samuel Rocca, *Herod's Judaea: A Mediterranean State in the Classical World*, 57。
② 参见 Norman Gelb, *Herod the Great: Statesman, Visionary, Tyrant*, 74。
③ 参见 Josephus, *Jewish Antiquities*, 15. 112-115。
④ 同上,15. 131-132。
⑤ 同上,15. 132。
⑥ 同上,15. 161。
⑦ 同上,15. 195-196。Josephus, *The Jewish War*, 1. 392.
⑧ 参见 Josephus, *Jewish Antiquities*, 15. 161-162。

处决。[1] 之后,大希律前往罗德岛拜见屋大维。在临行前,他对自己死后的事情提前作出了安排。相对于前往老底嘉前的安排,大希律这次就显得尤为绝望。他将国家交给自己的兄弟费洛拉斯(Pheroras)管理,将自己的母亲、姐姐和孩子们送往马萨达[2]——整个犹地亚地区最为安全的地方。显然,大希律已经开始考虑家人的安全问题。除此之外,他的妻子米利暗被送到亚历山大里亚,并置于自己亲信的监视之下。他指示手下,如果自己遭遇不幸,就立刻处死米利暗。[3]

公元前30年春,大希律抵达罗德岛。约瑟夫斯对此叙述颇为详细。大希律在屋大维面前摘下王冠,但又不失国王的体面。在与屋大维的交谈中,他坦率地承认了自己与安东尼的友谊。他还向屋大维解释了自己没有参战的原因,同时提到自己曾在战争中为安东尼提供物资。[4] 在这次谈话中,大希律充分展示出对自己庇护人的忠诚。屋大维听后并未惩罚大希律,而是将王冠重新戴回到他的头上,并再次确认了他的犹太王身份。然后,大希律带着荣耀重新返回了犹地亚。[5] 卡舍尔认为,这次谈话在某种程度上可以被视为"第二次加冕礼"。大希律故意在新的庇护人面前表现自己,头上没有王冠是为了表示谦卑,目的是在新庇护人面前发出信号,表示他只保留了罗马赋予的权力,并在等待屋大维加冕。[6] 同时,这也象征着他承认屋大维有能力确认或废除他的地位。从本质上来看,大希律的这次表现更像是在绝望处境下的政治赌博。通过这次谈话,大希律成功地加入了屋大维的阵营。后代学者对此评价颇高,认为大希律成功地驾驭了权力政治的潮流,巧妙地转变了立场,实属不易。[7] 大希律也积极回报自己的庇护人,他穷尽奢华地接待了前来视察的屋大维。根据约瑟夫斯的记述,屋大维对大希律的表现非常满意,并且对大希律的忠诚和捐助更有信心。[8] 事实上,在过去的30年里,安提帕特和他的儿子们一直支持着罗马在东方的优势,屋大维知道他可以指望大希律有效地转移他的忠诚。同时,将犹太这个动荡的国家置于罗马的有效统治下,除了让大希律继续他的统治以外,没有任何实际的替代办法。同年,屋大维进军埃及,大希律赶往埃及与屋大维会面。在这次会面中,

---

① 参见 Josephus, *Jewish Antiquities*, 14. 383, 15. 172-173; Norman Gelb, *Herod the Great: Statesman, Visionary, Tyrant*, 71-72。

② 参见 Josephus, *Jewish Antiquities*, 15. 183-184。

③ 同上,15. 184-186。

④ 同上,15. 187-193。

⑤ 同上,15. 194-198。Josephus, *The Jewish War*, 1. 393.

⑥ 参见 Aryeh Kasher, *King Herod: A Persecuted Persecuted*, 161。

⑦ 参见 Peter Richardson and Amy Marie Fisher, *Herod: King of the Jews and Friend of the Romans*, 389。

⑧ 参见 Josephus, *Jewish Antiquities*, 15. 201。

大希律收获颇丰。屋大维授予他大量的领土，包括克里奥帕特拉曾经从他手中夺走的土地，还有加达拉、希普斯、撒玛利亚等。之后，大希律护送屋大维到安条克，然后返回犹地亚。[①]

大希律还重修了斯特拉顿塔，并更名为凯撒利亚。[②] 约瑟夫斯在文本中细致地描述了这座城市的辉煌。大希律将其中一座最为壮观的塔命名为"德鲁苏"(Drusus)，以纪念奥古斯都早逝的儿子。[③] 除此之外，大希律还为奥古斯都修建了神庙，里面矗立着奥古斯都的雕像。[④] 从严格意义上来说，大希律的这种行为违背了犹太律法。罗科认为，在犹太人眼中，建立罗马神庙和奥古斯都神庙可以被看作一种政治行为，而不是一种宗教行为。他通过分析约瑟夫斯的文本，进一步发现犹太人没有因为大希律的行为发动骚乱。[⑤] 此后，大希律将自己的孩子亚历山大和阿里斯多布鲁斯送到罗马。这一做法符合藩属国的惯例，并有利于加强藩属国与罗马帝国之间的联系。[⑥] 之后，奥古斯都授予他指定继承人的权力，并将特拉可尼(Trachonitis)、巴坦尼亚(Batanaea)、奥瑞纳提斯(Auranitis)和利萨尼亚(Lysanias)交予大希律。[⑦] 公元前 20 年前后，奥古斯都巡视叙利亚。面对加达拉人对大希律的控告，他保护了大希律，并宣布后者无罪。[⑧] 约瑟夫斯对此评价称，奥古斯都以友好的态度对待大希律，并且没有因为这次骚乱改变对他的友善。[⑨] 在芝诺多罗斯(Zenodorus)死后，奥古斯都将他的领土授予大希律，并任命大希律为叙利亚总督。[⑩]

除政治关系外，奥古斯都多次主持解决大希律的家庭矛盾。公元前 12 年，大希律奔赴罗马，在奥古斯都面前，他谴责自己的两个儿子——阿里斯多布鲁斯和亚历山大密谋杀害他并意图篡位。[⑪] 根据约瑟夫斯的记载，大希律在这次控

---

① 参见 Josephus, *Jewish Antiquities*, 15. 215-217。

② 同上，15. 331-341。

③ 同上，15. 336-337。

④ 同上，15. 339-340。大希律在各地大量修建以"凯撒"命名的建筑物。参见 Josephus, *The Jewish War*, 1. 402-416。

⑤ 参见 Samuel Rocca, *Herod's Judaea: A Mediterranean State in the Classical World*, 48。

⑥ 参见 David M. Jacobson, "*Three Roman Client Kings: Herod of Judaea, Archelaus of Cappadocia and Juba of Mauretania*," 26。

⑦ 参见 Josephus, *Jewish Antiquities*, 15. 343-346。

⑧ 同上，15. 357。

⑨ 同上，15. 354-359。

⑩ 同上，15. 359-360。事实上，奥古斯都很可能任命大希律为科勒—叙利亚总督，而非叙利亚总督。相关讨论参见 Josephus, *Jewish Antiquities*, 15. 360. note. c。

⑪ 参见 Josephus, *Jewish Antiquities*, 16. 90-93。

告中歇斯底里地控诉自己的儿子们,并请求奥古斯都惩罚他们犯的严重错误。[①]面对父亲的控诉,阿里斯多布鲁斯和亚历山大在痛哭流涕的同时又感到困惑。奥古斯都看出了他们的困惑,认为他们没有犯罪,只是胆怯和缺乏经验。[②] 亚历山大以真挚的语气进行了辩护。他对父亲的过错用表示尊敬的沉默应对,却语言犀利地为自己和兄弟辩护。同时,他斥责安提帕特的恶劣行径,并表示自己问心无愧。最后,亚历山大讲道,如果父亲依然觉得他有罪,可以把他处死。[③] 奥古斯都没有给亚历山大和阿里斯多布鲁斯定罪,而是力促他们和解并成功地使他们达成了协议。[④] 根据《犹太战记》的说法,大希律放弃了指控,但仍然怀疑自己的儿子们。[⑤] 但是,在《犹太古史》中,约瑟夫斯明确提到大希律已经与两个儿子和解。[⑥] 在此后的几天时间里,大希律将 300 塔兰特的礼物赠送给奥古斯都。奥古斯都则将塞浦路斯铜矿一半的收入交给大希律,并委托他管理另一半收入。除此之外,奥古斯都还允许大希律选择继承人。[⑦] 回到犹地亚后,大希律宣布了第三封遗嘱:第一继承人为安提帕特,其次是亚历山大和阿里斯多布鲁斯。[⑧] 约瑟夫斯在这里的记载表明,大希律的遗嘱存在继承顺序。在《犹太战记》中,大希律是将王国分给三个儿子,每一个儿子都是国王。[⑨] 不论如何,总体来看,大希律对于此事的和解非常满意。然而,事情并未到此终结。此后,大希律先后处死了亚历山大、阿里斯多布鲁斯和安提帕特,最终立亚基帕为继承人。

在大希律与奥古斯都交往的过程中,也出现过信任危机。锡勒乌斯到奥古斯都面前指责大希律侵略阿拉伯并屠杀阿拉伯人。奥古斯都听后立刻询问周边的人,以调查控诉是否属实。当得到肯定的答复后,他愤怒地给大希律写信予以斥责。[⑩] 处于愤怒中的奥古斯都甚至拒绝接见大希律派来的使团[⑪],这是二人长达 30 余年的交往中最为严重的一次危机。在第一次出使失败后,大希律派遣大马士革的尼古拉斯再次出使罗马。在奥古斯都面前,尼古拉斯不为大希律辩护,而是指责锡勒乌斯的罪行,从而获得机会解释大希律的行为。同时,在这次会议

---

① 参见 Josephus, *Jewish Antiquities*, 16. 91-99。

② 同上,16. 103。

③ 参见 Josephus, *The Jewish War*, 1. 452-454; Josephus, *Jewish Antiquities*, 15. 357。

④ 参见 Josephus, *Jewish Antiquities*, 16.124-126; Josephus, *The Jewish War*, 1. 453-454。

⑤ 参见 Josephus, *The Jewish War*, 1. 455。

⑥ 参见 Josephus, *Jewish Antiquities*, 16. 131。

⑦ 同上,16. 127-129。

⑧ 同上,16. 133-134。

⑨ 参见 Josephus, *The Jewish War*, 1. 258-259。

⑩ 参见 Josephus, *Jewish Antiquities*, 16. 287-291。

⑪ 同上,16. 293。

上,阿拉伯人的使团也谴责锡勒乌斯的罪行。当奥古斯都得知锡勒乌斯对大希律的控诉都是编造的时候,他愤怒地判处后者死刑,并与大希律和解。[①]

总体来看,罗马现在需要的是大希律对内部管理的效率和对屋大维的忠诚。屋大维在政治上信任他,并喜欢他个人。接下来的 20 年是帝国对自称"罗马之友"和"凯撒之友"的藩属王大希律的青睐。大希律与奥古斯都的关系主要基于政治利益。最直接的证据是,大希律曾要求民众向奥古斯都和他本人宣誓效忠[②],这无疑是对二者关系的最直接表达。在奥古斯都建立的新秩序中,藩属王被认为是皇帝本人的封臣。用斯特拉波的话来说,"国王、王朝和教区过去和现在都是皇帝(帝国)的一部分"[③]。因此,大希律只是奥古斯都众多的"封臣"之一。然而,大希律高超的政治能力使得他备受关注。奥古斯都多次扩展大希律的领土,表明了他对大希律政治能力的肯定。这也生动地说明了藩属王作为一种手段,将边远地区与罗马帝国紧密结合并建立有效的渠道,传播罗马文化的影响。[④] 大希律时期是犹太从独立王国到罗马行省的过渡阶段,真正奠定了将犹太王国并入罗马行省的基础。在第一次犹太起义被镇压后,大希律建造的凯撒利亚取代了耶路撒冷成为该地区的行政中心。[⑤]

结语

公元前 2 世纪中叶,犹太人就已经开始了希腊化,并引发了严重的派别对立。在大希律统治期间,他大举推行希腊化,这并非出于他对希腊文化的认同,而是具有一定的政治因素。对于王国内部来说,他通过兴建各类建筑,强调自己与奥古斯都的友好关系,以稳定自己的统治。同时,对于一个多民族国家来说,尊重各地区和各民族的风俗习惯,采取"因地制宜"的统治策略,才是最为适合的政治手段。对于王国所处的外部环境来说,希腊文化是"世界"的主流文化,推行希腊化政策有利于犹太王国融入主流文化体系中,从而提高大希律个人、犹太国家和犹太民族的政治和文化地位。

藩属王取得罗马信任的常用手段之一是亲自拜访权力中心罗马或当时的权

① 参见 Josephus, *Jewish Antiquities*,16. 335-353。

② 同上, 17. 42。

③ David M. Jacobson, "Three Roman Client Kings: Herod of Judaea, Archelaus of Cappadocia and Juba of Mauretania," 25; Strab. xvii. 3. 25。

④ 参见 David M. Jacobson, "Three Roman Client Kings: Herod of Judaea, Archelaus of Cappadocia and Juba of Mauretania," 28。

⑤ 同上,34。

要人物。①大希律先后与安东尼和屋大维建立起了良好的私人关系。这种关系的核心要素是政治利益。作为藩属王的大希律在效忠庇护人的同时,也获得了相应的政治回报。对于大希律来说,只有维系好自己与罗马显贵人物的关系,才能维持住自己的国王地位。因此,在担任犹太王期间,他通过兴建大量的城市和公共设施、举办赛会、军事援助等方式,宣示了自己的忠诚。对于罗马而言,大希律的王国在罗马帝国东部最为混乱的地区,民族成分最为复杂,如何有效地维持该地的政治秩序是罗马帝国考虑的首要问题。大希律家族从安提帕特开始就与凯撒、安东尼、屋大维建立了良好的关系。同时,事实证明,藩属王大希律很好地维持了该地区的政治秩序。支持大希律成为犹太王符合罗马的政治利益。因此,个人关系与国家利益是相互统一的。良好的个人关系有利于维护国家的政治利益,正因如此,大希律时期的犹太王国才得以保持高度自治。

① 参见宋立宏,〈犹太战争与巴勒斯坦罗马化之两难〉,72。

A Study of the Hellenistic and Romanization Strategies of Herod the Great

ZHANG Shuai

Abstract: Herod the Great was the Jewish client king of Rome in the first century BC. In the face of the complex political environment, he took a series of measures to maintain the political status of the country. In terms of culture, he pursued the Hellenistic policy, promoting the Jewish Kingdom to integrate into the "world" cultural system, thus enhancing his personal and Jewish national influence. In terms of politics, he pursued the political strategy of Romanization. The key to this strategy is to establish a good personal relationship with the Roman rulers. While loyal to the patronage, Herod the Great also received political rewards. Because of this, the Jewish kingdom was able to maintain a high degree of autonomy.

Key Words: Herod the Great, Hellenization, Romanization, Patronage

论两种真理观的形而上学基础：经验实在性与基督教信任情感实在性*

贺方刚**

【摘要】对于形而上学的研究，人们往往都注重经验论和唯理论两大流派的辩驳与抗争，因为它们不仅对西方思想史的发展起了推动作用，而且也因其早已为人们所熟知而变得更易于被接受。就经验论和唯理论都仰赖人的"理性"这一心灵机能而言，学界给予了足够的重视，但另一个重要的心灵机能——情感——却往往被忽略。由情感所奠定的哲学基础，在整个形而上学的发展中发挥了重要作用，应该引起我们更多的关注。情感，尤其是信任情感所产生的实在性，为自然科学的发展乃至创新性发现提供了不同于经验实在性的另一种哲学基础，指出这一点，对于促进自然科学的创新大有裨益。

【关键词】真理观；形而上学基础；经验实在性；基督教；信任情感实在性

在西方思想史上，实在性大致可以归纳为两种，一种是以经验为基础的实在性，经验论者大多倚重于此；唯理论者虽强调观念、思想的至上性，但其思想的最终落脚点，也会追溯到经验领域。另一种是以信任情感为基础的实在性，这主要由基督教哲学所引发，学界过去往往多从理性为信仰服务的角度讨论之，鲜有揭示其实在性之意义的研究。我们经过研究发现，信任情感实在性在自然科学思维中也发挥着重要作用。这两种实在性的发展与西方形而上学的真理情结有

* 本文系国家社科基金项目"康德宗教哲学情感分析研究"(15XZJ008)、山东工艺美术学院教学改革项目"'思政+设计'双融共育机制下的思政课教学研究"(2021M08)、山东工艺美术学院校级科研项目"胡塞尔'前谓述经验'理论研究"(X21KY21)、山东省人文社会科学专项研究课题"大思政课视域下高校'思政'+'设计'双融共育机制研究"(2022-XXDY-34)的阶段性成果。

** 贺方刚，山东工艺美术学院教师。

关，首先发端于人的生存，因为但凡有建树的思想家，不管其所建构的体系有多庞大，也不管其所研究的领域有多宽泛，大都会关注人的生存选择问题，即人在生存中都选择善的东西，找到生存所依赖的"真理"。这一现象虽然和我们今天所熟知的自然科学意义上的"真理"不直接相关，但从发生学的视角来反观真理，它最初就是为了解决生存选择的根据问题。这一观点最先由柏拉图系统地提出，被称为"人皆求善"原则；也就是说，人求善是为了获得生存选择的根据——真理。从善的选择标准来看，其间有一个判断根据的问题，因为每个人的生存处境不同，人生际遇迥异，在 A 看来是善的东西，在 B 看来就可能不是。从生存体验来看，对人在生存中的判断标准进行分析不纯然是抽象的理论建构，它还要求分析者有设身处地的生存体验[①]，否则就会形成一种"没有生气的讨论"，作者可以随意发挥，好像思想可以在真空中自由运转一样，问题在于"在真空中产生的思想是不可能感染他人的，因为思想只能在共同的生存关注中传递"[②]。在这个意义上来对西方思想史上两种重要的实在性进行"生存分析"[③]，就要求我们深入思考这样一个问题：以经验实在性为主导的求善方式是否能找到真正的善？若不能，那真正的善只是一个虚幻的假设？再进一步追问，若没有真正的善，人的生存得以持续下去的选择标准在哪里？按柏拉图的求善原则，真理要靠人的理性去认识、寻找，但古希腊怀疑主义摧毁了这种可能性。奥古斯丁在一定意义上受到了新柏拉图主义者求善情结的感召而寻求真理[④]，当然，他前期没有跳出怀疑主义的窠臼，"他正经历着学院派哲学家所具有的那种怀疑"[⑤]，在遇到基督教哲学后，他体会到了主动彰显给他的善——真理。这种思维方式背后的形而

① 我们提出这种观点，不是强调分析某一生活模式或某一宗教信仰下的生活模式，就必须成为该种生活模式的成员或成为某一宗教的信众。但一个不争的事实是，有某一宗教信仰且又能客观中立地对其所处的生活状况进行分析，比没有这一宗教信仰者的分析无疑要深刻得多。比如西方的许多基督徒学者，他们能比非基督徒发现更多的东西。又比如国内著名的佛教哲学专家方立天教授，虽不是佛教徒，在刚开始研究佛教时，为了加深对佛教的理解，住到法源寺亲身体验僧人的生活，并听他们讲经说法，以此切身体会佛教的教义教理。参见方立天 Fang Litian，《方立天讲谈录》[Fang Litian's Lectures]（北京[Beijing]：九州出版社[Jiuzhou Press]，2014），4。对这一现象进行更深入的讨论不是本文的主题，在此只是指出这一现象。

② 谢文郁 Xie Wenyu，〈回归文本，回归生存〉[Return to the Text, Return to the Existence]，《世界哲学》[World Philosophy]，2007 年第 6 期[2007, Issue 6]，3。

③ 在《自由与生存》这本专著中，作者采用的是"生存分析法"，即体会不同思想家的生存关注，分析他们在生存中所重视的问题，具体表现为：第一，在概念上如何表达生存关注；第二，在理论上如何回答生存关注的问题；第三，理论回答是否有效。本文借鉴了这种方法。

④ 参见 Francis Ferrier 弗朗西斯·费里埃，《圣奥古斯丁》[Saint Augustine]，户思社 Hu Sishe 译（北京[Beijing]：商务印书馆[The Commercial Press]，1998），34。

⑤ 同上，29。

上学基础是信任情感的实在性，它和经验论的形而上学基础——经验的实在性——之间有一种张力。这种张力对没有信任情感实在性这一视角的人来讲，往往体会不深，所以也容易被忽略；但信任情感的实在性在西方思想史上却发挥了重要的作用，不仅对于形而上学的发展，而且对于自然科学的一些思维模式也产生了重要影响。本文以分析这两种真理观的实在性为契机，期望学界对后一种实在性给予更多的关注。

一、理性真理观的经验实在性

生存意味着自我保存，这在生物界是有目共睹之事。对于人来说，由于人具有理性，便不同于其他生物靠本能活着，而是有自己的选择能力。这一选择在给人带来很大优势的同时，也使人在面对诸多选择项时莫衷一是、难以抉择：生存中人虽然会选择对自己好或善的东西，但什么是好或善的标准呢？是不是每个人都会选择同一个善呢？柏拉图在《枚农篇》里借苏格拉底之口，从讨论品德入手来探讨善的问题，从而引出"人皆求善"原则。在苏格拉底看来，品德是使人成为好人的东西，是善的。基于此，他便向枚农请教品德是什么。枚农认为，男人、女人、老人、小孩等，都各有其自己这一类人所属的品德。苏格拉底觉得这种回答并未能给出品德的定义，因为不同的品德"虽然各种各样，却带有一个同一的型，正是由于这个型，它们才能是品德"①。

柏拉图在此显然是用他的"理型分有说"来对品德进行界定，即尽管不同类型的人都有自己的品德标准，但能称得上品德的东西里面有一个共同的关于品德的理型，正因为如此，"所有的人都是以同样好的东西成为好人的。他们有了这样东西，就成了好人"②。按枚农的观察，他却认为有的人在追求好东西，但有的人却在追求坏东西，且所谓的追求"就是指它(指被追求的东西——引者注)成为他们"③，也就是说，被追求的东西成为追求者的一部分，或对被追求者产生作用。就这个作用而言，枚农肯定是指那些被追求的东西能促进或有益于追求者的生存。苏格拉底看出了其中的问题，因为既然"追求"就是指被追求的东西成为追求者的一部分，那么有人追求坏东西就与人的生存背道而驰或有损于人的

---

① Plato 柏拉图，《柏拉图对话集》[The Collected Dialogues of Plato]，王太庆 Wang Taiqing 译(北京[Beijing]：商务印书馆[The Commercial Press]，2012)，157。"型"的希腊文为 ειδος，是指 ειδω(看)的对象，也就是指一个东西被人所看上去而呈现出来的样子，按王太庆先生的观点，ειδος 译为"型"较为合适，后来谢文郁教授认为译为"理型"更恰当，本文采后者。

② 同上，158。

③ 同上，165。

生存了，所以他反问枚农：

“依你看，那些知道坏东西坏的人认为坏的东西有益吗？”

枚农：“我不这么看。”

苏格拉底：“那些追求坏东西的人是不知其为坏东西，他是在追求自己以为好实际上却坏的东西。所以是那些不知道一件东西坏却以为它好的人，在追求那看来好的东西。”[①]

对上述二人的对话，我们可以进一步展开，作如下推论：第一，生活中有人求善(A)。第二，生活中有人求恶，其中的一大类是明知为恶而求恶，可再细分为知其为恶但对自己有利而追求之(B)，知其为恶且对自己有害而追求之(C)；另一大类是以恶为善而求善(D)。

我们可以看出，B类人虽然是在追求恶，但这个恶是第三者从真正的善出发来作出的判断，对追求者而言，他所追求的仍然是善；D类人仍然是在追求善；C类人并不存在，是空项，因为这种选择是在走向自我毁灭。由此我们就可得出结论：人在生存中都是求善的[②]，且这个善“不是一种观念性的东西，而是一种现实中的生存力量”[③]。

有学者指出，在柏拉图的“人皆求善”原则里，人所追求的善是受自己的欲望支配的，这些欲望有两种，一种是必要欲望，另一种是奢侈欲望。[④] 按柏拉图的观点，第一种欲望主要是指满足身体基本需要的欲望。初看起来，这个定义非常符合常识且易于理解。但细究之下，我们难免会质疑：在不同的生存状况之下，人们身体上的需要是不同的。实际上柏拉图将这种欲望的辨别标准放到了人的灵魂与智慧上，即只有那种使灵魂追求到智慧并达到清晰程度的欲望，才能被称为必要欲望。我们可以看出，在柏拉图这里问题变得复杂起来，他并没有将必要欲望局限于人的生理需求，而是引向了人的灵魂和智慧。众所周知，柏拉图对西方哲学的重大贡献之一在于他划分了理型世界和现象世界，并指出灵魂存在于理型世界，在这个世界里处于最高地位的是善，其余一切都是对善的分有(μέθεξις)。由于灵魂起初是与善同处于一个理型世界里的，所以它刚开始时知道什么是善。但灵魂在进入人体

① 柏拉图，《柏拉图对话集》，166。

② 谢文郁 Xie Wenyu，《形而上学与西方思维》[Metaphysics and Western Thinking](南宁[Nanning]：广西人民出版社[Guangxi People's Publishing House]，2016)，56—61。

③ 谢文郁 Xie Wenyu，《自由与生存：西方思想史上的自由观追踪》[The Concept Of Freedom: The Platonic-Augustinian-Lutheran-Kierkegaardian Tradition]，张秀华 Zhang Xiuhua、王天民 Wang Tianmin 译(上海[Shanghai]：上海人民出版社[Shanghai People's Publishing House]，2007)，3。

④ 参见 Plato, *The Collected Dialogues of Plato*, eds. E. Hamilton and H. Cairns (Princeton: Princeton University Press, 1961), 558D。

后由于喝了冥河水而忘记了何谓真正的善。按这种说法,追求真正的善就成了一个回忆的过程,且这种回忆是要靠学习哲学、追求智慧实现的。

通过上述分析可以看出,柏拉图提出必要欲望虽然是从本于身体的基本需要开始的,但它的判断标准已从处于现象界的肉体上升到了处于理型世界的灵魂那里。质言之,柏拉图提出的第一种欲望是要寻求真正的善的标准,它是有利于人的灵魂提升的东西;与此相对应,柏拉图强调的第二种欲望——奢侈欲望,则与此相反,它有损于人的灵魂,柏拉图于此所给出的例子是暴饮暴食,除此外并无过多分析。按照柏拉图的灵魂说及其对理型世界的设定,追求真正的善最后转化为一个认识论问题,即要靠学习哲学净化灵魂从而摆脱肉体欲望的束缚,才能臻达至善——真正的善。而这种认识论意义上的判断标准有一个无穷后退的问题,也就是说,要看一个东西能否用来评判真正的善,就要有一个是真正的善的东西,而这个关于真正善的东西还要有一个作为判断标准的标准……如此一来,就会引起一个无限追溯的链条。况且柏拉图把善的理型作为善的选择标准,只是一种理论建构,并未解决生存中的选择问题,因为善的理型虽然从理论上为人们指出了一个可供选择的目标,但它并不能充当真正的选择对象。但问题在于:真正的善到底在哪里?柏拉图并未向人们陈明。对这一问题有深刻体会的是奥古斯丁,他作为一名新柏拉图主义者,如柏拉图在《理想国》中所号召的那样,以自己的灵魂应对各种善恶,走向上的路,靠智慧来实践正义(亦即至善——引者注)。[①] 他追随柏拉图,靠自己的理性和哲学的智慧苦苦地追求至善。但他依然没有找到真正的善,最后在皈依基督教后的体验中体会到善已主动呈现在他的面前,这就是另一种善观念——在恩典中主动彰显的拯救的善(下一部分展开详细的论证)。

二、拯救真理观的实在性

奥古斯丁对于靠自己的理性追求真理而不得和作为一名基督徒在信仰、信任耶稣而白白地得到真理这二者之间的张力,在他的《忏悔录》中表现得极为清晰,他认为前者是“预设”,后者是“忏悔”。所谓预设,说明柏拉图的求善原则只是一种理论假设;而忏悔则意味着人的无能,无法靠自己的力量寻求到真正的善。奥古斯丁所体会到的这种预设与忏悔之间的张力,无疑是受古希腊怀疑主义的影响与冲击,因为怀疑主义通过无穷后退的逻辑困境,已否定了真理的存

① 参见 Plato, *The Republic*, ed. G. R. F. Ferrari (Cambridge: Cambridge University Press, 2000), 621c, 345。

在，最后的结果只能是在悬置判断中继续寻求真理。[①] 这种情况是与人的生存实际相悖的。奥古斯丁之所以能在基督教哲学中继续追求真理，一方面是对怀疑主义的不满与补救；另一方面也是以一种不同的方式在延续柏拉图倡导的求真之路。在基督教哲学中，真理靠耶稣基督主动彰显给世人，只要信靠、追随耶稣，就能得到真理。《约翰福音》里是这样说的："道成了肉身，住在我们中间。"(《约翰福音》1:14)耶稣在回答多马关于道路的问题时说："我就是道路、真理和生命。"(《约翰福音》14:5-7)(在希腊文《圣经》中，关于知，使用了 Yνωσιs，指真正的知识或真理性知识，与柏拉图的真理是同一个词。)对于这两种真理观，就其与人的关系来看，有的学者将其看作一种"动力性的张力"[②]，也就是说，在柏拉图的求善原则那里，真理是被追求的，它可以静止不动，要靠人的理性作为动力来追求；而在基督教的真理观里，真理借着耶稣来到人世间，变成了一种具有动力性的主动显现者。这种对于真理的言说模式，"实际上是在我们追求真理的过程引入一种外在力量。这种外在力量并不是在我们的控制之下，而是主动地向我们走来"[③]。也就是说，认识主体面对真理，可以有两种方式来获得：一种是像柏拉图那样，靠理性能力主动追求它；另一种则如奥古斯丁所言，真理主动向我们显示出来。奥古斯丁提出这种方式的理由是，人的理性虽有主动性，但囿于能力而不能获得真理。真理主动向人彰显的这种谈论方式，在基督教中被称为"恩典"，即真理是白白地向信仰者赐予的；但其前提条件是，接受真理者必须信仰耶稣为基督、为真理的显现者，而没有真理情结和不信任耶稣为基督的人体会不到这种真理的实在性。

奥古斯丁对基督教拯救真理观的接受有一个循序渐进的过程。他在求学的早期主要是靠自己的理性来追求真理。[④] 即便是在成为基督徒后，他也并没有完全顺服在对耶稣的信任情感中，这从他对自由意志的态度即可窥其端倪。按基督教的传统，人不认识真理是因为人一出生就带有原罪，这种罪的状态使人处于黑暗中，而真理则象征着光明，有罪之人与光明是隔绝的。要想摆脱这种状况，就必须信靠耶稣并顺从其带领。奥古斯丁敏锐地抓住了这一点并提出了质疑，他反问道："我们是否应该接受'人的自由意志是恶的起源'这一断言？"[⑤]因为，按《圣经》的说法，既然上帝在造人时赋予了他自由意志，且上帝是善的，那么

① 参见谢文郁，《自由与生存：西方思想史上的自由观追踪》，43。

② 同上，45。

③ 同上。

④ 参见弗朗西斯·费里埃，《圣奥古斯丁》，20。

⑤ 谢文郁，《自由与生存：西方思想史上的自由观追踪》，51。

自由意志也应该是善的。如此一来,引出的问题就是:恶从何而来?人与上帝的其他被造物同出一辙,为何单单自由意志是恶的,或自由意志带来了恶?奥古斯丁认为这是人使用或误用了自由意志的缘故,也就是说,自由意志在上帝造人时是善的,或曰自由意志中有善的成分;人在使用它作选择时会产生恶,说明自由意志里面也有恶的成分,否则不会从善的东西引出恶来。按奥古斯丁的观点,我们只能作如此推论,这样一来,就需要对自由意志作更多的分析。奥古斯丁接下来认为自由意志和上帝的其他被造物不一样,它是能动的,有一种选择的能力,就其有向善的一面来说,自由意志中有一种本性,他指出:"我所说的'本性'(nature),指的是所谓的'实体'(substance)。也就是说,任一实体或者是上帝,或来自上帝,正如善要么是上帝,要么从上帝而来。"[①]至于如何解释人在自由意志支配下选择恶的问题,奥古斯丁认为人的自由意志中还有另一部分,他称其为"自愿"的部分,这一部分引导人追求非永恒性的(指非善的)或世俗的东西,这样一种追求,奥古斯丁认为它"仅仅属于灵魂因而是志愿的;因此,应该受到责备"[②]。

奥古斯丁早期关于自由意志的学说,明显流露出他从柏拉图求善原则向基督教拯救式的善观念过渡的痕迹。他将自由意志的组成部分一分为二,虽然可以解释恶的问题,但却带来了这么一个疑问:自由意志作为上帝创造的一个整体,为何其中的"自愿"部分是恶的呢?显然,这是他把选择能力归诸自由意志的缘故。及至奥古斯丁中、晚期,特别是在他与佩拉纠主义者的论战中[③](佩拉纠及佩拉纠主义者是在当时和奥古斯丁观点不一致的一批人,他们认为人在今生靠着自己的意志和个人的努力就可以无罪),又进一步修改了关于自由意志的理论,提出"自由意志是一种中性的力量"的观点。关于佩拉纠及佩拉纠主义者,历史上留下的文字材料不多,我们只能从奥古斯丁对他们的反驳中还原其思想。佩拉纠派关于自由意志的观点,集中表现在自由意志选择善恶、接受恩典的能力上:

> 上帝在我们身上根植了一种在两个方向上行动的可能性。我们出生时……非善非恶,但取决于我们所做的:因为我们出生时并没有充分发展,而是拥有一种亦此亦彼的能力……在人的正当意志行动之前,他身上只有

① 谢文郁,《自由与生存:西方思想史上的自由观追踪》,53—54。

② 同上,54。

③ 参见 Saint Augustine 奥古斯丁,《原罪与恩典——奥古斯丁反佩拉纠主义文选》[On Original Sin and Grace: Against the Pelagians],周伟池 Zhou Weichi 译(香港[Hong Kong]:道风书社[Logos and Pneuma Press],2005),1。

上帝赋予给他的东西。[①]

佩拉纠所意欲说明的是，人受造于上帝，人的自由意志也得自上帝，且有充分的能力选择善恶。按这种观点，我们可以进一步推论，人既然是由自己选择了善恶，就应该完全为自己的行为负责；上帝虽然是善的，却不会对人的善恶负责。在这种情况下，面对人的善恶，上帝应处于一个什么地位或有什么作用呢？佩拉纠认为，上帝只起到帮助、教育、启蒙的作用，有人称其为“教育拯救学说”[②]，我们遵循这种说法。其实，这种说法和奥古斯丁早期的观点并无多大差别，只不过佩拉纠并没有像奥古斯丁那样将自由意志细分为本性和自愿两种成分而已。但随着奥古斯丁对基督教信任情感的加深，他已完全不能接受佩拉纠的这种观点，他认为人的意志虽然“是自由的，但却是没有能力的”[③]，因为自由意志的选择能力来自恩典。

这两种观点之间的分歧，虽然表现在自由意志的力量上，但其根源却在于如何看待恩典的态度上。按佩拉纠的教育拯救说，上帝在恩典中给予人的善，只能把它理解成一种知识，一种关于犹太教律法和信仰的知识。在佩拉纠看来，人通过学习这种知识，就有了辨别善恶、选择善恶的能力，上帝的恩典只是一种助推力，是在人的能力不足时的一种辅助性力量，因为“上帝的帮助通过教导去掉了人的无知，使得他知道在行为上应该避免什么，追求什么；从而借助于在本性上属于他的自由选择能力，他就可以走上那给他指明的道路”[④]。而在奥古斯丁这里，他放弃了早期谈论求善时由于“无知”而陷入的困境，因为在柏拉图哲学语境中，“无知”是“遗忘”的同义词，应对无知的办法是靠哲学的智慧来净化灵魂并回忆起关于善的知识。这种关于善的知识是否有人得到过，并没有被证实，它只是一个理论预设和生存方向而已；相反，倒是成为基督徒的体验使奥古斯丁觉得真理的获得“必须是上帝启示的，而不是通过自我追求”[⑤]。他对求善原则的这一调整，使我们注意到，在他看来，人可以追求其他知识，但是不能追求关于善的知识，善的知识只能来自上帝的恩典。如此一来就会导致这么一种结局：人要么在信仰基督中接受真理，要么因拒绝接受耶稣而和真理无缘。其原因在于“创造者赋予理性灵魂在本性上拥有选择自由（的力量），这只是一种中性的力量；既可以

① 谢文郁，《自由与生存：西方思想史上的自由观追踪》，68。
② 同上。
③ 同上。
④ 同上，70。
⑤ 同上，72。

被用来走向信仰,也可以引向不信”[①]。

通过分析奥古斯丁和佩拉纠的争论,就可以得到两种关于接受真理的方式。一种是佩拉纠式的,它完全靠个人的自由意志,这基本上是柏拉图求善原则的延续,只不过又增加了基督信仰以作为一个助推力量而已。而另外一种接受真理的方式则完全颠覆了柏拉图的求善原则,让真理和善主动向追求者呈现。若从认识论的角度来看,前一种方式还是在经验论者认识事物的顺序上来谈论真理问题,它把恩典当成一个认识对象,我们可以将其模式概括为“自由意志→信仰→恩典”,亦即人靠自己的意志和理性去认识、辨认信仰对象和真理,在得到确认并认可后才接受恩典。而后一种方式则把信仰作为获得真理的起点和主要途径,在认识顺序上与前一种相反,它是一种“恩典→信仰→自由意志”的模式,其实在性是以信任情感为基础的,它在西方思想史上影响深远且余绪不断,同时也对自然科学的思维产生了很大影响。

三、信任情感实在性给我们的启发

实在是人类理解事物的基础,也是人类思维得以深入发展的基点。按中国哲学的观点,我们的实在性被理解为“有”,特别是在形而上与形而下相区分的思路中,形而下的器、物主要指事物的“有”或“在场”,这只相当于西方形而上学中的“存在者”“显现者”,与西方形而上学中的“在”相去甚远。因为整个西方形而上学的发展过程,主要就是解释作为呈献给我们的事物背后的那个“在”,正是由于它作为“存在者”“显现者”的事物才被我们所认识。这种对“在”与“存在者”或“显现者”的区分,在柏拉图那里是以理型与事物的形式存在的,在康德那里是以物自体与现象的形式存在的,在海德格尔那里是以存在与存在者的形式存在的。综观西方形而上学的整个发展过程,虽然有古典实在论与唯名论之争,以及后来的经验论与唯理论之争,但其实在性问题的基石仍然奠立在经验事物之上,古典实在论与唯理论所谈论的纯粹理智的、思维的对象好像远离经验事物,或与经验事物分属不同的领域(或世界),但它仍是由对经验事物进行逻辑推论和抽象概括而得出的。

这种由经验对象推论、概括出的实在性虽然不在经验世界里,但其基点仍然是经验对象。这一想法尽管和经验论者以感官对象为基础的思路不同甚或在一定程度上造成对立,但其最终所指向的对象是一致的。而本文所指出的“求善原

① 谢文郁,《自由与生存:西方思想史上的自由观追踪》,74。

则"和"拯救原则"之间的实在性则是完全对立的,因为在经验论者看来,拯救原则所揭示的"善一真理"只是一种可能性,且这种可能性转化成现实性的基础是信任情感,由此会令人生疑:这种可能性实现的程度有多大?我们还是回到奥古斯丁与佩拉纠的争论当中,看看到底应如何理解这种善观念及其实在性。奥古斯丁和佩拉纠的争论中所涉及的对象仅仅是信任情感所指向的对象:"骆驼穿过针的眼"(《马太福音》19:24),"有 12000 军团的天使为基督作战"(《马太福音》26:53),等等。我们在上面已经指出过,这种可能性的实在性没法从经验出发加以验证,它的可能性只存在于信任情感当中。基于此,我们"只能以可能性为出发点来看待,也就是说,它们发生的可能性是上帝恩典的结果,我们无法从经验的角度加以验证"[①]。换言之,当信任者产生这种情感时,这种善观念的实在性就实实在在地出现了,由此而产生的实在性虽然是由基督教的信任情感引发出来的一种谈论真理的方式,但其影响却不止于此,而是在以经验对象为主导的科学理性中也发挥了重要的作用。比如伽利略当年所做的斜塔实验,他所面对的压力是自亚里士多德以来的物体下降理论:重者快,轻者慢。在进行实验之前,他怀着一种强烈的信任情感,认为上帝所创造的这个世界是最圆满的,最圆满的东西是一定能用数学来揭示其规律的,所以就是在这种信任情感的驱使之下他最终发现了自由落体定律。这种由信任情感而引发的情怀对科学研究的影响,在牛顿那里也表现得很明显,当 1693 年剑桥大学校长本特雷博士问牛顿"如果这个世界是用这种重力的机械原理制造出来的,那么这和唯物主义有什么不同"时,牛顿回答道:"写作《原理》的目的,是向思索着的人们灌输上帝存在的信仰……重力可以使行星运动,然而没有神的力量就绝不能使它们作现在这样的绕太阳而转的圆周运动。因此,由于这个以及其他原因,我不得不把我们系统的结构归之于一个全智的主宰。""这最美丽的太阳、行星、彗星的系统,只能从一位智慧的与无所不能的神的计划与控制中产生出来。"[②]牛顿运用具体的数学、物理学原理及方法来解释自然现象是毫无疑问的,但背后支撑他预设了宇宙现象的完满、完美且必定能够被解释的是一种坚定的信念,因为在作出合理的解释之前他并不能预知其结果如何,只是凭着一种强烈的信念,这就是一种信任情感。在爱因斯坦那里,这种情感成了科学思维的原创力,他说:"我们所能有的最美好

① 贺方刚 He Fanggang,〈奥古斯丁"恩典一信仰"观的认识论困境〉[The Epistemological Dilemma of Augustine's "Grace-Faith" View],《甘肃社会科学》[Gansu Social Sciences],2014 年第 1 期[2014, Issue 1]。

② H. S. Thayer 塞耶编:《牛顿自然哲学著作选》[Newton's Philosophy of Nature Selections from His Writings],王福山 Wang Fushan 等译(上海[Shanghai]:上海人民出版社[Shanghai People's Publishing House],1974),62。

的经验是奥秘的经验，它是坚守在真正艺术和真正科学发源地上的基本感情。……我们认识到有某种为我们所不能洞察的东西存在，感觉到那种只能以最原始的形式为我们感受到的最深奥的理性和最灿烂的美——正是这种认识和这种情感构成了真正的宗教感情。”[①]当然，我们揭示信任情感对科学家的思维所产生的影响，并不是否认理性认识的作用，也不是说科学家在进行发现探索的过程中像普通信众那样陷入虔诚的敬拜祈恩，毕竟他们秉持的是和普通信众不同的一种情感，“这种宗教感情同普通人的不一样。……他的宗教感情所采取的形式是对自然规律的和谐所感到的狂喜的惊奇，因为这种和谐显示出这样一种高超的理性，同它相比，人类一切有系统的思想和行动都只是它的一种微不足道的反映”[②]。再比如在机械制造、桥梁建设等工程中，虽然有前人所进行的无数次试验，但对未来所建造的对象，经验并没有给出一点指示以说明以后的工程会成功，施工者只是凭着对以往经验和工程师的信任来开展面向未来的工作。

综上所述，实在性问题是形而上学中的一个核心问题，它构成了人类思维的基础。人类的知识和思维从经验开始是毫无疑问的，但并不唯一来源于经验[③]，其中逻辑所发挥的重要作用也是有目共睹的并引发了深入的讨论。但除此之外，信任情感也不容忽视，我们不能因为它由基督教哲学所引发而轻视、漠视之。对这一问题加以重视，不仅有助于我们更加科学合理地看待基督教的信任情感，而且也有助于我们揭示科学家的原创性思维中所包含的情感性因素，进一步厘清情感与理性、科学与宗教之间的关系。实际上，从人类心灵机能的统一性来看，它们二者同出自人类的思维能力，孕育于同一个母体之中，将二者割裂开来便于分析得更透彻，但综合起来亦是对其加以客观全面考察的必然。经验实在性侧重于经验和逻辑，这已为许多学科所证实并成为其必不可少的工具；信任情感的实在性则更多地倚重于情感，且由基督教哲学所提供，许多习惯于经验、逻辑思维者会觉得其有些陌生，但它对人类思维能力的贡献是不容忽视的。

---

① E. Ainstein 爱因斯坦，《爱因斯坦文集》(第 3 卷)[Einstein Collected Works (Volume III)]，许良英 Xu Liangying、赵中立 Zhao Zhongli 译(北京[Beijing]：商务印书馆[The Commercial Press]，1979)，45。

② 同上，283。

③ 康德早已指出，人类的知识除了经验外，还有先天的东西(康德用拉丁文 *a priori* 来表示，不同于中国哲学语境中的“先天”“天生”因素，强调逻辑在先；齐良骥先生认为，康德使用的“先天”概念既有逻辑在先的意思，也有时间在先之意)，如时空观、先天范畴、知性的先天原理等。参见 Kant 康德，《纯粹理性批判》[Critique of Pure Reason]，邓晓芒 Deng Xiaomang 译(北京[Beijing]：人民出版社[People's Publishing House]，2017)，导言Ⅱ、Ⅲ。康德在《判断力批判》中专门探讨人类的情感，不过主要是揭示审美情感的先天法则以及审美情感与目的论的关系，其在《实践理性批判》中的情感因素，尤其是将道德法则作为一个情感指向的对象，值得我们重视。参见贺方刚 He Fanggang，〈论康德的“敬重感”〉[On Kant's Respect Feeling]，《齐鲁学刊》[Qilu Journal]，2013 年第 4 期[2013，Issue 4]。

On the Metaphysical Foundations of Two Views of Truth: Experiential Reality and Believing-Sentiment Reality in Christianity

HE Fanggang

Abstract: As to the study of Metaphysics, people often pay attention to the dialectics and conflicts between two schools—empiricism and rationalism. Because they not only improve the development of the history of Western thought, but also become acceptable owing to their familiarity to the people. But the philosophical foundation of empiricism and rationalism lies in this mind function—"reason"—while the other mind function—"sentiment"—has often been ignored. The philosophical foundation put by sentiment plays an important role in all of the development of metaphysics; we must pay more attention to it. Sentiment, especially the reality effected by believing-sentiment, supplies another philosophical foundation differing from the experiential reality for the development of natural science and innovative creation. Pointing out this will be beneficial to improve the development of natural science.

Key Words: View of Truth, Metaphysical Foundation, Experiential Reality, Christianity, Believing-Sentiment Reality

容器破裂:奥兹克《斯德哥尔摩的弥赛亚》中的喀巴拉书写*

隋莹莹**

【摘要】美国著名犹太女作家辛西娅·奥兹克的作品体现了鲜明的犹太性,这种犹太性彰显了作者对当代美国犹太文化中犹太传统缺位所进行的深刻思考。奥兹克擅长使用犹太喀巴拉神秘主义意象表征传统的犹太主题,探究回归犹太传统的手段与形式,《斯德哥尔摩的弥赛亚》便是极佳的例证。本文从犹太喀巴拉神秘主义出发,以《斯德哥尔摩的弥赛亚》为例,剖析"炖锅"这一容器意象所蕴含的犹太喀巴拉神秘主义维度,探索奥兹克如何利用犹太喀巴拉神秘主义因子,言说其对美国主流文化的批判和对自身犹太文化的反思。"容器破裂"蕴含着强大的解构力量,能在某种程度上去除蕴含在美国主流文化中的偶像崇拜元素。奥兹克利用"容器破裂"旨在冲破美国主流文化的桎梏,回归并彰显犹太传统。

【关键词】辛西娅·奥兹克;《斯德哥尔摩的弥赛亚》;喀巴拉神秘主义;容器破裂;反偶像崇拜

引言

辛西娅·奥兹克(Cynthia Ozick)是美国著名犹太作家,曾获得1971年美国国家犹太图书奖。奥兹克出生于纽约,后移居至布朗克斯,是第二代美国犹太移民。童年经历对她日后的文学创作产生了不可忽视的影响。当她路过教堂时,被人叫作"杀害耶稣的刽子手"。作为犹太人,她以演唱圣诞歌为耻,却被同学无

* 本文受北京语言大学校级项目(17ZDJ09)资助(中央高校基本科研业务费专项资金)。

** 隋莹莹,中国人民大学博士生。

情嘲笑。多年后,奥兹克仍然认为这种创伤“永远无法完全修复”[①]。幸运的是,家人给予她极大的支持,她获得了精神力量。奥兹克的父亲是一位犹太学者,经常为女儿解读《塔木德》(*Talmud*)经文,朗读美丽的希伯来语文段。家族中浓厚的文学氛围为她的写作生涯奠定了基础。因其作品思想深沉,艺术凝聚力强,美国著名文学评论家丹尼尔·露丝(Daniel Rose)称其为“犹太人中的艾米莉·狄金森”。

与狄金森不同的是,奥兹克十分关注并思考自己的犹太人身份,且经常在作品中借犹太喀巴拉神秘主义因子书写犹太传统,如《普特梅塞故事集》(*The Puttermesser Papers*)和《斯德哥尔摩的弥赛亚》(*The Messiah of Stockholm*)。在这些作品中奥兹克描写了当代美国犹太传统所面临的危机,并试图提供维系犹太传统的契机与途径。《斯德哥尔摩的弥赛亚》(以下简称《弥赛亚》)便是极佳例证。《弥赛亚》的主人公拉尔斯是一名文学评论编辑,其所在的杂志社如同一个容器——“炖锅”(Stewpot)[②],那是一个由美国主流文学和公共娱乐主导的世界。因为鲜有读者关心他的周一专栏,他在杂志社中处在边缘地位,无人重视。他杜撰自己是著名波兰籍犹太作家布鲁诺·舒尔茨(Bruno Schultz)的遗腹子,试图寻找舒尔茨的遗作《弥赛亚》的手稿,以证明自己所研究的犹太文学的价值。

小说《弥赛亚》备受评论家青睐。国外学者对《弥赛亚》中的喀巴拉神秘主义维度尚未系统探究,但这一研究视角从未被忽视。学者米歇尔·格林斯坦(Michael Greenstein)致力于奥兹克审美艺术研究,他认为主人公拉尔斯的世界是“奥兹克创作的一个喀巴拉式的世界”[③]。斯蒂文·卡茨(Steven Katz)从修辞学角度出发探究了喀巴拉神秘语言论对奥兹克创作的影响,认为“《弥赛亚》中的文学语言可被称为上帝之言”[④]。伊莲·柯娃(Elaine Kauvar)强调《弥赛亚》是“一场有关文学先驱的辩论,一种关于写作本身的思考”[⑤]。上述研究都与本文所讨论的喀巴拉神秘主义思想相关,但这些研究只是把神秘主义当作研究背景

---

① Elaine Kauva, *Cynthia Ozick's Fiction: Tradition and Invention* (Bloomington: Indiana University Press, 1993), 385.

② “炖锅”在原著中为 Stewpot,本文将其译为“炖锅”。炖锅指的是一种炊具,炖锅类食物是各种食物的大杂烩,包括各类蔬菜和食物的混合。炖锅类美食不仅仅是一种食物,也具有文化内涵,暗示着人口和文化等的多元化特征。本文中的炖锅,指的是主人公拉尔斯工作的杂志社,它如同一个充斥着美国主流文学作品的大炖锅。

③ Michael Greenstein, “The Muse and the Messiah: Cynthia Ozick's Aesthetics,” *Studies in American Jewish Literature* 8 (Spring 1989): 59.

④ Steven Katz, “The Epistemology of the Kabbalah: Toward a Jewish Philosophy of Rhetoric,” *Rhetoric Society Quarterly* 25 (Annual Edition 1995): 107.

⑤ Elaine Kauva, *Cynthia Ozick's Fiction: Tradition and Invention*, 6.

简要提及,并没有深刻挖掘《弥赛亚》中的喀巴拉内涵,也没有阐明喀巴拉神秘主义和反偶像崇拜主题之间的联系。国内尚无将犹太喀巴拉神秘主义思想与《弥赛亚》结合研究的先例,未发现《弥赛亚》具有犹太喀巴拉神秘主义的维度。本文从神秘主义角度出发,挖掘奥兹克的喀巴拉神秘主义书写,剖析"容器破裂"(Shevirah)的内涵,揭示文本中的"容器破裂"意象与反偶像崇拜主题之间的关系,展示奥兹克如何以犹太传统中的反偶像崇拜精神诊治当下美国社会弊病。

一、奥兹克与喀巴拉神秘主义

喀巴拉(Kabbalah)是希伯来语(קבל)的音译,意为"传统"(tradition)或"接受"(reception)。犹太喀巴拉神秘主义思想家肖勒姆(Gershom Scholem),将其解读为"传统之教义"[①]。犹太喀巴拉神秘主义者认为,上帝在传授给摩西成文律法的同时,也将一些不能以书面形式记录下来的口传律法传授给他,这些口传律法成为喀巴拉神秘主义的源头。喀巴拉主义者的任务是通过研究上帝口传律法,探索有限性与无限性、内在性与超越性合一的途径,从而在这一过程中重塑犹太传统并实现救赎。当生活中的某些现象暂时无法通过人类理性来获得合理解释时,人们往往诉诸神秘主义的方式进行思考。此外,喀巴拉不仅是简单的自省,更是一种身份认同层面的追求,"通过自我反省,喀巴拉主义者寻求自我的统一和超越,以加深对最高生活秩序的理解"[②]。喀巴拉提供了一种维系与上帝关系的方式,这种关系跨越了任何媒介,是一种具有直接性的联系,"所有对上帝的认识都是建立在一种上帝与造物的关系上"[③]。喀巴拉神秘主义者试图与上帝所彰显出来的诸多属性进行直接沟通,通过探究人与上帝关系来接受神圣传统。在某种意义上,他们尽力缩小上帝与人类沟通的鸿沟,将此视为终身事业。喀巴拉主义者认为,宇宙的演变就其本质而言,是一种回归的过程,人类需要回溯创世,思考前伊甸园时期的原始状态,因为在这一状态中,人类无需任何媒介便可与上帝直接交流,领受没有携带原罪的传统。喀巴拉神秘主义并不能简单地理解为一种宗教流派思想,它具有明显的跨界性质,是犹太人认识世界、阐释世界的重要途径,也超越了犹太宗教语境对文学批评和文学写作产生影响。一方面,

---

① G. G. Scholem 索伦,《犹太教神秘主义主流》[Major Trends in Jewish Mysticism],涂笑非 Tu Xiaofei 译(成都[Chengdu]:四川人民出版社[Sichuan People's Publishing House],2003),1。

② 陈影 Chen Ying,〈认识批判序言中的喀巴拉思想解读〉[A Kabbalistic Interpretation of Walter Benjamin's "Epistemo-Critical Prologue"],《外国文学评论》[Foreign Literature Review],2019 年第 3 期[2019, Issue 3],37。

③ 索伦,《犹太教神秘主义主流》,11。

喀巴拉神秘主义对文学批评观产生内在影响，甚至已经内化成为一种思维模式。美国著名评论家哈罗德·布鲁姆(Harold Bloom)将喀巴拉视为“一种书写理论”，他认为，喀巴拉“除了对思维中的创造直接描述外，更为展示诗的影响生成的过程提供最佳范例，为充满疑问的诠释之路提供一种图示”[①]。另一方面，喀巴拉神秘主义中的意象直接为作家提供创作资源，D.H.劳伦斯、叶芝、乔伊斯等人作品中都蕴含着喀巴拉神秘主义的意象。奥兹克的《普特梅塞故事集》中的“戈伦”(Golem)和《弥赛亚》中的“容器破裂”都是直接取材于犹太神秘主义意象。

“容器破裂”与奥兹克所珍视的作家想象力密切相关，她本人也与犹太喀巴拉神秘主义之间有很深的渊源。1980 年，奥兹克拜访了肖勒姆，她在此次谈话中明确了犹太喀巴教神秘主义对宗教和文学的影响，她认为作家“会不由自主地沉迷于神秘的宗教”，认为肖勒姆对喀巴拉的诠释“决定了人们审视自我与看待世界的方式”[②]。奥兹克意识到喀巴拉喷泉般的活力，并将喀巴拉视为“一个增殖系统，象征性地描述了创世与启示”[③]。她认为，喀巴拉神秘主义激发了作家的想象力，为理解犹太传统价值观提供了新的视角，“肖勒姆对喀巴拉的重新解读，使理性犹太教能重振神话和神秘主义的血统，并以众泉喷涌之活力焕发了宗教想象力”[④]。换言之，喀巴拉与人的想象力息息相关，而作家需要想象力来进行文学创作。奥兹克一生都在用富含想象力的方式讲述犹太故事，“容器破裂”正是想象力在其作品中的重要载体，喀巴拉隐喻的“火花点燃了奥兹克的想象力”[⑤]。

以撒·卢里亚(Isaac Luria)在前人经典著作的细枝末节中，创造性地发展了一些概念。“容器破裂”是卢里亚喀巴拉(Lurianic Kabbalah)理论中的一个关键术语，是创世过程中的重要一环。要把握容器破裂的内涵，首先要将其置于上帝创世的语境中来考察。上帝创世过程为：第一步是神光收缩、回归(Tsimtsum)，第二步是容器破裂，第三步是修补(Tikkun)。创世的第一步是否定，即上帝的收缩、回归，这是一种带有辩证性的否定，是一种以退为进的智慧，因为“上帝的收缩过程使宇宙的存在成为可能”，“如果没有一切，上帝将如何从无到有创造世界”。[⑥]创世之前，神光无处不在，到处是上帝的在场，没有多余的空间来进行创造，因此

① Harold Bloom, *Kabbalah and Criticism* (New York: Bloomsbury Press, 1975), 25.
② Cynthia Ozick, *Art and Ardor* (New York: Alfred A. Knopf Inc, 1983), 139.
③ 同上，135。
④ 同上，139。
⑤ 同上，139。
⑥ 索伦，《犹太教神秘主义主流》，11。

上帝不得不舍弃自身一部分,为原始世界腾出空间。创世本身是减少、收缩,而不是增加、繁殖。创世过程并非总是向前发展。相反,其运行机制是双向的,即“每一个新的散发和表现都会先出现集中和缩回”①。因此,神光收缩使创世成为可能。神光收缩之后,需要一个空间(或曰容器)来保存神光。但是当神光注入容器时,上帝之光过于强大,容器的外壳(Kelipah)无法承受神光涌入,发生破裂,外壳的碎片四散而去,这是创世的第二步。在容器破裂之后,神光的一部分回到了上帝自身,也有一部分附着于四散的碎片落于物质世界。“容器破裂之后,便进入神光流溢和创造的其他阶段;一切都以某种方式破裂,一切都有缺陷,一切都没有完成。”②既然缺陷存在,就有继续创造的必要。“容器破裂的概念表达了这样的一个观点,即在世界建造完成并变得完美之前,上帝最初的创造必须被彻底改造甚至摧毁。”③容器的碎片携带着一部分神光坠入原始空间,此刻进入创世第三步,人类寻找神光的碎片,进行容器“修补”。可见,在神光收缩→容器破裂→神光修补这一过程中,容器破裂是创世的关键阶段。

容器破裂是一个动态概念,其内涵随时间推移不断丰富。如前文所述,在前人启发下,卢里亚发展了这一概念的内涵。而肖勒姆在《犹太教神秘主义主流》(*Major Trends in Jewish Mysticism*)等作品中将其进一步深化。他认为,“就像种子破裂以发芽开花,头一批的碗必须打碎,以便圣光、宇宙的种子起它的作用”④。在创世过程中,容器破裂是上帝更新自身的重要一环,它象征着创造和新生。现代犹太喀巴拉神秘主义研究学者德罗布(Sanford Drob)在《喀巴拉符号:哲学与心理学视角》(*Symbols of the Kabbalah: Philosophical and Psychological Perspectives*)和《喀巴拉和后现代主义》(*Kabbalah and Postmodernism*)两部作品中继续对其进行现代和后现代行诠释。在他看来,“容器破裂是一种破坏行为,也是一种创造行为”⑤。换言之,容器破裂本身携带辩证维度:一方面,容器破裂破坏了原先的创造,带来了危机,产生了灾难性的后果;另一方面,装满神光的容器破碎,意味着上帝进行下一个创造的开始。这体现了创世神话中矛盾与统一的辩证规律。德布罗还指出,“容器破裂瓦解了各种权威,使我们敞开胸襟,接受新的可能性”⑥。容器破裂是“对我们的所处的文明世界的结构的挑战”⑦。容器破裂象征着对权

① 索伦,《犹太教神秘主义主流》,255。
② 同上,113。
③ Sanford Drob, *Kabbalah and Postmodernism* (New York: Peter Lang Publishing Inc, 2009), 93.
④ 索伦,《犹太教神秘主义主流》,262。
⑤ Sanford Drob, *Kabbalah and Postmodernism*, 31.
⑥ 同上,103。
⑦ 同上,297。

威的质疑，通过其中所蕴含的毁坏力量，鼓励着人们挑战权威、打破权威；容器破裂提供了一种建立完美世界的可能性，暗示着可推翻绝对价值和秩序的旧系统，迎接新世界的到来。容器破裂所蕴含的毁坏力量，鼓励人们挑战权威。对于美国犹太人来说，容器破裂中蕴含的反权威精神，鼓励其冲破美国主流文化的束缚，积极拓展本民族文化发展道路的可能性。

二、作为容器意象的“炖锅”

“按卢里亚的说法，上帝被迫放弃自身中的一部分，为世界让出空间，一种神秘的原始空间，上帝退出是为了在创造和启示的行动中再回来，这是 En-sof，无限的存在的首次行动。”[①]容器，作为承载神光的器皿，是上帝或者说无限者本体(En-sof)借以体现自身的工具。喀巴拉学者德罗布以卢里亚喀巴拉思想中对容器破裂的解读为基础，进一步丰富了容器的内涵，扩大了容器破裂神学内涵的适用范围。“容器，其功能是一种包含作用的器皿(containers)，是一种使某种文明成为可能的结构(structure)。”[②]在《弥赛亚》中，作为容器意象的“炖锅”是一个重复出现的线索，它不仅与故事情节的走向息息相关，也反映着主人公拉尔斯所处世界的本质——炖锅是一种具有“包含”作用的结构。这一结构有两个特点：无处不在性与封闭性。

作为一种无处不在的结构，具有封闭性的炖锅束缚着拉尔斯，使其无法逃离。拉尔斯把工作的编辑部想象成“炖锅”。这是一个文学世界，人物的一切活动都与文学相关。“斯德哥尔摩秋日的天空，半透明的黄昏开始降临，笼罩整个椭圆状的、空气潮湿的小城，如同一个鸡蛋壳保护着蓝黑色的鸡蛋黄。”[③]此处展现了拉尔斯的压抑之感，因为炖锅被一层坚硬的外壳所保护，炖锅这一容器不是开放的，而是封闭的。学者露丝(Elisabeth Rose)认为这是“对神秘主义的公开参考”[④]。喀巴拉神秘主义认为上帝是无限的。假如上帝向人们揭示关于自身的知识，其自身能够以某种确定的方式被认知，那么上帝便成为有限性的上帝。而在喀巴拉的思想中，神是无限的，能通过神光收缩、容器破裂、容器修补的过程无限地给人以启示。喀巴拉思想中的宇宙演变与人类历史的演进具有同一性，

① 索伦，《犹太教神秘主义主流》，254—255。

② Sanford Drob, *Symbols of the Kabbalah: Philosophical and Psychological Perspectives* (Maryland: Jason Aronson Inc, 1999), 296.

③ Cynthia Ozick, *The Messiah of Stockholm* (New York: Alfred A. Knopf Inc, 1987), 9.

④ Elisabeth Rose, "Cynthia Ozick's Liturgical Postmodernism: *The Messiah of Stockholm*," *Studies in American Jewish Literature* 1 (September 1981): 94.

承载神光的容器势必破裂，因为空间有限的容器无法承载无限的上帝。炖锅是承载美国主流文化的容器，人们在有限的文化空间内，所以犹太文化为了发展必须突破空间的有限性。主人公工作的杂志社编辑部是美国主流文化盛行的犹太社区的缩影。拉尔斯所在的杂志，刊登着美国名人的娱乐八卦，致力于推广美国的生活方式。他尽量不与其他人交流，但是他没有打字机，"与加纳和安德斯不同，拉尔斯没有工作单间，这可能因为他的周一专栏总是那么默默无名……他通常在周日的晚上十点出现在公司。如果安德斯不在，他通常就用安德斯办公室的打字机，或者加纳不在，他则用加纳的"①。在与别人共享打字机的过程中，"打字机将他与炖锅联系在一起"②。炖锅，是一个外壳坚硬的容器，将拉尔斯困在其中。拉尔斯的研究方向不受欢迎，经常受到其他主流文学编辑的冷嘲热讽，其专栏之所以鲜有人问津，是因为犹太知识分子被束缚在美国主流文化统治的容器中，逐渐被同化。大多数犹太人不再关注犹太文学与文化，而是选择美国主流文化与文学为崇拜对象。

在容器炖锅内部——犹太传统被边缘化的世界中，主流文化试图将边缘性的、异质性的文化收编、纳入自己结构内。"炖锅正在沸腾"③，这暗示着主流文化欣欣向荣。然而，这种生命力并不属于拉尔斯，因为拉尔斯是个"被捕的灵魂""被推离赛道的人"，"属于别处"④。在炖锅这一容器中，拉尔斯是一个被边缘化的人，生活中没有亲人，工作中被人孤立。其他畅销文学评论编辑都拥有属于自己的火热的专栏日，而"拉尔斯总是困在周一"⑤。因为周一的专栏无足轻重，开始上班的读者困意重重，鲜少注意他的专栏；而周一之外的专栏，比如说加纳的美国文学和安德斯的娱乐轶事，备受读者欢迎。这暗示着读者对美国文学主流文化的追捧，而犹太传统被忽视，被边缘化"在犹太人生活的某些时刻，如家庭聚会、婚礼和葬礼上，记住并强调它已经很不容易了"⑥。面对犹太传统正遭遇危机的社会现实，奥兹克的危机意识激发其进行文学创作，她试图"通过小说来重建集体记忆"⑦。在《弥赛亚》中，拉尔斯正是通过打破美国主流文化的容器的方

---

① Cynthia Ozick, *The Messiah of Stockholm*, 9.

② 同上，6。

③ 同上，62。

④ Cynthia Ozick, *Art and Ardor*, 234.

⑤ Cynthia Ozick, *The Messiah of Stockholm*, 2.

⑥ Samuel Heilman, *Portrait of American Jews: The Last Half of the 20th Century* (Seattle: University of Washington Press, 1995), 66.

⑦ Peter Kerry Powers, "Disruptive Memories: Cynthia Ozick, Assimilation and the Invented Past," *MELUS* 3 (Autumn1995): 80.

式,希望以犹太文学的力量改变犹太文化被边缘化的地位,繁荣犹太文化,唤醒犹太人对传统的记忆。在某种程度上,拉尔斯这一人物身上有着奥兹克的影子,因为在现实中奥兹克本人也希望诉诸写作的力量,回归犹太传统。她在演讲中曾说:"我们的声音似乎很遥远,但是如果我们选择全人类而不是犹太人,那么我们的声音将完全消失。"①由此可见,奥兹克认为犹太人应该勇敢发声,繁荣犹太文化。"作为犹太人,我是一个自学者。"②自学者意味着犹太人必须自觉保持犹太身份,因为保持犹太人的身份是避免犹太文化消亡的方法。面临犹太文化被边缘化的现状,奥兹克利用容器破裂中蕴含的反权威力量,警示犹太人应该继承犹太传统。

容器破裂意味着向某一封闭性的结构提出挑战。喀巴拉神秘主义将上帝创世或世界演化与历史进程同一,试图将上帝创世的历史纳入一种有规律的体系中。上帝通过"收缩""回归"为创世腾出空间,通过"容器破裂"完善自身,通过"修补"回到原初创造的起点。"卢里亚喀巴拉因以'无限者''收缩'和'容器破裂'三种否定力量,产生解构所有绝对价值、教条和偶像的效果。"③喀巴拉上帝创世的进程的启发是,人类的历史演进也需要容器破裂这一创造性的行动。如果只是将某一文明、文化当成一种崇拜的对象,那么一方面异质文明和文化将被边缘化;另一方面会导致陷入教条主义、思想僵化的误区。在炖锅这一容器内,异质性的犹太文化被边缘化,美国主流文化盛行,成为部分犹太人崇拜的偶像。

三、反偶像崇拜主题的回归与深化

在奥兹克的喀巴拉神秘主义书写中,主人公拉尔斯生活的炖锅容器内充斥着偶像崇拜的现象,而容器破裂这一意象的使用达到了反对偶像崇拜的效果。

作为犹太文学中最流行的主题之一,反偶像崇拜具有深刻内涵。"一神论的真正特性在于对偶像崇拜的否定。"④反偶像崇拜是保持犹太教特性的重要一环。"相信不相信或遵守不遵守犹太人与上帝所立的契约,对犹太人来说是赖以生存的大事情,抑或说是检验犹太人信教与背教的试金石。"⑤上帝与摩西之约、

① Cynthia Ozick, "We Ignoble Savages," *Evergreen Review* 3 (November 1995): 90.

② 同上,150。

③ Sanford Drob, *Kabbalah and Postmodernism*, 93.

④ Leora Batnitzky, *Idolatry and Representation* (Princeton: Princeton University Press, 2000), 35.

⑤ 傅勇 Fu Yong,〈"契约观":美国犹太小说的潜结构〉[The Concept of "Covenant": On the Substructure of American-Jewish Fiction],《汕头大学学报(人文社会科学版)》[Journal of Shantou University (Humanities & Social Sciences Edition)], 2014 年第 5 期[2014, Issue 5], 31。

上帝与亚伯拉罕之约都强调了反偶像崇拜。摩西十诫警示不可偶像崇拜,“你不可有其他的神”反映了犹太教中一神崇拜的思想。[①] 亚伯拉罕之父他拉因雕刻木制神像而受到上帝的惩罚,亚伯拉罕摔碎异教神像,尊上帝为唯一的神。这是《旧约》中有最早关于偶像崇拜与反偶像崇拜的记录。另外,“拜金牛犊”的故事也警示人们偶像崇拜的严重后果。西奈山下,以色列人制造金牛犊,违背上帝律法,遭到上帝的击杀,付出沉重代价。更重要的是,犹太人身份的定义来源于与上帝的契约,因为“在神学范畴内,从相反的方向去描述,是最能行之有效抑或最简明扼要地定义犹太人的方法:犹太人是避免偶像的群体,是最不应该期待成为他拉——塑造偶像者——的群体”[②]。犹太人想维持与上帝的关系,就必须牢记上帝之言,并在日常生活中遵守律法。可见,反偶像崇拜已然成为一种道德伦理。“道德一神教信仰激励着文化建构。”[③]反偶像崇拜引导犹太人保持民族特色,构建独特的民族文化。“《希伯来圣经》中有关于神观的特征是无像崇拜(aniconicworship),一切神像皆禁止作为对耶和华之崇拜。”[④]犹太人的独特性在于其在任何环境下都能坚持与上帝的契约,杜绝偶像崇拜。一旦违反了偶像崇拜这一律法,也就不再有唯一的神之说。而犹太人的历史也证明,这种内化于犹太人日常生活中的反偶像崇拜思想,已然成为犹太人流失家园情况下避免被其他文化同化、保持民族特性的有效工具。

《弥赛亚》中的偶像崇拜具体表现为炖锅内部对美国主流文化的崇拜。这种偶像崇拜的根源,是西方文化统治之下犹太信仰的缺失和犹太文化的缺位。大屠杀的阴霾尚未消失,部分犹太人怀疑自身信仰,而移民美国后异教文化渗透到他们的日常生活中,他们便以美国主流文化为崇拜对象。文本展现了部分犹太人移民美国后崇拜美国主流文化的社会现象。“拉尔斯的风格十分纯粹,而加纳恰恰相反,他是完全的美国风格。加纳喜欢一切美国性的东西,包括他们的人造芝士。每次去纽约旅行他都会带六磅的维尔维塔牌芝士当作礼物送给妻子。”[⑤]加纳便是一个崇拜偶像的例子,他将美国主流文化视为潮流,因受其熏陶而沾沾

---

① 《圣经》(中英文和合本)[The Bible: In Chinese and English(Chinese Union Version)](上海[Shanghai]:中国基督教三自爱国运动委员会[National Committee of Three-Self Patriotic Movement of the Protestant Churches in China],2017),6。

② Cynthia Ozick, *Art and Ardor*, 234.

③ Leora Batnitzky, *Idolatry and Representation*, 11.

④ 李炽昌 Archie LEE,〈《希伯来圣经》中的无像的神和中国的神像宗教〉[The Aniconic God and Chinese Iconolatry],收录于《犹太研究》(第14辑)[Jewish Studies (14)],傅有德 Fu Youde 主编(济南[Jinan]:山东大学出版社[Shangdong University Press],2016),3。

⑤ Cynthia Ozick, *The Messiah of Stockholm*, 2.

自喜。“奥兹克强调犹太教中的‘契约观’，一方面说明她对犹太教‘契约’精神一往情深，坚持犹太传统中最根本的东西；另一方面，她也在强调犹太人的道德责任而非偶像崇拜。”[①]偶像崇拜和反偶像崇拜之间的斗争从未停止，人们应该时刻提醒自己不要违反法律并制造偶像。“奥兹克在一个充满基督教世俗价值观的社会中，为维护犹太教和犹太文化而努力。”[②]由此可见，奥兹克从未忘记作为一个犹太作家的责任，一直在写作中践行犹太传统。

奥兹克利用犹太神秘主义中的容器破裂意象对传统反偶像崇拜主题进行了现代、后现代诠释。后现代思想的一个重要的特征是，打破曾经使世界变得有意义的思想和结构，使原有的不可侵犯的基础发生破裂。“容器破裂”这一观念的内涵与后现代主义精神中的“基础的破坏”是一致的。而“容器破裂”中对“基础的破坏”这一内涵，赋予拉尔斯击碎偶像的能力，达到了反偶像崇拜的效果。再者，德布罗也注意到了后现代思想与犹太神秘主义之间的关联。“据卢里亚喀巴拉学派，容器破裂是一种对船舱甲板的清理、一种崭新的开始、一种对现有的我们所处的文明生活结构的挑战。”换言之，喀巴拉神秘主义中的“容器破裂”蕴含着强大的解构力量。“容器破裂”这一意象进一步成为奥兹克在《弥赛亚》这一文本中书写反偶像崇拜主题的有力工具。主人公拉尔斯用“容器破裂”来表达自身的文化诉求，试图打破美国主流文化的偶像，回归犹太传统，引起人们对犹太传统的关注。拉尔斯打破容器的尝试具体体现为反抗他所在的杂志社中盛行的对美国主流文化的崇拜思想。拉尔斯经常受到公司内的畅销文学专栏作者的嘲讽。他声称自己是著名犹太作家舒尔茨的儿子，坚信一旦找到舒尔茨的遗作手稿，就不仅能够证明身份，从而使自己所做的研究在“炖锅”这个世界里有一席之地，还能重振父亲在文坛的声望，“他的父亲生来就是作家名人堂中的一员——拉格洛芙、史努克·哈姆生、托马斯·曼……这份冗长的获奖者的名单。他的父亲如果仍然在世的话会拿到这份大奖——这是不言自明的事实。”[③]这份名单中的作家都曾赢得当年的诺贝尔文学奖，拉尔斯认为舒尔茨也应在名单之列，于是他将全部身心投入搜索舒尔茨的遗作中。拉尔斯为打破容器采取了一种疯狂的尝试，他杜撰身份以证明自己所推崇的犹太文学的重要性。容器破裂代表着我们所处的世界中的基础的价值观念被置换、被打碎，它们的碎片四散，在打破容器之后人类通过重组碎片，抛弃旧的僵化的思想，迎接新生与进步。无论容器是否破裂甚至被毁坏，无论基础是否被打碎，这种正在努力打碎它的勇气是具有积

① 傅勇，〈“契约观”：美国犹太小说的潜结构〉，31。

② Sanford Drob, *Symbols of the Kabbalah: Philosophical and Psychological Perspectives*, 1.

③ Cynthia Ozick, *The Messiah of Stockholm*, 2.

极意义的。拉尔斯希望利用犹太文学与文化作为唤醒犹太同胞的武器,尝试打破炖锅所代表的偶像。在此,奥兹克用小说戏剧性的方式表现了拉尔斯的反偶像崇拜精神。容器破裂也是一种"替代力量"①。在奥兹克所处的时代,有许多作家并不关心犹太人的传统。他们经常关心美国主流社会的问题,而忽略了自己的文化,逐渐被美国主流文化所同化。奥兹克赋予拉尔斯一种置换或替代的能力。拉尔斯对犹太作家舒尔茨作品的复兴着迷,源于对犹太文化的热爱和对犹太身份的追求,他尝试着以犹太文学与文化置换美国主流文学与文化,改变犹太文化被边缘化的地位,其价值选择鼓励他努力打破以西方主流价值观的为本质的偶像。

关于犹太喀巴拉思想与后现代精神的在《弥赛亚》这一作品中的互动,其中缘由在奥兹克的后现代艺术中可见端倪,因为奥兹克被称为美国犹太后现代主义的代言人。学者露丝认为:"后现代主义成为表现奥兹克艺术性的最完美的工具。"②后现代思潮"反对用单一的、固定不变的逻辑、公式和原则以及普适的规律来说明和统治世界,主张变革和创新,强调开放性和多元性,承认并容忍差异"③。奥兹克也曾公开表达了对多样性和差异性的尊重,她曾对文学的目的作出以下总结:"拒绝'普遍的'模糊性;去区分一个人相比于另一个人的生活的差异性;去照亮多样性;去言明最小生命单位的生命的存在;去展现一个实实在在的个体相较于他人的特殊性;在其令人惊诧的特质中,言说最小生命单位的独特的生命圣洁性。"④因此,我们可以看出奥兹克尊重差异性和特殊性,反对世界具有同一性、一致性和中心性的话语。在《弥赛亚》中,奥兹克对容器破裂的书写颇具后现代意味,拉尔斯为了打碎炖锅作了一系列的尝试,只有炖锅破裂之后拉尔斯才能摆脱束。炖锅这一意象代表着犹太喀巴拉神秘主义中的容器,暗示着只有新的事物才有被创造出来的空间和可能性,暗示着只有原先统一的、普遍适用的模式被抛弃,事物的多样性才能显现出来。这正是容器破裂内涵的体现。基于此,喀巴拉传统中的容器破裂这一核心概念所蕴含的破除权威、打破僵化现状的维度,也与后现代思潮的内涵达成了契合,二者都体现了对权威的质疑。奥兹克对容器破裂的后现代式书写,是对现有价值体系的质疑,旨在以容器破裂的破坏力量和颠覆力量粉碎权威,创造一个多元异质的世界。

---

① Cynthia Ozick, *Art and Ardor*, 234.

② Elisabeth Rose, "Cynthia Ozick's Liturgical Postmodernism: *The Messiah of Stockholm*," 106.

③ 陈世丹 Chen Shidan,《美国后现代主义小说详解》[A Study of American Postmodernist Fiction](天津[Tianjin]:南开大学出版社[Nankai University Press],2010), 106。

④ Cynthia Ozick, *Art and Ardor*, 234.

结语

容器破裂是犹太喀巴拉神秘主义中的关键概念之一。在《弥赛亚》中，炖锅实则为犹太喀巴拉神秘主义中的容器，作者奥兹克利用容器破裂这一意象来反抗美国主流文化，回归并彰显犹太传统。西方现代语境中犹太传统的缺位激发了奥兹克对反偶像崇拜主题的书写动力，奥兹克将蕴含着反权威力量的容器破裂视为反偶像崇拜的工具，旨在以犹太传统中的反偶像崇拜精神诊治当下社会弊病。奥兹克利用犹太喀巴拉神秘主义对传统反偶像崇拜主题进行了后现代诠释，试图冲破美国主流文化的桎梏，倡导实现个体犹太性的回归，彰显了对犹太文化未来的关注，深化了反偶像崇拜主题。犹太喀巴拉神秘主义意象为奥兹克的反对偶像崇拜提供了创作题材，点燃了奥兹克的文学想象力，深化了其作品主题。奥兹克为犹太作家的身份而感到自豪，她呼吁犹太人坚持犹太律法，珍惜祖先遗留的精神财富，避免偶像崇拜。奥兹克用文学创作与任何形式的偶像崇拜作斗争，以高超的艺术技巧，成熟地驾驭了美国犹太文学传统主题，赢得了文学界的赞誉。

参考文献

(一)中文参考文献

1.陈世丹,《美国后现代主义小说详解》,天津:南开大学出版社,2010。

2.[德]索伦,《犹太教神秘主义主流》,涂笑非译,成都:四川人民出版社,2003。

3.陈影,《认识批判序言中的喀巴拉思想解读》,《外国文学评论》,2019 年第 3 期。

4.傅勇,《"契约观":美国犹太小说的潜结构》,《汕头大学学报》(人文社会科学版),2014 年第 5 期。

5.李炽昌,《〈希伯来圣经〉中的无像的神和中国的神像宗教》,《犹太研究》,2016 年第 14 辑。

6.《圣经》(中英文和合本),上海:中国基督教三自爱国运动委员会,2017。

(二)外文参考文献

1.Cynthia Ozick, *Art and Ardor* (New York: Alfred A. Knopf Inc, 1983).

2.Cynthia Ozick, *The Messiah of Stockholm* (New York: Alfred A. Knopf Inc, 1987).

3. Cynthia Ozick, "We Ignoble Savages," *Evergreen Review* 3 (November 1995).

4. Elaine Kauva, *Cynthia Ozick's Fiction: Tradition and Invention* (Bloomington: Indiana University Press, 1993).

5. Elisabeth Rose, "Cynthia Ozick's Liturgical Postmodernism: *The Messiah of Stockholm*," *Studies in American Jewish Literature* 1 (September 1981).

6. Harold Bloom, *Kabbalah and Criticism* (New York: Bloomsbury Press, 1975).

7. Leora Batnitzky, *Idolatry and Representation* (Princeton: Princeton University Press, 2000).

8. Michael Greenstein, "The Muse and the Messiah: Cynthia Ozick's Aesthetics," *Studies in American Jewish Literature* 8 (Spring 1989).

9. Peter Kerry Powers, "Disruptive Memories: Cynthia Ozick, Assimilation and the Invented Past," *MELUS* 3 (Autumn 1995).

10. Samuel Heilman, *Portrait of American Jews: The Last Half of the 20th Century* (Seattle: University of Washington Press, 1995).

11. Sanford Drob, *Kabbalah and Postmodernism* (New York: Peter Lang Publishing Inc, 2009).

12. Sanford Drob, *Symbols of the Kabbalah: Philosophical and Psychological Perspectives* (Maryland: Jason Aronson Inc, 1999).

13. Steven Katz, "The Epistemology of the Kabbalah: Toward a Jewish Philosophy of Rhetoric," *Rhetoric Society Quarterly* 25 (Annual Edition 1995).

Shevirah: On the Kabbalistic Writing in Ozick's *The Messiah of Stockholm*

SUI Yingying

Abstract: Cynthia Ozick, a famous American Jewish female writer, focuses on the distinctive Jewishness in her works, which demonstrates her deep thinking about the absence of Jewish tradition in the modern Western context. Ozick excels at representing traditional Jewish themes by using the mystical image and explores the means of returning to Jewish tradition in this writing process. *The Messiah of Stockholm* is a perfect illustration concerning this point. From the perspective of Jewish Kabbalistic mysticism, this paper takes *The Messiah of Stockholm* as an example to analyze the mystical dimension of "Stewpot" so that it explores how Ozick makes use of Jewish mysticism element to air her rebellion against mainstream American culture and her reflection on her own Jewish culture. With its deconstructive power, Shevirah can to some extent remove the idolatry elements contained in the mainstream American culture. With the aid of Shevirah, Ozick aims to shatter the shackles of mainstream American culture and achieve the goal to inherit the Jewish tradition and maintain the identity of Jewishness.

Key Words: Cynthia Ozick, *The Messiah of Stockholm*, Kabbalistic Mysticism, Shevirah, Anti-Idolatry

陨落的方舟：莫里斯·威廉犹太难民移华计划探析*

王宵飞**

【摘要】1939年，国民政府面临着内外交困的局面：国内日寇铁蹄侵略大江南北，国军连连败退；国外求助无援，反被苛责抗日决心不足。为了改善国际形象，争取国际援助，国民政府计划将深受迫害的欧洲犹太人移民中国西南，这一计划得到了许多国外有识之士的关注和称赞，纷纷为国民政府出谋划策。在此历史背景下，活跃在美国政坛上的犹太裔牙医莫里斯·威廉博士向国民政府提出了自己的犹太难民移华计划，得到了国民政府的青睐。莫里斯·威廉计划自德国纳粹迫害犹太人伊始构想，中国全面抗战时期正式提出，但最终由于美国政府的不支持、中国的现实战争困境和威廉个人的过于理想化而流产。莫里斯·威廉计划虽然失败了，但通过对该计划系统的考察，可以证明近代中国对深陷囹圄的犹太民族抱有同情、援助之心，具有国际人道主义精神、国际责任担当感和扶助弱小民族的历史关怀，契合当代构建人类命运共同体的现实主题。

【关键词】莫里斯·威廉计划；犹太难民；抗日战争；中犹民族交往；人类命运共同体

犹太经典著作《塔木德》(*Talmud*)在讲述"什么是真正的朋友"时写道："一个忠实的朋友是一个安全的庇护所，谁找到这样一个朋友，谁就找到了财宝。"①对于20世纪30年代流亡中国的犹太难民而言，中国是一个得以庇护身家性命的圣所，中华民族是犹太民族患难与共的真朋友。中国人民的接纳使欧洲犹太

* 本文受中央民族大学研究生科研实践项目(SZKY2022079)资助。

** 王宵飞，中央民族大学历史文化学院硕士研究生。

① Senia塞妮亚编译，《塔木德》[Talmud](昆明[Kunming]：云南人民出版社[Yunnan People's Publishing House],2006),105。

难民获得了生存的希望,也使大量为了民族未来夙兴夜寐的犹太精英看到了民族复兴的新曙光,莫里斯·威廉(Maurice William)正是其中之一。威廉博士是美国的一位犹太裔牙医,不仅在美国犹太政治圈有着重要地位,在华也具有重要影响力。孙中山先生是威廉思想上的挚友,曾从其著作《历史的社会解释》(*The Social Interpretation of History*)一书中汲取大量思想智慧,完善了他的"三民主义"思想体系。《改变世界历史的牙医》("The Dentist Who Changed World History")一文评价威廉时称:"即使他没有改变世界历史,但至少影响了中国的历史进程。"[①]威廉以对华友好而著称。抗日战争期间,他曾担任美国医药助华会(the American Bureau of Medical Aid to China)主席、秘书和美国援华联合会筹款委员会(the Fundraising Committee of the United Council for Civilian Relief in China)会长。[②] 早在1934年,威廉在与爱因斯坦(Albert Einstein)的通信中就提出了"为德国犹太人在中国寻找新家"的构想[③],1935他更是以国民党驻美东支部宣传部股长的身份撰文宣传中国是解决世界问题的关键[④]。纳粹党大规模迫害犹太人后,威廉加紧制订了他的犹太难民移华计划。

当前关于二战来华犹太难民的研究,学界成果颇丰,主要集中于犹太难民在华生活、就业和文化交流等方面。[⑤] 涉及国民政府对犹太难民政策的研究,也有数篇论文问世,主要关注的是孙科计划、龙云计划、白尔克拉斯计划(the Jakob

① "The Dentist Who Changed World History", https://www.international.ucla.edu/china/MauriceWilliamsArchives/bio,上网日期:2022年11月9日。该文与《哈珀杂志》(*Harper's Magazine*)1943年12月的一篇文章同名。

② 关于威廉身份的记载,参见 *History of the American Bureau for Medical Aid to China* (New York: ABMAC, 1954), Columbia archives, https://indianamemory.contentdm.oclc.org/digital/collection/WMIC/id/1694,上网日期:2022年11月9日;D1.014, ABMAC Bulletin for November 1941, Volume III, No. 10, 6, https://www.international.ucla.edu/media/files/D1.014.pdf, 上网日期:2022年11月9日。

③ 参见 A7.001, *Letter from William to Dr. Albert Einstein regarding the relocation of German-Jews to China*, 1/30/1934.Maurice Williams Archives, https://www.international.ucla.edu/media/files/A7.001.pdf,上网日期:2022年11月10日。

④ 参见 D3.008, *China: The Key to World Problems?* 10/1935. Maurice Williams Archives, https://www.international.ucla.edu/media/files/D3.008.pdf,上网日期:2022年11月9日。

⑤ 关于二战来华犹太难民的研究的代表作参见潘光 Panguang,《犹太人在中国》[Jews in China](北京[Beijing]:五洲传播出版社[Intercontinental communication center],2003);潘光 Panguang,《艰苦岁月的难忘记忆:来华犹太难民回忆录(1933—1945)》[Jewish Refugees Memoirs: Their Experiencein Wartime China](北京[Beijing]:时事出版社[Current Affairs Press],2015);王健 Wangjian,《逃亡与拯救:二战中的犹太难民与上海》[Escape and Rescue: Jewish Refugees and Shanghai in World War II](上海[Shanghai]:上海交通大学出版社[Shanghai Jiao Tong University Press],2016)。

Berglas Plan)。[①] 遗憾的是,相关研究过于依赖国内的档案资料,缺乏国外史料的补充佐证。更遗憾的是,莫里斯·威廉计划尚未有国内学者关注,而该计划的重要性丝毫不亚于其他三个计划。相比于白尔克拉斯计划,该计划虽同样缺乏翔实的国内史料,但国外资料较为丰富,亦有国外学者关注。[②] 鉴此,本文试图基于加州大学洛杉矶分校中国研究中心的莫里斯·威廉档案(The Maurice Williams Archives-UCLA Center for Chinese Studies)、台湾地区国民政府档案,并结合美国的在线解密档案和相关中外文研究文献来厘清该计划的历史脉络,分析该计划失败的原因。

一、莫里斯·威廉计划提出的背景

20 世纪 20 年代,欧洲反犹主义出现了新的特点,即法西斯主义盛行背景下的反犹主义与反共主义相结合,欧洲对犹太人的迫害在 30 年代迎来了大高潮。德国成为反犹主义的急先锋和大本营,纳粹党党魁希特勒在其自传《我的奋斗》(*My Stuggle*)中写道:"雅利安人最大的对立面就是犹太人。""要是犹太人靠马克思主义信条战胜了世界人民,那么这顶胜利的桂冠将是全人类的坟墓,而后地球就会像数百万年前一样再次变得荒无人烟在太空中翱翔……所以,现在我确

---

① 关于国民政府对犹太难民政策的研究论文代表作,参见刘亦实 Liu Yishin,〈在大西南安置犹太人计划的幕后〉[Behind the scenes of the Jewish Resettlement program in the Great Southwest],《文史月刊》[Historical Monthly],2002 年第 10 期[2002, Issue 10];殷昭鲁 Yin Zhaolu,赵飞飞 Zhao Feifei,〈抗战时期国民政府计划容留 10 万犹太难民始末〉[During the Anti-Japanese War, the National Government Planned to Accommodate 100,000 Jewish Refugees],《文史月刊》[Historical Monthly],2007 年第 2 期[2007,Issue 2];曹晓飞 Cao Xiaofei,〈云南:犹太难民的希望之乡〉[Yunnan: The hometown of Hope for the Jewish Refugees],《云南行政学院学报》[Journal of Yunnan University of Administration],2007 年第 3 期[2007, Issue 3];吴鹏 Wu Peng,〈云南犹太难民安置计划探析〉[A Study on the Resettlement Plan for the Jewish Refugees in Yunnan Province],《昆明学院学报》[Journal of Kunming University],2016 年第 5 期[2016,Issue 5];杨智友 Yang zhiyou,〈档案揭秘:二战前夕,国民政府曾筹划在云南为犹太人开设避难特区〉[Archives Disclosure: On the Eve of World War II, the Chinese Nationalist Government Planned to Open Special Shelters for Jews in Yunnan],《云南档案》[Yunnan Archives],2017 年第 4 期[2017,Issue 4];姚江鸿 Yao Jianghong,〈抗战初期国民政府对犹太人的关注与处置〉[In the Early Days of the Anti-Japanese War, the National Government Paid Close Attention to and Disposed of the Jews],《社会科学研究》[Social Science Research],2018 年第 6 期[2018,Issue 6]。

② 汉学家 Tiberiu Weisz 在"Shanghai Jews:The Berglas Plan"一文中简单提到了莫里斯·威廉计划;北卡大学威尔明顿分校的 Gao Bei 教授在著作"Shanghai Sanctuary: Chinese and Japanese Policy toward European Jewish Refugees during World War II"的第二章(2011 年已作为论文"The Chinese Nationalist Government's Policy toward European Jewish Refugees during World War II"发表)涉及莫里斯·威廉计划。

信要遵循万能上帝的意愿抵抗犹太人，为上帝的事业而奋斗。”[①]1933 年希特勒执掌德国大权后，公然宣称，现在是人类历史上的“关键时刻”，自由资本主义已经分崩离析，“犹太一布尔什维克主义”正在策划征服欧洲和全世界，作为“优良种族”的雅利安人，必须通过“永久性的革命”来消灭犹太人及其马克思主义，以争取更多的“生存空间”。[②] 随后，纳粹政府实行大规模排犹政策，党卫军强迫犹太人离开德国，却不允许他们携带自己的财产。至 1939 年，约一半德国犹太人，共计 30 万人，身无分文地离开了德国。[③] 1938 年 3 月，德国吞并奥地利。同年 11 月 7 日，犹太青年赫舍尔·格林斯潘(Herschel Grynszpan)刺杀了德国驻巴黎外交官恩斯特·冯·拉特(Ernst vom Rath)。纳粹政府以此为由掀起了更大规模的排犹浪潮。刺杀事件发生两天后，德国、奥地利和捷克斯洛伐克的苏台德地区爆发了针对犹太人的“水晶之夜”[④]暴乱，其间 177 个犹太教堂被毁，无数犹太商店和企业被洗劫和烧毁，死伤的犹太人不计其数，4 万犹太人被抓进集中营，无数犹太家庭支离破碎，数以百万计犹太人不得不走上流亡他乡的道路。[⑤]德国闪击波兰之后，又造成了大量的欧洲犹太难民。雪上加霜的是，此时欧洲犹太人逃出欧洲愈加困难，因为他们难以获得外国的入境许可。许多犹太难民的首选避难目的地是犹太人口众多的美国，但美国接收的犹太人数量有限且附有严苛条件，难民们必须等待移民配额的增加，有时长达一年甚至更久，而纳粹的迫害却迫在眉睫。

1938 年的埃维昂会议(the Evian Conference)上，西方各国均对接纳犹太难民态度冷漠。当西方世界集体抛弃绝望的犹太人时，中国上海成为犹太难民出乎意料的“诺亚方舟”，犹太难民能够获得前往上海的签证，并且不需要缴纳任何保证金。自 30 年代前期德国大规模排犹开始，反对法西斯暴行、帮助犹太难民成为中国自民间至政府的共识。对于纳粹针对犹太人的迫害活动，中国人民予以严正谴责，各类中文报刊纷纷撰文声援欧洲犹太人，抗议纳粹党的反犹暴行。当大批的犹太难民来到上海时，上海群众给予了他们无私的帮助，号召为难民捐

---

① Adolph Hitler 阿道夫·希特勒，《我的奋斗》[My Struggle]，王诚 Wang Cheng 译(新加坡[Singapore]：南洋出版社[Nanyang Press]，2016)，230、51。

② 参见潘光 Pan Guang，《犹太研究在中国三十年回顾：1978—2008》[The Thirty Years' Review of Jewish Studies in China：1978-2008](上海[Shanghai]：上海社会科学院出版社[Shanghai Academy of Social Sciences Press]，2008)，106。

③ 参见 John S. Conway, "The Holocaust and the Historians," *The Annals of the American Academy of Political and Social Science* 450 (1980)：153-164。

④ 德文原文为 Kristallnacht，中文又译作“玻璃破碎之夜”。

⑤ 参见 John S. Conway, "The Holocaust and the Historians," 159。

款捐物，帮助其共渡难关。相比于民间扶助弱小民族的纯粹感情，国民政府对欧洲犹太难民的态度则比较矛盾复杂：一方面是此时的中国正处于战火之中，日本法西斯使中华大地生灵涂炭，中华民族自身岌岌可危，援助犹太人势必会加重政府负担，还会招致欧洲法西斯国家的敌对；另一方面则是犹太人在西方尤其是美国具有举足轻重的影响力，救助犹太人是国民政府树立良好国际形象、获得更多国际援助的一个重要渠道。此外，救助犹太人也有利于中国获得大量犹太人精英的帮助来支持国防建设和社会发展。早在 1933 年，蒋介石电讯兵工署署长俞大维军用化学工厂事宜时，便要求每月出资十万元招聘犹太人中的化学人才来帮助生产。[①] 抗战初期国民政府军队节节败退，武汉会战之后更是疲于应战，西方媒体普遍认为国民政府是一个消极抗战、无法保护人民的政权，不值得同情和援助。随着日寇侵略范围的扩大，国军军费开支的大幅增加，民间要求抗战到底的呼声也越来越高。国民政府不得不考虑救助犹太难民以改善国际形象，获取更多国际援助。在这种历史背景下，莫里斯·威廉提出了自己的犹太难民移华计划，得到了国民政府的青睐。

二、莫里斯·威廉计划的出台

(一)计划的雏形

20 世纪 30 年代，莫里斯·威廉一直关注欧洲同胞的悲惨命运，为他们摆脱纳粹囹圄之境而在政界奔走呼号。在欧美主要资本主义国家不肯对犹太人施加援手之际，大批犹太难民逃往中国上海，他看到了欧洲犹太人生存的希望。一份关于提议中国向德国犹太技工开放国门的备忘录更是吸引了威廉的注意，备忘录建议国民政府利用希特勒排犹的契机大规模引进德国犹太技工，犹太人会感恩中国的善举，日后致力于中国建设。中国驻华盛顿大使施肇基也对犹太技术人员来华表示欢迎，他保证凡是由美国犹太人支持的以向中国输送德国犹太技工为目的活动都会得到他的全心支持。一旦相关计划成熟，他将向国民政府强烈推荐，以此作为中国获得发展的一个特殊机会。[②] 备忘录和施肇基大使的保证给了威廉很大希望，认为犹太人大规模移民中国具有很大现实性和可操作性。

---

① 《巩固国防(四)》，台北“国史馆”，数位典藏号：002-090102-00004-125，1。https://ahonline.drnh.gov.tw/index.php?act=Display/image/2402937PYVzoFk#a3J，上网日期：2022 年 11 月 12 日。

② D3.013, *Proposal for China to Open up to German-Jewish Technicians Fleeing from the Hitler Regime*, Undated. Maurice Williams Archives, https://www.international.ucla.edu/media/files/D3.013.pdf.上网日期：2022 年 11 月 12 日。

1933 年 12 月,威廉写信给埃米尔·希尔布(Emil Hilb)[①],表明德国犹太人此刻正处于危难之中,他希望利用自己在华的威望来保护犹太人的利益,认为犹太人移华无论对中国人还是对犹太人来说都是双赢。[②] 次年 1 月,希尔布在回信中赞同了他的想法,并表示已经与爱因斯坦讨论了该想法的可行性和存在的问题。[③] 通过希布尔作为中间人,威廉迫不及待地与爱因斯坦取得了联系。他告诉爱因斯坦中国驻华盛顿大使施肇基欢迎犹太人来华,还在信中透露,他已经与美国最高法院的法官路易斯·布兰代斯(Louis Brandeis),教育学家、哲学家约翰·杜威(John Dewey),哥伦比亚大学历史学教授、国际劳工组织创始人詹姆斯·肖特维尔(James T. Shotwell)进一步讨论了这个想法,并得出结论:"中国是希特勒受害者们的最大希望,我们应尽其所能地利用在华(拯救犹太人)的机会。"[④]在 2 月给威廉的回信中,爱因斯坦对威廉的计划大加赞赏,认为这是一个充满希望和具有可行性的方案,但是他对中国是否能够给犹太人提供充足的就业机会表示怀疑,为此,他建议由美国犹太人基金会出资调查犹太人移民中国的可能性。[⑤] 4 月 4 日,威廉在给华纳兄弟影业集团总裁秘书露比·马克斯(Ruby Marks)女士的信中进一步提出了帮助犹太难民移华的构想,他写道:"我相信我本人对帮助在华的犹太人有一些用武之地。碰巧,在帮助犹太人在华有一个新的开始的过程中,我也乐意为中国效劳,因为中国需要那些被希特勒驱逐的拥有丰富经验的聪明犹太技工。"[⑥]同日,他去信给友人哈里·戈德堡(Harry A. Goldberg)博士,在解释他的计划能够给中国带来什么回报时,威廉认为这是一个既能解决德国犹太人问题又能处理中国问题的一箭双雕的好办法,"历史的

---

① 莫里斯·威廉档案馆收录数篇威廉与此人的通信,但具体身份不详。

② A11.002, *Letterfrom William to Hilb regarding the plight of the German-Jews*, 12/6/1933. Maurice Williams Archives, https://www.international.ucla.edu/media/files/A11.002.pdf. 上网日期:2022 年 11 月 11 日。

③ A11.003, *Letter from Hilb instructing William to send a letter to Einstein regarding his ideas on the relocation of German-Jews*, 1/22/1934. Maurice Williams Archives, https://www.international.ucla.edu/media/files/A11.003.pdf.上网日期:2022 年 11 月 11 日。

④ A7.001, *Letter from William to Dr. Albert Einstein regarding the relocation of German-Jews to China*, 1/30/1934. Maurice Williams Archives, https://www.international.ucla.edu/media/files/A7.001.pdf. 上网日期:2022 年 11 月 12 日。

⑤ A7.002, *Reply from Einstein regarding the possibility of William's plan*, 2/13/1934. Maurice Williams Archives, https://www.international.ucla.edu/media/files/A7.002.pdf. 上网日期:2022 年 11 月 12 日。

⑥ A13.002, *Follow-up letter from William regarding his efforts to relocate German-Jews to China*, 4/4/1934.Maurice Williams Archives, https://www.international.ucla.edu/media/files/A13.002.pdf. 上网日期:2022 年 11 月 12 日。

轮回这次将在中国上演，与历史上美国和犹太民族间的互帮互助、投桃报李如出一辙，中国帮助犹太人未来将会获得类似的结果”[①]。至此，莫里斯·威廉犹太难民移华计划已初具雏形，计划的核心思想是中国收留无家可归的犹太难民，犹太人为中国建设提供相应的服务。威廉很清楚，他曾经在中国的声誉为他赢得了中国人民的尊重，他愿意利用在华的人脉关系为受难的犹太同胞服务。[②] 包括爱因斯坦在内的诸多犹太领袖对威廉的移民计划纷纷表示支持，希望威廉进一步完善该计划。

（二）游说中国外交官与国民政府对外宣传的转向

1939 年前，中德关系处于蜜月期，国民政府不希望因为犹太人问题惹恼德国人，威廉没有机会直接向国民政府兜售他的移民计划，于是把重点放在了游说国民政府外交官员身上。1934 年，威廉与中国驻华盛顿大使施肇基探讨了犹太难民移华的初步计划，施肇基对威廉计划十分感兴趣，并表示中国“愿意”接受那些遭受希特勒迫害非自愿离开德国的犹太人。与施肇基的交流无疑给了威廉极大的信心，他立即将这一好消息告诉了爱因斯坦，并表示他已经与施肇基大使探讨了许多关于犹太难民移华的细节。[③] 然而，施肇基是否将威廉的初步计划转告国民政府不得而知，后续也再无证据证明大使对该计划有过更多的过问。1936 年，时任中国驻美大使王正廷帮助威廉加入中国国民党，使其成为唯一一位非华裔的美籍国民党党员。[④] 王正廷热衷慈善事业，同情欧洲犹太人的悲惨遭遇，他的另一重身份是中国红十字会会长，自 1934 年起，担任该职长达十余年。美国医药助华会自成立就与中国红十字会交接捐赠工作，长期担任该会高级官员的威廉与王正廷公务往来颇多，私交也甚密。1937 年的国联大会和《九国公约》签字国会议对日本侵华采取了姑息态度，抗日战争必不可免地爆发了。王正廷在美国的工作重点也从争取国际干预转移到了力争美国对华援助上。在这个问题上，王正廷采取了两条腿走路的方法：一面对美国国会和各政要进行游说，力争能在政策上给予中国最大的支持；一面积极向美国民间进行宣传，争取

① A10.002, *Letter from William explaining his thoughts on the relocation of German-Jews to China*, 4/4/1934. Maurice Williams Archives, https://www.international.ucla.edu/ccs/MauriceWilliamsArchives/correspondence.上网日期：2022 年 11 月 12 日。

② Gao Bei, *Shanghai Sanctuary: Chinese and Japanese Policy toward European Jewish Refugees during World War II* (New York: Oxford University Press, 2013),41.

③ 莫里斯·威廉档案馆的 A7.001 文件记载了威廉与施肇基大使探讨犹太难民的过程。除此文件外，笔者再无找到相关资料证明二人有更深入的沟通。

④ D3.011, *Essay by Maurice Zolotow regarding William, originally printed in Harper's Magazine*, 12/1943. Maurice Williams Archives, https://www.international.ucla.edu/media/files/D3.011.pdf.上网日期：2022 年 1 月 12 日。

民间力量的支持，转而能影响美国政府的决策。[①] 在威廉的影响和游说下，王正廷相信中国只要帮助犹太人就能够得到美国犹太财团的经济援助，于是他向国民政府提出援助德国犹太人的建议，但是被国民政府拒绝。究其原因，王正廷在自己的回忆录中给出了答案，他表示自己早些时候曾向国民政府提出过援助德国犹太难民的问题，然而，国民政府认为不应该得罪德国，所以他没有进一步提出这一意见。[②]

暂时的失败并没有使莫里斯・威廉气馁，他在等待时机使国民政府能够接受他的计划。1939 年，由于战事吃紧，来华犹太难民日益增多，问题频发，更重要的是此时德国已经完全倒向了日本一边。美国驻华代办佩克(Peck)在给国务卿赫尔(Hull)的外交文件中说："中国的经济部长黄文浩抱怨德国外交大臣里宾特洛甫(Ribbentrop)表现得非常亲日，德国拒绝为中国提供制成完备的军事武器，但只有这样的装备才能在中国组装使用。蒋介石也十分反感纳粹政府对中国的政策，因为德国撤出了所有在华的德国军事顾问。"[③]另外，早在前一年，陶德曼调停失败后，德国便承认了伪满政权，不再对华军售和培训中国军队。于是，国民政府决定不再顾虑德国人的感受，着手解决犹太难民问题。立法院院长孙科筹划在中国西南省份安置犹太难民，其理由：一是遵从总理遗教，扶助弱小民族；二是援助犹太人，可以增进英国一般民众对我国之同情，且英国的远东政策实取决于在远东之巨商与银行家，而此巨商与银行家以犹太人为多；其三是此案实施之后，能获得美国一般人民之好感；其四是犹太人财力丰盈，人才尤多，若能结其好感得其协助，实为我国莫大之臂助。该计划还明确表示，因为犹太难民生活困苦，度日艰难，有必要在职业介绍上给予帮助。[④] 值得注意的是，这一时期，国民政府出台在西南省份安置犹太人的计划主要是为了解决无国籍的犹太人问题，因为此时在华的犹太难民除了少数无国籍的白俄犹太人外，都保留着原国籍。他们所属的一些国家在中国仍然享有领事管辖权，

---

① 参见毛庆根 Mao Qinggen,《中国奥运之父：王正廷传》[The Father of China's Olympic Games: The Biography of Wang Zhengting]（杭州[Hangzhou]：浙江大学出版社[Zhejiang University Press]，2012)，485。

② 参见 Gao Bei, *Shanghai Sanctuary: Chinese and Japanese Policy toward European Jewish Refugees during World War II*, 42。

③ The Chargé in China (Peck) to the Secretary of State, March 28, FRUS, 1939, The Far East, Volume III, pp. 662-663, https://history.state.gov/historicaldocuments/frus1939v03/d624. 上网日期：2022 年 11 月 12 日。

④ 《犹太人移居西南边案》，台北"国史馆"，数位典藏号：014-020500-0030，10—11。https://ahonline.drnh.gov.tw/index.php? act=Display/image/2398430blbPLl2#HC8e，上网日期：2022 年 11 月 12 日。

如果允许他们在内地居住，国民政府难以对他们行使行政管辖权。在有国籍的难民中，德籍犹太人数量较多，德国虽然在一战后丧失了在华的领事裁判权，并且按照德国1935年公民法规定，这些犹太人早已被剥夺国籍，“非阿里安人（雅利安人），不得为德公民”[①]，但如果此时收留安置德籍犹太难民，在中德关系严重恶化的背景下，国民政府极有可能在外交上因为犹太人问题被纳粹政府指摘，处于被动的地位，德国也会变成中国的敌人，甚至会以“护侨”为由联合日本干涉中国内政。鉴于这种情况，国民政府优先考虑安置无国籍犹太难民。这种做法在当时来看无疑是最为明智的，因为它既没有得罪以德国为首的原籍国的外交顾虑，也不妨碍国民政府对进入内地的犹太难民进行管理。

国民政府也开始对外宣传拯救犹太难民的计划。1939年，在谈及国际宣传问题时，国民政府外交部记载：“最近德大使馆秘书康培曾以闻有此项提议，来部表示意见……至于扶助弱小民族一点，素以拥有殖民地之英法所不喜闻，在此有求于该两国时期，似亦不便加以宣传，免致引起该两国不快。”[②]因此，国民政府将宣传的重点放在人道主义与贫穷救济上，宣传的对象侧重于犹太人口众多的美国，争取美国的国际援助。国民政府的宣传策略是成功的，在国际社会上引起了剧烈的轰动，欧洲战事大规模爆发后，大量外逃的犹太人选择避难中国，至1941年上海犹太人难民数量已达2.5万人之多。[③] 美国政府此时也开始关注在华的犹太难民问题。上海总领事高斯（Gauss）在给国务卿赫尔（Hull）的机密文件中写道：“来自欧洲的大量贫困犹太难民的涌入，导致上海市议会要求外国领事代表通过有关组织和航运公司采取措施防止此类难民进一步涌入，因为上海已经无法应对严重的难民问题，并且社区或市政当局无法为大量难民提供住宿和生计。”[④]高斯建议提醒各国政府注意上海的局势，并建议欧洲犹太人委员会立即采取紧急行动，向上海犹太人委员会提供大量资金，以支持已经到达和继续抵达的难民。

① 《德将颁公民法犹太人与非阿里安人不得为德公民》，台北“国史馆”，数位典藏号：002-080200-00451-001，1。https://ahonline.drnh.gov.tw/index.php? act＝Display/image/2507560jEhzgf0#8al.上网日期：2022年11月13日。阿里安人即雅利安人。

② 《犹太人移居西南边案》，台北“国史馆”，数位典藏号：014-020500-0030，28—29。https://ahonline.drnh.gov.tw/index.php? act＝Display/image/2398430blbPLl2#vHic，上网日期：2022年11月13日。

③ 潘光，《犹太研究在中国三十年回顾：1978—2008》，243。

④ The Consul General at Shanghai (Gauss) to the Secretary of State, January 3, 1939, FRUS, 1939, GENERAL, THE BRITISH COMMONWEALTH AND EUROPE, VOLUME II, Document 37, p.56. https://history.state.gov/historicaldocuments/frus1939v02/d37.上网日期：2022年11月13日。

(三)计划的完善出台与国民政府的回应

德裔犹太富商白尔克拉斯最先响应国民政府的移民计划,他于1939年5月前往重庆,游说国民政府高层,提出了自己的移民计划:"(甲)拟准十万犹太人移住中国内地,中国政府予以保护;(乙)不论职业、阶级,中国政府当在各方面尽量予以援助;(丙)移来犹太人编纳入中国经济之内。"具体办法规定:每一移民到达中国前应向指定银行缴交英金五十镑保证金。① 急缺外汇的国民政府对保证金一项非常感兴趣,但是日后白尔克拉斯与国民政府谈及保证金问题时,国民政府将金额提升至英金二百镑,白尔克拉斯却表示保证金应该用于移民运输、饮食和创办工业,资金由合办银行掌控。② 言下之意是这笔钱取之犹太人,尽数用于犹太人。此外,国防最高委员会对该计划进行审查后认为十万人的规模远远超出了国民政府的计划人数,该计划也没有交代清楚移民的国籍问题,在地点上明确选择内地也与原来规定的通商口岸有出入。审查处还认为由犹太人组织运输公司有垄断之忧。最后,审查的结论为:"此事所关甚大,似有作详尽考虑之必要,不能遂予准许。"③出于这些原因,国民政府搁置了该计划。

1938年9月,胡适正式接任中国驻美大使一职,他也是美国医药援华互助会的成员,一直关注在华犹太人问题,同样希望借助救助犹太人的契机争取美国犹太人团体的对华援助。在1939年中国对美宣传拯救犹太难民之后,莫里斯·威廉与胡适取得了联系,向他询问国民政府关于犹太人移华的具体政策。5月6日,胡适将国民政府制订的犹太人寄居区计划的英译本转发给威廉。④ 可以肯定的是,威廉对国民政府的移民计划非常感兴趣,他希望能够投入美国资金开发中国西南诸省,以此解决之前与爱因斯坦通信时所担心的犹太人在华就业问题。据1939年12月19日的国民政府军事委员会电报称,威廉曾于5月30日去信给国民政府,提出开发中国西南地区的建议,投资规模约一千万美元。该电报记载:"旅美华侨李泰初、陈称美、犹太资方波绯氏及威廉氏愿供给技士、资本在华西察勘煤油、石油,发展电、钢铁等重工业及变换产品。本年五月卅日犹资方由威廉氏领衔函国府贡献意见:(一)派员来华商洽投资方式与程序;(二)费用统由

---

① 《犹太人移居西南边案》,台北"国史馆",数位典藏号:014-020500-0030 ,78—79。https://ahonline.drnh.gov.tw/index.php? act=Display/image/2398430blbPLl2#yLgt.上网日期:2022年11月14日。

② 同上,97。

③ 姚江鸿,《抗战初期国民政府对犹太人的关注与处置》,163。

④ 《划定犹太人寄居区域》,台北"国史馆",数位典藏号:020-070900-0062,54。https://ahonline.drnh.gov.tw/index.php? act=Display/image/2515595PR==seb#PVM9.上网日期:2022年11月16日。

资方承担;(三)请勿对外发表。”[①]5 月 31 日,威廉致电胡适解释他的完整计划,作为对国民政府贡献意见的补充。第一,中国人和犹太人都是侵略战争的受害者,应该精诚合作,相互援助。德国犹太人可以向中国提供科学技术上的培训、工商业经验、技术和资本。在提出这个问题时,威廉特别强调,德国犹太人并不是孤立无援的,他们能够得到世界犹太人尤其是美国犹太人的支持,他们将给中国带来各国犹太人的善意。第二,美国犹太人能够对中国的抗日战争提供帮助。中国未来将是一个巨大的市场,现在美国却将它拱手让给日本。不过,威廉相信美国的犹太人可以发出强有力的声音,使美国援助中国,制裁日本。作为回报,他希望国民政府能够邀请美国犹太人代表到中国调查建立犹太人定居点的可能性。为此,威廉提出了三个建议:(1) 美国犹太人派遣可靠的代表赴华与中国领导人洽谈移民问题并考察在华安置犹太难民的实际可能性;(2) 调查将由美国人自费进行;(3) 代表回国后将向美国犹太人组织述职。此项活动不会有任何形式的宣传。第三,美国是世界上犹太人口最多的国家,富有的美国犹太人为海外救济提供的资金也是最多的。然而,用于救济的资金只是治标不治本,不能一劳永逸地解决犹太难民问题,只有中国的安置计划才能提供建设性的解决方案。如果该计划能够成功,它将对中国的经济发展产生积极影响,也将对美国公众产生刺激性的影响,公众舆论最终可以促使美国援助中国的抗战。[②]

如前所述,国民政府出于行政管理、外交的顾虑,安置计划考虑的对象主要是无国籍的犹太人,而威廉计划首要解决的则是在华德籍犹太人的安置问题。对此,威廉给出了自己的解决方案。6 月 5 日,胡适向外交部转呈威廉计划时补充了威廉的方案,即“至领事裁判权问题,则因德国人已失去此项权利,德国犹太人当无享受可能亦愿逐渐入中国籍”[③]。在行政院讨论划区域安置犹太难民问题期间,威廉又于 6 月 27 日及 7 月 11 日先后函陈国民政府询问关于犹太人移民中国的情况。7 月 3 日,威廉在给王正廷的信中透露,美国红十字会主席诺曼 · 戴维斯(Norman H. Davis)十分支持他的犹太难民移华计划,并鼓励他尽快实施。威廉还通过美国犹太人协会和美国医药助华会为他的计划发起了一次

① 《犹太人移居西南边案》,台北“国史馆”,数位典藏号:014-020500-0030,193。https://ahonline.drnh.gov.tw/index.php? act=Display/image/2398430blbPLl2#Jztn.上网日期:2022 年 11 月 16 日。

② 《划定犹太人寄居区域》,台北“国史馆”,数位典藏号:020-070900-0062,49—53。https://ahonline.drnh.gov.tw/index.php? act=Display/image/2515595PR==seb#Nz29. 上网日期:2022 年 11 月 16 日。

③ 同上,54。

全国性的募捐活动,目前已经筹集到了一万五千美元的经费。[①] 王正廷立刻将此消息转达外交部。7 月 21 日,外交部发函给王正廷,称先前胡适寄送的莫里斯·威廉计划书已在部内讨论,关于此事,孙科院长提议于先,他建议将行政院院长孔祥熙审查白尔克拉斯计划时签署的意见作为附件发送威廉。附件大概内容是中央召集与移民有关系的各部开会讨论,因领事裁判权及内地杂居问题影响重大,决定对有国籍犹太人入境及居留可照现行条约办理,不必特定方法,无国籍犹太人则给予入境之便利。职业介绍方面,中国本着人道主义观念将在可能范围内特予协助,实施办法正在筹划中。[②] 行政院于 8 月 9 日去信给威廉,内容如下:"台端本年六月二十七日及七月十一日先后函陈关于犹太人移植中国一案,兹奉院长谕嘱转告:如旅美犹太人代表自费来华考察我国境内将来移植为德所逐之犹太难民情形,我政府表示欢迎。即希登照。又关于台端所论及之白尔克拉斯氏建议计划,本院原已定有办法,兹抄附英译本以借参考。"[③]在信中,行政院向威廉表示国民政府欢迎任何来自美国的代表前往中国实地考察犹太人移民的可能性,满足了威廉计划派代表考察中国的请求。这反映出国民党高层非常希望能够与美国犹太人领袖进行沟通,以获得美国政府的支持,但将针对白尔克拉斯计划的"定有办法"的英译本抄附,又从侧面反映了国民政府不希望得罪德国的心理。同日,行政院又函复威廉表示愿意接受"彼等准备投资一千万美金等语",对内则宣称"此事既经行政院函复有案,希即查案签复候核为要中正效侍秘渝"。[④] 可见国民政府对待威廉来信极度重视,将行政院对威廉的函复作为高级别机密文件记录在案,查看时需要蒋介石的秘谕批准,完全遵守威廉"请勿对外发表"的要求。

三、莫里斯·威廉计划的流产及其原因

日本在中国的军事侵略咄咄逼人,打破了美国一直主张的门户开放政策,1939 年 1 月,派克在致赫尔的外交文件中表示:"日本当局坚持认为,目前的情况只是'一段时间内'不允许第三国船只使用(中国的)主要港口,从而断然拒绝

---

① 《划定犹太人寄居区域》,台北"国史馆",数位典藏号:020-070900-0062,101。https://ahonline.drnh.gov.tw/index.php? act=Display/image/2515595PR==seb#ldkg. 上网日期:2022 年 11 月 16 日。

② 同上,111。

③ 《犹太人移居西南边案》,台北"国史馆",数位典藏号:014-020500-0030,195。https://ahonline.drnh.gov.tw/index.php? act=Display/image/2398430blbPLl2#uCmn. 上网日期:2022 年 11 月 16 日。

④ 同上,193。

了美国大使馆关于采取步骤恢复美国公司在华进行合法自由贸易的请求。”[①]日本挑战美国在华商业利益引起了美国的极大反感，美国政府对日本提出了强烈抗议，但收效甚微。1939 年 7 月 26 日，忍无可忍的美国政府通知日本，将终止 1911 年的《美日商业条约》。[②] 美国的这种政治反应对中国产生了巨大的影响。蒋介石认为它代表着美国与日本决裂的开始，缓解了中国极其危急的局面，这将使中国取得抗战胜利成为定局。[③] 同年 11 月，美国国会修改了 1937 年《中立法案》中的禁运条款，取而代之的是“现款自运”，但罗斯福总统仍没有说服国会授权他改变政府的中立政策和对日禁运战略物资。

威廉相信罗斯福总统会在援华抗日的过程中认识到推动中美关系进一步发展的机会，于是他将犹太难民移华计划带到国务院，试图以个人名义将该计划转达给国务院。1939 年 8 月 31 日，国务院欧洲司的罗伯特·佩尔(Robert T.Pell)会见了威廉，威廉详细解释了他的计划，希望国务院能够向总统积极推荐他的计划。然而，佩尔建议威廉应该先与总统咨询委员会取得联系，随后为威廉开了介绍信。尽管威廉在 1939 年 10 月 31 日自豪地告诉爱因斯坦，他与国民政府关于犹太难民移华的谈判非常成功，但并没有提及美国总统咨询委员会是否响应了他的计划。[④] 此后，无论是中方资料还是美方资料，都没有找到关于威廉犹太难民移华计划有进一步推进的相关记录。莫里斯·威廉计划和孙科计划、白尔克拉斯计划一样，都走向了失败的宿命，但其背后失败的原因值得思考。

首先，缺乏美国政府的支持是该计划失败的重要原因。一方面，20 世纪 30 年代美国深陷经济危机之中，国内孤立主义倾向严重，美国民众既普遍反对修改移民法增加移民数量，又反对动用美国财政来救济海外的犹太难民，因为犹太移民会挤占本来就为数不多的就业机会和各种社会资源，救济海外犹太难民会加重国内税收。另一方面，1940 年的总统选举迫在眉睫，罗斯福不能忽视公众支

---

① The Chargé in China (Peck) to the Secretary of State, January 17, 1939 ,*FRUS*, 1939, The Far East, Volume III, Document 318. https://history.state.gov/historicaldocuments/frus1939v03/d318. 上网日期:2022 年 11 月 18 日。

② Memorandum by the Assistant Secretary of State (Sayre) of a Conversation With the Counselor of the Japanese Embassy (Suma), July 26, 1939, *FRUS*, 1939, THE FAR EAST, VOLUME III, Document 531, 560. https://history. state. gov/historicaldocuments/frus1939v03/d531. 上网日期:2022 年 11 月 18 日。

③ The Ambassador in China (Johnson) to the Secretary of State, July 31, 1939, *FRUS*, 1939, The Far East, Volume III, Document 534, 563. https://history. state. gov/historicaldocuments/frus1939v03/d534. 上网日期:2022 年 11 月 18 日。

④ Gao Bei, *Shanghai Sanctuary: Chinese and Japanese Policy toward European Jewish Refugees during World War II*, 48.

持的重要性。当公众舆论与国会意见着重于国内事务,反对大量接纳难民和冒险卷入任何国外战争时,罗斯福感到只能作出象征性姿态来对待犹太难民,他本人并不愿意强求让更多的犹太移民进入美国,不愿因要求改变移民法而同国会发生冲突,因为这正是他需要国会支持,以在外交事务上发挥更大作用的时候。[1] 罗斯福准确地评估了民间和国会的反难民情绪,他不愿冒着失去政治选票的风险对海外犹太难民进行人道主义救济,反而收紧移民政策,减少拯救欧洲犹太危机的资金。在这种情况下,美国政府必定不会考虑支持威廉这种"劳民伤财"的犹太难民移华计划。

其次,国民政府的现实利益考量和中国的战争困境是该计划失败的另一个原因。中国当时仍处于抗战的艰难阶段,尚有千万百姓流离失所,根本没有现实条件为犹太难民提供安居乐业的环境。此时国民政府愿意帮助犹太难民移华也的确另有所图,即改善自己在西方尤其是美国眼中的国际形象以求取更多国际援助。让国民政府失望的是,美国犹太人对美国政府的影响力并不像国民党高层想象的那么大,尽管确实有许多美国犹太人积极抗议政府对华的不作为行为,但美国政府并不愿意为该计划提供帮助,美国犹太人组织为该计划的捐款也十分有限。起初,威廉承诺的一千万美元投资十分吸引国民政府,但后来国民政府发现这仅仅是一张空头支票而已,因为美国犹太人组织甚至连威廉本人并没有响应国民政府的请求来华考察犹太人移民问题。[2] 出于现实利益的考量,国民政府绝不可能自己出资实施该移民计划,如果不能使该计划给中国带来经济回报,干脆放弃是明智的,因为中国还有许多其他更为迫切的问题需要解决。

最后,莫里斯·威廉的过于理想化是该计划失败的主观因素。威廉是一个极其理想化的人,他认为自己有责任帮助中美建立密切的关系。威廉曾提出:"美国应该向中国市场出口更多的美国产品,以避免一战后的大萧条,应该提供贷款帮助中国发掘巨大的经济潜力。这样一来,不仅会帮助中国,还会充实美国。"[3]威廉的计划也正是基于他的这种使命感提出的。然而,他高估了该计划的现实性。一方面,他天真地以为美国政府会无条件地支援中国,但实际上1935 年他去信邀请戴维斯参加援华会议时便被婉拒了。戴维斯来信提醒威廉,

---

① 马广东 Ma Guangdong,〈试论罗斯福总统对待欧洲犹太难民的态度〉[On President Roosevelt's Attitude towards the Jewish Refugees in Europe],《前沿》[Forward Position],2008 年第 2 期[2008, Issue 2],185。

② Evansville Press 1942 年 3 月 8 日的报纸"'Greatest Living Influence' on China is New York Dentist"记载威廉从未去过东方,由此可以推测至少在 1942 年之前威廉并未到过中国。C4.003, https://www.international.ucla.edu/media/files/C4.003.pdf. 上网日期:2022 年 11 月 20 日。

③ Maurice Zolotow, *Maurice William and Sun Yat-sen* (London: R. Hale, 1948), 121.

“由于他的官方工作，他不能对美国的对外友好使命承担任何道德责任”①。这时威廉应该觉察出美国政府对援助中国的态度并不友好，但是他还是一厢情愿地认为只要中国接纳犹太难民便能得到美国犹太人的支持，从而影响美国政府支持中国抗战。另一方面，他又乐观地估计了当时中国的状况。中国已陷入多年战争，无力启动该计划，中国内部也并不完全对犹太难民持欢迎的态度。正如布鲁诺·鲍威尔在1843年的《犹太人问题》中讨论犹太人解放问题时所持的狭隘观点：“在德国，没有人在政治上得到解放。我们自己没有自由。我们怎么可以使你们自由呢？”②和19世纪的德国人民一样，1939年的中国人民生活在国民政府的专制统治下，也没有获得政治解放，即使中国人民对犹太难民抱有同情之心，仍有许多反对者不能接受犹太人大规模地移民中国。以上这些因素的最终结果就是莫里斯·威廉计划如空中楼阁一般难以实现，甚至不如白尔克拉斯计划那么现实，走向失败是其最终的必然命运。

结语

因其著作《历史的社会解释》对孙中山先生的重大影响，莫里斯·威廉蜚声中外。日本侵华之后，他投身援华运动，为中国抗战作出了巨大贡献，赢得了中国人民的普遍好感。作为中国人民的老朋友，莫里斯·威廉在华具有巨大的名人光环，当他提出犹太难民移华计划并宣称可促进中犹互助时，得到了许多人的支持。该计划自纳粹德国大规模迫害犹太人时萌芽，威廉游说中国外交官和国民政府对外宣传转向后得以完善出台，最终由于种种因素的阻碍而不了了之。该计划虽然失败了，但是通过对该计划的探析可以得出以下结论。

首先，莫里斯·威廉计划是一个非常不完善的计划。和平年代安置数万移民已经是一个浩大的工程，战争时期安置数万流亡他乡的犹太人更是难上加难，需要多方考虑。威廉认为白尔克拉斯安置难民的措施是片面的，只是单纯从犹太人的角度要求中国帮助解决难民问题，而他的计划则是基于互帮互助的原则，利用犹太人的力量来帮助国民政府抵抗日本，最终获得抗战的胜利，犹太难民在中国安居乐业是他们促进中国发展后获得的回报。表面上看似乎并无问题，但

① A6.029, *Letter from Davis reminding William that he had stated he could not take any moral responsibility for the American Good-Will Mission due to his official work*, 5/10/1935. Maurice Williams Archives, https://www.international.ucla.edu/media/files/A6.029.pdf，上网日期：2022年11月20日。

② 《马克思恩格斯全集》第3卷[The Complete Works of Marx and Engels, Vol. 3](北京[Beijing]：人民出版社[People's Publishing House],2002),163。

通过前文的考察可知，莫里斯·威廉计划从构想、筹备到出台并没有形成一个完备的方案，相比于不完善的白尔克拉斯计划，是一个更加不完善的计划。

其次，莫里斯·威廉计划反映了国民政府高层"以犹太为中心"的错觉。许多国民党高层精英看待英美政局时有一种"以犹太为中心"的误解，这导致国民政府认为犹太团体对英美政治有着决定性的影响，犹太人可以左右英国和美国的政治。所以，他们的政策逻辑是实行帮助犹太难民的国家行为来触动英美犹太人精英改善对华印象，再由他们利用影响力操纵英美，帮助中国对抗日本。威廉成功把握住了国民政府高层的这一错觉，在计划中不断渲染犹太人尤其是美国犹太人的国际影响力，以此吸引国民政府的注意力。

最后，莫里斯·威廉计划具有反法西斯的特点。中华民族与犹太民族都是热爱和平的民族，历史上的民族命运多次交织，尤其是近代面对法西斯主义的威胁，两个民族选择共渡难关，中国在危急时刻接受了大量欧洲难民，世界犹太人反过来也为中国的抗战捐款捐物。莫里斯计划的目的是使犹太民族逃离德国法西斯的迫害，中国支持该计划也是希望借助国际力量击败日本法西斯。从这点上看，该计划为中华民族和犹太民族的战时合作提供了一种可能性，反映了两族人民希望战胜法西斯获得和平的美好愿望。

总之，莫里斯·威廉计划是中犹两族患难与共、同舟共济的历史见证。中华民族与犹太民族是友好互助的民族，历史上的交往体现了构建人类命运共同体的历史渊源。中国自古以来就具有扶助弱小民族的传统，犹太民族是这个传统的受益者。中国在唐宋时期就接纳了大批来华的犹太人，中华民族对犹太民族持包容心态，两族人民一直其乐融融，相安无事。近代中国积贫积弱，虽处于抗日战争的险恶境地，但仍然接受了大批的欧洲犹太难民。国民政府虽然出于利益考虑没有实行莫里斯·威廉计划，但是也没有违背这一传统。

The Fallen Ark: An Analysis of Maurice William's Plan for the Migration of Jewish Refugees to China

WANG Xiaofei

Abstract: In 1939, Kuomintang government was faced with internal and external difficulties: the Japanese invaded many parts of China, Kuomintang army was defeated one after another, and there was no help from abroad, but it was harshly accused of insufficient determination to resist Japan. In order to improve its international image and seek international assistance, Kuomintang government planned to immigrate the persecuted European Jews to Southwest China. This plan received attention and praise of many foreign people of insight, who gave advice to Kuomintang government. Against this historical background, Dr. Maurice William, a Jewish dentist who was active in American politics stage, proposed his Jewish immigration plan, which was favored by Kuomintang government. Conceived from the start of the Nazi's persecution of Jews in Germany, the Maurice William's plan was formally proposed during the period of China's full-scale war of resistance, but was ultimately aborted due to the lack of support from the U. S. government, the realities of China's war plight, and William's idealization. Although this plan failed, through the systematic investigation of the plan, it can be proved that modern China has sympathy and assistance for the imprisoned Jewish people, has an international humanitarian spirit, a sense of international responsibility, and historical concern for helping weak and small peoples, which is in line with the contemporary practical theme of building a community with a shared future for mankind.

Key Words: Maurice William Plan, Jewish Refugees, the War of Resistance Against Japan, Association between the Chinese and Jewish Peoples, a Community with a Shared Future for Mankind

关于犹太人到达开封时间问题的再思考*

李大伟**

【摘要】关于犹太人到达开封的时间，有周代之前说、周代说、汉代说、唐代说、宋代说、明代说等。综合看来，汉代之前的说法难以被确证，唐代说也缺乏足够证据，近些年来出现的明代说显然缺少证据支持，难以成立，在论证分析时存在对文献错误解读之嫌。传统的宋代说更为可信，不能被轻易否定，开封犹太人的碑刻记载，尤其是明弘治二年碑的价值不能被忽视。

【关键词】开封犹太人；唐代说；宋代说；明代说

开封犹太人是古代中国犹太人一个最为重要的群体，备受关注。关于犹太人到达开封的时间，有周代之前说、周代说、汉代说、唐代说与宋代说等，但是迄今所知犹太人入华的考古发现以及文献记载最早出现在唐代，汉代之前的说法难以被确证。① 目前，关于开封犹太人入华时间比较流行的说法是宋代说，但是还有唐代与明代等说法。其中唐代说目前尚未有明确的证据，近些年来新出现的明代说则对传统的宋代说提出了新的质疑，颇为引人关注。② 为揭示犹太人抵达开封的时间以及古犹太人入华的历史状况，本文依据开封犹太人文献资料

---

* 本论文受到2022年国家社科基金重大项目“世界历史上主要文明之间的比较、互动与互鉴研究”(22&ZD249)、2020年国家社科基金后期资助项目“古犹太人入华研究”(20FZSB063)等资助，系其阶段性研究成果。

** 李大伟，陕西师范大学历史文化学院副教授。

① 参见李大伟 Li Dawei，〈古开封犹太人入华研究述评〉[A Review of the Study of Ancient Kaifeng Jews Entering China]，收录于《犹太研究》(第13辑)[Jewish Studies (13)]，傅有德 Fu Youde 主编(济南[Jinan]：山东大学出版社[Shangdong University Press]，2015)，231—236。

② 参见 Yu Peng, “Revising the Date of Jewish Arrival in Kaifeng, China, from the Song Dynasty (960-1279) to the Hung-Wu Period (1368-98) of the Ming Dynasty,” *Journal of Jewish Studies* 68 (2017): 369-386。

（包括四个碑刻与其他资料）与其他有关古代中国犹太人的文献和考古资料，在对唐代说介绍的基础上，着重对宋代说与明代说进行新的探讨。

一、唐代说

迄今所知，犹太人最早在唐代入华，且已被相关考古与文献记载证实。相关资料共有7则。其中考古发现为1901年斯坦因（A. Stein）在新疆于阗丹丹乌里克遗址获得一封8世纪中叶犹太商人所写的犹太—波斯文（Judeo-Persian）信件，现存大英博物馆[1]；2004年中国国家图书馆入藏了一份新疆和田（古称于阗）出土的编号为BH1-19的犹太—波斯文书信，张湛、时光对此文书进行了解读，认定该信件也出自丹丹乌里克遗址，与斯坦因所获为同一时期、同一人所写的书信[2]；1908年伯希和（P. Pelliot）在敦煌藏经洞中发现一份8—9世纪犹太人的希伯来文祈祷书，现存巴黎国家图书馆。[3] 文献记载包括：916年阿拉伯史地学家阿布·赛义德（Abu Saiyid）记载回历264年（877年9月至878年9月）黄巢在广州（Khānfū）屠杀城中经商的伊斯兰教徒、犹太教徒、基督教徒、拜火教徒等[4]；10世纪阿拉伯史地学家马苏迪（Al-Masudi）记载广州犹太商人；[5]9世纪中叶阿拉伯史地学家伊本·胡尔达兹比赫（Ibn Khurdāhbeh）记载拉唐（Rādhānites）犹太商人沿陆路与海路入华[6]；953年波斯人巴佐尔·本·萨赫里亚尔（Buzurg ibn Shahriyar）记载阿曼犹太人商人艾萨克（Isaac）入华贸易；[7]10世纪

---

① 参见 D. S. Margoliouth, "An Early Judaeo-Persian Document from Khota, in the Stein Collection, with Other Early Persion Documents," *Journal of the Royal Asiatic Society of Great Britain and Ireland* (Oct. 1903): 735-760。

② 参见张湛 Zhang Zhan、时光 Shi Guang，〈一封新发现犹太波斯语信劄的断代与解读〉[The Chronology and Interpretation of a Newly Discovered Jewish Persian Letter]，收录于《敦煌吐鲁番研究》（第11卷）[Study on Dunhuang and Turpan(11)]（上海[Shanghai]：上海古籍出版社[Shanghai Classics Publishing House]，2009），71-99。

③ 参见 M. Pollak, *Mandarins, Jews and Missionaries, the Jewish Experience in the Chinese Empire* (Philadelphia, 1980), 260。

④ 参见 Abu Sayyid 阿布·赛义德，《中国印度见闻录》[Akhbār al-Sīn wa'l-Hind]，卷二[Vol.2]，黄倬汉 Huang Zhuohan 译（北京[Beijing]：中华书局[Zhonghua Book Company]，1983），96。

⑤ 参见 Al-Masudi 马苏第，《黄金草原》[The Meadows of Gold]，耿昇 Geng Sheng 译（北京[Beijing]：人民出版社[People's Publishing House]，2013），165-167。

⑥ 参见 Ibn Khurdādhbih 伊本·胡尔达兹比赫，《道里邦国志》[Kitāb al-Masālik wa'l-Mamālik]，宋岘 Song Xian 译注（北京[Beijing]：中华书局[Zhonghua Book Company]，1991），164。

⑦ 参见 Jacob R. Marcus, *The Jew in the Medieval World: A Source Book*, 315-1791(New York: Atheneum), 355。

阿拉伯史地学家伊本·穆哈利尔(Ibn Muhalhil)记载吐蕃、于阗有犹太人。[①] 以上有关唐代中国犹太人的考古发现,证实了中世纪时期诸多阿拉伯与波斯史地学家关于唐代犹太人入华的记载,犹太人在唐代已经到达中国,甚至久居中国已成为事实。

同时,有些学者也主张犹太人在唐代到达了开封。孔宪易主张,开封犹太人"自唐传入开封后,已历千年,岁月既久,教徒逐渐汉化,教中除'满喇'等少数人认识希伯来文外,其它一般人经营商业、手工业,和一些人学习儒家经籍,作为猎取功名的工具"[②]。他指出,唐代各色西域人等沿着丝绸之路进入中国,犹太人进入也在情理之中。"安史之乱"之后,唐朝政治、经济等中心东移,开封地位逐渐提高。同时,唐朝为了避免汉蕃混杂,规定:"大历十四年(779)诏,回纥诸蕃住在京师者,各服其国之服,不得与汉相参。"开封也受此限制,故犹太人在土市子居住。宋代也同样不可能让这些西域蕃人居住在城内,尤其是大内东华门附近,所以他们祖祖辈辈在土市子定居,并有可能已经建立祠庙,只有他们族人自己知道,影响不大因而不为人知。他进一步指出,从唐宋以来因为其祠庙名不见经传,很难摄入文人的笔下。明代开封人李濂与犹太族人李应元,不仅是同乡,还同是进士,先后都在山西省太原居官,李濂不能不知开封犹太人,但其名著《汴京遗迹志》只字未提一赐乐业礼拜寺一事。清代开封人刘昌为康熙碑撰文者,与该族重要人物赵映乘等私交甚好,同时其府第就在礼拜寺旁边,可是在其修撰的《河南通志》《开封府志》中亦只字未提开封犹太人礼拜寺。清代嘉兴人周城作为一个外省人,在《宋东京考》中亦只字未提就可想而知了。开封犹太人历经金元明等朝代,适应中国环境,读儒家书者甚多,有些更是应试从政,开封籍的缙绅纵然熟知他们是犹太人,也不好意思提及,这也是中国人的恒情,不足为怪。同时,该寺一直坐落在土市子东背后的小巷中,故非熟于开封当地情况者,很难知晓。[③] 高望之认为,虽然目前尚无史料可以断定,但从唐代中西交通历史来看,开封犹太人可能在唐代到达。高望之指出,在唐代极有一部分犹太人从广州、扬州到达开封定居。他认为,虽然目前尚无史料可以断定,但是从唐代中西交通的

① 参见 Gabriel Ferrand 费琅,《阿拉伯波斯突厥人东方文献辑注》[Annotations of Eastern Documents of Arab Persian Turks],耿昇 Geng Sheng、穆根来 Mu Genlai 译(北京[Beijing]:中华书局[Zhonghua Book Company],1989),233、238。

② 孔宪易 Kong Xianyi,〈开封一赐乐业教钩沉〉[An Analysis of Kaifeng Israeli Religion],《上海师范大学学报》[Journal of Shanghai Normal University],1985 年第 3 期[1985, Issue 3],68。

③ 上述引文为孔宪易关于开封犹太人唐代进入开封的论证,参见同上。

历史来看,对于开封犹太人而言,并非如陈垣所言“非宋以前所至”。[①]

潘光旦亦认为开封犹太人的一部分在唐代到达开封。他根据1605年艾田告诉利玛窦族里的一个传说,即“当帖木儿征服波斯之时,他们也征服了中国,并将很多摩尔人、基督教徒和犹太人带进中国。这大约是八百年前的事情”,认为大概是在明代,中东犹太人和开封犹太人还是有些接触,他们把帖木儿席卷中东一带的侵略行动,当故事一般说给开封族人,因而演成了这样一个牛头不对马嘴的传说。但是其中两点是对的:一是“大约在八百年前”,即唐中叶以后;二是同来的还有基督教徒和回教徒等。据此,他认为在开封犹太人中间,多少总有一部分人的祖先是唐代来的。除此之外,他还引用五代时期何光远《鉴诫录》中所记波斯人李珣在中国参加科考等事迹,类比开封犹太人,说明开封犹太人至少有一部分是在唐代入华。[②]

但是,现存开封犹太人碑刻与其他文献资料中,并没有提及犹太人在唐代到达开封。以上学者主要是基于一种可能性的判断,并没有提出明确的证据。通过唐代犹太人的考古与文献材料,可以看到唐代犹太人多因贸易入华,主要活动在中国边境贸易城市,如于阗、敦煌、广州,乃至吐蕃等地。迄今为止,尚未发现犹太人在中国内地活动的证据。但是,若为贸易之便,犹太人最有可能首先选择到达唐代都城长安,因为长安不仅是中国经济贸易中心,而且由于古代中国奉行朝贡贸易,犹太人来到长安之后会得到唐廷大量赏赐。唐代开封的地位较之东都洛阳都相差甚远,更遑论长安,因此似乎没有什么优势能够吸引犹太人前去。因此,开封犹太人唐代入华说尚有待确凿证据证明,至少目前不能得出明确结论。

二、关于宋代说的再认识

开封犹太人宋代入华说主要基于明弘治二年(1489年)《重建清真寺记》与明正德七年(1512年)《尊崇道经寺记》的记载。明弘治二年《重建清真寺记》记载:

---

① 参见高望之 Gao Wangzhi,〈关于中国犹太人〉[About Chinese Jews],收录于 Sidney Shapiro 沙博理,《中国古代犹太人——中国学者研究文集点评》[Ancient Chinese Jews — Comments on the Research Works of Chinese Scholars],殷罡 Ying Gang 译(北京[Beijing]:新世界出版社[New World Press],2008),133。

② 参见潘光旦 Pan Guangdan,《中国境内犹太人的若干历史问题——开封的中国犹太人》[Several Historical Issues of the Jews in China — The Chinese Jews in Kaifeng](北京[Beijing]:北京大学出版社[Peking University Press],1983),36—37。

教道相传,授受有自来矣!出自天竺,奉命而来,有李、俺、艾、高、穆、赵、金、周、张、石、黄、李、聂、金、张、左、白七十姓(十七姓之误)等,进贡西洋布于宋,帝曰:“归我中夏,遵守祖风,留遗汴梁。”宋孝隆兴元年(1163)癸未,列微五思达领掌其教,俺都剌始建寺焉。①

明正德七年《尊崇道经寺记》亦记载:

厥后原教自汉时入居中国,宋孝隆兴元年(1163年)癸未,建祠于汴(开封)。②

明弘治二年《重建清真寺记》的记载更为翔实,意指十七姓开封犹太人来自天竺(印度),向宋朝贡奉西洋布——西洋在明代之前主要指东南亚与印度洋沿线国家,晚清之后主要指西方欧美国家,古代印度以盛产棉布闻名,西洋布显然指印度棉布,宋朝皇帝允诺他们久居开封。宋孝隆兴元年(1163年),开封犹太人俺都剌首次建寺,即犹太会堂。寺在古代中国初指佛教寺庙,但之后也用以指代其他宗教活动场所,如唐代入华的聂斯托利派基督教(景教)教堂被称为“大秦寺”“波斯寺”,穆斯林 Mosque 被称为“清真寺”等。列微即 Levi,犹太人的祭祀阶层。五思达即 Oustad,在波斯语中类似犹太人拉比,管理宗教事务。明正德七年《尊崇道经寺记》记载开封犹太人建立犹太会堂的时间与明弘治二年《重建清真寺记》一致,不同的是将犹太会堂称为“祠”。祠为古代中国祭祀祖先的地方,即祠堂,此处又一次借用了汉语词汇来称谓犹太会堂,应是因为犹太会堂发挥类似祭祀的功能。

明弘治二年《重建清真寺记》与明正德七年《尊崇道经寺记》刻写的“隆兴”(1163—1164年)是南宋(1127—1297年)皇帝宋孝宗赵昚的年号。1127年之后,金朝(1115—1234年)灭亡北宋(960—1127年),占领开封;北宋皇室赵构(1107—1187年)流亡到中国南部,在应天府(今河南商丘)称帝,建立南宋。因此,1163年开封犹太人显然是在金人统治时建立犹太会堂。明代开封犹太人在立碑之时,没有采用金朝统治年号,这是因为宋朝与明朝皆为汉族政权,金朝非汉族所建立政权,因此开封犹太人选择宋朝皇帝年号表述时间,以示正统。

如明弘治二年《重建清真寺记》与明正德七年《尊崇道经寺记》所记,1163年开封犹太人既已建立犹太会堂,那么犹太人在此之前即金朝或北宋肯定已到达开封。金朝在大定元年(1161年)七月迁都开封,距1163年犹太人建立会堂仅

---

① 陈垣 Chen Yuan,《陈垣史学论著选》[Selected works of Chen Yuan on Historiography](上海[Shanghai]:上海人民出版社[Shanghai People's Publishing House],1981),66—67。

② 同上,69。

有两年时间，从犹太人朝贡到建寺时间太过短促。[①] 明弘治二年《重建清真寺记》记载这批犹太人来自印度，并进贡西洋布于宋，显然是经海路入华。1161 年之后金朝与南宋对峙，南宋控制中国南部地区，犹太人不可能途径中国南部沿海地区到达开封。

关于开封犹太人入华时间，陈垣称："自汉至明，千有余年，犹太人若久居中国，不应无一人一事一建筑物足述。何以弘治碑之始，于本教传入源流，止溯于宋，而不及于宋以上？……故谓汉以前已有犹太人曾至中国则可，谓开封犹太人为汉所遗留则不可。"[②]针对陈垣的论述，Yu Peng 认为陈垣不仅不接受开封犹太人汉来说，而且怀疑宋来说。[③] 其完全误解了陈垣的意思。陈垣显然是以明弘治二年《重建清真寺记》将开封犹太人历史追溯至宋代的记载来驳斥汉代说，并非质疑宋代说，所谓"自汉至明，千有余年，犹太人若久居中国，不应无一人一事一建筑物足述"，则是强调为何在汉代没有关于中国犹太人的记载或事迹。而且，陈垣在下文紧接着又称：

> 及之唐世，欧亚交通渐盛，景教、回教皆接踵而来，犹太人亦当继至，亚拉比（阿拉伯）人阿布·赛义德《东洋行纪》有曰：唐末黄巢之乱，因贸易而至广府之回教徒、犹太教徒与基督教徒等十二万人，皆死于难。此足为唐末犹太人至中国之确证。……今试以种种方法，证明开封犹太族非宋以前所至。宋敏求《东京记》，颇注意于祠庙……而于一赐乐业教寺无闻；张邦基《墨庄漫录》……而于一赐乐业教寺无闻……足见宋时一赐乐业教尚无人能道，其非宋之前所至，可断言也。[④]

可见陈垣通过引用阿布·赛义德所记黄巢在广州屠杀犹太教徒的事迹说明唐代中国已经出现了犹太人，又称宋代历史地理著作中没有提到开封犹太人，是因宋代开封"一赐乐业教"（即以色列教）不为人所知，开封犹太人非宋之前所至，可断言也。因此，陈垣的主要观点是开封犹太人不是在宋代之前来到开封，恰是支持宋代说。

目前，除了明弘治二年《重建清真寺记》与明正德七年《尊崇道经寺记》记载之外，确实没有其他有关宋代说的证据，但这是否意味着犹太人不可能在宋代到

① 参见魏千志 Wei Qianzhi，〈中国犹太人定居开封时间考〉[A Study on the Time of Chinese Jews Settling in Kaifeng]，《史学月刊》[Journal of Historical Science]，1993 年第 5 期 [1993, Issue 5]，41。

② 陈垣，《陈垣史学论著选》，83。

③ 参见 Yu Peng, "Revising the Date of Jewish Arrival in Kaifeng, China, from the Song Dynasty (960-1279) to the Hung-Wu Period (1368-98) of the Ming Dynasty," 371。

④ 陈垣，《陈垣史学论著选》，83—84。

达开封?

首先,除了明弘治二年《重建清真寺记》与明正德七年《尊崇道经寺记》关于犹太人在开封建立会堂的记载一致,皆称宋孝隆兴元年(1163 年)癸未建立会堂,元至元十六年己卯重建会堂,明代历经重修等。尽管清康熙二年(1663 年)碑记载"教……周时传于中州,建祠于大梁"——前述此已被证明可信度不大,但是清康熙二年碑仍然强调其寺俺都剌始创于宋孝隆兴元年,重建于元至元十六年。虽然此三碑存在差异,但关于开封犹太人宋代建立会堂的记载完全一致,而且越是年代久远的碑刻可信度越高,因此不能轻易否定弘治二年碑的价值。

其次,明弘治二年碑对犹太会堂称谓的记载,经历了从寺、古刹清真寺到清真寺的流变,即宋孝隆兴元年癸未始建寺,元至元十六年己卯重建古刹清真寺,明代数次重修清真寺。[①] 前述寺或古刹为中国古代佛教寺庙称谓,但常用来称呼其他宗教场所。清真寺称谓出现在明代,专指穆斯林宗教场所,开封犹太人被汉人称为"蓝帽回回"(穆斯林),因此可以理解犹太会堂在弘治二年被称为"清真寺",元代古刹清真寺则应是明代人对元代开封犹太人重建会堂的称呼。从寺、古刹清真寺到清真寺称谓的演变,显示犹太人在明代之前就已到达开封,那么便是元代或宋代,且弘治二年碑明确提及宋代建寺、元代重建古刹清真寺,显示开封犹太人在元代对宋代的犹太会堂进行了重建,因此犹太人在宋代应已到达开封。

这里需要注意明正德碑关于犹太会堂称谓的记载。明正德碑记载:"宋孝隆兴元年癸未,建祠于汴。元至元十六年己卯重建,其寺古刹也,以为尊崇是经之所。"[②]其中祠与寺同,为借用汉语词汇来称谓犹太会堂。李渡南称陈垣对该碑的断句,显示元至元十六年重建的"尊崇是经之所"(即犹太会堂)是由一座古刹改建而来,起初并非作为犹太会堂。[③] 李渡南应是误解了此段内容的意思。明正德碑中没有提及"清真寺"这一称谓,碑名也被称为《尊崇道经寺记》,"道经"即指摩西五经。这是因为明代中叶大量伊斯兰教场所都被称为清真寺,已占据绝对优势,开封犹太人在明正德碑中刻意不再使用该词,应为避免穆斯林的影响,担心被同化的危险。因此,明正德碑所记元至元十六年的"古刹"实际上为弘治二年碑所记"元至元十六年古刹清真寺",指的就是犹太会堂,是作为"尊崇是经之所",并非如李渡南所言元至元十六年的犹太会堂是从古刹改建而来。

明弘治二年《重建清真寺记》与明正德七年《尊崇道经寺记》的记载显然可以支持宋代说,但最为重要的是北宋时期犹太人是否具备到达开封的可能性与必

---

① 参见陈垣,《陈垣史学论著选》,66—67。

② 同上,69。

③ 参见 Lesile, *The Survival of the Chinese Jews* (Leiden: Brill, 1972), 79-80。

要性？前述唐代中国犹太人的资料，显示唐代犹太人已经开通了入华的陆路与海路，犹太人出现在于阗、敦煌与广州等地贸易。元代犹太人也已出现在中国各地，尤其是东南沿海地区。马可·波罗曾记载："元朝皇帝忽必烈对基督徒、伊斯兰教徒、犹太人和佛教徒等同样的礼遇。"[①]阿拉伯旅行家伊本·白图泰入华时曾记载："由犹太人进入第二城，杭州城内居民为犹太和基督教人以及崇拜太阳的土耳其人，他们人数很多。"[②]1605 年开封犹太人艾田会见利玛窦时，也提到杭州犹太人要比开封多，那里有一所礼拜堂。[③] 1326 年天主教传教士安德鲁(Andrew)在写给罗马教会的一封信中，提到很难规劝泉州犹太人改宗基督教。[④] 杭州、泉州位于中国东南沿海，在元代为重要的贸易港口，这些犹太人肯定是为贸易入华。既然唐代与元代犹太人已经入华，那么宋代完全有可能入华，因为宋代是海上丝绸之路最为繁荣的时期，波斯、阿拉伯、印度与东南亚等地商人都入华贸易，大量国库收入都来自海外贸易税收。历史上印度西海岸地区一直作为印度犹太人的主要分布区域，信德赛义姆尔(Saymur)、孟买南部 20 英里处孔坎(Konkan)、梵答剌亦纳(Pandaraina)、僧急里(Cyngilin)以及锡兰等地皆有大量犹太人流散。[⑤]据戈尼萨文书(Genizah Documents)记载，北非、亚丁等地大量犹太人 11 世纪已到达印度西海岸等地，并与印度犹太人有贸易联系，如马达姆·哈桑(Madm ūn b. Hasan)在给亚伯拉罕·伊居(Abraham b. Yiju)的信中让他转达对印度商人艾萨克(Ishaq)等人的问候[⑥]，亚伯拉罕·伊居在印度铜

---

① Marco Polo 马可·波罗，《马可波罗行纪》[The Travels of Marco Polo]，冯承钧 Feng Chengjun 译(北京[Beijing]：中华书局[Zhonghua Book Company]，2004)，305。

② Ibn Battuta 伊本·白图泰：《伊本·白图泰游记》[The Travels of Ibn Battuta]，马金鹏 Ma Jinpeng 译(银川[Yinchuan]：宁夏人民出版社[Ningxia People's Publishing House]，2000)，551。

③ 参见 Moule 穆尔，《1550 年前的中国基督教史》[The History of Christianity in China before 1550]，郝镇华 Hao Zhenhua 译(北京[Beijing]：中华书局[Zhonghua Book Company]，1984)，3。

④ 参见张星烺 Zhang Xinglang，《中西交通史料汇编》[A Corpus of Reference on the Traffic Histories Between China and Western Countries](北京[Beijing]：中华书局[Zhonghua Book Company]，2003)，334。

⑤ 参见 Joan G. Roland, "The Jews of India: Communal Survival or the End of a Sojourn?" *Jewish Social Studies* 42 (1980): 77; Walter J. Fischel, "Bombay in Jewish History in the Light of New Documents from the Indian Archives," *Proceedings of the American Academy for Jewish Research* 38/39 (1970-1971), 123-125; David G. Mandelbaum, "The Jewish Way of Life in Cochin," *Jewish Social Studies* 1 (1939): 424; Benjamin, *Travels of Rabbi Benjamin, Son of Jonah, of Tudela* (London: Oxford University Press, 1907), 93。

⑥ 详见戈尼萨文书 TS 6J4 f. 14; TS 18J2 f. 7; TS 12, 416; TS 20. 130; TS NS J 241; TS NS J240; TS 20. 137; TS NS J1 等记载。G. D. Goitein and Mordechai Akiva Friedman, *India Traders from the Middle Ages: Documents from the Cairo Geniza* (Boston: Brill Leiden, 2008), 311-318, 328-351, 373-374.

厂中雇佣了亚伯拉罕等印度犹太人。[①] 因此,印度西海岸与锡兰犹太人应早已活跃在印度洋贸易中,完全有可能在宋代经海路到达中国。古代中国奉行朝贡贸易,异域商人尤喜向中央王朝朝贡,因此可获得远比贡奉之物更多的赏赐。所以,这些印度犹太人完全有理由来到北宋都城开封,贡奉西洋布于宋并定居开封。

开封犹太人碑刻与《托拉》卷轴(*Torah* scroll)显示,开封犹太人受到波斯地区犹太人影响颇深,如碑刻所记"五思达"即为波斯语,开封犹太人《托拉》与波斯犹太人的《托拉》相同,开封犹太人圣所建筑风格在波斯地区也极为常见。[②] 这些因素表明开封犹太人应来自波斯,因此很多学者对明弘治二年碑所记来自天竺产生怀疑,质疑弘治二年碑的真实性。[③]

但是,需要注意的是,明弘治二年碑所记来自印度的犹太人可能是最早到达开封,其与宋孝隆兴元年癸未掌教五思达与俺都剌建立犹太会堂的犹太人应是不同批次到达,因为犹太人到达开封不可能立即建立犹太会堂,后者显然来自波斯,因此不难理解开封犹太人受到波斯犹太人的影响。

明正德七年《尊崇道经寺记》中提到了"天竺西域"这一地名:

> 至于一赐乐业教,始祖阿耽(亚当),本出天竺西域,稽之周朝,有经传焉。[④]

其中"西域"指中国以西的内陆地区,"天竺"西域的称谓说明明代开封犹太人久居中国对犹太教发源地信息非常模糊,因此以来源地表示犹太教发源地,即分别来自印度与西域——西域自然包括波斯以及中亚等其他地区,清康熙碑刻则记载教起于天竺。这些记载说明开封犹太人来源的多样性,开封犹太人应是分不同批次入华,但是最早一批有可能是来自印度。Yu Peng 将明弘治二年碑、明正德七年碑与清康熙碑记载的"天竺""天竺西域",错误地理解为开封犹太人宗教的来源地,并指出开封犹太人提供了混乱的信息。[⑤] 实际上,只有明弘治二年碑记载了开封犹太人的来源,后两者则是记载开封犹太人宗教的来源,所指并不相同。

---

① 详见 TS 20.137 文书记载,同上,638。

② 参见 W. C. White, *The Chinese Jews* (Toronto,1942), Vol. II, 21, 144。

③ 参见 Yu Peng, "Revising the Date of Jewish Arrival in Kaifeng, China, from the Song Dynasty (960-1279) to the Hung-Wu Period (1368-98) of the Ming Dynasty," 377。

④ 陈垣,《陈垣史学论著选》,69。

⑤ 参见 Yu Peng, "Revising the date of Jewish arrival in Kaifeng, China, from the Song Dynasty (960-1279) to the Hung-wu period (1368-1398) of the Ming Dynasty," 376。

当然历史上印度犹太人与波斯联系密切,而且大部分都是从波斯迁徙而来,如僧急里犹太人便被认为是5世纪受到萨珊波斯的迫害迁徙到印度。[①] 中世纪时期,尤其是8—11世纪印度西海岸诸地、锡兰犹太人与波斯、阿拉伯乃至西班牙等地犹太人联系密切,彼此熟知。11世纪早期印度犹太人就诸多宗教与犹太律法等问题问巴比伦地区加昂亥(Geon Hai),加昂亥以“答问”(Responsa)答之。[②] 因此,这些来到开封的印度犹太人本身就可能继承了波斯犹太人的传统与习俗。

虽然Yu Peng称在《册府元龟》中没有找到有关犹太人进贡西洋布的记载[③],但并不能因此全然否定宋来说。古代中国官方史书不可能完全记载所有朝贡事宜,而且古代汉人常将穆斯林与犹太人混淆,如明清时期开封犹太人便被汉人称为蓝帽回回,因此不排除宋廷误将犹太人视为穆斯林的可能。尽管目前没有发现宋来说的其他证据,但基于上述分析显示开封犹太人应在北宋到达开封,宋代说不能被轻易否定,尤其是明弘治二年碑的价值不能被忽视。

三、关于明代说的商榷

Yu Peng认为开封犹太人在元代入华,最早到达开封的时间为明洪武年间(1368—1398)。具体而言,其称元代开封犹太人与回回共同被蒙古人带到中国,元代灭亡后这些犹太人在明初来到开封,由于明朝是汉人政权,不再对蒙古时期的色目人实行优待,甚至出台了一些歧视性政策,因此开封犹太人在碑刻中伪造了他们的历史,追溯至宋代、汉代甚至周代,说明犹太人与汉人一样久居中国;而声称来自印度,是因为印度在中国人心目中是一个佛教国家,佛教早在汉代便传入中国,这样便能掩饰他们曾经作为蒙古元代统治阶层的历史,以避免受到明廷的迫害与歧视。[④]

为论证此说,Yu Peng力求证明开封犹太人碑刻所记宋孝宗隆兴元年建立

① 参见 Walter J. Fischel, “The Exploration of the Jewish Antiquities of Cochin on the Malabar Coast,” *The Journal of the American Oriental Society* 87 (1967):231; Werner Keller, *Diaspora*, *The Post-Biblical History of the Jews*, Harcourt (New York:Brace&World, Inc, 1966),106-108; H. H. Ben-Sasson, *A History of the Jewish People* (Cambridge:Harvard University Press, 1999), 380。

② 中世纪印度犹太人与阿拉伯等地犹太人交往,详见 Werner Keller, *Diaspora*, *the Post-Biblical History of the Jews*, 156-157。

③ 参见 Yu Peng, “Revising the Date of Jewish Arrival in Kaifeng, China, from the Song Dynasty (960-1279) to the Hung-Wu Period (1368-1398) of the Ming Dynasty,” 372。

④ 同上,375-378。

犹太会堂的俺都剌就是明代永乐年间的俺诚(或俺三),犹太会堂首次在明代永乐年间建立,开封犹太人故意将会堂建立时间篡改到北宋。[①] 如其所述,尽管开封犹太人碑刻与《明实录》中关于开封犹太人俺诚(或俺三)身份、姓名等记载存在差异,但不容否认的是开封犹太人碑刻所记俺诚与《明实录》所记俺三为同一人,而且曾因举报周王谋反被赐姓赵(也称为赵诚),授予锦衣卫指挥等职位。[②] 如明弘治二年碑记载:"俺诚医士,永乐十九年奉(1421)周府定王令,赐香重修清真寺,寺中奉大明皇帝万万岁牌。永乐二十一年以奏闻有功,钦赐赵姓,授锦衣卫指挥,升浙江都指挥佥事。"[③]《明实录》记载:"擢河中护卫军丁俺三为锦衣卫指挥佥事,赐姓名赵诚,以其告周王橚不轨,得实也。"[④]

康熙十八年,(1679年)开封赵姓犹太人(即俺诚家族)立《清真寺赵氏牌坊并开基源流序》碑刻,纪念赵氏家族从赵诚到清代的历史与开封犹太会堂的建造情况。该碑记载:"由今追昔,创地(犹太会堂)者,吾俺都喇锦衣公也。"[⑤]其中"俺都喇"即宋孝宗隆兴元年建立犹太会堂的俺都剌,锦衣应指锦衣卫,"公"在古代汉语中意为长者或老者,常用来尊称先辈。锦衣卫是明代专有官职,专门进行军政情报搜集的机构,开封犹太人中只有俺诚曾担任锦衣卫。因此,Yu Peng 据"俺都喇锦衣公"的记载,认为俺都剌就是俺诚,指出开封犹太人故意将1421年俺诚建寺的事迹追溯至1163年。

古代中国若后世出将入相、称王称帝,则将会此份荣耀追溯至其先祖,此为惯制,如明太祖朱元璋建立明朝之后便将其父朱世珍尊为皇帝,谥号淳皇帝。需要注意的是,《清真寺赵氏牌坊并开基源流序》将俺都剌称为锦衣公而非锦衣卫。若如 Yu Peng 所言俺都剌与俺诚为一人,则仅记为"俺都喇锦衣卫"即可,因此"俺都喇锦衣公"的记载,显示应是后人将俺诚生前担任锦衣卫的荣耀追溯至俺家先祖俺都剌,将其称为锦衣公。而且,《清真寺赵氏牌坊并开基源流序》明确记载:"永乐时,俺诚□□□□□代孙,以奏闻有功,钦赐赵姓。"[⑥]虽然中间五个字模糊无法辨认,但显然是指俺诚为开封犹太人俺家子孙,其意应是俺诚为俺都剌

---

① 参见 Yu Peng,"Revising the Date of Jewish Arrival in Kaifeng, China, from the Song Dynasty (960—1279) to the Hung-Wu Period (1368—1398) of the Ming Dynasty,",384。

② 同上,373-383。

③ 陈垣,《陈垣史学论著选》,67。

④ 《明实录》[Mingshilu],卷二三二[Vol. 232],第1页,总第2242页,台湾"中央研究院"历史语言研究所校印,收录于李景文 Li Jingwen,《古代开封犹太人——中文文献辑要与研究》[Ancient Kaifeng Jews-Summary and Study of Chinese Literature],30。

⑤ 同上,43。

⑥ 同上,42。

数十代子孙，显示其并非俺家先祖俺都剌。因此，俺诚与俺都剌不可能为同一人。

同时，Yu Peng 援引怀履光称明洪武初年，一支李姓犹太人从北京迁徙到开封，说明这支犹太人就是开封李姓犹太人，并由此证明整个开封犹太人群体明初从北京迁往开封。[①] 元代灭亡后，北京犹太人在明初迁徙到开封，为自然之事，因为明代开封犹太人与中国各地犹太人联系密切，如明代天顺年间(1457—1464)宁波犹太人为开封犹太人呈送本教道经(*Torah*)一部，宁夏犹太人金瑄为开封犹太会堂购置供桌、铜炉、瓶子与烛台等；明正德七年重建犹太会堂时，扬州犹太人又为开封犹太人请道经一部，宁夏犹太人为开封犹太会堂修建碑亭等。[②] 但是，这支李姓犹太人的迁徙仅能说明明初有北京犹太人迁徙到开封，并不能说明整个开封犹太人群体都是从北京而来。

因此，Yu Peng 的主张并没有说服力。这里需要强调的是，尽管开封犹太人碑刻关于犹太人入华时间记载存在出入，如明正德碑与清康熙碑分别记载汉代与周代，但是关于宋代开封犹太会堂建立的时间完全一致，皆记载宋孝隆兴元年俺都剌建立犹太会堂。在古代中国碑刻中，越是久远的碑刻越能接近事实，真实性越大，新近的碑刻则包含一些后人添加的内容，同类碑刻之间难免会有出入，因此不能完全否定开封犹太人三个碑刻的价值，想当然地认为这种差异是开封犹太人篡改历史所引起的。即使如其所言，开封犹太人三个碑刻是经过篡改、伪造的，但是难以想象能够伪造得如此精确，如明弘治二年碑精确地记载了元代建寺的时间、地点，称："元至元十六年己卯，五思达重建古刹清真寺，坐落土市字街东南，四至三十五杖。"[③]

同时，Yu Peng 言称"明朝不对蒙古时期色目人实行优待，甚至出台了一些歧视性政策"，但是，开封犹太人三个碑刻字里行间仍然清晰地表明其所信奉的宗教为异域宗教，其亦非汉人，如此何以躲避明朝的迫害与歧视？反而是明弘治二年碑明确记载："殆我大明太祖高皇帝开国初，扶绥天下军民，凡归其化者皆赐地以安居乐业之乡，诚一视同仁之心也。"[④]显示在明朝建立之初，明太祖允诺只要异域族群(包括犹太人)能够归服中央受其教化，便可赐地让其安居乐业。明代开封犹太会堂中奉大明皇帝万万岁牌，就表明开封犹太人接受明廷的统治，并

① 参见 W. C. White, *The Chinese Jews*, Vol. III, 158, 221; Yu Peng, "Revising the Date of Jewish Arrival in Kaifeng, China, from the Song Dynasty (960-1279) to the Hung-Wu Period (1368-1398) of the Ming Dynasty," 385。

② 陈垣，《陈垣史学论著选》，67、70。

③ 同上，66-67。

④ 同上，67。

没有受到迫害与歧视,否则俺诚何以能够在明廷中担任锦衣卫指挥此等要职。

明朝对于境内异族的政策,主要体现在取消他们在元代享有的优待,鼓励异族与汉族通婚,限制族内通婚,达到同化他们的目的。《明会典》记载:“洪武三年,令蒙古色目人氏,既居中国,许与中国人家结婚姻,不许与本类自相嫁娶,违者男女两家抄没,入官为奴婢。”[①]这项政策便主要是通过联姻促使异族同化,并非对异族进行迫害与歧视。因此,明代开封犹太人只要能够归服中央受其教化,便可足以安居乐业,避免迫害与歧视。Yu Peng 所谓开封犹太人为避免受到明廷迫害与歧视而伪造历史的主张,夸大了这些政策对异族的危害性,而且最为重要的是并没有提出足以支撑其主张的历史证据。因此,其关于开封犹太人元代入华与明代到达开封的说法不足为信。

结语

虽然学术界关于犹太人到达开封时间有诸多不同说法,由于迄今所知犹太人最早在唐代入华,因此唐代之后(包括唐代)的说法具备一定的可能性,但是,综合开封犹太人碑刻记载、宋代犹太人流散与贸易状况等诸多因素分析,宋代说更为可信,而明代说显然缺少证据支持。因此,期望通过对开封犹太人入华时间的再思考,能够进行尽量客观的探讨与研究,揭示更多有关开封犹太人的历史真相。

① 《明会典》[Minghuidian],《户部七》[Hubuqi],卷二十[Vol. 20](北京[Beijing]:中华书局[Zhonghua Book Company],2004),135。

Reconsider the Problem of Jews' Arrival Time of Kaifeng

LI Dawei

Abstract: As for the time when the Jews arrived in Kaifeng, there are some arguments about before the Zhou Dynasty, the Zhou Dynasty, the Han Dynasty, the Tang Dynasty, the Song Dynasty and the Mind Dynasty. In general, it is difficult to confirm the arguments about before the Han Dynasty, and the argument of Tang Dynasty still lacks sufficient evidence. The argument of Ming Dynasty in recent years is obviously lack of evidence support, which is difficult to establish, and there is a suspicion of misinterpretation of the literature in the argument and analysis. The traditional Song Dynasty argument is more credible and cannot be easily denied, and the value of the inscriptions of Kaifeng Jews, especially the monument of the second year of the reign of Emperor Hongzhi of the Ming Dynasty cannot be ignored.

Key Words: Kaifeng Jews, Tang Dynasty, Song Dynasty, Ming Dynasty

JEWISH STUDIES
犹太研究
第21辑

犹太人大流散——以犹太阿威罗伊主义回应迈蒙尼德*

拉赫莉·哈利瓦**
沈剑彧***译

【摘要】传统上认为，犹太人的大流散是因为违背上帝的旨意而受到神圣的惩罚。迈蒙尼德以及其他犹太理性主义思想家曾试图用更自然主义的观点来解释，但甚至连他们也没有脱离"犹太人犯罪导致流亡"的经典解读范式。根据迈蒙尼德的观点，犹太人被驱逐出家园是因为他们从事占星术活动。在他看来，这是犹太律法所禁止的，也导致他们未能制定出合适的军事战略。本文中，我将介绍艾萨克·波卡尔的自然主义观点，其观点与迈蒙尼德等人提供的自然主义解释背道而驰。根据波卡尔的说法，犹太人被驱逐出他们的土地是因为他们严格遵守

* 探讨波卡尔对犹太人大流散态度的研究，参见 Hannah Kasher, "'Why Is the Land in Ruins?' (Jeremiah 9:11): Religious Transgression versus Natural Historical Process in the Writing of Maimonides and His Disciples," in *Hebrew Union College Annual*, Cincinnati (1998): 143-156. [Hebrew]; Shlomo Pines, "Some Topics on Polqar's Treatise '*Ezer ha-Dat* and Their Parallels in Spinoza's View," in *Studies in Jewish Mysticism, Philosophy and Ethical Literature, Presented to Isaiah Tishby on His Seventy-Five Birthday*, eds. Joseph Dan and Joseph Hacker (Jerusalem: Magnes, 1986), 395-457 [Hebrew]; Shlomo Pines, "Spinoza's *Tractatus Theologico-Politicus* and The Jewish Philosophical Tradition," in Jewish Thought in the Seventeenth Century, eds. Isadore Twersky and Bernard Septimus (Cambridge, MA: Harvard University Press, 1987), 499-521; Shalom Sadik, "Negation of Political Success in the Thought of Rabbi Isaac Pulgar," *AJS* 39 (2015): 1-13 [Hebrew]。沙洛姆·萨迪克(Shalom Sadik)在他的文章中试图将政治成功与犹太—基督教论战中的"奇迹理论"联系起来。本文中，我根据他的老师迈蒙尼德的观点考察了波卡尔的惊人论点，强调了两者的共同目的——否定占星术及其实践。然而，除了反对关于犹太人流放原因的传统观点外，波卡尔还隐晦地批评了迈蒙尼德的观点，即犹太人从事占星术是犯罪。

** 拉赫莉·哈利瓦(Racheli Haliva)，山东大学犹太教与跨宗教研究中心教授。

*** 沈剑彧，耶路撒冷希伯来大学犹太思想系博士研究生。

了上帝的诫命，而遵守诫命使得犹太人以道德的方式约束自己和对待他人。而列国不受上帝诫命的约束，因此无法阻止他们以不道德的方式对待他人。鉴于道德准则的差异，犹太人特别容易被那些不受道德约束的国家所征服、压迫和流放。

【关键词】布尔戈斯的阿布纳；犹太大流散；迈蒙尼德；艾萨克·波卡尔；犹太教—基督教对话

绪言

犹太传统看法认为，大流散是对背弃上帝诫命的神圣惩罚。[①] 在对这种"违法—惩罚"关系的众多解释中，迈蒙尼德(Maimonides)提出的自然主义解释脱颖而出。在迈蒙尼德看来，使用犹太律法所禁止的占星术是犹太人忽视战争之术的原因，这导致他们丧失土地。[②] 14 世纪的哲学家艾萨克·波卡尔 (Isaac Polqar) 是迈蒙尼德的学生之一，他对这种解释提出了质疑。他的论证最终得出了一个看似矛盾的结论：犹太人的大流散不是违背上帝律法的结果，而恰是服从的结果。波卡尔对大流散的解读，为理解降临在犹太人身上的最大灾难之一提供了全新的思考方式。其论述质疑了关于"犹太人在自己命运中所扮演角色"的既定理念，同时也表明其不愧为一名有主见的迈蒙尼德门徒。

---

① 关于犹太人大流散的传统解读，即犹太人因违背上帝而受到惩罚，参见 Augustine, *Contra Faustus*, 12:12; Judah ha-Levi, *The Kuzari*, 2:23, 3:11, 4:23; Nachmanides, *Kitvei ha—Ramban*, A, 294; Cf. Moshe Halbertal, *By Way of Truth-Naḥmanides and Creation of Tradition* (Shalom Hartman Institute, 2006), 230, 246 [Hebrew]; Ehud Krinis, "Galut and Ghayba: The Exile of Israel and the Occultation of the Shī'ī Imām — Comparative Aspects (Judah Halevi and Early Shī'ī Literature)," *Jerusalem Studies in Arabic and Islam* 40 (2013): 245-299; Shlomo Pines, "The Probability of the Re-establishment of the Jewish State According to Joseph Ibn Caspi and Spinoza," *Iyyun* 14 (1964): 289-317 [Hebrew]; James M. Scott, *Exile: Old Testament, Jewish, and Christian conceptions* (Leiden & New York: Brill, 1997); Stephen K. Wright, *The Vengeance of Our Lord: Medieval Dramatization of the Destruction of Jerusalem* (Toronto: University of Toronto Press, 1989)。

② 参见 Maimonides, "Letter on Astrology," in *A Maimonides Reader*, West Orange, ed. I. Twersky (Millburn N.J.: Behrman House, 1972), 463-473。汉娜·卡舍尔(Hannah Kasher)在"'Why Is the Land in Ruins?' (Jeremiah 9:11): Religious Transgression versus Natural Historical Process in the Writing of Maimonides and His Disciples"中讨论过其中几种观点，除波卡尔的论点外，还分析了叶达雅·哈-佩尼尼(Yeda'ya ha-Penini)、约瑟夫·伊本·卡斯皮(Joseph Ibn Caspi)以及摩西·纳尔博尼(Moshe Narboni)的观点。参见 Elijah Del-Medigo, *Behinat ha-Dat*, Introduction。

波卡尔的思想在许多方面与迈蒙尼德的思想是连续的,尤其是注重以哲学的方式解释犹太教。波卡尔和他同时代的人都是犹太阿威罗伊主义哲学学派的成员,包括撒母耳·伊本·提本(Samuel Ibn Tibbon)、闪·托夫·伊本·约瑟夫·法拉奎拉(Shem Tov Ibn Joseph Falaquera)、约瑟夫·伊本·卡斯皮(Joseph Ibn Caspi)、摩西·纳尔博尼(Moses Narboni)和艾萨克·阿尔巴拉格(Isaac Albalag)等。他们的主要目标是用伊本·鲁世德[①]对亚里士多德的评论,为世界的起源、上帝的非物质性和预言的本质等宗教难题提供哲学解决方案。

作为历史研究解读的对象,波卡尔最广为人知的身份是其前任老师布尔戈斯的阿布纳[②]的主要反对者。[③] 波卡尔著作中的很大一部分致力于反驳阿布纳对自己信仰出身的攻击。阿布纳赞同古典基督教证明犹太教虚假性的论点,声称基督教的真理源于犹太人受压迫和堕落的状态。[④] 在其著作《正义之师》(*Moreh Ẓedeq / Mostrador de Justicia*)的序言中,他描述了自己皈依基督教的内心斗争:

> 我看到犹太人身负重担,而我是犹太人的后裔。在长期被俘的历史中,

① 译者注:伊本·鲁世德(Ibn Rushd,1126—1198),即阿威罗伊(拉丁语 Averroes),安达卢斯著名哲学家,亚里士多德哲学的大力支持者与传播者,其著作涉及哲学、医学、律法、神学等诸多领域,对中世纪伊斯兰教、犹太教、基督教的思想都产生重要影响。

② 译者注:布尔戈斯的阿布纳(Abner of Burgos,即 Alfonso de Valladolid,约 1260—1347)是 14—15 世纪犹太西班牙"改宗拉比"运动中最重要的哲学家之一。在人生前半段,他曾是亚里士多德派的犹太哲学家,后皈依基督教,成为一名新柏拉图式的基督徒,这使他成为中世纪为数不多的在哲学思想和宗教上产生过极大转变的哲学家之一。其著作大部分是辩论性的,常试图说服曾经的犹太同胞像自己一样皈依基督教,下文引用的段落亦能体现这一主旨。

③ 关于布尔戈斯的阿布纳和波卡尔之间关系的其他研究,参见 Isaac Baer, *A History of the Jews in Christian Spain* (Philadelphia & Jerusalem: The Jewish Publication Society, 1961), 331, 333, 348, 357-358; Isaac Baer, *A History of the Jews in Christian Spain* (Tel-Aviv: ' Am ' Oved Publishing house, 1965), 194-197, 202-203, 213 [Hebrew]; Shoshan Gershenzon, "A Study of Teshuvot La-Meḥaref by Abner of Burgos," Thesis for the degree of Doctor of Hebrew Literature in Jewish History (the Graduate School of the Jewish Theological Seminary of America, 1984), 14-16, 18, 23-26; Jonathan Hecht, "The Polemical Exchange between Isaac Pollegar and Abner of Burgos/ Alfonso of Valladolid according to Parma MS 2440," A Dissertation for the Degree of Doctor of Philosophy, Skirball Department of Hebrew and Judaic Studies (New York University, 1993), 51-88; Ryan Wesley Szpiech, "From Testimonia to Testimony: Thirteenth-Century Anti-Jewish Polemic and the Mostrador de Justicia of Abner of Burgos/Alfonso de Valladolid," A Dissertation for the Degree of Doctor of Philosophy (Yale University, 2006), 1n2, 170-171, 192, 209-210, 233-235, 257-258, 288, 311-316, 322-323, 329-331, 334-336, 496。

④ 数位基督教思想家都强调了一个公认的论点,即犹太人受苦而基督徒繁荣,是因为前者拒绝接受耶稣为弥赛亚。参见 Augustine, *Contra Faustum*, 12:12。

他们被沉重的税负压迫、击垮，不堪重负，这个民族已经失去了曾经拥有的荣誉和荣耀，而那些本身没有任何帮助或影响。一天，我正苦思这个困境，带着内心巨大的呼喊和苦楚，我走进了会堂，向主祈祷说："主啊，我求你怜悯，求你看见我们所处的磨难。为什么会这样？这是基于什么？长期以来，你对你的人民——你羊群的羔羊——大发烈怒的理由是什么？为什么外邦人会说：'他们的上帝在哪里？'主啊，求你垂听我的祷告祈求，照耀你已毁坏的圣所，怜悯你的百姓以色列。"我给自己带来了极大的焦虑，疲倦得睡着了。在梦中，我看到一位伟人对我说："你为什么睡着了？明白我要对你说的话，振作起来，因为我告诉你，犹太人被虏这么久，是因为他们愚蠢糊涂，也因为缺乏公义的良师来告诉他们真理。这就是上帝对你说的话，平平安安地去吧。"①

传统犹太人将流亡的苦难解释为犹太人违背了上帝的诫命。正如我们在这段话中看到的，阿布纳接受了这种将流放视为对罪恶的惩罚的传统观点。然而，对他来说，犹太人被驱逐出自己的家园，真正的罪因是没有一位老师可以引导他们走上正确的道路。② 此处"老师"可能指耶稣——第二圣殿时期，他的教训和预言被他的犹太同胞拒绝。然而，这里的"老师"更可能指的是阿布纳本人——书名 *Moreh Ẓedeq* 即"正义的老师"，此书旨在通过说服犹太人皈依基督教来拯救自己。

除了解释犹太人为何遭受如此长久的流放之外，阿布纳还提出了另外两个理论。在《对亵渎者的回应》(*Teshuvot la-MeẒaref*)——这是阿布纳给波卡尔的信《对异教徒的回应》(*Teshuvat Apikoros*)的回复中，阿布纳通过一个内部神学问题探讨了犹太人的现状：

解释诗篇的米德拉什③中写道："拉比约书亚·本·利未(Joshua ben

① Abner of Burgos, *Mostrador de Justicia*, 12r/1:13, trans. Ryan Wesley Szpiech, *Dissertation*, 216. 参见 214—226 页斯皮耶奇(Ryan Wesley Szpiech)对这段话的讨论。Isaac Baer, *A History of the Jews in Christian Spain* (1961), 328-330; Isaac Baer, *A History of the Jews in Christian Spain* (1965), 202.

② 在 *Mostrador de Justicia* (230v/2: 198)的另一章节中，阿布纳提出了经典的基督教指控，声称犹太人遭受了漫长而痛苦的流放，是因为塔木德圣贤拒绝接受耶稣为真正的弥赛亚。在阿布纳看来，只有那些接受基督教弥赛亚启示的人才配称为"以色列人"，而拒绝承认耶稣应验了这一启示的人则被判流放。参见 Szpiech, *Dissertation*, 383-384。

③ 译者注：米德拉什(Midrash)作为文学类型，指犹太教拉比们对《圣经》的注解，主要分为解释律法的米德拉什(Midrash Halacha)以及解释律法外其他经文的米德拉什(Midrash Aggadah)。另外，米德拉什(Midrash)亦指使用这种解经模式对《圣经》进行注释的著作，后文提到的《创世记注》(*Genesis Rabbah*)即是一部对《圣经》中《创世记》(*Genesis*)一书进行解释的米德拉什著作。

> Levi)说:为什么以色列人在这个世界上祈祷,却没有得到回应?因为他们不知道神不可言说之名。但在来世的时间里,神圣唯一的主,赞美归于祂,将使祂的名字广为人知……《创世记注》(*Genesis Rabbah*)13:2 中写道:"以色列人都为圣殿祈求,'何时建造?'他们每天祷告:'看看我们的苦难,为我们战斗。快救赎我们,完成救赎……'拉比约书亚说:'他们的祈祷没有得到回应,因为他们不知道神不可言说的名字。'"圣名是对神圣唯一的主——赞美归于祂——内在关系的认识,暗指三个基本属性:"智慧""理解"和"知识"。祂通过这些创造了世界。正如解释过的那样,神在每个人身上的化身和人类在两个世界中的救赎必随之而来……由于(不知主名)这罪,圣殿被毁,他们陷入流放。因为这罪,他们的结局(以及他们被放逐的结束)没有被揭示,他们也无法脱离流亡。他们没有为这罪悔改,因为他们不知道这是一种罪。①

此处,阿布纳不再声称犹太人流亡是因为拒绝承认耶稣是真正的弥赛亚,而是依托拉比的说法,指出犹太人的福祉直接取决于他们是否知道上帝不可言说之名。由于他们不再知道,因此没有得到承诺的安乐生活。之后阿布纳的神学解释转了个弯,辩称遗失的知识是三位一体的"智慧""理解""知识";接受耶稣教导的基督徒现在拥有了通往美好生活的钥匙,他们目前的政治、经济和宗教地位明确地证实了这一点。

在后来的《对亵渎者的回应》中,阿布纳又对犹太人的长期流放提出了完全不同的解释:

> 他们(犹太人)说,根据塔木德的教导,救赎并没有随弥赛亚而来,因为他们对弥赛亚怀有毫无来由的仇恨(sina'at ḥinam)。因此,他们没有被救赎,永远生活在流放中,是因为塔木德。②

第二圣殿被毁、犹太人被流放是因为毫无根据的仇恨,这一拉比文学的观点发生了有趣的曲解:认为犹太人内部的无端仇恨导致了圣殿被毁和民族流亡的经典解释不再,反之,无端的仇恨被理解为从犹太人尤其是塔木德圣贤指向耶稣。他们拒绝去接受、去爱真正的弥赛亚,因而惹祸上身。

---

① *Teshuvot la-MeẒaref* 28a-b. Jonathan Hecht trans., *Dissertation*, 195-197. 阿布纳在《给拉比约瑟夫·沙洛姆的第三封信》("Third Letter to Rabbi Joseph Shalom")中持相同观点,参见 Judah Rosenthal, "The Third Letter of Abner of Burgos," *Studies in Bibliography and Booklore* 5 (1961): 42-44。

② *Teshuvot la-Me ḥaref* 33b.

波卡尔认为，除了反驳本土基督徒和基督教皈依者的批评外，重要的是重新审视自己所在的犹太社区也认同的对犹太人流亡的传统解释。如前所述，传统犹太人认为自己目前的处境是由于他们违反了上帝的诫命。他们认为，遵守诫命可以保证安全和福祉，而不遵守上帝的律法会招致神圣的惩罚，例如流散于各国之中。在这方面，我们看到基督徒和犹太人对犹太人被流放所提出的原因恰巧趋同：双方都认为这是对罪的惩罚，只是对该罪的本质有分歧。对于基督徒来说，其本质是拒绝承认耶稣为真正的弥赛亚、拒绝他的律法，而对于犹太人来说，罪在于违反摩西律法。

一、迈蒙尼德对大流散的解释

波卡尔并不是第一个质疑关于犹太人流亡的传统观点的人。迈蒙尼德也广泛地讨论过这个问题，其作品为波卡尔所熟悉。因此，在引出波卡尔的论证之前，让我们先参考一下迈蒙尼德对这个问题的处理方法——虽然其与波卡尔的方法有很多共同之处，但仔细考察会发现，它们在许多关键方面存在显著差异。

迈蒙尼德曾就占星术给蒙彼利埃(Montpellier)的圣贤写信，信中直接谈到犹太人流散的话题[①]，并将犹太人的流散与第二圣殿时期犹太领袖参与占星术活动联系起来[②]。在其另外两部作品即《律法再述》(*Mishneh Torah*)和《〈密释纳〉评注》(*Commentary on Mishnah*)中，迈蒙尼德大量地解释了他对占星术的否定。

在关于占星术的信中，他写道：

> 这(即追求占星术)就是为什么我们丢了王国，为什么我们的圣殿被毁，为什么我们被带到这里(即流放)；我们的先祖因犯了罪而不复存在，他们发现了许多关于观星者的书籍……他们没有忙于战争或征服土地，却认为研究这些会对他们有所帮助。因此，先知称他们"愚顽"(《耶利米书》4:22)。他们是真正的傻瓜，"因为他们随从那糊涂无益的神"(《撒母耳记上》12:21，

---

① 关于该信的权威性，参见 H. A. Davidson, *Moses Maimonides, the Man and His Works* (Oxford: Oxford University Press, 2005), 494-501。

② 尚不明确迈蒙尼德指第一圣殿还是第二圣殿被毁；最有可能的解释是，两座圣殿的被毁被理解为一个连续事件。

《耶利米书》2:8)。[①]

在此,迈蒙尼德试图将圣殿的毁坏和随后的流散解释为犹太领袖不负责任、非理性的迷信行为的自然结果。犹太领导人没有认真研究战争之术,以保护他们的人民,扩大他们的领土,却专注于无用的占星术书籍和占星实践,这在迈蒙尼德看来是犹太律法所禁止的;这些做法让他们错误地认为自己受到了星星的保护。在这封信的后文中,迈蒙尼德辩称,天文学是关于天体及它们的位置和运动的真实知识,占星术则不同,是一门伪科学,因此必须反对。

在其著作《〈密释纳〉评注》中,迈蒙尼德对占星术的虚假性进行了进一步的科学论证:

> 你们要知道,完美的哲学家不相信护身符。他们嘲笑护身符和那些认为它们(对肉体)有作用的人。这解释很长。我已经这么说了,因为我知道大多数人——实际上可能所有人,都被这个大骗局和许多其他类似的事情给愚弄了,认为它们是真理。可它们不是。(骗局是如此之大)以至于即便是我们托拉之民中最虔诚的人也以为它们是真实的,但这是被禁止的,因为托拉禁止这些。他们没有意识到它们是托拉警告过的荒谬虚假的事物,就像警告我们不要(相信)谎言一样。他们尊崇星星,将不属于它们的事迹归

① Maimonides, "Letter on Astrology," 464-473. 参见 Gad Freudenthal, "Cosmology: The Heavenly Bodies," in *The Cambridge History of Jewish Philosophy*, eds. Steven Nadler and Tamar Rudavsky (Cambridge: Cambridge University Press, 2009): 302-361; Gad Freudenthal, "Maimonides' Stance on Astrology in Context: Cosmology, Physics, Medicine, and Providence," in *Moses Maimonides*, eds. Fred Rosner and Samuel S. Kottek (Northvale, NJ: Jason Aronson, 1993), 77-90; Michael Katzman, "Maimonides' Rejection of Astrology," *Beloved Words*, Yeshivat Chovevei Torah Rabbinical School, 2, v. 2 (2006): 105-120; Howard Kreisel, "Maimonides's Approach to Astrology," *World Congress of Jewish Studies* (1994): 25-32 [Hebrew]; Tzvi Langermann, "Maimonides' Repudiation of Astrology," *Maimonidean Studies* 2 (1992): 123-158; Sarah Pessin, "Maimonides' Opposition to Astrology: Critical Survey and Neoplatonic Response," *Al-Masaq* 5 (1992): 1-15; Ralph Lerner, "Maimonides' Letter on Astrology," *History of Religion* 8 (1968): 143-158; Aviezer Ravitzky, "The Ravings of Amulet Writers: Maimonides and His Disciples on Language, Nature and Magic," in *Between Rashi and Maimonides: Themes in Medieval Jewish Thought, Literature, Exegesis*, eds. Ephraim Kanarfogel and Moshe Sokolow (New York: Yeshiva University Press, 2010), 93-130; Shlomo Sela, "Astrology in Medieval Jewish Thought (Twelfth-Fourteenth centuries)," in *Science in Medieval Jewish Cultures*, ed. Gad Freudenthal (Cambridge: Cambridge University Press, 2011), 292-300; Shlomo Sela, "Queries on Astrology Sent from Southern France to Maimonides: Critical Edition of the Hebrew text, Translation, and Commentary," in *Aleph: Historical Studies in Science and Judaism*, volume 4 (Bloomington: Indiana University Press, 2004), 89-190; Schwartz Dov, *Astral Magic in Medieval Jewish Though* (Ramat Gan: Bar-Ilan University Press, 2004), 92-121, 241-242, 263-266 [Hebrew]。

功于星星。他们(早期的偶像崇拜者)摸清了星辰的规律(以借助它们的力量),制定了魔法、咒语、降灵、与星辰对话、恶魔、鬼魂、各样的诡计、通灵以及许许多多这类被托拉的真理之剑毁灭的东西。它们是偶像崇拜及其衍生物的根源。第一个骗局是(建立)占星术,我们可以通过经验和科学推翻其基本前提。他们(占星家)说,这颗特定的星星是吉兆,其他则是凶兆;他们还说,天体的某一部分与某颗星相容,与另一颗星不相容,然而它们(天体)是一个整体,根本没有部分或组成部件。这两个观点是占星术的基础,如果被证伪——已经被证伪了,那么所有的细节到最后就分崩离析。[①]

迈蒙尼德强调,科学已经证明,每个天体都是同质且不变的物体。[②] 然而,占星家持有的两个主要假设都与这一事实相矛盾:首先,一些星星是吉星,而另一些是灾星[③];其次,每颗星星的球体上都有一个与该特质对应的"位置"。鉴于构成占星学的基本前提是科学错误,因此预言家、占卜师和占星家的结论仅出于偶然的关联,在完全相同的情况下会导致不同的结果。

迈蒙尼德对其论点的犹太律法式辩护,即我们在上述关于占星术的信中看到的那样,从事占星术与居住在应许之地的神圣契约之间的联系,这一点在《律法再述》中也得到了详细论述:

这些做法(占星术和巫术)都是虚假的、具有欺骗性的,是古代偶像崇拜者用来欺骗各国人民,诱使他们成为自己追随者的手段……任何人要是相信这类事物,并在心中认为尽管托拉禁止,但它们是真实的、科学的,这些人不过是傻瓜,缺乏理解力,与理智不成熟的妇女和儿童属于同一阶层。拥有智慧、知识完备的人都清楚地知道,所有这些律法所禁止的做法,都是没有科学依据的,都是空想和空洞的;只有那些缺乏知识的人才会被这些愚蠢行为所吸引,并因为它们的缘故放弃真理之道。因此,托拉禁止所有这些愚蠢

① Maimonides, *Commentary on the Mishnah*, *Avodah Zarah*, 4:7; Cf. Dov Schwartz, *Astral Magic in Medieval Jewish Thought*, 104-106.

② 茨维·朗格曼(Tzvi Langermann)的文章《迈蒙尼德对占星术的否定》("Maimonides' Repudiation of Astrology")132 页为迈蒙尼德在《迷途指津》(*The Guide of the Perplexed*)中忽略了这一观点提供了一种可能的解读,他认为《迷途指津》2:19 探讨了球体的不均匀性,以解释神圣意志创造世界。

③ 波卡尔在《信仰之助》(*'Ezer ha-Dat*)第 112 页用了同一观点。本文中所有引用《信仰之助》的段落皆出自莱文格(Levinger)的希伯来语评述版(Tel-Aviv University, 1984)。英译本参见"Charles Manekin's (trans.) Selected Chapters," in *Medieval Political Philosophy*, second edition, eds. Joshua Parens and Josheph C. Macfarland (Ithaca, N.Y.: Cornell University Press, 2011), 208-219。

行为,并告诫我们:“你要在耶和华你的神面前做完全人。”(《申命记》18:13)。[①]

根据迈蒙尼德的观点,必须反对参与占星术的原因有两个:第一个是哲学原因,虽然他没有在此处详细说明这个论点;第二个是历史神学原因。首先,他断定占星术在科学上是错误的,因此,任何追随占星术的人“都只是一个缺乏理解力的傻瓜”。其次,他指出占星术实践与偶像崇拜之间的历史联系:占星术是偶像崇拜者试图欺骗大众、巩固其地位的工具。他们自我赋予特殊力量,如预测未来[②]、通过占卜医治病人等[③],并声称自己知道如何利用星星的放射物来达成这些目的。

那么,在迈蒙尼德看来,不可从事占星术一是因为占星术不基于科学/哲学研究,二是因为占星术在历史与神学上都与偶像崇拜相关。由此可见,由于圣殿时期的犹太领袖倾向于相信占星术,所以他们非但没有为群体的福祉做出贡献,反而给同胞带来了难以想象的灾难。迈蒙尼德出于历史和神学的缘由反对占星术,这使他有理由公开批评流亡前时期的犹太领袖。这些犹太领导人忽视了从事占星术危险致命的后果,导致犹太人被驱逐出他们的家园。

上述迈蒙尼德的科学论证对本文的论点至关重要,原因有二。首先,它是波卡尔确立其自然哲学论点的基础。[④] 其次,迈蒙尼德的方法——提供自然主义的解释——被波卡尔当作工具,以达成《信仰之助》(‘*Ezer ha-Dat*)的写作目标之一,即识别犹太社群内部的危机,主要指那些反对哲学研究的人的意见。[⑤] 非

---

① Maimonides, *Mishneh Torah*, Laws of Idolatry and Ordinances of the Heathens, 11.16, Twersky, *Maimonides Reader*, 75-76.含一些改动:迈蒙尼德在《也门书信》(“Epistle to Yemen”)第3章中表达了同样的想法,并探讨了如何计算救赎日期,称尽管努力预测,该日期“没有人能够精准地确定”。参见 Maimonides, “Epistle to Yemen” in *A Maimonides Reader*, 450。

② *Mishneh Torah*, Laws of Idolatry and Ordinances of the Heathens, 11:6.

③ 同上,11:12。

④ 参见‘*Ezer ha-Dat*, Treatise Three, 105-153。在这篇论文中,波卡尔介绍了两位对话者,一位是学者,另一位是占星家。学者在对话中的主要目的是反驳占星家的说法,即占星术是一门解释星星对人类影响的学科。波卡尔使用迈蒙尼德的论证方法来反对——或至少谨慎对待——没有科学依据的领域,该方法在这篇论文中尤为显著。参见‘*Ezer ha-Dat*, 111。文中的学者是波卡尔的代言人,他以轻蔑幽默的方式将占星者所做的比作儿童游戏:占星者将人类的属性赋予一个个星球,正如孩子们给彼此安排不同的身份和角色,如国王、大臣等。孩子们和占星者之间的区别在于,前者知道自己在玩游戏,他们采用的所有人格都是虚构的,而占星者却相信自己虚构的理论是真实的。波卡尔称只有通过理智获得的知识才是真正的知识。同上,50。

⑤ 在“‘*Ezer ha-Dat*, Treatise Four”中,波卡尔主要关注几个犹太群体,他们将自己视为信仰的捍卫者。但事实上,波卡尔认为他们严重破坏了宗教原则。这些团体的成员包括传统主义者和占星者,威胁到了“那些从事真正的科学的人”(‘*Ezer ha-Dat*, 155)。

理性主义者，包括占星家和传统主义者，不通过论据来证明自己的论点。然而，哲学家拒绝任何没有科学证据支持的论点。因此，关于星星可以影响人类的说法，或者换句话说，上帝因为违背祂的诫命而惩罚犹太人的说法，由于缺乏科学依据，应完全否定。

至此，我们已经列举了三种解释犹太人大流散的不同观点。其中基督徒和基督教皈依者以及传统犹太人这两方的论点，从神学的角度解释了犹太人的流散，将其理解为对罪的神圣惩罚。第一种解释认为，犹太人的困境是由于他们拒绝耶稣为真正的弥赛亚，而第二种则认为这是犹太人不服从上帝诫命的后果。迈蒙尼德提出的第三种论点，试图证明犹太人的大流散是犹太领导人参与占星术的自然结果，这使他们忽略了研究战争之术。尽管迈蒙尼德改良了传统的神学解释，但他仍然采纳了这种解释的基本前提，即"犹太人的罪导致他们被流放"。然而，对他来说，罪是犹太人迷信占星术的后果，而对这种罪的惩罚是自然的而不是超自然的方式。

二、波卡尔对犹太人大流散的自然主义解释

乍一看，波卡尔的解释似乎并没有偏离传统的观点，即流放是对罪的惩罚——无论是神圣的还是自然的。[①] 这是因为波卡尔借鉴了迈蒙尼德的方法，在同一论述中向不同受众传达不同的信息。[②] 因此，我们发现，在整个关于大流散的论述中，波卡尔对此提出了两种解释。第一种支持传统观点，这无疑是针对传统的犹太读者的。以该种方式提出这一论点，传统犹太读者会认为波卡尔也赞同传统观点。第二个论点对大流散提出了自然主义的解释，针对的是哲学读者。这种双重信息与波卡尔的声明一致，他在《信仰之助》的序言中提到，将在几个地方隐藏自己的真实观点，以避免被社区同胞误解，指控他为异端。[③]

波卡尔在《信仰之助》中如此开始他对犹太人大流放的讨论：

> 我们长期流亡，过着多灾多难的生活，为我们的灵魂所憎恶，但思想家们没必要将此作为证据，以证明我们的律法缺乏正当性，或者我们信仰的真实性不存在。相反，他们应该相信这恰恰标志着我们宗教的真实性、我们律法的公平性以及我们法规的公正性。明眼人该知道，越是精绝巧妙、非同寻

① 参见 Shalom Sadik, "Negation of Political Success in the Thought of Rabbi Isaac Pulgar," 11-12. 作者为波卡尔传统的和理性的两种相互矛盾的观点提供了几种解释。

② Maimonides, *The Guide of the Perplexed*, Introduction (Pines' edition, 18).

③ '*Ezer ha-Dat*, 27.

常的宗教信仰(这是由理智的本性所证明的,它才是正确的评断者),就越不可能被大多数人所接受。[①]

波卡尔在这里指出,理智的人绝不会认为,长期流放是摩西律法的"错误内容"导致的直接结果,相反,托拉反映了终极真理;然而,很少有人有能力去把握它的真正含义,大多数人追求的是肉体的欲望,不从事理论科学的研究,结果,他们无法理解导致特定事件——此处指犹太人大流散——发生的自然因果链。这种观点在哲学家中很普遍。在他们看来,只有少数人能够充分欣赏哲学,而大多数人却在削弱它的重要性。所以,只有少数人重视"真正的宗教",而庸俗的人只会追随显然在政治上更成功的大众宗教。

这段论述后不久,波卡尔写道,犹太人被流放不是因为他们犯了罪,而是因为他们严格遵守诫命。波卡尔指出,在遵守上帝的律法时,犹太人受到道德准则的约束,而其他国家则不受此约束。因此,波卡尔称:

> 因为我们完美的律法禁止、告诫我们不要行这毫无价值的道路,并阻止我们犯上述卑鄙特质(嫉妒)的恶行;由此可见,我们将位于被压迫者,而不是压迫者的行列;是被侵犯的一方,而不是侵犯者。[②]然而,肉体的欲望,包括[嫉妒]这种特质,对其他民族来说并不被禁止,所以他们会成为压迫者和侵犯者。因为他们内心的邪恶倾向,即欲望,他们无法警惕犯罪。他们不明白邪恶是真真实实的邪恶。[③]

具有讽刺意味的是,波卡尔在此讲大流散描述为犹太人遵守诫命的不可避免的结果。只要犹太人忠实地遵守上帝的律法,他们就永远属于"被压迫者"和"被侵犯者"。于是,这种激进的观点将流散解释为犹太人顺服上帝的结果,而不是他们所犯的任何罪的惩罚。

波卡尔对这一观点的阐述,是通过解释导致第二圣殿被毁和大流散的历史事件。在另一个段落中,他令人惊讶地写道:

> 当我们在自己的国家,扎根于自己的土地时,我们区别于周围所有的民

---

① ʻ*Ezer ha-Dat*, 51. 与波卡尔"真理不在多数"的观点相反,Origen 等基督教思想家认为,一个宗教的教徒人数证明了它的真实性和正确性。参见 Origen, "On First Principles," in *Origen An Exhortation to Martyrdom*, *Prayer and Selected Works*, book iv, chapter one, 2 (Paulist Press, 1979), 172-173。

② 汉娜·卡舍尔认为,波卡尔的观点从犹太人的角度表达了一种顺从和谦卑的态度。我认为,波卡尔的论点仅说明了犹太人在遵守诫命的情况下必须考虑的伦理因素,我将在下文进行论证。参见 Hannah Kasher, "Why is the Land in Ruins?", 154-156. [Hebrew]。

③ ʻ*Ezer ha-Dat*, 55; *Medieval Political Philosophy*, 219.着重号为作者所加。

族并高于他们。我们遵守自己值得称颂的律法诫命,这些诫命禁止各种身体的欲望,让我们远离它们……于是我们不再欺压他人。此外,我们有义务日日夜夜地研究律法和各种科学,这也是律法所规定的。而现在这却削弱、耗尽了我们的力量。[①] 另外,怜悯和温柔的特质被植入我们内心[②],我们开始忙于祭祀仪式和圣殿礼拜。结果,(开展)战争被我们遗忘了,武器也被废弃了。以色列人和犹大人忘却了他们曾学过的拉弓技能……因为我们想要远离邪恶而行善,寻觅追求和平。此时,我们周围民族的特征与正义的特征相反……他们心中充满了刚硬和残忍,因为他们对我们所拥有的东西有着巨大的欲望和嫉妒,正如大卫所说:我愿和睦,但我发言,他们就要争战。(《诗篇》120:7)……因为他们的方式是像野兽、熊和狮子一样攻击。他们不与我们讲和,而是咬牙合力毁了我们的殿,掳走我们作俘虏。我们这些幸存下来的极少数人流散在各处的土地上。[③]

波卡尔对圣殿被毁后犹太人处境的最初解释,引起了对其他民族伤害犹太人的严厉批判,毕竟犹太人只是寻求和平。波卡尔称,目前的情况体现了犹太人的律法与其他民族法律之间的主要区别。他严厉地批评了圣殿时期迫害犹太人的外邦人,指责他们缺乏道德规范来约束自己在社群内的行为,以及对其他民族的行为。

波卡尔的解释与迈蒙尼德一样,试图用自然主义的术语来阐释大流散。然而,虽然迈蒙尼德批评犹太领袖依赖观星,但波卡尔却为犹太人的道德行为辩护,并指责其他国家缺乏道德约束。更重要的是,对于迈蒙尼德来说,大流散是犹太人违法的结果;而对波卡尔来说,则源于对同一律法的忠实遵守。此外,波卡尔同意迈蒙尼德的观点,即犹太人未能制定战争策略、征服土地。然而,迈蒙尼德认为,犹太人没能研究发展战争之术,是因为他们忙于从事占星术——在他

---

① 参见 *Babylonian Talmud*, *Tractate Sanhedrin*, 26:b, "תורה מתישה כחו של אדם."

② Spinoza, *Theological-Political Treatise*, chapter 3, "Signum circumsicionis etiam hac in re tantum posse existimo, ut mihi persuadeam, hoc unum hanc nationem in aeternum conservaturum, imo nisi fundamenta suae religionis eorum animos effoeminarent, absolute crederem, eos aliquando, data occasione, ut sunt res humanae mutabiles, suum imperium iterum erecturos, Deumque eos de novo electurum." ("在我看来,割礼是非常重要的标记,我甚至可以说服自己,该标记会永远保护这个民族。不,我甚至相信,若不是他们的宗教基础使他们的灵魂变得软弱,他们甚至可以——如果机会允许,毕竟人的事情如此多变——重新建立自己的帝国,上帝可能会再度选择他们。")在斯宾诺莎看来,是犹太教的根基削弱和软化了犹太人的灵魂,造成他们被流放的处境。参见 Shlomo Pines, "Some Topics on Polqar's Treatise '*Ezer ha-Dat* and Their Parallels in Spinoza's View," 440; Shlomo Pines, "Spinoza's *Tractatus Theologico-Politicus* and the Jewish Philosophical Tradition," 718。

③ '*Ezer ha-Dat*, 55-56; *Medieval Political Philosophy*, 219.

看来这是犹太律法所禁止的。因此,犹太人的罪是他们从事被禁止的行为,结果受到惩罚并被逐出自己的家园。相比之下,波卡尔则认为,犹太人并没有专注于研究战争之术和战略,是因为他们忙于学习《托拉》(*Torah*)和科学,因此他们比其他民族更羸弱,最终遭到侵略,并从自己的土地上被驱逐。

然而,在本话题讨论的最后一段,波卡尔似乎用更传统的神学观点取代了他对犹太人大流散的激进的自然主义解释。粗略读来,他倾向于传统观点,视大流散为对罪的惩罚:

> 我们虽然接受了对上帝的真实信仰,成为圣洁且尊于其他所有民族,但却身陷痛苦和流亡。至此,我已经用基于自然的演示和论证为大家阐释了其中原因。至于那些嫉妒我的人,不要质疑我违背了严格的信仰路线,根据自然来进行论证。因为,事实上,我这样写只是为了"知道如何回应异端"。我相信应让人们知道,我们的城市因我们的罪而被毁,我们的圣殿因我们无数的过犯而荒废,我们因自身的罪过而被逐出自己的土地。上帝将以祂的怜悯为我们的诸多赎罪行为救赎我们,并将分散的同胞聚集在一起。祂将拯救我们,并带领我们屹立在我们自己的土地上。①

汉娜·卡舍尔(Hannah Kasher)在关于该主题的分析中对波卡尔的真实观点持怀疑态度。② 卡舍尔认为,波卡尔是出于反驳基督徒的理由提出了激进的自然主义观点。在她看来,波卡尔提出这种有争议的解释,动机是针对他自己的社区,向他们证明"历史上的以色列"是真正的以色列。虔诚善良的犹太人通过遵守诫命获得了这些道德品质,而基督徒因为犹太人遵守诫命而厌恶他们。卡舍尔总结道,这种自然主义的解释并不反映波卡尔的真实观点,因为从神学和历史的角度来看,这个论点是薄弱的。从神学上讲,它削弱了"犹太人赎罪后会得到上帝救赎"的整个犹太信仰理念。从历史上看,波卡尔的论点与《圣经》的解释并不相关,《圣经》将圣殿被毁与以色列人的罪直接联系起来。

与卡舍尔的观点相反,我建议对波卡尔关于犹太人大流散的讨论进行不同的解读。我认为,波卡尔不太可能在不厌其烦地对犹太人的灾难阐述了创新独特的见解之后,最终再提出常见的传统神学理由。在我看来,关于犹太人的流

---

① '*Ezer ha-Dat*, 56. Manekin's translation, 219.

② 参见 Hannah Kasher, "'Why Is the Land in Ruins?'(Jeremiah 9:11): Religious Transgression versus Natural Historical Process in the Writing of Maimonides and His Disciples," 155-156; Shlomo Pines, "Some Topics on Polqar's Treatise '*Ezer ha-Dat* and Their Parallels in Spinoza's View," 432-438; Shlomo Pines, "Spinoza's *Tractatus Theologico-Politicus* and the Jewish Philosophical Tradition," 506-508。

亡，波卡尔实施了迈蒙尼德的策略，即一边向大众进行通俗易懂的解释，一边向细心的读者提供隐晦教导。波卡尔在《信仰之助》的序言中明确强调，由于政治和社会环境，他必须隐藏自己的真实观点，以避免被那些无法理解他的哲学方法的人指责为异端。[1] 因此，他故意提出这种传统观点，以防止他的社群成员指责他违背传统的神学观点。[2]

于是，在上文引用的段落中，波卡尔假意声称自己提出自然主义观点“只是”作为对异端的回应，上下文暗示异端指的是布尔戈斯的阿布纳。然而，他提到那些“嫉妒”他的人、那些可能指责他捍卫哲学观点而不是神学观点的人，从中可以清楚地看出，他以这种方式结束该章节是出于为教义辩护的原因。因此，他并没有指责外邦人缺乏道德准则，并利用犹太人遵守律法而欺压他们，而是强调外邦人迫害犹太人，摧毁他们的城市，并将他们驱逐出自己的土地，这都是犹太人咎由自取。

在他对犹太人大流散的最后一段讨论中，波卡尔向传统主义者发表了讲话。我认为，他是带着歉意甚至虚伪选择赞扬——至少部分地赞扬传统方法。因此，波卡尔选择在讨论的结尾重归传统主义的观点，将大流散视为违背上帝律法的惩罚。波卡尔以传统观点结束他的讨论，旨在强化自己社群成员的精神——他们无视基督徒和基督教皈依者的指责，依旧接受传统的解释。如果说阿布纳和他的同类遵循的是基督教的神学主张，即上帝抛弃犹太人是因为他们不接受耶稣是真正的弥赛亚，波卡尔在此则是强调了犹太人的对应论点。他转向传统的犹太神学观点，根据该主张，流放是对犹太人不遵守上帝诫命的惩罚。因此，结论是犹太人必须继续遵守上帝的律法，为自己赎罪，同时拒绝耶稣是真正的弥赛亚，耐心地忍受他们目前的处境。他们应这样做，直到上帝出于祂的怜悯，因忠实遵守律法奖赏他们、救赎他们。

结论

波卡尔遵循迈蒙尼德使用的隐晦方法，针对两种不同受众，提出两种关于犹太人大流散的不同解释。一种是针对传统主义者的神学解释，而另一种是他原

---

① 参见 *'Ezer ha-Dat*，27。

② 波卡尔多次应用迈蒙尼德的方法，例如，关于预言，他提出了“传统”观点——此处也是迈蒙尼德的观点，即先知高于哲学家（*'Ezer ha-Dat*，158）。另一方面，他与后来斯宾诺莎的观点相呼应，提出了相反的主张，即哲学家高于先知，因为他们可以解释如何获得知识并教导他人，而这两项技能是先知所缺乏的。参见 *'Ezer ha-Dat*，44，88。

创的激进解释，针对的是更有洞察力的读者。通过这种做法，他为传统犹太人提供了标准的神学论据，以削弱当地基督徒和基督教皈依者的神学指控。同时，他为细心的读者提供了一种激进的自然主义的解释，以削弱基于无法证明的超自然因素或迷信的论点。

波卡尔反对传统的犹太观点，即犹太人因违反上帝的诫命而受到惩罚。他进一步反驳了基督徒和基督教皈依者的观点，他们认为犹太人的罪是拒绝耶稣为真正的弥赛亚。波卡尔认为，犹太人因严格遵守上帝的诫命而遭受漫长痛苦的流放。遵守上帝的律法，意味着受道德准则约束的虔诚人比不遵守任何法律的人遭受更多的痛苦。因此，通过遵守诫命，犹太人寻求的不是外在的物质利益，而是内在的益处。

既然大流散是犹太人严格遵守上帝诫命和列国不道德行为的结果，根据此逻辑，流亡将在以下两个事件之一发生时结束，即犹太人违背上帝的诫命 ，并因此变得与其他民族一样不道德；或者，其他民族将采用一种道德准则约束自己，并以道德的方式对待他人，包括犹太人。

The Jewish Exile—A Jewish Averroistic Response to Maimonides

Racheli Haliva Tr. SHEN Jianyu

Abstract: Jewish exile is traditionally perceived as a divine punishment resulting from the Jews' disobedience to God's will. Even Maimonides and the Jewish rationalists who attempted to naturalize this traditional view did not break from the classical paradigm of the Jewish exile resulting from the Jewish people's transgression. According to Maimonides' view, the Jews were exiled from their homeland because they engaged in astrological practices, which, in his view, are forbidden by Jewish law. As a consequence, they failed to develop proper military strategies. In this paper I wish to present Isaac Polqar's naturalistic view, which deviates from the naturalistic explanation provided by Maimonides and others. According to Polqar the Jews were exiled from their land because they strictly obeyed God's commandments. Observing these commandments resulted in the Jews behaving ethically towards others and among themselves. The nations, on the other hand, were not bound by God's commandments, and therefore lacked norms that would prevent them from treating others in an unethical manner. Given their ethical code, the Jews were a particularly easy target for the nations who, unconstrained by ethical considerations, could conquer, oppress, and exile them.

Key Words: Abner of Burgos, Jewish Exile, Maimonides, Isaac Polqar, Jewish-Christian Dialogue

《以赛亚书》居鲁士形象探析*

孟振华**

【摘要】《以赛亚书》中对居鲁士的描述和《圣经》其他经卷一样，不乏溢美之词。他也成为《希伯来圣经》中一位特殊的外邦君主。对居鲁士的提及和记载，可能并非同时代作者的描述（或预言和期待），而是源于更晚年代的书写和编辑。对他的塑造基本反映了后流放时期以色列作者的真实态度。在通过这位外邦君主传播一神信仰观念的同时，先知作者或许还尝试将这一形象与古代以色列的重要人物联系起来，以消除社群中不同传统之间的冲突。

【关键词】《圣经》；波斯；犹大；族群关系

《希伯来圣经》记载了为数众多的外邦人，其中既有被描绘为以色列人朋友，甚至被接纳为一份子的正面人物，也有恶贯满盈、被人鄙视或仇恨的反派形象。而经文提及的外邦君主同样呈现出多样性，难以一概而论。但波斯帝国（阿契美尼德王朝）的统治者居鲁士大帝，则是这些外邦君主中相当特别的一位。他在《圣经》中被直接提及名字的次数便不下20次，分散在记录历史的《历代志》《以斯拉记》和先知作品《以赛亚书》等书卷中。①

呈现历史记载风格的《以斯拉—尼希米记》，其叙事背景基本都是在波斯帝

* 本文系教育部人文社会科学研究青年基金项目“族群关系视角下的《希伯来圣经》正义问题研究”（19YJC130007）、教育部人文社会科学重点研究基地重大项目“文明交流互鉴视角下的希伯来圣经研究”（22JD730003）的研究成果，并受到中央高校基本科研业务费专项资金资助。

** 孟振华，南京大学哲学系（宗教学系）、南京大学犹太和以色列研究所教授。

① 《历代志下》36:22，23；《以斯拉记》1:1，2，7，8；3:7；4:3，5；5:13，14，17；6:3，14；《以赛亚书》44:28；45:1，13（原文作“他”）；另在启示文学作品《但以理书》也曾被提及（《但以理书》1:21；6:28；10:1）。

国统治时期。在作者的笔下,犹太人与波斯政权相处融洽,利益一致,因此他们可以也应该共存,并通力合作。[①]具体到居鲁士,他领导此前名气不大的波斯迅速取代了盛极一时的新巴比伦王国,下诏允许被掳的犹太人回归耶路撒冷,并允诺和资助他们重建圣殿。《尼希米记》第5章犹大省的社会矛盾与近百年前的居鲁士没有直接关系;而《以斯拉记》中,波斯当局禁止犹太人重建圣殿(《以斯拉记》4)之后,也因为犹太人援引居鲁士的命令(《以斯拉记》5:13—17)上书大利乌(大流士)王查考、确认其诏命(《以斯拉记》6:1—5)而再次允准了圣殿的重建,促成第二圣殿最终完工。如果说,从《以斯拉记》和《尼希米记》字里行间可以看出回归的犹太人与波斯之间发生的不愉快事件,使波斯帝国的正面形象多少打了一点折扣,那经文对于居鲁士的提及就完全没有这样的元素。相反,他之前的诏命(《以斯拉记》5—6)还为缓和关系提供了重要的帮助和支撑。居鲁士的行为被作者归于耶和华的大能,是耶和华"激动"了他的心,使他"下诏通告全国"(《历代志下》36:22;《以斯拉记》1:1)。而《以斯拉记》中的居鲁士诏命显示,他对耶和华也具有一定的认识(《历代志下》36:23;《以斯拉记》1:2—3)。总的来说,居鲁士的个人形象在《以斯拉记》《尼希米记》,以及在末尾提及他准许回归诏命的《历代志》这些历史书卷中臻于完美。

而在作为先知作品的《以赛亚书》中,尽管居鲁士被直接提及的次数并不算很多,但地位比起历史作品中似乎有过之而无不及。第二以赛亚把居鲁士称为耶和华所拣选的"牧人",必成就耶和华所喜悦的,且"必下令建造耶路撒冷、发命立稳圣殿的根基"(《以赛亚书》44:28)。还称他是"耶和华所膏的",耶和华"搀扶他的右手,使列国降伏在他面前",又"放松列王的腰带,使城门在他面前敞开,不得关闭"(《以赛亚书》45:1)。接下来,耶和华还对他直接说:

> 我必在你前面行,修平崎岖之地。我必打破铜门,砍断铁闩。我要将暗中的宝物和隐秘的财宝赐给你,使你知道提名召你的,就是我耶和华以色列的上帝。因我仆人雅各、我所拣选以色列的缘故,我就提名召你。你虽不认识我,我也加给你名号。(《以赛亚书》45:2—4)

耶和华将"受膏者"的名号赐予并不了解自己与其关系的居鲁士,本身便令

① 详见孟振华 Meng Zhenhua,〈圣经中的波斯形象——以历史记载为中心的考察〉[The Image of Persia in the Bible: An Observation based on Historical Accounts],《华中学术》[Central China Humanities],2018年第3期[2018, Issue 3],221-229。

人惊讶,对被掳以后《以赛亚书》的读者解读此书也非常重要。① 除此之外,第二以赛亚还有更多的经文被认为可能和居鲁士有关。②他是耶和华凭公义所兴起的,他侍奉耶和华,耶和华也给他丰厚的回报(《以赛亚书》45:13—14)。外邦君主受耶和华控制和支配的描述在《希伯来圣经》中固然并不少见(如《出埃及记》7:3; 9:12; 10:20, 27; 11:10; 14:8;《耶利米书》25:9; 27:6 等),他们对以色列的上帝有所认识的例子在后期书卷(如《历代志下》35:21;《但以理书》2:47; 4:34—37)中也曾出现,但居鲁士在《以赛亚书》中获得的荣宠程度在《希伯来圣经》中可谓绝无仅有,成为外邦君主中一个显著的特例。

第二以赛亚对居鲁士的提及和描写,是同时代作者对居鲁士的描述,还是包括了更晚年代犹太精英对居鲁士的回忆与塑造?第二以赛亚对居鲁士的真实态度是什么样的?塑造这样的居鲁士形象有何目的?这些问题对于研究波斯时期以色列人对外邦人的态度以及他们的历史与宗教观念都有重要的意义。

一、《以赛亚书》相关经文的成书背景

现代《圣经》学术一般不会把《以赛亚书》第 40—55 章看作公元前 8 世纪的先知以赛亚所作的预言,而认为出自被掳以后的作者(第二以赛亚)之手笔。但对具体的成书时间和背景仍然存在较大的争议。

19 世纪末,德国学者基特尔(R. Kittel)指出了第二以赛亚经文与居鲁士圆柱铭文的相似性,并推测两份文献都源于"巴比伦宫廷风格"。③史密斯(Morton Smith)则指出,如果说《以赛亚书》的第 40—48 章和圆柱铭文为平行关系,那么之后剩余的章节中并没有这样的对应关系。④同时,《以赛亚书》和铭文后半部分居鲁士对巴比伦宣告统治政策的内容并没有相似点,说明第二以赛亚的书写早于居鲁士对巴比伦的占领。可见,这是在居鲁士征服巴比伦前不久,他的代理人

① Goran Eidevall, "Propagandistic Constructions of Empires in the Book of Isaiah," in *Divination, Politics, and Ancient Near Eastern Empires*, eds. Alan Lenzi and Jonathan Stokl (Atlanta: Society of Biblical Literature, 2014), 124.

② 除了 44:24—28; 45:1—7 (8)之外,可能还包括 41:1—4 (5—7), 21—29; (42:5—9); 45:9—13; 46:(5), 9—11; 48:12—15 (16a)。Kristin Joachimsen, "The Book of Isaiah: Persian/Hellenistic Background," in *The Oxford Handbook of Isaiah*, ed. Lena-Sofia Tiemeyer (Oxford: Oxford University Press, 2020), 181.

③ 参见 R. Kittel, "Cyrus und Deuterojesaja," *Zeitschrift für die alttestamentliche Wissenschaft* 18 (1898):149 ff. 转引自 Morton Smith, "II Isaiah and the Persians," *Journal of the American Oriental Society* 83 (1963): 415。

④ 参见 Morton Smith, "II Isaiah and the Persians," 415。

在巴比伦发布的宣传纲领，为居鲁士的行动铺平道路。[①]犹太人和巴比伦人的利益和期待有所区别，而对波斯来说，后者的利益显然更为重要，因此居鲁士把犹太人复仇的梦想放在一边，竭尽所能安抚巴比伦人。这使第二以赛亚非常失望，因此在48章之后的预言中，居鲁士也就此消失。[②]德尔比（Josiah Derby）则推测，第二以赛亚可能亲自参加了居鲁士发布圆柱铭文宣言的仪式，这激励他用兴高采烈和期待的话语表达异象。他大胆运用耶和华取代马尔杜克，并宣称是耶和华兴起了居鲁士。从居鲁士的角度而言，重建耶路撒冷圣殿的建议与他宣布的政策本来就是一致的。犹太人不可见的上帝授予他的崇高头衔也令他受用。如果居鲁士接受这个神祇的指示，神祇可能会继续保佑他；如果他拒绝接受，则有可能受到阻碍或伤害。[③]因此居鲁士愉快地接受了祝福，并下诏支持了第二圣殿的建设。

史密斯的对比分析似乎有些道理，但忽略了圆柱铭文后半部分的28—30行和《以赛亚书》45:14之间的对应关系，这使得他对第二以赛亚成书时间的推测依据产生怀疑[④]；而把第二以赛亚、居鲁士圆柱铭文和拿波尼度的宫廷文献所做的联系，也不免有些牵强。[⑤]德尔比则是全盘接受了《以斯拉记》所记录的波斯诏命的真实性，把第二以赛亚的书写看作先知的一次赌博，目的在于救赎其同胞，让被流放者回到耶路撒冷，在他们的历史家园恢复他们的民族存在，并最终获得了成功。[⑥]这两种看法共同的问题在于，过于依赖经文中的记录和铭文中的自我宣传，同时也多少高估了犹太人在居鲁士心目中的地位。公元前6世纪中期的犹太人作为巴比伦的阶下囚，连同被毁灭的耶路撒冷，恐怕很难引起波斯的关注。铭文在谈及多个城市、民族和政权的同时，对犹太人和耶路撒冷只字未提。

史密斯和德尔比把第二以赛亚的成书地点定为巴比伦，认为其反映了公元前539年居鲁士征服新巴比伦帝国的历史背景，这一假设在学术界是比较流行的。不过，和《希伯来圣经》的大多数篇章一样，把第二以赛亚的16章经文归于

---

① 参见 Morton Smith, "II Isaiah and the Persians," 417。

② 同上，418。

③ 参见 Josiah Derby, "Isaiah and Cyrus," *Jewish Bible Quarterly* 24 (1996):174-175。

④ 铭文28—30行的译文为："所有住在从波斯湾到地中海、大地四方的宫殿里的君王……所有住在帐篷里的西土的君王，向我纳上丰富的贡品，在巴比伦城亲吻我的双脚。"参见 Philip Davies, "God of Cyrus, God of Israel," in *Words Remembered, Texts Renewed: Essays in Honour of John F.A. Sawyer*, eds. Jon Davies, Graham Harvey and Wilfred G.E. Watsonp (Sheffield: Sheffield Academic Press, 1995), 210。

⑤ 参见 Joseph Blekinsopp, *Isaiah 40-55: A New Translation with Introduction and Commentary* (New York: Doubleday, 2002), 250-267。

⑥ 参见 Josiah Derby, "Isaiah and Cyrus," 174, 177。

同一位作者的假设受到了挑战。而布雷肯索普(Joseph Blenkinsopp)在把第二以赛亚的写作时间定为巴比伦统治期最后十年的同时,指出 45:1—7 涉及居鲁士的情节可能完成于公元前 6 世纪末 5 世纪初的大流士一世时期。[①]与此相关的质疑是,为何先知兼诗人一定是实际上在巴比伦生活的?为什么必须亲身经历了被掳?[②]

塞茨(Christopher R. Seitz)基于第二以赛亚的经文总结了这些质疑的要点:(1)对被掳的描述并非站在巴比伦的立场上,而是有北方、南方、东方和西方(《以赛亚书》43:5—6; 49:12);(2)居鲁士被描述为从东方/北方兴起(《以赛亚书》41:2, 25),“从远方来”(《以赛亚书》46:11);(3)对雅各/以色列未能献燔祭的批判(《以赛亚书》43:22—24)在被掳期间并不适用;(4)对锡安/耶路撒冷和犹大(《以赛亚书》40:9; 44:26)以及重建圣殿(《以赛亚书》44:28)的高度关注;(5)对巴比伦的描述是“到巴比伦去”(בבלה שלחתי)(《以赛亚书》43:14),另有“向列国举手,向万民竖立大旗”(אשא גוים-אל ידי, עמים-ואל ארים נסי)(《以赛亚书》49:22);(6)“这百姓是被抢被夺的,都牢笼在坑中,隐藏在狱里”(《以赛亚书》42:22)与被掳无关。[③]戴维斯(Phillip Davies)进一步提出,第二以赛亚的开场宣告(《以赛亚书》40:1—2)即是针对耶路撒冷而非被掳民众的[④],认为第二以赛亚产生于被掳巴比伦的看法忽略了文本的耶路撒冷源头,同时把第一和第二以赛亚的结合看作是偶然或外部强加的,忽略了两者的有机联系。[⑤]至于《以赛亚书》对巴比伦神祇的提及(《以赛亚书》46:1)和对巴比伦被血腥占领的预言(《以赛亚书》46—47),戴维斯指出,无论是被掳者还是留居者,都曾被巴比伦人管制数十年,犹太人熟悉其文化,用巴比伦神名来称呼外邦神合情合理。如果说预言可能出错,记忆和记录也有可能不准确。摧毁巴比伦的行为被第二以赛亚安排在了居

---

① 参见 Joseph Blenkinsopp, “The Theological Politics of Deutero-Isaiah,” in *Divination, Politics and Ancient Near Eastern Texts*, 136,及该页 note 13 所列有关编修层次讨论的更多文献。

② 参见 Philip Davies, “God of Cyrus, God of Israel,” 213; Christopher R. Seitz, *Zion's Final Destiny: The Development of the Book of Isaiah. A Reassessment of Isaiah* 36-39 (Minneapolis: Fortress Press, 1992), 205。

③ 参见 Christopher R. Seitz, *Zion's Final Destiny: The Development of the Book of Isaiah. A Reassessment of Isaiah* 36-39, 205。

④ 参见 Philip Davies, “God of Cyrus, God of Israel,” 213。

⑤ 参见 Christopher R. Seitz, *Zion's Final Destiny: The Development of the Book of Isaiah. A Reassessment of Isaiah* 36-39, 206-207。

鲁士身上。[①]戴维斯进而断言,《以赛亚书》40—55 章产生于巴比伦的可能性微乎其微。[②]

第二以赛亚谈及耶路撒冷和犹大城市时,承诺这位母亲会拯救其失去的子女(《以赛亚书》49:20—25; 54:1),从"列国"(גוים)、"万民"(עמים)中带来(《以赛亚书》49:22)。这或许可以联系到波斯允许犹太人回归的政策,但更有可能和公元前 5 世纪波斯对犹大省的日益重视和经济复兴的目标有关。[③]对人口不足的焦虑固然贯穿了几乎整部《希伯来圣经》的主题;而在波斯时期的犹大省,这个问题又尤其突出。人丁不旺是犹大省的现实危机,增加人口则是犹大省的当务之急。第二以赛亚对此的关注或许就是对这一状况的反应。

克拉茨(Reinhard G. Kratz)提出了更为复杂和系统的编辑过程假设,他将第二以赛亚分为五个不同的编辑层面,将第三层称为"居鲁士补编",追溯到大流士一世统治时期(公元前 520—515 年)。在分析第 45 章第 1—7 节时,他将第 1 节和第 3 节的一部分,以及第 2、4、6、7 节归为"基本层",居鲁士被称为耶和华的受膏者,其任务是征服巴比伦,并解放耶和华的仆人雅各/以色列。而在"居鲁士补编"(包括第 1 节一部分、3b 和第 5 节)中,居鲁士被认定为耶和华的仆人,他对雅各/以色列的拯救成为外邦人的光。[④]不过,这样的重构同样存在问题。克拉茨在批评过往学者将第二以赛亚的居鲁士与圆柱铭文的居鲁士生硬联系的同时,自己不免也将前者和阿契美尼德王室铭文简单结合起来,作为重构编修过程的依据,但忽略了希伯来、亚述、巴比伦等传统中创造的主题和更深厚的文化背景,同样显得简单化和牵强。[⑤]

总的来说,第二以赛亚的成书背景仍在存在很大的争议,难以定论。当代学者一般认为,其中的经文可能经历了不同时期、不同群体的编修。要想将每节经

① 参见 Philip Davies, "God of Cyrus, God of Israel," 214-215。另有看法认为,第二以赛亚中无论是直接点名提及,还是通常被认为指称居鲁士的经文(42:5—7; 45:11—13; 48:12—15),实际所指的是大流士一世。参见 Rainer Albertz, "Darius in Place of Cyrus: The First Edition of Deutero-Isaiah (Isaiah 40.1-52.12) in 521 BCE," *Journal for the Study of the Old Testament* 273 (2003), 371-383。关于反对意见,参见 Reinhard G. Kratz, "Isaiah and the Persians," in *Imperial Visions: The Prophet and the Book of Isaiah in an Age of Empires*, eds. Reinhard Gregor Kratz and Joachim Schaper (Göttingen: Vandenhoeck & Ruprecht, 2020), 158-159。

② 参见 Philip Davies, "God of Cyrus, God of Israel," 215。

③ 同上,221。

④ 参见 Reinhard G. Kratz, *Kyros im Deuterojesaja-Buch: Redaktionsgeschichtliche Untersuchungen zu Entstehung und Theologie von Jes* 40-55 (Tübingen: Mohr Siebeck, 1991), 175-191; Joachimsen, "The Book of Isaiah: Persian/Hellenistic Background," 188, n. 56; Kratz, "Isaiah and the Persians," 155-161。

⑤ 有关介绍与批评,详见 Joachimsen, "The Book of Isaiah: Persian/Hellenistic Background," 188-189。

文都准确定位到某个确切年代似乎更是难以完成的任务。但无论如何,把所有的章节都归于居鲁士征服巴比伦之前(或之后很短的时间内)所作,显然是不明智的。其中相当一部分内容,包括对居鲁士的提及和记载,可能并非同时代作者的描述(或预言和期待),而是源于更晚年代的书写和编辑。作者关注的群体和设定的受众,或许不仅仅是身处巴比伦的被掳者及其后裔,已经回归到耶路撒冷和犹大省各地的犹太人同样是先知言说的重要对象。在这一背景下,第二以赛亚又是如何看待居鲁士和波斯的呢?

二、第二以赛亚对居鲁士和波斯的态度

古代以色列先知曾经多次对周边的一些政权宣告耶和华(或他们自己)声色俱厉的批判,但先知文学中并没有任何关于耶和华对波斯的惩罚或审判的文字。《以赛亚书》中对巴比伦的反对和对波斯的亲近似乎是一脉相承的,而居鲁士更被描绘成上帝的代理人、犹太人的解放者甚至世界的征服者[①],呈现出高大、完美的正面形象。

第二以赛亚和其他犹太知识分子一样,有充分的理由赞美和歌颂居鲁士。这位君主是一位伟大的领袖,他以和平的方式帮助犹太人战胜敌人。他承诺让被掳的犹太人重返家园,并资助他们重建圣殿,展现出无比的慷慨与仁慈。此外,他还是一位睿智的统治者,下达的命令总能得到快速而有效的实施。对于波斯委任的犹大省的领导人,以及与第二圣殿密切相关的祭司群体而言,居鲁士和他的波斯帝国是他们现实世界中权柄的来源,忠于波斯的统治者理所当然,甚至还倾向于将“上帝律法”和“王的命令”(《以斯拉记》7:26)相提并论。而第二以赛亚很可能也属于这样一个精英群体。[②]哪怕是普通的巴比伦犹太囚虏(及其后裔),无论是否在波斯国王许可下返回故土,对居鲁士产生感激之情都是自然而然的。把这种感激书写在自己的宗教文本中表达出来,并向民众传颂,对于居鲁士和波斯当局来说也是喜闻乐见的现象。犹太的政治未来将在波斯国王的统治下,而作者并没有暗示未来会有一个本土的独立政权。就思想层面而言,“受膏者”的角色不仅传给了居鲁士,也传给了波斯人,因为耶路撒冷作为世界国王的中心这一角色意味着一个世界帝国,而这只能是波斯帝国。耶路撒冷的命运不是等待波斯帝国的毁灭,而是在它内部实现的:耶路撒冷将作为波斯帝国的一座

① 关于居鲁士除了“解放者”“征服者”之外的形象,详见 Philip Davies, “God of Cyrus, God of Israel,” 216。

② 参见 Goran Eidevall, “Propagandistic Constructions of Empires in the Book of Isaiah,” 124。

城市延续,也许会取代巴比伦成为一个宗教和文化中心。①这得到了犹太人的广泛认可。当然,波斯君主似乎并没有排他性的一神宗教信仰,这从居鲁士圆柱铭文中把他本人打扮成马尔杜克的代言人就可以看出来。而在《圣经》中,居鲁士成了弥赛亚、受膏者,拥有上帝赋予的统治犹大的权威(《以赛亚书》44:24—28;45:1—8),这种对政治现实的神学辩护也将犹大被殖民的状况加以合法化。②简而言之,犹太人政治上接受了波斯的统治,思想上认可了波斯的统治,同时还为这样的现实进行了辩护。

然而,这是不是《圣经》作者尤其是第二以赛亚对待居鲁士和波斯的真实态度呢?学者注意到,居鲁士在《以赛亚书》44:24 至 45:13 中并没有被称为波斯国王或统帅,第二以赛亚也并没有直接提及波斯。③爱德瓦尔(Goran Eidevall)据此推测,居鲁士的波斯身份头衔以及波斯帝国在先知语言中的缺失,表现出作者对这个政权的矛盾心理。犹太知识分子(包括先知和文士)不敢公然反对他们那个时代的外国压迫者,因为他们恐惧报复。④爱德瓦尔把尼希米祷告中的怨言(《尼西米记》9:36—37a)看作对波斯的批评,认为其中提到的苦难是犹太人在波斯统治下所遭受的。而先知的预言往往就是在危机中产生的。在这种情况下,很可能有一部分人会通过斯科特所说的"隐藏文本"(hidden transcripts)来表达自己的观点,也就是"变相的公众异议"(disguised forms of public dissent)。持不同政见者采取的策略之一是匿名(包括使用假名),而第二以赛亚选择了匿名,这可能就是针对波斯的。居鲁士因为对犹太人作出了一些贡献而被授予了"弥赛亚"的称号。但这只是对他个人的,没有理由将耶和华拣选的观念延伸到他的王位继承人即波斯统治者身上。第二以赛亚在此故意不提他们和他们的帝国,属于"被压制的反对"(suppressed opposition)⑤。除此之外,爱德瓦尔把《以赛亚书》33:1 也看作对波斯的谴责,认为一些针对亚述或巴比伦的神谕对于波斯同样适用;《以赛亚书》30:27—33 的"反亚述"预言可能起源于波斯时代,使用"亚述"作为实际压迫者波斯的代号。因此,波斯和亚述、巴比伦的命运一样,帝国崛起后,最终注定衰落,被人遗忘。当历史实现它的最终目标时,耶和华将创

① 参见 Philip Davies, "God of Cyrus, God of Israel," 218。

② 参见 Jon L. Berquist, "Postcolonialism and Imperial Motives for Canonization," *Semeia* 75 (1996): 22。

③ 事实上,《以赛亚书》40—48 章除居鲁士外,并未提其他君主,也未提其他的帝国、总督、高官的名字,或军队、税收等信息。参见 Joachimsen, "The Book of Isaiah: Persian/Hellenistic Background," 177。

④ 参见 Goran Eidevall, "Propagandistic Constructions of Empires in the Book of Isaiah," 125。

⑤ 同上。

造一个“新天新地”(《以赛亚书》66:22)[①]。换言之,第二以赛亚用刻意的沉默和对重要信息的忽略,表达了对波斯的不满。

然而,居鲁士作为波斯的君主,在公元前6世纪中期以后的巴勒斯坦、巴比伦乃至整个古代近东社会,都是广为人知的。当人们谈论居鲁士时,首先想到的便是他建立强大帝国的丰功伟绩。他甚至被视为“波斯的化身”[②]。居鲁士和波斯帝国之间很难真正分离开来。约西姆森(Kristin Joachimsen)则从另一个角度理解这一现象,指出居鲁士未被称为波斯人的国王,而这个外邦人被纳入了耶和华的计划:波斯国王征服巴比伦拯救了耶和华人民。在《以赛亚书》未来的愿景(《以赛亚书》66:22)中,当所有人都承认耶和华的时候,外来的民族和锡安、耶路撒冷和以色列一样都是被包括的。[③]不过,约西姆森并不认为居鲁士就得到了真正的尊宠。他进一步指出,当第二以赛亚将居鲁士描绘为救世主,并嘲弄其他神祇及其崇拜者时,居鲁士其实和拜别神者一样,在这些预言中的任务不过是揭示耶和华与以色列的身份。更确切地说,这些文本既不是反巴比伦,也不是亲波斯,而是亲耶和华。[④]按照这样的分析,不管居鲁士在这里被授予什么样的头衔,不过是个工具人而已。

应当承认,爱德瓦尔等学者对主流观点的质疑和约西姆森等人的回应与分析都有一定根据,除了第二以赛亚中“波斯”的缺失和居鲁士“波斯头衔”的缺失之外,历史上波斯对统治下的各个民族确实可能并没有想象中那么宽容。不过,如果据此便断言第二以赛亚乃至《圣经》其他的作者反对波斯又慑于其淫威而不敢公开批评波斯,未免失之偏颇。毕竟,犹太回归者是得到波斯的允准回到故土的,耶路撒冷上层人士的权柄也是由波斯当局赋予的,这对包括第二以赛亚之内的《圣经》经卷写作和编纂产生了不小的影响。

显而易见的是,后流放时期的经卷中,波斯帝国和历史上其他强大政权(如亚述和巴比伦)往往是被区别对待的,波斯的形象得到了美化。这样的话语逻辑能间接地增强回归者的合法性,同时也可以提升耶路撒冷在犹太人中的中心地位,凸显圣殿的作用。[⑤]居鲁士在第二以赛亚中和其他先知作品中被提及的次数不多,主要原因可能在于先知书将大量注意力集中于国破家亡的惨剧以及犹太

---

① 参见 Goran Eidevall, “Propagandistic Constructions of Empires in the Book of Isaiah,” 125-127。

② Ehud Ben Zvi, “The Yehudite Collection of Prophetic Books and Imperial Contexts: Some Observations,” in *Divination, Politics, and Ancient Near Eastern Empires*, 157.

③ 参见 Joachimsen, “The Book of Isaiah: Persian/Hellenistic Background,” 179。

④ 同上,186。

⑤ 参见 Ehud Ben Zvi, “The Yehudite Collection of Prophetic Books and Imperial Contexts: Some Observations,” 155。

人未来的乌托邦式设想。居鲁士时期正好处于这两个事件之间,因而未能受到更为广泛的关注。从更深的层次看,正如波斯时期的第二圣殿在宏观意义上并没有过去的第一圣殿和未来乌托邦式的圣殿重要,因此不值得被"记住";居鲁士也没有未来乌托邦式的国王重要。将来取代波斯帝国的政权比波斯帝国本身更加重要,也更值得被铭记。[①]先知书作者写作的目的并非为居鲁士个人树碑立传,其更为在意的还是犹太民族自身的命运。居鲁士和波斯或许并不是他们的核心关切。

不过,作者对居鲁士形象着墨不多,绝不意味着《以赛亚书》对居鲁士和波斯帝国的否定。至于"工具人"的推测,应当指出的是,居鲁士和其他的以色列人与外邦人一样,不但仍然在上帝拯救万民的计划之中,还扮演了重要的角色。即使经文未提他的外邦身份和头衔,考虑到外邦君主在《圣经》书卷中较为普遍的负面形象,他所受的荣宠也会给受众留下更为深刻的印象。若他只是一个普通的工具,作者则完全没有必要将各种溢美之词叠加在这个外族国王身上。

接下来的问题是,连耶和华都不认识的外邦君主居鲁士(《以赛亚书》45:4—5)又能否被如此高举呢?在第二以赛亚的论述逻辑中,即使是伟大的居鲁士,也不知道耶和华,不知道他成功的原因或他努力的"真正"目的。先知告诉大家,耶和华是世界的创造者和统治者,但在世俗世界中,这个神往往不为人知;耶路撒冷应该是处于世界中心的城市,但在现实中,它是一个"世界"的大多数居民都不知道的非常小的村庄,很难想象可以履行它的宇宙角色。因此,在波斯帝国的世界里,"真理"似乎是一个"秘密",只有犹太人知道。他们能够通过阅读权威的宗教典籍,获得这样隐秘的知识。[②]对这个"秘密"的掌握足以令多数犹太人在心理上接受波斯的统治和对居鲁士的溢美。

同时,在第二以赛亚乃至其他被掳后的先知中,有一股强大的潮流,它记住了一个未来的帝国,在这个帝国的中心,传统的国王和神的形象将会合二为一;在未来的帝国里,只有耶和华是国王。而居鲁士的成功,恰恰证明了这位独一神的大能。因此,波斯人居鲁士成为受膏者,并不会影响到耶和华信仰和先知对犹太人教导的权威性。[③]毕竟,作者深信也试图让其受众相信的是,耶和华才是王。而居鲁士的成功,在《圣经》作者的描述中,就不知不觉变成了耶和华和以色列的成功。作者将波斯的传统化为己用,不但使犹太人能够更好地融入帝国之中,也

① 参见 Ehud Ben Zvi, "The Yehudite Collection of Prophetic Books and Imperial Contexts: Some Observations," 158。

② 同上,159。

③ 同上,161。

有助于犹太社群自身的稳定和发展。

总的来说,犹太精英群体有充分的理由赞美和歌颂居鲁士,而第二以赛亚很可能也属于这样一个精英群体,也是既得利益者。返回故土的犹太人对居鲁士产生感激之情毫不意外。而当《圣经》作者通过宗教文本将居鲁士的作为解释为独一神的功绩之时,思想上对耶和华的虔敬和现实中对波斯政权的臣服与支持便能够较为和谐地统一起来。居鲁士的正面形象基本反映了以第二以赛亚为代表的犹太精英对波斯及其统治者的真实态度。

三、第二以赛亚居鲁士形象塑造对回归群体的作用

第二以赛亚所塑造的居鲁士的正面形象,并不违背《圣经》作者对他的态度和本意。不过,用以色列的方式和逻辑来谈论居鲁士,把它纳入《圣经》的话语体系,显然也会面临调和的困难。"'他者'被部分地'以色列化'的问题,必然会引发'他者'是否会改变到足以加入未来帝国中心的问题。"[①]不过,正如前文指出,先知关注的焦点,并非某位外族领袖或某个外邦政权。先知的预言并不只是为了表达情感,更不是单纯向波斯示好的阿谀奉承。预言的目的还是向特定的受众传递自己的思想,以解决现实中存在的问题。相比之下,以色列民族所面临的现实困难和思想困境,是先知乃至经文的受众更为在乎的问题。

在后流放时期的以色列社群中,存在争议的一个重要问题,是亚伯拉罕传统与摩西传统哪个才是以色列精神的正统。这种争论不仅关乎土地所有权,更关乎社区内部宗教和政治领导权的把握。《以赛亚书》的经文反映了社群身份归属问题和冲突,即权力社团自居为"亚伯拉罕"或"以色列"的正统,拒绝接纳继承摩西传统的边缘社团,认为他们不是社群成员;而后者则要求分享主流权力社团的应许、权力和社群身份。[②]亚伯拉罕—大卫之约(无条件应许)和摩西之约(有条件应许)这两大传统的竞争和冲突贯穿了古代以色列宗教的发展历程,从被掳之前延续到了流放中回归的社群。在第二以赛亚和第三以赛亚的经文中,不但可以看到这种张力的呈现,也可以看到作者或编者进行改造的尝试。而对居鲁士形象的塑造,在某种程度上也可以为传统的继承和融合服务。

---

① 参见 Ehud Ben Zvi, "The Yehudite Collection of Prophetic Books and Imperial Contexts: Some Observations," 164。

② 参见姜宗强 Jiang Zongqiang,《〈以赛亚书〉研究》[A Study of the Book of Isaiah](北京[Beijing]:民族出版社[The Ethnic Publishing House], 2020), 224—225。关于《以赛亚书》所反映的后流放时期社群冲突的问题,可详见该书 100—121 页、199—227 页的分析,及所列更多参考文献。

第二以赛亚的经文里提到了三个“无条件应许”的约，包括上帝和亚伯拉罕的约(《以赛亚书》51:1—3)、和大卫的约(《以赛亚书》55:3—5)以及先前和挪亚的约(《以赛亚书》54:7—10)。关于居鲁士和亚伯拉罕的关系，琼斯(Gwilym H. Jones)从类型学的角度，通过对语言、词汇、情节设定等方面的分析，提出了具有创见的观点。[①]琼斯选取了以往受关注较少的《创世记》第14章的情节，强调了亚伯拉罕的军事生涯和军事角色，并将其与居鲁士的军事征服联系起来。[②]他指出，对于《以赛亚书》第41章(尤其是41:2—4, 25ff)的描述，单独用亚伯拉罕解释或将其与居鲁士联系起来都是不够的。而当把两种理解结合起来，沿着类型学线索解释作者的思维方式时，上述两种理解所产生的困难似乎就消失了。第二以赛亚故意选择了他的措辞，以便在主要描述居鲁士时能够回忆起过去历史的某些部分，特别是那些与居鲁士时代事件平行的亚伯拉罕历史部分。先知将亚伯拉罕作为原型，将居鲁士作为反原型/对型(anti-type)。这种类型学方法允许先知将亚伯拉罕和居鲁士的形象统一起来，将过去的历史与当前的事件加以联系。因为亚伯拉罕是以色列的代表，耶和华对亚伯拉罕的承诺，现在便通过居鲁士重复、更新和实现。和亚伯拉罕一样“从东方来”的居鲁士，为以色列人取得了胜利。这一特点似乎更牢固地连接了亚伯拉罕和居鲁士：通过这两个勇士，耶和华一直都在为以色列人考虑。[③]布雷肯索普进一步指出，召唤居鲁士和支持他行动的神是从一开始就召唤几代人的同一位神，亚伯拉罕是他的代理人(《以赛亚书》41:4a)；他也和那些后来的人，即居鲁士和他的军队同在(《以赛亚书》41:4b)。正因如此，先知提醒了同时代的犹太人，他们是上帝的朋友亚伯拉罕的后裔(《以赛亚书》41:8)。[④]

相比于亚伯拉罕式的无条件之约在经文中的多次出现，以及居鲁士和亚伯拉罕形象和事迹之间存在的联系，西奈之约在第二以赛亚中似乎并没有被直接提及。不过，第二以赛亚所包含的“第二次出埃及”的意象也得到了认可和接受。姜宗强指出：“在40—55章中虽然没有直接提到摩西的名字，但并不等于‘摩西’在‘第二以赛亚’的‘第二次出埃及’的传统中没有地位；恰恰相反，之所以不提摩西，可能是因为回归社群中‘受苦仆人’所代表的社团，已经取代摩西，视自己为

① 参见 Gwilym H. Jones, “Abraham and Cyrus: Type or Anti-type?” *Vetus Testamentum* 22 (1972): 304-319。

② 同上，309。

③ 同上，315-316，319。

④ 参见 Joseph Blenkinsopp, “Abraham and Cyrus in Isaiah 40-48,” in *New Perspectives on Old Testament Prophecy and History: Essays in Honour of Hans M. Barstad*, eds. Rannfrid I. Thelle, Terje Stordalen, and Mervyn E. J. Richardson (Leiden: Brill, 2015), 35。

摩西自由解放传统的承担者,愿意为完成上帝交付使自己和通报获得自由解放的使命,而主动承担责任(53:12)。”[①] 而居鲁士和历史上的摩西之间同样存在诸多共同点。

通过对第二以赛亚中有关居鲁士的诗歌(《以赛亚书》44:24—28;45:1—13)与《出埃及记》中对摩西的呼召情节(《出埃及记》6:2—8)的比较分析,奥格登(Graham S. Ogden)揭示了这两个重要形象之间的联系。[②]他指出,先知借鉴了以色列过去的另一种传统,即《出埃及记》对摩西的记载,特别是摩西的召唤,表明他将居鲁士的崛起置于以色列救世传统的背景下。[③] “以赛亚之歌”是一个复合作品,包含了不同的文学类型,开头强调了耶和华作为造物主、以色列的圣者和救赎主的角色,而创造—救赎的主题被应用于一个具体的对象——以色列,并通过居鲁士这个具体的人物实现。[④]

在文学层面上,先知刻意将居鲁士呈现在摩西传统内部。第一,对耶和华“救赎主”(גאלך יהוה)的称呼(《以赛亚书》44:24)是第二以赛亚的关键主题之一(《以赛亚书》41:14; 43:14; 44:6, 24; 48:17; 49:7—8, 26; 54:5),对这个词根的使用基本上与出埃及有关(《出埃及记》6:6; 15:13),被理解为上帝的行为,在异国他乡实现了对奴役的拯救。第二,“我(是)耶和华”(אנכי יהוה/אני יהוה)的表达(《以赛亚书》44:24; 45:3, 5, 6, 7)在第二以赛亚(如《以赛亚书》41:4; 42:6, 8 等)和整个被掳回归时期比较常见,和对摩西的呼召也非常吻合:耶和华对摩西的神谕(《出埃及记》6:2, 6, 7, 8)反复出现**אני יהוה**的句式。这种处理不仅统领了居鲁士之歌和摩西神谕,为它们提供了神学基础,还是一种重要的修辞手段。《出埃及记》的 6:2 和 6:8 构成了该次对摩西所宣告的神谕的开场白和结束语;而在居鲁士的例子中,耶和华关于居鲁士的话语在 44:24 以**אני יהוה**形式开始,在 45:7 中以相同的方式结束。第三,耶和华“使说假话的兆头失效,使占卜的癫狂,使智慧人退后,使他的知识变为愚拙”(《以赛亚书》44:25)。这与《出埃及记》中摩西和法老及其手下的埃及法师斗法的情节遥相呼应,而埃及的法师术士如同诗句中的占说谎者、占卜者、“智慧人”一样,遭到了可耻的失败。第四,耶和华“论到犹大的城邑说:‘必被建造,其中的荒场我也必兴起’”(《以赛亚书》44:26),耶和华的救赎能力将在恢复中得到具体的体现,也是《出埃及记》

---

① 姜宗强,《〈以赛亚书〉研究》,197。

② 参见 Graham S. Ogden, “Moses and Cyrus: Literary Affinities between the Priestly Presentation of Moses in Exodus vi-viii and the Cyrus Song in Isaiah xliv 24-xlv 13,” *Vetus Testamentum* 28 (1978): 195-203。

③ 同上,196。

④ 同上,197。

主题的重新应用,从赐予土地发展为耶路撒冷城的重建。第五,居鲁士被描述为并不认识耶和华(《以赛亚书》45:5),但这可以理解为先前的情况;因为“从日出之地到日落之处”,人们都将知道这位独一神(《以赛亚书》45:6)。这和摩西叙事的情节也是对应的:先祖们先前不知道耶和华的名(《出埃及记》6:3),但民众渐渐认识了他和他的大能,进入了新的理解和关系(《出埃及记》6:7)。第六,民众对神谕的反应同样有相似性。摩西向以色列人传达神言后,他们“因苦工愁烦,不肯听他的话”(《出埃及记》6:9)。而第二以赛亚同样记载了与造物主争论的言论(《以赛亚书》45:9—10)。听到神谕的人都曾不信和拒绝。这个主题似乎进一步巩固了摩西和居鲁士之间的纽带。[①]

居鲁士形象和摩西之间联系的问题,还值得进一步讨论。但这些相似点很难说都只是巧合。《圣经》作者常常把具有代表性的重要人物或者记忆场所进行整合,建立过去的“伟大英雄”和当下的知名人物之间的联系。而第二以赛亚将居鲁士与亚伯拉罕和摩西这两位以色列历史上重要的人物都巧妙地联结起来,居鲁士这位既“政治正确”又得到犹太社团普遍认可和拥护的形象,同以色列民族的祖先和领袖的杰出品质与赫赫功绩交相辉映,这对于团结更多的受众,获得更多的共鸣,无疑会有积极的作用。

除此之外,古代以色列另一个重要的赐予无条件应许的约是大卫之约,被认为和亚伯拉罕之约一脉相承,在第二以赛亚中也有所提及(《以赛亚书》55:3—5)。居鲁士和大卫具有的相似点显而易见——他们都是伟大的君王,开疆拓土;大卫让古代以色列人真正获得了独立,走向强大;居鲁士让犹太人重获自由,走向复兴;大卫为第一圣殿的建设作了准备,居鲁士为第二圣殿的建设颁发了许可。作为受膏者的大卫获得了耶和华无条件的应许,而同为受膏者的居鲁士也同样获得了召唤和赏赐。弗莱德(Lisbeth S. Fried)表示,第二以赛亚使当代居鲁士合法化为“大卫的君主,大卫王位的继承人”,并用埃及和巴比伦的参照案例来说明这一说法:“像埃及的乌加特女神和巴比伦的马尔杜克的祭司一样,第二以赛亚把‘耶和华的受膏者’的犹大王室头衔以及与之相关的整个犹大王室神学交给了居鲁士。”[②]本-兹维(Ehud Ben Zvi)也认为:“圣殿的重建者必须被解释为一个非常正面的人物。他不是以色列人,因为他只能是波斯人;但可以看出作者将他部分地大卫化的倾向。”[③] 然而,对于

① 有关的详细分析与讨论,参见 Ogden, “Moses and Cyrus,” 198-202。

② Lisbeth S. Fried, “Cyrus the Messiah? The Historical Background to Isaiah 45:1,” *Harvard Theological Review* 95 (2002): 390.

③ Ehud Ben Zvi, “The Yehudite Collection of Prophetic Books and Imperial Contexts: Some Observations,” 156.

第二以赛亚如何看待以大卫之约为代表的王室神学,仍然存在争议①;在波斯前中期的语境中,《圣经》作者又是否敢于唤起和强调大卫传统,也是一个需要继续探讨的问题。因此,分析居鲁士和大卫之间的联系时,或许应当更加谨慎。

总的来说,《以赛亚书》中的居鲁士是一个正面形象。耶和华以公义兴起的这位外邦领袖在其指引下为以色列人乃至世界所作出的贡献,成为独一神大能的体现。而作者在刻画这一形象时,有意无意将其和古代以色列历史上的英雄人物联系起来,既有亚伯拉罕这位无条件应许的代表,又有摩西这样有条件应许的代表。不同传统的支持者,都可以在居鲁士身上找到自己认同的人物具有的特征。也就是说,在后流放时期犹太社群存在分歧、思想也难以统一之时,居鲁士成为沟通两种约传统的一座桥梁,第二以赛亚以此来丰富回归犹太社团的信仰体系,消弭潜在的冲突,使整个社群更加团结、更加和谐、更加有序。

① 详见姜宗强,《〈以赛亚书〉研究》,152—159。

The Image of Cyrus in Deutero-Isaiah

MENG Zhenhua

Abstract: The Book of Isaiah depicts Cyrus, much like in other biblical books, in a predominantly positive light, considering him a special foreign ruler in Hebrew scripture. The accounts of Cyrus might not have been originally composed by the contemporaneous author(s) but could have emerged from later writing and editing. The portrayal of Cyrus reflects the actual attitude of Israelite authors during the post-exilic period. While propagating monotheistic beliefs through this foreign king, the prophetic author attempted to link this image with significant figures in ancient Israel in an effort to reconcile conflicts between different traditions within the community.

Key Words: *Bible*, Persia, Judah, Ethnic Relations

迈蒙尼德哲学中的神秘主义因素

赵同生*

【摘要】迈蒙尼德往往被宗教哲学研究者视为重要的理性主义者，而他作为犹太人社群中宗教领袖和虔诚信徒的另一面，往往没有得到应有的重视。本文尝试就迈蒙尼德在对哲学与启示传统进行融合过程中表现出的理智神秘主义思想特征进行一番考察，通过分析迈蒙尼德接受中世纪阿拉伯—犹太哲学世界观背后的逻辑思路，以及他如何从该世界观出发对犹太教圣经—拉比传统进行神秘主义解读，揭示他的宗教哲学思想，尤其他的先知论、神佑论以及认识论思想中蕴含的神秘主义因素，并进一步考察他对上帝之爱（'āhav）这一概念的神秘主义阐释。

【关键词】神秘主义；神佑；爱；虔敬

历史上的迈蒙尼德一直都是一位充满争议的犹太学者，他一生笔耕不辍，著作内容涵盖犹太教教义、律法、《圣经》诠释、哲学、医学等，有些犹太教徒将其尊为宗教律法权威①，但也有人因《迷途指津》一书而指责他接受希腊化哲学、背弃犹太教传统②。20世纪中期以来，有诸多犹太研究者将其塑造为一位理性主义的文化英雄，称赞他面对雅典和耶路撒冷之间的对峙而选择前者，在隐微写作的

---

* 赵同生，烟台大学外国语学院副教授，烟台大学翻译研究中心主任，山东大学犹太教与跨宗教研究中心兼职研究员。

① 根据迈蒙尼德的书信记载，当时常有人登门求教，咨询各类问题，如他在一封著名的信中对也门犹太人有关弥赛亚的问题进行了解答。

② 如迈蒙尼德与另一位在巴格达的宗教领袖撒母耳·本·埃里（Samuel ben Eli）的争论；又如，他的作品在其生前即遭欧洲多国毁禁；等等。

掩护下向世俗青年揭示了自己普世主义的理性立场[①]。这一倾向在很大程度上是由研究者自己对哲学与宗教的态度决定的。近代以来,人们普遍倾向于接受理性与哲学乃通往现代社会必由之路的观点,而神秘主义因其隐晦、秘传、体验等特征往往被视为理性的天敌,甚至是中世纪文明史上的糟粕。即使是一些犹太教学者,也往往试图证明犹太教是一种理性的伦理一神教,而否定神秘主义在犹太教传统中的重要地位。[②] 本文认为,神秘主义往往是宗教的内核,犹太教中的神秘主义传统是该教拥有强劲生命力的重要源头,神秘主义是犹太教传统文化研究中的重要部分,考察迈蒙尼德宗教哲学中的神秘主义因素,对于研究其先知论、神佑论以及认识论思想具有重要的启发意义。

一

犹太学者沃尔夫逊(Harry Wolfson)以哲学观念史的写作方法,通过详细分析迈蒙尼德作品中的语言特征以及前后期思想的连贯性,探究其中诸如上帝属性以及创世论等较为重要的中世纪宗教哲学主题,分析迈蒙尼德在阿拉伯哲学和基督教哲学传统中的影响。但沃尔夫逊没有讨论迈蒙尼德作为虔诚犹太教徒其作品中所涉及的宗教体验的问题,在他那里迈蒙尼德在理性上的追求显然高于宗教以及宗教体验诸问题。皮那斯(Shlomo Pines)作为迈蒙尼德哲学代表作《迷途指津》最重要的英译本翻译者,同样也是从理性主义的视角出发,通过梳理迈蒙尼德哲学思想背景与脉络,分析其否定神学的理智主义倾向,指出人的认知探索对于迈蒙尼德而言止于对于质料的分析探究,而形而上学的知识超越人的理智认知能力的界限,仅仅属于信仰的领域。

然而,在犹太神秘主义研究者那里,迈蒙尼德思想中的神秘主义因素也没有得到应有的重视。索伦(Gershom Scholem)同哲学研究者一样将迈蒙尼德视为理性主义者,认为其思想与注重个人神秘体验和戏剧性情感表现的神秘主义之间没有多少共同之处。在述及 13 世纪喀巴拉神秘主义代表亚伯拉罕·阿布拉菲亚的思想背景时,索伦就曾明确表示那种“神秘主义者与伟大的理性主义者的结合”是“令人诧异的”。[③] 索伦作品中归纳出神秘主义的表现形式,诸如默卡巴

---

① 如列奥·施特劳斯等人的观点。

② 参见刘精忠 Liu Jingzhong,《犹太神秘主义概论》[Introduction to Jewish Mysticism](北京[Beijing]:中国社会科学出版社 [China Social Sciences Press],2015),3。

③ Gershom Scholem 索伦,《犹太教神秘主义主流》[Major Trends in Jewish Mysticism],涂笑非 Tu Xiaofei 译(成都[Chengdu]:四川人民出版社 [Sichuan People's Publishing House],2000),123。

神秘论中的诸多天使及其魔法姓名，中世纪哈西德主义的禁欲苦修与魔法符咒，喀巴拉的通神术、召唤弥赛亚等，显然与迈蒙尼德对个人理智能力的限制格格不入。在索伦看来，神秘主义植根于对神秘符号的操作以及狂迷的情感体验，而非系统的理性思考。

法国犹太学者瓦伊达(Georges Vajda)受到阿拉伯哲学研究者迈德库(Madkour)以及加德特(Gardet)①等人的影响，率先在犹太教研究中提出"默观神秘主义"的概念。他认为，一方面中世纪犹太哲学家并非单一的逻辑学者，他们往往还是虔诚教徒和神秘主义者；另一方面中世纪犹太神秘主义者也不单纯是沉湎于魔法或者狂迷的人，他们还是推崇理智主义的学者。关于犹太神秘主义，瓦伊达指出：

> 就其源头而言，喀巴拉是诺斯替思想的一种形式；如果必须用"某某主义"来表述它，那么它与其说是犹太神秘主义，不如说是诺斯替主义。因为这一诺斯替思想声称要教导其追随者如何实现所谓的"涉神的内心体验"(la vie intérieure de la divinité)，人们完全可以据此称之为"通神论"。……在某种意义上，我们可以说古典喀巴拉就属于中世纪的犹太—阿拉伯神学和哲学。②

瓦伊达认为，在涉及知识、体验和虔诚等概念之间的相互关系时，哲学与神秘主义之间的边界开始消融。当然，他所谓神秘主义并非指一般意义上那种狂迷状态下的人神合一，而是灵智追求与禁欲苦修实践的结合，是对理智达到通透澄明状态的体验。他在大英百科全书中对"犹太神秘主义"这一词条进行解释时就曾指出，神秘主义与形而上学、宇宙论、通神论、巫术崇拜、神智论等概念之间往往难以划定明确的界限；犹太历史上出现过三种类型的神秘主义——狂迷式、默观式和秘传式，它们相互之间也并非界限分明，在现实中往往出现彼此重叠和混杂的情况。③ 在述及迈蒙尼德时，瓦依达曾提到：

> 说到底，所谓知识乃是趋向上帝之旅，自然知识仅仅是以神为主要和最高目标的形而上学知识的准备阶段，它不是有关神秘合一的问题。迈蒙尼德所谓对上帝的虔诚显然带有默观的(contemplative)特征。虔诚的终极状

① 迈德库将阿拉伯哲学家法拉比的思想称为"理智神秘主义"，而加德特将阿维森纳的哲学标为"理性神秘主义"。参见 I. Madkour, *La Place d'Alfarabi dans l'ecole philosophique musulmane* (Paris: Adrien-Maisonneuve, 1934); L. Gardet, *La pensee religieuse d'Avicenne* (Paris: Vrin, 1951)。

② Georges Vajda, *Introduction à la pensée juive du Moyen Age* (Paris: J. Vrin, 1947),198-199.

③ 参见 Georges Vajda, "Jewish Mysticism," *Encyclopedia Britannica* 10:183。

态则是进入幸福的异相(la vision béatifique)……总之,默观式虔诚(la piété contemplative)才是他在《迷途指津》中想要表达的关键概念。[1]

瓦伊达所谓"默观式"神秘主义乃是按照形而上学的沉思方法进行理智探索以求达到极致的尝试,这一概念的提出在中世纪犹太教研究领域引起了两方面的变化,一是在哲学研究中对虔诚一神秘因素的发掘,二是对神秘主义研究中理智一哲学因素的重视。正是在这个意义上,迈蒙尼德在对哲学与启示传统进行融合过程中表现出的理智神秘主义思想特征值得我们进行一番考察。通过分析迈蒙尼德接受中世纪阿拉伯—犹太哲学世界观背后的逻辑思路,以及他如何从该世界观出发对犹太教圣经—拉比传统进行解读,我们可以揭示他的宗教哲学思想,尤其他的先知论、神佑论以及认识论思想中蕴含的神秘主义因素。

二

在宗教传统中人人皆可拥有一种灵性能力,它使人们在日常生活范围之外能够以某种方式认识并体验到某种终极力量的存在。这种超越性存在者在一神教传统中被称为上帝,而在其他形式的宗教中则拥有不同的名称,信徒对于这些存在者的体验也各不相同。所谓"属灵的追求"即是接受并努力探求这种超越性存在以期达到与其同在的一种生存状态。

犹太学者布鲁曼瑟(David Blumenthal)指出神秘主义是灵性的一种,对终极存在的神秘主义体验应具备两个特征:其一,至高者沿着一个秩序井然的等级序列从上往下"流溢",同时人的理智须由这一等级序列的底端向上不断探索方能够获得神秘"启蒙",而且人在向上跨越之前需要进行专门的知识储备。其二,个人所获得的这种"启蒙"本身具有抽象、无法以言语表述的特征。[2] 根据布鲁曼瑟这一定义,圣经宗教是"灵性的"但不是"神秘主义的"。《圣经》中上帝是一个具有人格的至上神,他按照自己的意志行事,可以任意降临某人,随意选择先知。在一般圣经宗教中,任何人皆可通过简单的言语形式向上帝祈祷,无须预先进行任何形式的教育准备。即便到后来的拉比犹太教那里,上帝仍然任意而为,而个人仅需少量学习、作出简单准备即有可能体验其存在。根据布鲁曼瑟的界定,这些行为显然都不属于神秘主义的范畴。

在拉比犹太教初期出现的默卡巴主义(Merkava)提出,要向上超越介于人

---

① Georges Vajda, *Introduction à la pensée juive du Moyen Age*, 143-144.

② 参见 David Blumenthal, *Philosophic Mysticism: Studies in Rational Religion* (Ramat Gan: Bar-Ilan University Press, 2006), 24。

神之间的一系列天体,个人必须具备特殊的“灵智”(gnosis),接受特殊训练,掌握守门卫士的魔法名字,才能到达至高者王座所在的宫廷,获得有关“宝座”的异相,聆听到天上的颂歌。到中世纪犹太神秘主义诸流派兴起时,在这一等级序列的超越过程中又加入了法术和神秘体验等因素,但个体要达到理想的宗教状态同样需要一系列精神上和实践上的准备。在佐哈尔(Zoharic)神秘主义那里,若想登上“实在”之天梯并实现最终“救赎”(tikkun),需要精心研究并掌握十个上帝流溢之“显相”或创世神力(sefirot)的名称及其相互关系。卢里亚(Lurianic)神秘主义则认为只有掌握了四重天的复杂结构与运行机制,才能超越物质世界,上升到外在天体并恢复创世之初的神人关系,实现“神人合一”(yihudim)。在某些哈希德(Hasidic)神秘主义者那里,同样存在一个严密的等级序列,获得神秘体验也需要精神上作出特殊准备。综合这些犹太教神秘主义流派的观点可知,个体对上帝的体验不同于圣经犹太教和拉比犹太教传统中简单的人神对话,而更像是一种抽象的、能量的迁移。相比较而言,如果说灵性追求是普罗众生皆可实践的一种生存状态,神秘主义的诉求则主要来自受教育程度较高的精英阶层。

迈蒙尼德理性化的宗教思想没有脱离犹太教传统。他继承了犹太神秘主义传统中神人关系框架的设定,将先哲们的神秘智慧之学——“创世论”及“神车论”与阿拉伯哲学中的新亚里士多德主义宇宙观相结合,对个人理智实现神秘主义超越所需要的准备工作的性质作出哲学意义上的解读。他认为,通过对数学、逻辑乃至物理学与形而上学等科学知识的学习与把握,个人可以实现理智能力的提升,使自己的理智能够接收来自至高者的流溢。即是说,哲学意义上的知识和实践最终导向一种全新的神秘主义体验,而这种体验具有抽象的特征以及神秘的(或启示的)本质。将个体理智与神秘主义体验之间关系的打通,是迈蒙尼德理性主义宗教哲学的一个特征,抑或说,是他对犹太教神秘主义传统进行了独特的理性主义解读。

受中世纪新亚里士多德主义的影响,迈蒙尼德接受了一种融合亚里士多德主义宇宙结构理论和新柏拉图主义流溢思想的宇宙观。这一宇宙观所涉及的天体物理学和形而上学在现代学科体系中分别属于不同的两类学问,但是在12世纪的宗教哲学家那里,二者所涉及的内容仍属于同一个体系。他们认为,决定天体运动的机械原理和主宰宇宙的力量,都与一个秩序井然的天体序列相关。根据这一时期流行的物理学和天体物理学,宇宙中有物质与灵性两个存在等级序列。物质的等级体系囊括当时人们所能理解的整个宇宙,层层天体依次笼罩在大地之上,其间没有虚空。宇宙的中心是地球,往外依次覆盖着四层天体,它们通体透明又彼此相邻,分别由土、水、气和火四大元素构成。这四种元素混合形成物质世界中的一切物体,它们连同四重天体一起构成月球以下世界(sublunar

world)。四重天之外又有九层天体依次包裹覆盖,它们同样通体透明,由"第五元素"(quintessence)构成。这九层天体各含不同星体,又各自围绕地球运行。其中最低一层天体内含月球,其他天体分别含有水星、金星、火星、太阳、木星和土星,太阳居于中间一层天体中,而第八层天体包含其它星体。最外一层天体每二十四小时绕地球旋转一周,被称为"日周天"(diurnal sphere)。

和诸天体相对应的是一个始自神的灵性存在者的等级序列。但是该序列中的神不同于圣经传统和拉比传统所描述的人格上帝,它被抽象为超越的神性,远离一切具体的变化、运动、情感和行为。作为唯一的、至高无上的存在,此神是以自身为思考对象的纯粹理智,是融思考者、思考对象和思考行动为一体的存在。纯粹之思向外延伸被称为"流溢",中世纪哲学家们常常用两个比喻来描述它:如不竭的泉水汩汩而出,或者像太阳光芒一泻万里。但神性的流溢毕竟不同于物质世界里养育众生的泉水或恩泽万物的阳光,它汇聚形成一种非物质性存在,被称作"第一理智"(first intelligence)。[①] 它成为神性之外的第一个灵性存在,具备与神相似的思考能力,以神和自身为思考对象,并由此初步具备多样性。

当第一理智以神为对象进行沉思时,其思考流溢而出,形成"第二理智"。当第一理智以自身为对象进行沉思时,其思考流溢生成最高一层天体,即"日周天"。日周天位于宇宙中物质性等级体系的顶端,它亦是灵性存在者等级序列的延续。随后依次诞生灵性等级体系中第三至第九等级的理智,以及物质等级体系中的其它八层天体。当第九理智以第八天体为对象进行沉思时,其流溢产生第十理智;当它以自身为对象进行沉思时,其流溢产生最低一层天体——月球天体,以及月球之下的天体,即由四大元素构成的四层天体。

柏拉图认为物质世界中万物源于各自的理念,普拉提诺进一步指出这些理念存在于上帝的理智。到中世纪哲学家那里,这些理念则存在于第十理智。第十理智又称能动理智(agent intelligence),它以自身为对象进行沉思,流溢产生世间万物。当能动理智以高一等级的第九理智为对象进行沉思时,其流溢产生人的理智。能动理智作为人的理智和神圣理智序列的中介,在迈蒙尼德先知论和认识论思想中占据重要地位。

这一中世纪阿拉伯—犹太哲学世界观体现在迈蒙尼德的哲学作品中,也构

---

① 流溢产生的灵性存在者'aql 在中文里一般译为"理智",但它在不同语境中意义略有不同,这一点在英语译文中有所体现。在英语文献里它分别译为 intellect 或 intelligence,前者多用于新柏拉图主义语境,具有认识论意义;后者常出现在法拉比、阿维森纳等人的研究文献中,在宇宙论意义上使用。按照中世纪阿拉伯—犹太哲学传统,来自上帝流溢的最高一级"理智"(intelligence),通过流溢依次产生位于人类世界之上的诸天体及其灵魂(即低一级的"理智"),这一系列"理智"同时又具备某种认识能力(此时则为 intellect),使得它们能够以自身和上一级"理智"为对象进行沉思。

成了他心目中年轻学者需要掌握的基础知识。同时,他也充分利用这一跨宗教的思想资源,以这一世界观为基础对犹太教拉比传统进行解读。通过分析迈蒙尼德这一做法背后的逻辑思路,可以揭示他的宗教哲学思想尤其先知论、神佑论以及认识论中蕴含着的神秘主义因素。

三

迈蒙尼德坚持阿拉伯亚里士多德主义宇宙论,它与中世纪流行的世界观相比有一点不同,认为除了神性的存在之流自上而下的流溢之外,宇宙间还应有一种自下而上的超越。迈蒙尼德进而指出,这种自下而上的超越,就是犹太教传统中所谓"沿天梯攀登"的先知异相所要表达的隐秘之义,而这一"攀登",也与新亚里士多德主义的认知论和知识论密切相关。根据这一世界观,宇宙中每个事物都分有一个柏拉图意义上的理念,如人的善行分有了善的理念,而探究并阐明这些理念则是哲学家的工作。

人的感官以两种方式感知世上诸种现象:人灵魂中较低级的部分(如想象力和理性灵魂)形成有关事物的幻相并由此对其理念进行概括,高级的部分(直接来自第十理智的理智能力)将这些抽象的感觉数据与自身带来的理念的绝对标准进行比较,如果二者相符,则意味着获得了"真知"。有关理念的真知存储在人的理智之中,被称作"习得理智"(acquired intellect)。人获得的理念数量越多,他的习得理智能力也就越强,越接近第十理智。这也就意味着人的理智越接近上帝之理智,尽管是间接地。因此说,上帝是理智,上帝理智容纳理念,人的理智仿效上帝之理智也掌握了一些理念真知。迈蒙尼德正是在这个意义上谈论人对上帝的仿效,"存在"自下而上流动,"沿天梯而上"。

随之而来的问题是,人辨别、收获那些理念后又将如何? 人在收集了这些沿"存在之流"散落下来的光之后,能否进入更高层次的灵性境界? 在回答这一问题时,迈蒙尼德由理性迈入宗教神秘主义领域,将理性思考纳入拉比传统思想的框架体系,并由此探讨人对上帝的虔敬问题。

根据迈德库对阿拉伯哲学"理智神秘主义"的描述,一方面,对神的体验是哲学、理智方面准备完善后的结果,此体验进而可以给人带来哲学的、理智上的新知识;另一方面,人对神的体验又被描述为与神之理智进行"契接"的过程,或者被比作"接受光照"。这种体验不同于伊斯兰教传统中的苏菲神秘主义,后者将人神相契接的体验称为"神人合一",且这一状态的获得是弃绝一切世俗事务的结果。对此,9 世纪著名伊斯兰苏菲神秘主义者祝奈德(al-Junayd)曾有描述:"我们获得神人合一状态的途径,不是谈话或者教育,而是忍受饥饿,远离物质世

界，停止遵从所有习惯和欲望，断绝世俗友谊，放弃对已知或未明知识的追求。”[①]理智神秘主义的不同就在于它认可有关神的理智主义描述，承认人有理智能力，进而探求人的理智与神之理智进行“契接”的条件与本质，同时借鉴新柏拉图主义的“灵魂上升”学说来解释人如何实现理智完善，揭示人神理智契接的实质。

迈蒙尼德关于先知启示的解释体现了神秘理智主义的特征。他认为神意不会无条件到达个人，“越是智高德重，人从上帝神佑中享到的就越多……越是无知而背信弃义的人，上帝对他的神佑就越少”[②]。要获得神的启示，先知不仅在道德方面，更应该在理智上作好准备，然后来自上帝的神秘之流才会与先知理智进行契接，进而流向其想象力。同时，预言过程作为一种神秘体验也会改变先知本人的理智能力：

> 具备这些德性并且身体功能正常的人，当他进入“神秘花园”(pardes)并且持续对那遥远而又重大问题进行沉思时，如果他的理智具备一定感知和理解能力，如果他能够远离黑暗时期众人所行之道从而使自己保持圣洁，如果他能克制、警戒自己，不虚度时光于无用之事，不耗费心机于时人流行的奇思异想，而是将全部精力投入到对高高在上的神之宝座的追求，致力于对神圣的、纯粹形式的理解以及对上帝智慧——从第一形式到物质世界的核心——的沉思，当他从中获得有关唯一神的相关知识时，神圣精神随即降临于此人。当其时，他的灵魂达到第十级天使('ishim)，这给他带来颠覆性变化，且其本人也清楚自己已经异于以往，甚至超越了那些被称为“贤者”的灵魂水平，正如撒母耳对扫罗所说：“你就要与他们一同受感说话，变成另一个人。”(《撒母耳上》10:6)[③]

在迈蒙尼德那里，神佑与神知是密切相关的两个概念，上帝之知乃是神的流溢过程，其所及之处必然会有神佑的存在。而能够向上“攀登”进而与上帝之流溢进行契接的只有人的理智，因此他在将其他物种的个体排除出上帝认知范围的同时，保留了个体的人得到神佑的可能性。[④] 神佑的获得同样涉及理智与体

① I. Madhour, *La Place d'Alfarabi dans l'ecole philosophique musulmane*, 187.

② Maimonides 迈蒙尼德，《迷途指津》[The Guide of the Perplexed]，傅有德 Fu Youde 等译(济南[Jinan]：山东大学出版社[Shandong University Press]，1998)，431。

③ Maimonides, *Mishneh Torah*, “Hilkhot Yesodei ha-Torah,” 7:1.

④ 参见赵同生 Zhao Tongsheng，《迈蒙尼德宗教哲学思想研究》[A Study of Maimonides' Religious Philosophy](上海[Shanghai]：上海三联书店 [Shanghai SDX Joint Publishing Company]，2016)，181—184。

验两个层面,而且神佑流溢到个人的多寡与此人理智能力的大小及发展水平直接相关:

上帝如何对待其他生命,我的看法与亚里士多德一致。我也不相信树叶飘落是神意的结果,飞虫落入蜘蛛网的刹那是上帝的旨意使然,蚋碰巧被行人的一口痰淹死是上帝的意欲所为。水面上的虫子被鱼吃掉也并非上帝的安排。依我之见,所有这些,就像亚里士多德认为的那样,都纯粹出于偶然。上帝的护佑与其智力的影响有关,受上帝智慧影响的存在物会拥有智力,并能认识只有理性物才能认识的事物,因此,它们也受上帝保佑……我认为上天的保佑与拥有智力密切相关。因为只有有智慧的存在物才能受到保佑,而该存在物自身必是最完满的,因此,那些分享上帝智慧的存在物会以同样的比例分享到上帝的保佑。①

迈蒙尼德的认识论同样体现出理智与体验之间的平衡。他接受理智是人灵魂的形式的说法,将人的完善和认知联系起来,认为犹太教传统中所谓的“灵魂不灭”是指人的理智处于完善状态,即成为习得理智。尚未达到完善状态的个人理智,按照阿佛罗狄西亚的亚历山大的说法,叫“质料理智”(material intellect),这一称谓意在强调其潜在性,认为它具备接受某些“形式”的潜能。一旦它与形式结合到一起,潜在的质料理智也就实现了自身,成为一种现实的思考行为,达到了完善状态。② 人的感官所得材料被灵魂中的想象力进行抽象加工,然后理智将其与脑中已存的抽象理念进行对比从而确立真理即真知识。头脑中已有的那些理念来自外部,得自神圣理智赋予理智的流溢,所以,人的理智完善的过程也就是其与能动理智的契接过程,同时这也意味着人对上帝的认知水平受其理智能力的高低及其完善程度影响。

四

在《申命记》中,人对上帝之爱(’āhav)一方面体现在“遵守”(Shamar)、“行”(halakh)、“听从”(shama)、“畏惧”(yārē’)和“紧随”(dāvaq)等行为上,迈蒙尼德认为它们反映了宗教的实践层面。所谓爱上帝是由畏惧转变到服从,而那些普通信徒要紧随贤者及其学生,以他们为榜样,遵行上帝的诫命。迈蒙尼德将宗教实践视为在来世获得生命的首要前提。在此之外,还有一个概念“虔敬”

① 迈蒙尼德,《迷途指津》,428、430。

② 参见赵同生,《迈蒙尼德宗教哲学思想研究》,147。

('avad)得到了迈蒙尼德的特别关注。

在《迷途指津》第三篇末尾处,迈蒙尼德由人的理智认知过渡到人对上帝的体验:

> 本章是结论性的。同时,还要对人们,即那些由于认识了上帝的本质而对上帝独有的真正实在有所体会的人如何敬拜上帝做出解释,并为他们的敬拜指明方向,以帮助他们实现人生这一最高目的。最后要说明,他们获得永生前在现世是如何受到上帝保佑的。①

他抛弃了传统犹太神秘主义中诸如施魔法、去知识等非理性的因素,将宗教体验与新亚里士多德主义的存在序列相结合,于是哲学之道通往的终点就是对上帝的"虔敬"(al-'ibāda),反过来,虔敬本身蕴含理智的、沉思的因素。虔敬是人神之间的心灵交流,是人的心灵与上帝之灵进行契接后的独特体验。在有关上帝宫殿的比喻中,迈蒙尼德根据人们对上帝的认知水平进行分类,当认知达到极致状态,人对上帝的热爱就跃升为虔敬,即对上帝全身心的奉献:

> 有些人在神学上已得完善;之后,便排除一切杂念,一门心思侍奉上帝。他们用全部心智研究万物,试图从中找到上帝存在的证据并了解上帝统治万物的可能方式。这些人是朝中的大臣,也就是我们所说的先知……现在我们就言归正传,来劝诫那些已认识上帝的人,再一心一意地敬拜上帝。这种敬拜是那些认识了真正实在的人所独有的。他们越是默念上帝,与上帝同在,其崇拜之情就越是强烈。②

可见,迈蒙尼德由人对上帝之"爱"(al-mahabba, love)开发出一个更高的境界,即人对上帝的"虔敬"(al-'ibāda, worship)。前者属于理智的范畴,与个人对上帝的"理解"(al-'idrak, comprehension)直接相关,侧重理性、分析和哲思,而对上帝的虔敬则是由理性认知到宗教体验的跳转,是个人将自己完全投入对上帝的体验,是人在独处时才能更好体验到的一种"激情"(al-'ishq, passion),具备灵性、沉思、体验和神秘的特征。作为宗教体验的基础,个体理智上的准备是实现对上帝的虔敬的必由之路。迈蒙尼德指出有一类人在侍奉上帝时表面上看来似乎非常投入,实则不然,因为他们缺乏对上帝的理性认知:

> 有些人也思念上帝,经常说起上帝的名,但却没有真正认识上帝,而是凭想象或按别人的说教信仰上帝。在我看来,这些人与处在宫外且离宫很

① 迈蒙尼德,《迷途指津》,569—570。

② 同上,571。

远的人无异。他们所思念、所谈论的并不是真正的上帝。因为他们心里想的、口中说的并没有任何存在物与之对应,而完全是他们臆造的结果。①

在外部条件上,个人的生活方式也会对他的宗教体验产生独特的影响:

人的目的就是:在认识上帝之后,全心全意侍奉他,并将对上帝的永恒渴念与理智认识融为一体。一般而言,人只有在隐居和独处的条件下才能实现这一点。所以,虔敬的人常要与世隔绝,万不得已时才与人交往。②

此外,只有在爱上帝以及追求这种爱的过程中,个人理智所接受的神圣流溢才是最强的,人对上帝之爱的专注程度降低,就会削弱他对上帝的灵性体验:

所有的敬拜仪式,诸如诵经、祈祷以及其他一些教规等,目的只有一个,就是让人凝神聆听上帝的训导,并摆脱一切尘世的烦扰。因为由此你才会与上帝沟通,且不为俗事所扰。但如果你在面壁祈祷时用心不专,装模作样,视履行教规如在地上挖坑或在林中伐木一般,一点也不去想敬拜的含义、目的以及制定教规的上帝,就不能说你已达到了目的。③

迈蒙尼德甚至提出一系列训练步骤来增加人对上帝之爱乃至虔敬的强度:

你务必做的第一件事是:在背诵《经训》和祷文时要全神贯注;并且善始善终——不能凭借一时的喜好去背诵《经训》第一行或第一段祷文。在你坚持数载,已能成功地做到这一点时,再在读经或听经的过程中把全部心思都尽量放在对其内容的理解上。如此坚持训练上一段时间,再专心致志地去读先知的其他著作,乃至全部祷文,也要把精力放在对其内容及意义的理解上。不过,如果你在敬拜活动中已能一心不二,抛开一切日常事务的干扰,之后,就要训练自己在吃饭、喝水、洗澡,与妻子、孩子或别人交谈时去想生活中必做的或闲杂的事情,即一切世俗的事务。我想,人在一天中时间很多,已足够你去考虑钱财、家务或健康方面的事。但当你参加律法所规定的敬拜仪式时,就必须对你目前所做的专心致志,不得有一丝杂念。如果你独自一人躺在床上闭目养神,你就应该把这段珍贵的时间全用在对理智敬拜的沉思上,即以我已向你表明的那种方式,而不是借助虚幻的感情去接近上帝、服侍上帝。依我之见,通过这种训练,有学识的人就能获得最高完善,

① 迈蒙尼德,《迷途指津》,571—572。
② 同上,572—573。
③ 同上,573。

使其心灵的境界提升到应有的高度。[①]

迈蒙尼德所提的“虔敬”基于个人对上帝的理性认知，兼具理性与神秘主义的特征，具体体现在个人对上帝的感知与虔诚以及上帝对人的佑护上。在这一跳转过程中，理智上升为一种更高的“理智”，哲思变为虔敬，沉思变成信靠，对上帝的反思变为与上帝同在。由此看来，理性与神秘主义同为迈蒙尼德解读宇宙间神人关系时不可或缺的重要因素，而在人追求上帝的信仰旅途中，神秘主义的地位还要高于前者。

① 迈蒙尼德，《迷途指津》，574。

Elements of Mysticism in the Philosophy of Maimonides

ZHAO Tongsheng

Abstract: Maimonides is usually studied as an important rationalist in the field of religious philosophy, but the other image of Maimonides as a religious leader and a pious follower of Judaism is often neglected by Chinese scholars in this circle. This paper is a part of the effort to change the situation. It attempts to analyze the hidden logic in the world views of the medieval Arabic-Jewish philosophy Maimonides grew to accept, in order to investigate the element of mysticism in his interpretation of the Rabbinic traditions, reveal its influence on his ideas of prophecy, providence and epistemology, and then to look at how Maimonides explains the concept of Love of God ('āhav) from a mystic approach.

Key Words: Mysticism, Providence, Love, Worship